XML All-in-One Desk Reference For Dumm...

D0128081

Basic Parts of an XML Document

```
① <?xml version="1.0" encoding="utf-8" ?>
      ②
   <mnu:menu
③ xmlns:mnu="http://www.chucksmeals.com/2003/menu">
      ④      ⑤      ⑥              ⑦
      <mnu:entree id="1">Sunburnt Chicken</mnu:entree>
   </mnu:menu>
      ⑧
```

1. XML declaration
2. Start tag
3. Namespace declaration
4. Namespace prefix
5. Element name
6. Attribute (name-value pair)
7. Element content
8. Close tag

X-Team Roster

XML Technology	Purpose
XML	Defines elements that describes data they contain.
XML Schema	Defines the structure of an XML document that can be validated by a validating processor.
XSLT	Transforms XML documents into other formats, such as HTML.
XSL-FO	Describes a set of formatting rules for printing XML documents.
XPath	Locates nodes in an XML document.
XSL	Generic term that encompasses XSLT, XSL-FO, and XPath.
XLink	Defines links from XML documents to external resources.
XPointer	Defines pointers to resources inside of an XML document.
XForms	Defines XML-based form elements.
XHTML	Defines presentation of pages for Web browser (XML-compatible version of HTML).
SOAP	Defines a way to pass XML-encoded data over the Internet.
WSDL	Provides a way for a Web service to describe what it does, where it lives, and how you can activate it.
UDDI	Provides a way for a Web service to find other Web services on the Internet.

For Dummies: Bestselling Book Series for Beginners

XML All-in-One Desk Reference For Dummies®

XPath Shorthand

Shorthand	Equivalent	Definition	Example
(nothing)	child::	When no axis is defined, a value of child:: is assumed.	match="book" is the same as match="child::book"
@	attribute::	Selects an attribute of the context node	select="@id" is the same as select="attribute::id"
.	Self::node()	Selects the context node	.//book is the same as self::node()/descendant-or-self::node()/book
..	parent::node()	Selects the parent of the context node	../book is the same as parent::node()/book
//	/descendant-or-self::node()/	Search the entire source tree for a specific node set either by name or by type	//title is the same as /descendant-or-self::node()/title

XPath Location Step

```
     axis       node test  predicate
      |             |          |
   parent::book[first]
```

For Dummies: Bestselling Book Series for Beginners

XML

ALL IN ONE DESK REFERENCE

FOR

DUMMIES®

XML
ALL-IN-ONE DESK REFERENCE
FOR
DUMMIES®

**by Richard Wagner and
Richard Mansfield**

Wiley Publishing, Inc.

XML All-in-One Desk Reference For Dummies®

Published by
Wiley Publishing, Inc.
111 River Street
Hoboken, NJ 07030
www.wiley.com

Copyright © 2002 by Wiley Publishing, Inc., Indianapolis, Indiana

Published by Wiley Publishing, Inc., Indianapolis, Indiana

Published simultaneously in Canada

For general information on our other products and services or to obtain technical support, please con-tact our Customer Care Department within the U.S. at 800-762-2974, outside the U.S. at 317-572-3993, or fax 317-572-4002.

Wiley also publishes its books in a variety of electronic formats. Some content that appears in print may not be available in electronic books.

Library of Congress Cataloging-in-Publication Data:

Library of Congress Control Number: 2003101516

ISBN: 978-0-7645-1653-5

Manufactured in the United States of America

10 9 8 7 6 5 4

1B/RV/QV/QY/IN

WILEY   is a trademark of Wiley Publishing, Inc.

About the Authors

Richard Wagner is an experienced author of over 15 technical books, including *XSLT For Dummies* and *JavaScript Unleashed*. He also invented and architected the award-winning NetObjects ScriptBuilder and served as editor for the XML-based ECMAScript Components standard. In his non-tech life, Rich is author of *Christian Prayer For Dummies* and enjoys writing on his Web site called Digitalwalk.net (www.digitalwalk.net). Rich lives with his wife and three boys in Princeton, Massachusetts. He can be reached at rich@digitalwalk.net.

Richard Mansfield's recent titles include *Visual Basic .NET Weekend Crash Course, Visual Basic .NET Database Programming For Dummies, Visual Basic 6 Database Programming For Dummies* (all published by Wiley), *Hacker Attack* (Sybex), and *The Wi-Fi Experience: Everyone's Guide to 802.11b Wireless Networking* (Que).

From 1981 through 1987, he was editor of *COMPUTE! Magazine,* during which time he wrote hundreds of magazine articles and two columns. From 1987 to 1991, he was editorial director and partner in Signal Research and began writing books full-time in 1991. He has written 34 computer books since 1982. Of those, four became bestsellers: *Machine Language for Beginners* (COMPUTE! Books), *The Second Book of Machine Language* (COMPUTE! Books), *The Visual Guide to Visual Basic* (Ventana), and *The Visual Basic Power Toolkit* (Ventana, with Evangelos Petroutsos). Overall, his books have sold more than 500,000 copies worldwide and have been translated into 11 languages.

Dedication

To Kimberly, with a grateful heart. — *Richard Wagner*

This book is dedicated to Florence Mansfield. — *Richard Mansfield*

Authors' Acknowledgments

Richard Wagner: In writing this book, I'd like to thank Andrea Boucher for her guiding hand throughout the project and unwavering confidence that I'd pull through even when the deadline loomed ever near; Bob Woerner for his relentless push to get this book going and completed; and Richard Mansfield for making such a valuable authoring contribution to this book. Finally, I'd especially like to express earnest gratitude to my wife, Kimberly, and our three boys, the J-team, for their patience and grace throughout the entire project.

Richard Mansfield: I was very lucky to have two first-rate editors work with me on this book. Project Editor Andrea Boucher deserves much credit for her discernment and the exceptionally high quality of her editing. I've written 36 books now, and in my experience, truly outstanding editors are relatively rare. Andrea has just the right touch: She knows when you've been naughty and she knows when you've been nice. And her suggested changes are nearly always an improvement.

Technical Editor Chris McGee is also well above the average. He thoroughly reviewed the manuscript and carefully tested all the code. He made many important suggestions and considerably enhanced the book's overall quality.

I'd also like to thank Acquisitions Editor Bob Woerner for initiating this project and for his thoughtful advice throughout. To these, and all the other good people at Wiley who contributed to the book, my thanks for the time and care you took to ensure quality every step along the way to publication.

Finally, I want to give special thanks to my agent, Matt Wagner of Waterside Productions, who has been offering me good advice for over a decade.

Publisher's Acknowledgments

We're proud of this book; please send us your comments through our online registration form located at www.dummies.com/register/.

Some of the people who helped bring this book to market include the following:

Acquisitions, Editorial, and Media Development

Project Editor: Andrea C. Boucher

Acquisitions Editor: Bob Woerner

Technical Editor: Christopher McGee

Editorial Manager: Carol Sheehan

Senior Permissions Editor: Carmen Krikorian

Media Development Specialist: Travis Silvers

Media Development Manager: Laura Carpenter

Media Development Supervisor: Richard Graves

Media Development Coordinator: Sarah Cummings

Editorial Assistant: Amanda Foxworth

Cartoons: Rich Tennant (www.the5thwave.com)

Production

Project Coordinator: Dale White

Layout and Graphics: Amanda Carter, Jennifer Click, Carrie Foster, LeAndra Hosier, Kristin McMullan

Proofreaders: Laura Albert, John Tyler Connoley, Arielle Carole Mennelle

Indexer: Johnna VanHoose

Publishing and Editorial for Technology Dummies

    Richard Swadley, Vice President and Executive Group Publisher

    Andy Cummings, Vice President and Publisher

    Mary C. Corder, Editorial Director

Publishing for Consumer Dummies

    Diane Graves Steele, Vice President and Publisher

    Joyce Pepple, Acquisitions Director

Composition Services

    Gerry Fahey, Vice President of Production Services

    Debbie Stailey, Director of Composition Services

Contents at a Glance

Table of Contents

Introduction

Seemingly everyone I talk to these days wants to use Extensible Markup Language (XML) to help out what they do. Software makers see XML as a better way to exchange data with other applications. Web developers realize how much more efficient it is use XML rather than Hypertext Markup Language (HTML) to design Web pages. Heck, I could be wrong, but I think I even overheard my mailman talking about how to use XML to make his route go quicker!

Indeed, many people are hailing XML as the solution to many age-old problems in sharing and managing data. Given that fact, you'd think the technology would be so complex that it would take an MIT degree to understand. Yet, perhaps the most amazing aspect of XML is its overall simplicity and intuitive nature. Oh, there are certainly tricky XML concepts that do have a noticeable learning curve, but by and large, XML is a *Dummies*-like technology: approachable for normal folks like you and I.

Use *XML All-in-One Desk Reference For Dummies* as your guide for exploring the powerful, but approachable, world of XML

How This Book Is Organized

XML All-in-One Desk Reference For Dummies contains seven books, each of which is focused on a key XML-related topic. If you decide to read *XML All-in-One Desk Reference For Dummies* from cover to cover, you'll be turning the pages faster than you would a John Grisham thriller, waiting to see how the lawyer frees the innocent victim. Oops, wrong book! But, seriously, if you do decide to read the book from start to finish, you'll find that the topics are logically ordered, with each successive book and chapter rounding out the previous material.

However, don't think the book has to be read from front to back. *XML All-in-One Desk Reference For Dummies* is a reference, enabling you to easily access the specific information you need at any given moment.

Here are the seven books, and what they contain:

Book I: Describing Data with XML. Start off your exploratory journey into the world of XML by looking at why the markup language is a natural for describing data. You'll discover the basic building blocks of XML as well as how to construct a well-formed document.

Book II: Validating XML. This book takes you into the nuts and bolts of validating your XML documents with Document Type Definitions (DTD) and XML schemas. These validating solutions are so powerful, the store clerk won't even ask to see your ID!

Book III: Presenting XML. An XML document is not much to look at by itself; truth be told, it's actually ugly, filled with data and tags all jumbled up together in a mess of a document. It's enough to give you nightmares! Because XML has no built-in mechanism for formatting, it needs help from other technologies like Cascading Style Sheets (CSS) and Extensible Stylesheet Language Formatting Objects (XSL-FO) when you want to display XML in a browser or in print. This book dives into these styling options for XML and shows you how to use them.

Book IV: Transforming XML. As you read through this book, you'll discover how you can take an XML document and change it to look completely different, such as an HTML file or even a different XML structure. You don't need Doug Henning to perform these magic acts; instead, you need a mouthful-of-a-technology called Extensible Stylesheet Language Transformations (XSLT).

Book V: Working with the Rest of the X-Team. When you go to a McDonald's restaurant, there is one thing you can always count on — that the menu will be filled with McSomethings: McMuffin, McFlurry, McChicken, and so on. Well, after reading this book, you'll realize that a seemingly mandatory requirement of any XML-related technology is that it begins with an X. In this book, you'll discover four more of those emerging technologies with the familiar X at the start of their names: XLink, XPointer, XForms, and XHTML.

Ever wonder if McDonald's merged with the W3C, what kind of names we'd get? "I'd like a McLink, McPath, and a McSLT, but please hold the lettuce and tomato."

Book VI: Processing XML. The previous four books focus on XML and related technologies from the "inside." This book takes an "outside" look at how to work with and process XML documents from external applications using Simple API For XML (SAX) and Document Object Model (DOM), which are two different approaches for working with XML documents.

Book VII: XML Web Services. The final book dives into the emerging new world of XML Web services and introduces you to a new set of XML-based Web service technologies, some of which mysteriously do not contain the letter X in them: SOAP, XML-RPC, WSDL, UDDI, and VoiceXML.

Conventions Used in This Book

While *For Dummies* books are never one to bow to convention, you will want to keep the following in mind as you read this book:

✦ *Term definitions.* When a new term is introduced and defined in this text, that word is italicized. For example, consider the following excerpt:

> An *element* is made up of a start tag, an end tag, and content in between the two. The *start tag* is enclosed in angle brackets and is given a name that appropriately describes the data inside the element

✦ *Syntax definitions.* When a new programming concept is introduced and the syntax shown, you'll often have two parts of the syntax: parts that have to be typed exactly like they appear in the definition, while other parts are placeholders for the real values you'd plug into your code. In the book, code that must be entered exactly is shown in normal mono-space text, while pieces that you can define yourself are italicized. For example, as you'll find out in Book I, Chapter 4, the syntax for declaring a namespace is:

```
<elementName xmlns:prefix="URI">
</elementName>
```

In this example, `xmlns:` is text that must be written in your document exactly as shown, while *elementName*, *prefix*, and *URI* are all variables that you can define as you wish in your code.

✦ *Code samples.* Code samples are provided to help explain a new concept and illustrate how it works in the real world. For example, the following snippet demonstrates a particular use of XPath, which you'll find out about in Book IV, Chapter 3:

```
<xsl:template match="child::region">
  <xsl:value-of select="attribute::name"/>
</xsl:template>
```

If you enter code by hand, make sure you type the code exactly as is shown. Call XML picky if you like, but changes in case or missing brackets here or there will give you fits when you try to process the document.

✦ *Highlighting in code samples.* On occasion, when I want to point out something in particular to pay attention to in the code sample, I'll bold the text. For example, the following code sample highlights the name-space-related parts of the XML structure:

```
<dtv:dish xmlns:dtv="http://www.directv.com/2003/dish">
  <dtv:model>A32201-WZ-TURBO</dtv:model>
  <dtv:size>2.0 x 2.0 x .75</dtv:size>
  <dtv:weight>27 lbs.</dtv:weight>
</dtv:dish>
```

✦ *XML names and instructions.* When XML element names or instructions appear within the text of the book, they look like this.

Icons Used in This Book

Tips point you to key techniques that can use to save time and effort.

Remember icons are used to draw attention to something in the text that is particularly important and can greatly benefit your understanding of how to work with XML.

The Warning icon is synonymous with "Watch out, Buddy!" Pay attention to warnings so that they can save you from falling into XML quick sand.

The Technical Stuff icon is the used to highlight techno-mumbo-jumbo that is interesting for XML geeks and geek-wanna-bes, but is not essential for you to know.

What I Assume About You

In *XML All-in-One Desk Reference For Dummies*, I don't assume that you have any prior know-how of XML or related technologies when you start the book. In addition, if you've ever worked with HTML or a general programming language before, you'll find that background will give you a leg up as you explore the world of XML.

A Word About the W3C

Throughout the book, you'll find references to the W3C. I know, it sounds like a tax form that you have to fill out when you start a job in the U.S. But it actually stands for the World Wide Web Consortium (commonly referred to as the W3C). The W3C is a group of Web stakeholders, including universities, companies, and other technology geeks that come together under the W3C umbrella to define web-related standards (known technically as "W3C recommendations").

The W3C is the body responsible for defining XML. In addition to XML itself, the W3C defines recommendations for HTML, Cascading Stylesheets, and many XML-related technologies you'll be exploring throughout this book, such as XSLT (Extensible Stylesheet Language Transformations), XPath, and XLink. You can visit their web site at www.w3.org.

Where to Go from Here

If you have a specific topic that you'd like to immediately dive into, consider the following jumping-off points:

✦ For the basics of an XML document, go to Book I, Chapters 1-3.

✦ For an understanding of what namespaces are, go to Book I, Chapter 4.

✦ For the two key ways to validate XML documents, see Book II.

✦ For discovering how to make XML look presentable, jump to Book III.

✦ For what to do when you to change an XML document into another structure, check out Book IV.

✦ For a sneak peak into emerging XML technologies, go to Book V.

✦ For a discussion on how to work with and parse XML from other applications, see Book VI.

✦ For knowing how XML fits into the world of Web services, jump on over to Book VII.

Book I

Describing Data with XML

Contents at a Glance

Chapter 1: Introducing XML

Throughout the past decade, a myriad of technologies have been touted as the "next big thing." Yet, despite their initial acclaim and fanfare, most of these technologies are exposed as pretenders and eventually fade into that Great Fad Wasteland in the Sky, alongside the Pet Rock, Rubik's Cube, and a host of teeny pop idols.

Extensible Markup Language (XML), however, was not one of those wannabes. Yes, XML was bandied about by industry pundits from the start as the "next big thing." But as the years go by, XML is proving itself worthy of all the hype, as it is being used in practical and significant ways by untold thousands of developers.

As you begin your journey through the world of XML, this chapter introduces you to Extensible Markup Language and helps you understand where it came from, what it can do for you, and why XML is a natural way to work with all types of information.

Tipping a Hat to HTML

XML owes a lot to Hypertext Markup Language (HTML) for its emergence as the "technology of choice" for many developers today. First, if it wasn't for the widespread popularity of HTML, markup languages would have never been considered as a viable way to work with data. Second, if it wasn't for the major shortcomings of HTML, the need for proposing an alternative wouldn't have been compelling to so many people.

HTML: The information blender

The term "HTML" is synonymous with the World Wide Web. Heck, even my mother has heard of HTML. From the very get-go, HTML has been used as the standard data format to display content over the Web. Documents written in the markup language are stored on Web servers and then delivered to a Web browser when its Web address (also called a *URL)* is requested. The Web browser, which knows how to work with HTML documents, processes the document and renders it as a Web page.

HTML is a tag-based language that has a defined set of formatting tags or *elements* to define formatting instructions. An element is simply a special code inside a document that tells the browser how to display the information it contains. For example, suppose you'd like to format a sentence in a Web page so that it looks like this:

The **dog** ate *my* homework.

The HTML code you'd write might look something like this:

```
<p>The <b>dog</b> ate <i>my</i> homework.</p>
```

The p element is used to define a paragraph, so that everything within the open and close p tags is considered a paragraph. The b element is for bolded text, so text within the b element is bolded. Finally, the i element is for italicized text, so words inside the i element are italicized.

HTML is popular not only because you can display cool graphics and play annoying MIDI sounds when a Web page is loaded, but, as you can see from the simple example shown above, it is also very easy to learn and work with. Because HTML is just plain text, you can use a visual Web page software to design a Web page, but you can also use plain old Notepad and achieve the exact same result.

When people saw how easy it was to work with HTML, everyone and their brother began to build Web sites. As the Web became more and more popular, businesses in turn began to discover news ways in which they could reach customers through this emerging technology.

But the more people who began to develop innovative new ways to utilize the Web, the more the Web began to resemble an ever-expanding house with an inadequate infrastructure. Let me explain. Imagine a new furnace is installed into a one bedroom house and is designed to effectively heat that size of home. Yet, while keeping the same furnace, suppose you expand the house, constructing a second story and adding on more and more rooms, ultimately transforming the 1,000 square-foot dwelling into a 4,500 square-foot mansion. When the bitter cold of the winter comes, it would become very obvious to the homeowners that a furnace that worked well for a small home doesn't do nearly so well when its job becomes four times more difficult.

In the same way, HTML became a victim of the success of the Web. It was originally designed solely as a way to format and layout information. However, because people began adding more and more uses for the Web,

HTML has been forced to do far more than was ever intended for it, much like that little furnace in the big mansion.

One of the most prolific examples of HTML's inadequacy on the Web is displaying and manipulating information that is stored in a database. Consider a typical example of the Slurpbucks coffee roaster company who wants to allow customers to order coffee beans over the Web. The information about each coffee product is stored in a database that looks like the following:

Coffee	Origin	Taste	Price	Availability	Best With
Guatemalan Express	Guatemala	Mild and Bland	11.99	Year-round	Breakfast
Costa Rican Deacon	Costa Rica	Exotic and Untamed	12.99	Year-round	Dessert
Ethiopian Sunset Supremo	Ethiopia	Cheap but Expensive	14.99	Limited	Chocolate
Kenyan Elephantismo	Kenya	Solid yet Understated	13.99	Year-round	Elephant Ears

In order to be able to present this list of coffee beans on the Web, this information has to be extracted from a database and then converted into an HTML table that the browser can display. The HTML code would look something like this:

```
<table border="1">
  <tr colspan="5">
    <th>Coffee</th>
    <th>Origin</th>
    <th>Taste</th>
    <th>Price</th>
    <th>Availability</th>
    <th>Best With</th>
  </tr>
  <tr colspan="5">
    <td>Guatemalan Express</td>
    <td>Guatemala</td>
    <td>Mild and Bland</td>
    <td>11.99</td>
    <td>Year-round</td>
    <td>Breakfast</td>
  </tr>
  <tr colspan="5">
    <td>Costa Rican Deacon</td>
    <td>Costa Rica</td>
    <td>Exotic and Untamed</td>
    <td>12.99</td>
    <td>Year-round</td>
    <td>Dessert</td>
```

```
    </tr>
    <tr colspan="5">
      <td>Ethiopian Sunset Supremo</td>
      <td>Ethiopia</td>
      <td>Cheap But Expensive</td>
      <td>14.99</td>
      <td>Limited</td>
      <td>Chocolate</td>
    </tr>
    <tr colspan="5">
      <td>Kenyan Elephantismo</td>
      <td>Guatemala</td>
      <td>Solid yet Understated</td>
      <td>13.99</td>
      <td>Year-round</td>
      <td>Elephant Ears</td>
    </tr>
</table>
```

When you first look at this table in a Web browser, you might think "cool beans" because HTML provided a way to display a database table inside of a browser. While that is useful, only when you start to look closer do you begin to see the major weakness of HTML starting to appear in the cracks.

In this simple example, I transform meaningful collections of data into a table that displays inside of a browser. But the information is now not useful for much else. While inside the database, the prices of the coffees all were identified as "price" fields, and the database record served as the means to store a group of related information. However, when this information was outputted to HTML, the pieces of information lost their identify. They are now just raw pieces of text that have row and column formatting instructions around them. Any concept of a "coffee" record is now gone.

If Slurpbucks wanted to display only product information on its Web site and nothing else, then this lose of identity is no big deal. But like most other people who use the Web, Slurpbucks is discovering that they have needs that go far beyond that. They'd like to be able to work with the same database data inside the browser to perform additional functionality and would like to easily exchange data with the server.

Slurpbucks can create a Moo-Cow-A-Chino drink by mixing espresso, chocolate syrup, frothed milk, and whip cream together. But after these ingredients are blended, there's no practical way to extract the chocolate syrup from the drink. In the same way, it is hard to extract useful information from HTML documents because the data is mixed into the display instructions.

Therefore, you can think of HTML acting as an "information blender": start with a cup or two of data and then add a pinch of formatting instructions into a blender. Turn the blender's power on high, and, after a few seconds, out comes a pureed mixture of the two. The HTML page may look great, but don't try to use the raw materials again for a different purpose.

XML: Giving data the focus

XML was developed as a solution to the "information blender" effect of HTML. XML allows you to work with structured information on the Web without requiring the data to lose its identity. The inventors of XML wanted to be able to work with structured data in a format that was

✦ **Similar to HTML** so that it can be easy to read and work with, but

✦ **Different enough from HTML** that XML could effectively describe data in a manner that was separate from display instructions

Therefore, the inventors wanted to preserve the basic markup language capabilities of HTML. But instead of using the markup tags for formatting purposes, they wanted to use the tags for describing the data inside of it.

For example, suppose you start with a group of related information, expressed as a row in a database table:

Coffee	Origin	Taste	Price	Availability	Best With
Guatemalan Express	Guatemala	Mild and Bland	11.99	Year-round	Breakfast

As I show in the preceding section, if you output this cluster of information into HTML markup code, you lose its collective identity:

```
<tr colspan="5">
  <td>Guatemalan Express</td>
  <td>Guatemala</td>
  <td>Mild and Bland</td>
  <td>11.99</td>
  <td>Year-round</td>
  <td>Breakfast</td>
</tr>
```

In contrast, XML combines these two concepts (markup language and data identity) by using HTML-like markup code to describe and structure the data:

```
<coffee>
  <name>Guatemalan Express</name>
  <origin>Guatemala</origin>
  <taste>Mild and Bland</taste>
  <price>11.99</price>
  <availability>Year-round</availability>
  <bestwith>Breakfast</bestwith>
</coffee>
```

What is the W3C?

XML was developed by a group known as the World Wide Web Consortium, or the W3C. The W3C is a group of Web stakeholders, including universities, companies, and other technology geeks that come together under the W3C umbrella to define Web-related standards (known technically as "W3C recommendations").

In addition to XML itself, the W3C defines recommendations for HTML and many XML-related technologies you'll be exploring throughout this book, such as XSLT (Extensible Stylesheet Language Transformations), XPath, and XLink. You can visit their Web site at www.w3.org.

XML: A Natural Way to Describe Stuff

Another reason why XML is so popular is that it is such a natural way to describe the data that you work with on a day-in, day-out basis. Most every kind of information you deal with has an implicit structure to it and can be expressed as XML.

Consider the following letter to the editor:

November 31, 2003

Dear Recipe Digest:

Thanks for your recent article on snicker-doodle noodles. However, I don't think you gave enough credit to the cook who invented the original snicker-doodle noodle – Peter Pasta.

Warm Regards,
Mrs. Peter Pasta

Instead of thinking of the letter as a set of grouped paragraphs, it actually has far more structure to it. For example, the above letter could be expressed as XML as the following code:

```
<letter>
  <date>November 31, 2003</date>
  <salutation>Dear Recipe Digest:</salutation>
  <body>Thanks for your recent article on snicker-doodle
    noodles. However, I don't think you gave enough credit to
    the cook who invented the original snicker-doodle noodle
    - Peter Pasta.</body>
  <closing>Warm Regards,</closing>
  <signature>Mrs. Peter Pasta</signature>
</letter>
```

Or consider the dialogue from a movie, *The Princess Bride*:

Inigo Montoya: "Who are you?"

Dread Pirate Roberts: "No one of consequence."

Inigo Montoya: "I must know."

Dread Pirate Roberts: "Get used to disappointment."

Expressed as XML, this text could be structured as follows:

```
<dialogue film="The Princess Bride">
  <InigoMontoya>Who are you?</InigoMontoya>
  <DreadPirateRoberts>No one of
  consequence.</DreadPirateRoberts>
  <InigoMontoya>I must know.</InigoMontoya>
  <DreadPirateRoberts>Get used to
  disappointment.</DreadPirateRoberts>
</dialogue>
```

Finally, those Slurpbucks coffee beans could also be represented as an XML structure:

```
<coffees>
 <region name="Latin America">
  <coffee name="Guatemalan Express" origin="Guatemala">
    <taste>Mild and Bland</taste>
    <price>11.99</price>
    <availability>Year-round</availability>
    <bestwith>Breakfast</bestwith>
  </coffee>
  <coffee name="Costa Rican Deacon" origin="Costa Rica">
    <taste>Exotic and Untamed</taste>
    <price>12.99</price>
    <availability>Year-round</availability>
    <bestwith>Dessert</bestwith>
  </coffee>
 </region>
 <region name="Africa">
  <coffee name="Ethiopian Sunset Supremo" origin="Ethiopia">
    <taste>Cheap but Expensive</taste>
    <price>14.99</price>
    <availability>Limited</availability>
    <bestwith>Chocolate</bestwith>
  </coffee>
  <coffee name="Kenyan Elephantismo" origin="Kenya">
    <taste>Solid yet Understated</taste>
    <price>3.99</price>
```

```
        <availability>Year-round</availability>
        <bestwith>Elephant Ears</bestwith>
    </coffee>
    </region>
</coffees>
```

From these examples, you can see XML describes information in a very logical and straightforward manner — *put descriptive tags before and after the text values and you've just about got an XML document!*

While HTML is standardized with a fixed set of formatting elements, the only thing standardized about XML is its syntax rules, not the actual tag names. This aspect of XML shows you why it is so flexible in most any situation.

A set of defined XML tags used for a particular purpose is called an *XML vocabulary*.

The Life of an XML Document

XML may be a great technology, but unless you are among the geekiest of folks, you're not going to want to spend your days looking "under the hood" at a raw XML document. Clearly then, in order to make XML usable in the real world, you need to do something to an XML document to make it presentable or to be otherwise useful.

It may be thus helpful to think about the life of an XML document as flowing through three stages: create, parse, and consume. Each of these stages are described below and shown in Figure 1-1.

- ✦ **Stage 1: Creating an XML document.** The first stage is to create an XML document either by hand using an editor, such as Notepad, or to export data from another software application into XML format. Many databases now allow you to export data as XML documents, along with such everyday software applications as Microsoft Excel or Word.

- ✦ **Stage 2: Parsing the XML document.** After you've created the XML document, the second stage is to parse (or process) the document to check to see whether the document structure and content is acceptable for using the document in Stage 3.

    Many software applications that consume XML (see Stage 3) have an XML parser built into them. For example, if you display an XML document inside Microsoft Internet Explorer, it first parses the XML document and then renders it inside of the browser window.

Additionally, there are also several freely available XML parsers that enable you to work with XML documents for your own unique uses. These are discussed in greater detail in Book I, Chapter 3.

✦ **Stage 3: Consuming the XML document.** The final stage is actually doing something with the XML document that has been "approved" by the parser. Whereas an HTML document has one primary purpose — display in a Web browser — an XML document actually has several possible ways of being utilized by a variety of applications, as Figure 1-1 illustrates.

Some applications can render the XML and display the document in a presentable fashion. However, an XML document by itself does not contain formatting instructions, so the basic view of an XML document inside an application is usually going to either be the raw file (such as in Microsoft WordPad, shown in Figure 1-2) or perhaps as a tree structure (such as in Internet Explorer, shown in Figure 1-3). You discover in Book III that you can apply formatting instructions to XML documents using Cascading Style Sheets (CSS) or Extensible Stylesheet Language (XSL) to make XML documents look presentable in the fashion of an HTML document.

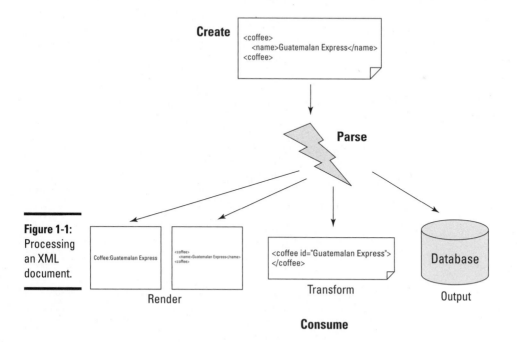

Figure 1-1:
Processing an XML document.

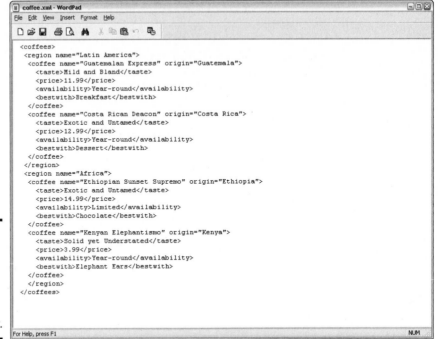

```
<coffees>
 <region name="Latin America">
  <coffee name="Guatemalan Express" origin="Guatemala">
   <taste>Mild and Bland</taste>
   <price>11.99</price>
   <availability>Year-round</availability>
   <bestwith>Breakfast</bestwith>
  </coffee>
  <coffee name="Costa Rican Deacon" origin="Costa Rica">
   <taste>Exotic and Untamed</taste>
   <price>12.99</price>
   <availability>Year-round</availability>
   <bestwith>Dessert</bestwith>
  </coffee>
 </region>
 <region name="Africa">
  <coffee name="Ethiopian Sunset Supremo" origin="Ethiopia">
   <taste>Exotic and Untamed</taste>
   <price>14.99</price>
   <availability>Limited</availability>
   <bestwith>Chocolate</bestwith>
  </coffee>
  <coffee name="Kenyan Elephantismo" origin="Kenya">
   <taste>Solid yet Understated</taste>
   <price>3.99</price>
   <availability>Year-round</availability>
   <bestwith>Elephant Ears</bestwith>
  </coffee>
 </region>
</coffees>
```

Figure 1-2:
Microsoft
WordPad
rendering
an XML
document
as plain text.

XML documents are used for more purposes than just rendering, however. Perhaps you need to change the document into a completely new structure for another purpose. XSLT is the XML-based technology that enables you to perform exactly these kind of transformations and is covered in detail in Book IV. Or perhaps you have a need to move the XML data into a traditional relational database. Many databases today support importing of XML documents.

XML is an extensible, flexible technology for defining data. The ways in which you can utilize XML are as extensive, too.

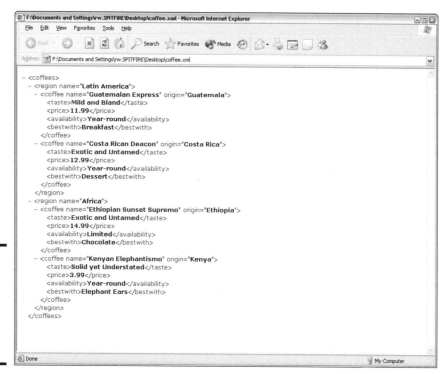

Figure 1-3:
Internet
Explorer
rendering
an XML
document
as a tree.

Yes, but Is XML Useful?

By now, you've discovered some of the basics of what XML is and how it works, but some of the implications of using XML in the real world may not be immediately apparent. While there are many reasons why XML is a useful technology, the following are but a sampling of some of these key uses.

✦ **XML allows you to create your own markup language.** Unlike HTML, XML has no predefined set of elements. You can create your own elements based on the specific needs of your application, company, or industry. Consider the following XML code snippet:

```
<coffee>
  <name>Guatemalan Express</name>
  <origin>Guatemala</origin>
  <taste>Mild and Bland</taste>
  <price>11.99</price>
  <availability>Year-round</availability>
  <bestwith>Breakfast</bestwith>
</coffee>
```

By reading the element names and then looking at their content, you can easily determine that the structure describes the details of a particular coffee. Check out Book I, Chapter 2 for more information on how to create your own set of XML elements.

✦ **XML data can be presented in a variety of ways.** XML concentrates on describing data, not on the appearance of the data. However, as I mention earlier in the chapter, you can display XML documents in a variety of ways based on CSS and XSL technologies. XML's ability to separate data from the presentation instructions allows you to change the way an XML document is displayed without changing the actual data.

✦ **XML enables more robust and efficient information exchange over the Web.** XHTML is considered the "next generation" version of HTML and adds many of the advantages of XML to the older HTML language. (See Book V, Chapter 4 for more on XHTML.) When browsers eventually support it, the data exchange between a browser and a Web server will be greatly optimized. For example, rather than reloading an entire HTML page, XHTML will enable you to download only the portion of the page that has changed since the last reload.

✦ **XML is well-suited as means of transferring data across platforms.** Businesses depend on reliable data interchange within and across companies. However, the age-old challenge in transferring data has been that everyone stores data in a different structure using different software tools. Fortune 500 companies have turned to such technologies as EDI (Electronic Data Interchange) as a standardized way to transfer data across companies. But EDI is very expensive and not practical except for the largest of companies. In contrast, XML provides a low-cost, low-barriers to entry solution to provide a universal data format that makes communication across heterogeneous platforms possible.

Yup, that "X" stands for *extensible*

Working with HTML and other legacy technologies is something like a goldfish swimming in a bowl. A goldfish can survive in a small bowl, but the goldfish's life is characterized by the severe limits of its confines. Studies show that even after you set a goldfish free in a lake, the goldfish will continue to swim in small circles, not realizing the vastness of its new domain.

In the same way, as you start to work with XML, you may find yourself "swimming in small circles" as you grapple with the extensible nature of XML. Those accustomed to working with HTML can be so used to describing data in a

way that makes sense to HTML's fishbowl that they find it hard to believe that XML actually enables them to describe data like it should be done — without forcing it into an artificial structure imposed by something outside.

Therefore, when you are defining an XML structure to describe data, don't fall into the trap of defining the information based on how it is going to be presented or utilized. Instead, try and look at the natural organization and types of data that you are trying to structure and produce an XML vocabulary accordingly.

25

XML and EDI

EDI (Electronic Data Interchange) is a technology that has been used over the last 40 years to transfer documents and data between businesses. Many see XML as a successor to this technology due to three reasons:

✔ **Lower cost:** XML does not require a high priced infrastructure like EDI does. Therefore, XML is a practical technology that even businesses large and small can utilize.

✔ **More flexible:** XML enables you to store data in a structured format using your own XML vocabulary. In contrast, EDI is far less flexible and does not, for example, allow individual business units in a company to define their own business rules. Instead, it has a fixed transaction set, which is required to be followed by all business units.

✔ **Easy to interpret**: EDI requires specialized translation software to map the EDI formats to the formats used by individual trading partners. In contrast, XML documents can be easily interpreted by the target systems by using an everyday XML parser, many of which are available for free download on the Internet.

Chapter 2: Dissecting an XML Document

*O*kay class, it's dissection time. But don't worry if you're squeamish — unlike your high school biology course, you won't have to put on a lab smock, smell formaldehyde, or gaze upon a cut-up frog. Instead, you can slice and dice your way through the relatively clean confines of an XML document.

In this chapter, you explore the innards of an XML document and discover what it takes to build one. You begin by looking at *elements* (the basic building blocks of XML) and then go on to explore a document's organization and structure.

Elements: The Basic Building Blocks

If you study the human body and want to understand how it works, you'd probably want to start with the cell, the basic building block of a human. Similarly, when you want to understand how XML works, you have to start with its most fundamental unit, the element.

An *element* is made up of a start tag, an end tag, and the content in between the two (see Figure 2-1). The *start tag* is enclosed in angle brackets and is given a name that appropriately describes the data inside the element. The *end tag* is also enclosed in angle brackets but is prefixed with a forward slash (/) after the opening bracket, followed by the same identifier as its companion start tag. The *content* is the stuff that falls in between these tags.

Figure 2-1:
An element
is the basic
building
block of
XML.

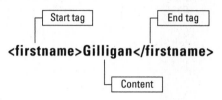

An element can contain text, other elements, or both inside its start and end tags. For example, each of the following are valid XML elements:

```
<quote>We thought you was a toad.</quote>

<quote>
  <spokenby>Delmar</spokenby>
  <source>O Brother, Where Art Thou</source>
  <text>We thought you was a toad.</text>
</quote>

<quote><spokenby>Delmar</spokenby> said: We thought you was a
    toad.</quote>
```

The first element contains text, the second element contains elements nested inside of it, and the third element contains a mixture of both text and elements.

If you've ever viewed the source of an HTML file, the syntax shown above should look familiar to you, since HTML follows a similar tag/content structure. However, XML permits a shortcut syntax that you can use that is not available in HTML. When you have an element that doesn't contain any content, you can combine the start and end tags to form an *empty element*. To combine, take the forward slash (/) from the end tag and add it onto the end of the start tag, like this:

```
<combo></combo>
```

is the same as:

```
<combo/>
```

To illustrate, suppose the `quote` element below has a `favorite` element that is used to denote the favorite film quote in the document:

```
<quote>
  <spokenby>Delmar</spokenby>
  <source>O Brother, Where Art Thou</source>
```

```
<text>We thought you was a toad.</text>
<favorite></favorite>
</quote>
```

Because the `favorite` element is used as flag, it doesn't need any content. Therefore, the `favorite` element syntax can be reduced to an empty tag, as shown in the following code:

```
<quote>
  <spokenby>Delmar</spokenby>
  <source>O Brother, Where Art Thou</source>
  <text>We thought you was a toad.</text>
  <favorite/>
</quote>
```

Attributes: Describing Elements

While elements contain information and a descriptive tag name that labels the content, you often have additional qualities that you'd like to associate with that piece of data. For example, consider the following quotes `element` that contains several `quote` elements:

```
<quotes>
  <quote>We thought you was a toad.</quote>
  <quote>To infinity, and beyond!</quote>
  <quote>It seems to me that, aside from being a little
    mentally ill, she's pretty normal.</quote>
  <quote>More isn't always better, Linus. Sometimes it's just
    more.</quote>
  <quote>Who are you really, and what were you before? What
    did you do, and what did you think, huh?</quote>
  <quote>Well, it's Groundhog Day... again...</quote>
  <quote>To the pain...</quote>
  <quote>Only one is a wanderer; two together are always
    going somewhere.</quote>
</quotes>
```

For each of the `quote` elements, suppose that you'd like to add an ID to identify the element and a category to classify each of the quotes. You can do so by adding attributes to the inside of the element's start tag. An *attribute* consists of a name and value bound together in a *name-value pair*. A name-value pair is formatted as follows:

```
name="value"
```

or

```
name='value'
```

The pair must always be connected using the equal sign, and the attribute value must always be enclosed in either single or double quotes.

You can add as many attributes to an XML element as you wish, so long as the names are unique and you separate the name-value pairs with one or more spaces. In this example, I'll add two attributes to each quote element:

```
<quotes>
  <quote id="101" film="O Brother Where Art Thou"
   category="Comedy">
    We thought you was a toad.</quote>
  <quote id="102" film="Toy Story" category="Children">
    To infinity, and beyond!</quote>
  <quote id="103" film="Benny & Joon"
   category="Comedy/Drama">
    It seems to me that, aside from being a little mentally
   ill, she's pretty normal.</quote>
  <quote id="104" film="Sabrina" category="Poignant">
    More isn't always better, Linus. Sometimes it's just
    more.</quote>
  <quote id="105" film="Casablanca" category="Romance">
    Who are you really, and what were you before? What did
    you do, and what did you think, huh?</quote>
  <quote id="106" film="Groundhog Day" category="Comedy">
    Well, it's Groundhog Day... again...</quote>
  <quote id="107" film="Princess Bride" category="Comedy">
    To the pain...</quote>
  <quote id="101" film="Vertigo" category="Romance">
    Only one is a wanderer; two together are always going
   somewhere.</quote>
</quotes>
```

What's In a Name?

In "XMLSpeak," the name of an element or attribute is referred to as a name token or *NMToken*. As I discuss in Book I, Chapter 1, XML has no fixed set of elements or attributes like HTML does. You are free then to name your NMTokens in any way that you please. However, be aware of the rules concerning permissible characters and case sensitivity.

Legal characters

There are some rules that you need to keep in mind as you work with NMTokens:

✦ **Starting character.** NMTokens must begin with an alphabetic letter or an underscore. You can't use a number or a special character.

✦ **Valid characters.** NMTokens can include any alphanumeric character, underscores, hyphens, and periods.

✦ **Invalid characters.** NMTokens can't include any white space or any other special character not mentioned in the valid characters list.

Table 2-1 lists some examples displaying valid and invalid element names.

Table 2-1	Valid and Invalid Element Names
Valid Name	*Invalid Name*
<darnquote>	<#&$!quote>
<film_quote>	<film quote>
<quote1>	<1quote>
<film.quote>	<.film.quote>
<_quote>	<quote>>

Case sensitivity

Unlike HTML, which ignores case altogether, XML element and attribute names are case sensitive. As a result, each of the following are considered different element names because their case is different:

```
<filmquote/>
<FILMQUOTE/>
<filmQuote/>
```

To avoid confusion, you should consistently use either all lower, all upper-case, or mixed case for the XML documents you create. I recommend standardizing on lowercase — it's the convention most developers follow.

Looking at XML through HTML eyes

You may be approaching XML after having already worked with HTML to create Web pages. If so, as you begin working with XML, you'll naturally look at the markup language through HTML eyes.

If you have an HTML background, you definitely have a head start as you begin to learn the syntax of XML. Use this section as a primer to reinforce some of the similarities and differences in the syntax of the two markup languages.

Similarities

1. Element is basic building block.

The element is the basic building block of XML, much like in HTML. For example, a paragraph in HTML is defined as:

(continued)

(continued)

```
<p>Only one is a wanderer; two
   together are always going
   somewhere.</p>
```

Similarly, a quote in XML can be defined to look something like this:

```
<quote>Only one is a wanderer;
   two together are always
   going somewhere.</quote>
```

2. Attributes are used to describe elements.

XML follows HTML's practice of using attributes (name-value pairs) inside elements to provide additional descriptive information about an element. For example, the `bgcolor` attribute provides additional information related to HTML's `body` element:

```
<body bgcolor="#FFFFFF">

</body>
```

In the same way, XML uses name-value pairs, as shown below:

```
<quote id="101">
 Only one is a wanderer; two
   together are always going
   somewhere.
</quote>
```

In this XML snippet, the `id` attribute provides additional information related to the `quote` element.

Differences

HTML and XML have definite similarities, but there are also important variations in syntax rules as well. The three most important are as follows.

1. XML is well-formed.

HTML has always been laid back in some of its syntax requirements, not always forcing you to have closing tags on some of the elements, such as the paragraph (`<p>`) element. For example, both of the following lines are valid HTML:

```
<p>Hello. My name is Inigo
   Montoya. You killed my
   father. Prepare to die.
```

and

```
<p>Hello. My name is Inigo
   Montoya. You killed my
   father. Prepare to die.</p>
```

In contrast, XML is much more rigid: All XML documents must be "well-formed," meaning that every begin tag needs to have a matching end tag:

```
<source>Princess
   Bride</source>
```

2. XML allows "shortcuts".

While XML requires any element to have an open and closed tag pair, it does allow you to combine the two tags if the element is *empty*, meaning that no text is provided between the open and closed tags. For example, the following two lines are equivalent:

```
<device
   id="3838-2020"></device>
```

and

```
<device id="3838-2020"/>
```

In contrast, HTML does not allow for empty tags using this notation.

3. XML is case sensitive.

HTML is case insensitive. As long as you spell out the tag syntax correctly, the document is processed appropriately. For example, each of the following are valid and identical HTML statements:

```
<body
   bgcolor="#FFFFFF"></body>
<BODY
   BGCOLOR="#FFFFFF"></BODY>
<Body
   Bgcolor="#FFFFFF"></Body>
```

On the other hand, XML is case sensitive, so the following statements are not considered equal:

```
<quote>Get used to disappoint-
    ment.</quote>
<QUOTE>Get used to disappoint-
    ment.</QUOTE>
```

If you can read HTML, you'll quickly discover that XML looks very much like HTML in terms of its markup language structure.

Putting the Pieces Together

When you've got a basic understanding of elements and attributes, you can begin to look at the XML document as a whole. An XML document is a collection of elements that describe a particular set of data. As you find out in Book I, Chapter 3, a valid XML document has a single element that serves as the container for all other elements in the file. This "mother-of-all-elements" is known as the *root element* (or sometimes called the *document element*).

To illustrate, consider the following XML structure of film quotes. The filmquotes element serves as the root element for this XML document because it contains all the other elements:

```
<filmquotes>
  <quote id="101">
    <spokenby>Sam</spokenby>
   <source>Benny and Joon</source>
    <text>It seems to me that, aside from being a little
    mentally ill, she's pretty normal.</text>
  </quote>
  <quote id="102">
    <spokenby>Sabrina</spokenby>
    <source>Sabrina</source>
    <text>More isn't always better, Linus. Sometimes it's
    just more.</text>
  </quote>
  <quote id="103">
    <spokenby>Delmar</spokenby>
    <source>O Brother, Where Art Thou</source>
    <text>We thought you was a toad.</text>
  </quote>
  <quote id="104">
    <spokenby>Inigo Montoya</spokenby>
    <source>Princess Bride</source>
    <text>Hello. My name is Inigo Montoya. You killed my
    father. Prepare to die.</text>
  </quote>
</filmquotes>
```

The `filmquotes` element contains the quote four elements, but you'll notice that the `quote` elements also contain elements themselves. As a result, `filmquotes` and `quote` are considered *container elements* because they enclose other elements inside their start and end tags. In contrast, the `spokenby`, `source`, and `text` elements don't contain any elements inside them.

When an element is inside a container element, it is considered a *child element* or *sub element*. Therefore, the `quote` elements are child elements of `filmquotes`, and the `spokenby`, `source`, and `text` elements are children of `quote`.

Keep in mind as you begin to create XML documents that there can't be more than one root element per document or you'll get errors trying to process the document. Therefore, you couldn't simply have the four `quote` elements be free to roam about outside of a container element in a document.

In addition to the root element, you also have additional parts that may be part of an XML document: XML declaration, processing instructions, comments, and entities.

In the end, designing an XML structure is more an art than a science. The longer you work with the data, the more you begin to get a feel for which data bits work best as attributes and which work as elements inside the container element for your particular needs.

Six one way, half a dozen the other

Because elements can contain attributes as well as other elements, it can be confusing to determine whether a given piece of data should be in the form of an element or attribute. After all, consider the following three `quote` elements. Each of them are valid ways of containing the inter-related information inside of an element:

Mixed

```
<quote id="101"
    category="Comedy">We
    thought you was a
    toad.</quote>
```

All elements

```
<quote>
<id>101</id>
```

```
<category>Comedy</comedy>
<text>We thought you was a
    toad.</text>
</quote>
```

All attributes

```
<quote id="101"
    category="Comedy" text="We
    thought you was a toad."/>
```

While each of these may be valid from an XML syntax perspective, which is the best way to express the data? In one sense, you could apply the old adage, "six one way, half a dozen the other" and say that it really doesn't matter. However, there are considerations to think about:

✔ **Verboseness of content.** If the content that you are storing is sizable, then you'll usually want to use an element. For example, because the text of the quotes in the elements can span multiple lines, putting the text inside an element is easier to work with than as an attribute value, which must be enclosed in quotes. For example, the first element below is far harder to work with than the second:

```
<quote id="105" text="Who are
    you
  really, and what were you
    before? What did
  you do, and what did you
    think, huh?"
  category="Comedy"/>


<quote id="105"
    category="Comedy">
Who are you really, and what
    were you before? What did
    you do, and what did you
```

```
    think, huh?
</quote>
```

✔ **Presentable data.** In some XML implementations, it is more straightforward to format and display element content than it is attribute values. Therefore, if you are certain that the data bit you are using must be presented to the user, then you may want to consider using an element instead of an attribute name-value pair.

✔ **Manageability.** Attributes can be easier to manage within an element than is a set of nested elements. For example, the following element:

```
<quote id="101"
    category="Comedy"/>
```

can be easier to work with than the following nested element:

```
<quote>
  <id>101</id>
  <category>Comedy</category>
</quote>
```

Declaring the XML document

An XML document is a normal text file that has a structure beginning with a root element that in turn contains more elements. However, in order to identify a XML document, you need to add an *XML declaration* at the top of your file that simply says to an XML processor, "Hey, I'm an XML file. Please process me!"

An XML declaration is a specific kind of *processing instruction* (PI), which is a special kind of XML markup tag that is used to instruct the XML processor on how to parse the document. While a PI is included inside the document, it is not considered part of the document's XML data and wouldn't ever be shown to a user or outputted in another fashion. You may find it helpful to think of a PI as being akin to Post-It note that you affix to a report you give to your coworkers for review. The yellow-sticky note tells your coworkers special instructions on what to double-check. But those notes are removed before you give the final report to your boss. In the same way, PIs are stripped out of the document by the processor during its parsing process.

A PI has a special syntax that uses a $<?$ to begin the tag and a $?>$ to end the tag. Inside the brackets, the processing instruction must always be lowercase:

```
<? processinginstruction ?>
```

A processing instruction is a single lowercase tag enclosed with the $<?$ and $?>$ characters. It doesn't have a corresponding end tag like a normal XML element does.

A basic XML declaration uses the following syntax:

```
<?xml version="1.0"?>
```

The $<?xml\ ?>$ identifies the tag as an XML declaration, and the `version` attribute denotes the version of XML that the document conforms to. Currently, there is only a single version of XML, so you'll always use `1.0` as the value. This instruction then tells the processor that the document should be parsed as if it is an XML 1.0 document.

The XML declaration is placed at the top of the XML document, before the root element, as shown in Listing 2-1.

Listing 2-1 filmquotes.xml

```
<?xml version="1.0"?>
<filmquotes>
  <quote id="101">
    <spokenby>Sam</spokenby>
    <source>Benny and Joon</source>
    <text>It seems to me that, aside from being a little
    mentally ill, she's pretty normal.</text>
  </quote>
  <quote id="102">
    <spokenby>Sabrina</spokenby>
    <source>Sabrina</source>
    <text>More isn't always better, Linus. Sometimes it's
    just more.</text>
  </quote>
  <quote id="103">
    <spokenby>Delmar</spokenby>
    <source>O Brother, Where Art Thou</source>
    <text>We thought you was a toad.</text>
  </quote>
  <quote id="104">
    <spokenby>Inigo Montoya</spokenby>
    <source>Princess Bride</source>
    <text>Hello. My name is Inigo Montoya. You killed my
    father. Prepare to die.</text>
  </quote>
</filmquotes>
```

Even though you can have only one root element, the XML declaration —
nor any PI for that matter — is considered part of the actual document
structure and therefore is not considered an additional root element.

There are also two other optional attributes that you can add to the XML
declaration, as shown in the following example:

```
<?xml version="1.0" standalone="yes" encoding="UTF-8"?>
```

The `standalone` attribute specifies whether or not the document is independent of other files for its markup declarations. If you use a `no` value, then
you tell the XML processor that you are using *external markup declarations*
within the document, which are usually defined in a document type definition (DTD). You can discover more about *external markup declarations* in
Book II, Chapter 2. If you don't include the standalone attribute, then the
processor defaults the value to `yes`.

The `encoding` attribute specifies the encoding scheme used in the XML
document. The *encoding scheme* is the standard character set of a language.
The XML processor uses this encoding information to know how to work
with the data contained in the XML document. *UTF-8* is the standard character set used to create pages written in English.

UTF stands for UCS (Universal Character Set) Transformation Format. This
character set uses eight bits of information to represent each character.
Therefore, UTF-8 stands for an 8-bit character set. UTF-8 supports characters compatible with computing systems based on ASCII text. However, if
you need to work with information in other languages, such as Japanese
Katana and Cyrillic, you need to set the encoding attribute to `UTF-16`.
UTF-16 character set uses 16-bits to store a character.

Getting descriptive with comments

A *comment* is descriptive text included in your XML document for "behind-
the-scenes" use that the XML processor ignores during its parsing process.
You may, for instance, want to use a comment to label a particular structure,
describe the purpose of a given element, or jot a note about something you
need to add to the document later. A comment is something used for development purposes only and is never output by the XML processor.

Just like in HTML, a comment is any text that is surrounded by a `<!--` prefix
and a `-->` suffix. For example, the following verbose XML document will be
parsed by an XML processor and produce the same output as the comment-
free structure shown earlier in the chapter:

```
<?xml version="1.0"?>

<!-- Developed by:  Gargan Zola -->
```

```
<!-- Last modified: 6/22 -->

<filmquotes>
  <!-- Note to self: Double-check this one again after seeing
    the movie -->
  <quote id="101">
    <spokenby>Sam</spokenby>
    <source>Benny and Joon</source>
    <text>It seems to me that, aside from being a little
  mentally ill, she's pretty normal.</text>
  </quote>
  <quote id="102">
    <spokenby>Sabrina</spokenby>
    <source>Sabrina</source>
    <text>More isn't always better, Linus. Sometimes it's
  just more.</text>
  </quote>
  <!-- This is my favorite quote! -->
  <quote id="103">
    <spokenby>Delmar</spokenby>
    <source>O Brother, Where Art Thou</source>
    <text>We thought you was a toad.</text>
  </quote>
  <quote id="104">
    <spokenby>Inigo Montoya</spokenby>
    <!-- Hey, no one will ever read this comment when it
        is output! -->
    <source>Princess Bride</source>
    <text>Hello. My name is Inigo Montoya. You killed my
  father. Prepare to die.</text>
  </quote>
</filmquotes>
```

Use comments freely in your XML documents. Doing so can make your XML document easier to read and work with than without them. This is especially true if more than one person works on an XML document.

You can do pretty much anything you want with comments, but there are a few rules that you need to follow:

✦ **Location.** You can add comments anywhere inside the XML document except: (a) above the XML declaration and (b) inside a start or end tag.

Therefore, the following are *invalid* comments:

```
<!-- Developed by:  Gargan Zola -->
<?xml version="1.0"?>
```

and:

```
<quote <!-- This is my favorite quote! --> id="103">
```

✦ **Permissible text.** You can type most any text inside a comment and span as many lines as you wish. However, you can't use two consecutive hyphens or you'll get an error. Consider the following *invalid* example:

```
<!-- Developed by -- Gargan Zola -->
```

Adding aliases to your documents

An *entity* is a shortcut or an alias to another piece of information. XML allows you to declare an entity either inside your document or in an external DTD. For example, if you have a long piece of text that you need to use throughout a document, you can define an entity once and then reference the entity in your document, saving you space and time.

XML also provides some built-in entities to enable you to use characters that have special meaning for XML documents. Suppose the content of an XML element needs to use an opening angle bracket, as shown in the following example:

```
<expression>(5*5)<(6*6)</expression>
```

An XML processor would generate an error trying to process that element because the < character must always refer to the start of an XML element. Therefore, to get around that problem, you can use the built-in entity < to represent the angle bracket in the expression:

```
<expression>(5*5)&lt;(6*6)</expression>
```

When the XML processor parses the element, it recognizes the entity and replaces the < with a < when it is rendered or output.

Entities are closely associated with DTDs. See Book II, Chapter 2 for complete details on using entities with your XML documents.

Thinking of Documents as Trees

So far, as you've explored the innards of an XML document, the focus has been on the syntax of the XML elements and document as a whole. I've alluded to the hierarchical structure of an XML document, but the focus has thus far been on a "flat" document. However, XML documents have a very clear hierarchy to them when you start to examine the various layers of a document. For example, Figure 2-2 illustrates the hierarchy of elements from the filmsquotes.xml file shown in Listing 2-1.

Figure 2-2:
Hierarchy of
elements.

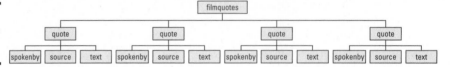

As you can see, an XML document has a natural hierarchy or tree-like structure. In the same way, a tree has a built-in structure or hierarchy to its various parts (see Figure 2-3). At the base layer is a root system directly
connected to the trunk, which is the most noticeable part of the tree's structure. At the next level, you have a multitude of branches, some large and
some small, that directly connect with the tree trunk. These branches then
either connect to smaller branches or else to leaves. In turn, the tinier
branches connect to leaves or to even smaller branches. If you started at
the trunk of the tree, you could trace a path to each branch and leaf within
the interconnected hierarchy of tree limbs.

Figure 2-3:
Various
parts of a
tree.

An XML document is quite similar in structure. A document's root element is the counterpart to a tree trunk, because it is the container of all other elements in the document. Elements directly inside of the root element are the equivalent of the first level of branches of a tree. Some of these elements will contain additional elements, like smaller branches on a tree.

When you start working with XSLT later in this book, you discover more about how to work with an XML document as a tree. See Book IV, Chapter 1 for more details.

Chapter 3: Creating Well-Formed XML Documents

In This Chapter

⮕ Exploring "well-formedness" and why it is critical to XML

⮕ Creating your first well-formed XML document

*C*lose only counts in horseshoes and hand grenades.

Boy, how many times I've heard that expression from someone, stressing the fact that simply being close oftentimes isn't good enough. In fact, consider the following scenarios:

✦ A student receiving a 1599 on the SAT nears perfection, but still loses out on a scholarship to the other student who received a perfect 1600.

✦ A baseball team mounts an incredible 5-run comeback in the bottom of the 9th inning but goes on to lose in the 11th by the homerun of the opposing team.

✦ While driving your brand new car down a road, you see a tree falling into the road. You swerve to avoid it; despite your valiant attempt, your car is totaled just the same, as the tree clips the tail end of the vehicle.

Being close in situations like these may provide a "moral victory," but in the harsh world that you and I live in, "moral victories" have no substance to them and only serve to make it easier for us to sleep at night.

In the same way, an XML document must be syntactically perfect to be a true XML document, adhering to the syntax rules discussed in Book I, Chapter 2. "Being close," such as missing a closing tag or mixing the case of elements, isn't good enough. Any error, regardless of how small it is, renders an XML document as unacceptable for processing by an XML parser.

In this chapter, I discuss what it means to have a well-formed XML document as well as discuss the how-to steps of structuring a XML document that goes beyond "being close."

Understanding "Well-Formedness"

Given the amazing popularity of diets these days, you can see that people both young and old are obsessed with being "well-formed." XML is similarly fanatical with well-formedness. It may not care about carbohydrates or fat grams, but XML *is* focused on the syntax of the XML document.

A *well-formed document* is one that is syntactically correct. For example, Figures 3-1 and 3-2 show examples of a well-formed document and a poorly formed document. An XML parser processes a well-formed document but spits back an incorrect document.

Figure 3-1:
A well-formed XML document.

```
<beverage type="Cola">
  <size>Small</size>
  <size>Medium</size>
  <size>Large</size>
  <value>6@lt;7</value>
  <special/>
</beverage>
```

Figure 3-2:
A poorly-formed XML document with several syntax problems.

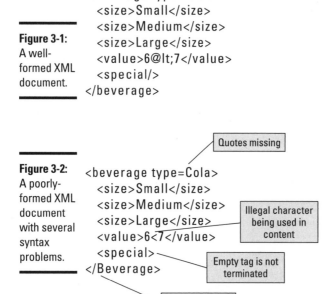

Book I, Chapter 2 discusses the syntax rules of XML, but use Table 3-1 as a quick checklist.

Table 3-1	Well-Formed Document Checklist	
Question		*Checkbox*
Document has a single root element		❏
Element and attribute names have consistent use of case		❏
All non-empty elements have a closing tag		❏

Question	Checkbox
All empty elements terminate properly	❑
No elements are overlapped and follow the "last open, first closed" rule	❑
Attribute values are enclosed by quotation marks	❑
Entities are used in place of special characters (such as < instead of <)	❑

While the terms sound synonymous, a *well-formed document* is not the same as a *valid document*. A valid document refers to one whose structure is tested against a Document Type Definition (DTD) or an XML Schema by validating parser. Book II covers the issue of validating XML documents.

Writing a Well-Formed XML Document

If you've read Book I, Chapter 2 and the first part of this chapter, you know how an XML document should look to be well-formed. However, it's time now to dive in and create an XML document from scratch — from concept to completion. In doing so, I follow a five-step process:

✦ Structuring your document.

✦ Declaring an XML document.

✦ Adding the root element.

✦ Adding the remaining data.

✦ Viewing the XML document

Each of these steps are discussed below.

Step 1: Structuring your document

Perhaps the most critical step in creating a well-formed document is to determine the appropriate XML structure that best describes the data. Consider, for example, the structured information shown in Table 3-2. It displays a listing of entrées on a menu for the world-famous Gilligan's By The Sea restaurant.

Table 3-2	List of Entrees for Gilligan's By The Sea			
ID	*Name*	*Features*	*Fat Grams*	*Description*
1	Sunburnt Chicken	Salad, vegetables, baked potato, and dessert	23	Chicken prepared so hot, you'll need a gallon of soda to wash it down. Bring sunscreen!

(continued)

Table 3-2 *(continued)*

ID	Name	Features	Fat Grams	Description
2	Filet Mig's None	Soup, vegetables, baked potato, and dessert	0	Our master chef Mig prepares a uniquely no-fat filet mignon. You won't believe how great it tastes!
3	Chicken Parmashaun	Soup, pasta, baked potato, and dessert	20	Our award-winning chicken parmesan prepared especially for you by our master chef Shaun.
4	Eggs Benelux	Bacon, sausage, and toast	35	No matter the time of day, enjoy our scrumptious breakfast cooked by our famous Belgian and Dutch master chefs.
5	Jerk Chicken	Soup, vegetables, and dessert	5	A delicious hot Jamaican dish prepared by our most obnoxious master chef.
6	Gusto Spaghetti	Soup, salad, and dessert	55	Our famous master chef Boyd Ardee prepares a succulent dish of spaghetti with zesty gusto!

This entrée list provides an example of how information that you and I work with every day has a natural structure to it. (See Book I, Chapter 1 for more on this topic.)

Suppose Gilligan's By The Sea wants to be able to work with their data more efficiently, storing the information in one place but using it to do a variety of tasks, such as outputting menus and table tents, updating an online menu on their Web site, and exchanging data with its sister restaurant Ginger & Mary Ann's. XML is seen as the solution, so the first responsibility is to convert the menu entrée list into an XML document structure.

***1.* Pick the organizing element that can serve as the container.**

Because all entrées are part of the menu, the menu is a logical choice to serve as the container.

```
<menu>
<menu>
```

***2.* Identify the second level of elements.**

The entrée is the primary piece of data inside a menu and serves as the main element for the XML document. All the data inside the rows of the table naturally can be contained by an `entree` element. The structure now looks like:

```
<menu>
 <entree></entree>
</menu>
```

3. **Determine the child elements and attributes.**

Each of the columns in the table can potentially be a child element of the `entree` element or else an attribute. (Book I, Chapter 2 discusses the nuances between deciding whether attribute or child element is the best choice.) For this structure, I'm going to use the ID as an attribute of the entree element but classify the other columns as child elements. The updated structure is now:

```
<menu>
  <entree id="">
    <name></name>
    <features></features>
    <fatgrams></fatgrams>
    <description></description>
  </entree>
</menu>
```

The structure I have defined now adequately accounts for the entrée information that I have on hand, yet is extensible as needs change over time.

Step 2: Declaring an XML document

The preliminaries are now over; the time for creating the document can begin. Using Notepad or another editor, create a new text file and enter an XML declaration at the start of the file:

```
<?xml version="1.0" encoding="utf-8" ?>
```

See Book I, Chapter 2 for more on XML declarations.

Step 3: Adding the document root

After the document has been designated an XML file using the XML declaration, you can add the root element, which is the element that contains all the other elements within the document.

You can't have more than one root element defined or you'll get an error.

Looking back at Step 1, you can see that the menu element was selected to be the root element and so is entered here:

```
<?xml version="1.0" encoding="utf-8" ?>
<menu>

</menu>
```

The root element is often used as a location to define additional information pertaining to the XML document, such as namespaces (see Book I, Chapter 4) and XML schemas (see Book II, Chapter 6).

Step 4: Adding the structured data

The menu container element is now ready to house the entrée data. Using the entree element structure that was developed in Step 1, can add each of the entrees to the document:

```
<?xml version="1.0" encoding="utf-8" ?>
<menu>
  <entree id="1">
    <name>Sunburnt Chicken</name>
    <fatgrams>23</fatgrams>
    <features>Salad, Vegetables, Baked Potato, and
  Dessert</features>
    <description>Chicken prepared so hot, you'll need a
  gallon of soda to wash it down. Bring
  sunscreen!</description>
  </entree>
  <entree id="2">
    <name>Filet Mig's None</name>
    <fatgrams>0</fatgrams>
    <features>Soup, Vegetables, Baked Potato, and
  Dessert</features>
    <description>Our master chef Mig prepares a uniquely no-
  fat filet mignon. You won't believe how great it
  tastes!</description>
  </entree>
  <entree id="3">
    <name>Chicken Parmashaun</name>
    <fatgrams>20</fatgrams>
    <features>Soup, Pasta, Baked Potato, and
  Dessert</features>
    <description>Our award-winning Chicken Parmesan prepared
  especially for you by our master chef
  Shaun.</description>
  </entree>
  <entree id="4">
    <name>Eggs Benelux</name>
    <fatgrams>35</fatgrams>
    <features>Bacon, Sausage, and Toast</features>
    <description>No matter the time of day, enjoy our
  scrumptious breakfast cooked by our famous Belgian and
  Dutch master chefs.</description>
  </entree>
```

```
<entree id="5">
  <name>Jerk Chicken</name>
  <fatgrams>5</fatgrams>
  <features>Soup, Vegetables, and Dessert</features>
  <description>A delicious hot Jamaican dish prepared by
 our most obnoxious master chef.</description>
</entree>
<entree id="6">
  <name>Gusto Spaghetti</name>
  <fatgrams>55</fatgrams>
  <features>Soup, Salad, and Dessert</features>
  <description>Our famous master chef Boyd Ardee prepares a
 succulent dish of spaghetti with zesty
 gusto!</description>
</entree>
</menu>
```

For each successive level of the document hierarchy, I indent two spaces to make the document structure easier to read. However, this indentation is purely optional.

After you've entered the data, save the file as menu.xml.

Step 5: Viewing the document

You can now view the results of the document in an XML document reader. No, you shouldn't need to download any new software to perform this task. Actually, the newer versions of Microsoft Internet Explorer and Netscape Navigator both have XML parsers built into them and display the XML document as a tree.

If you typed in the document as shown in the previous steps, the XML document is well-formed and will display properly by the document reader. To view, locate the menu.xml file you just saved in Windows Explorer and double-click it to open in your Web browser. Figure 3-3 shows the result when viewed in Internet Explorer 6.0.

However, because an XML document must be well-formed in order to be displayed, check out what happens when an error is in the document. Suppose I remove the menu element from the file so that I no longer have a single root element in the file. When I try to open up this incorrect document in Internet Explorer, the browser encounters the error during processing and then displays that error information inside its window instead of the document, as shown in Figure 3-4.

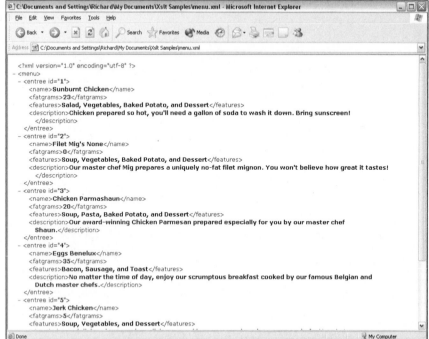

Figure 3-3:
Viewing an
XML
document in
Internet
Explorer.

The next steps

The menu.xml document is completed and viewable by an XML document reader. However, this basic XML document is often just the starting point to doing more. Therefore, consider jumping to one of the following parts of the book:

✦ To add an increased level of validation to the structure, see Book 2.

✦ To display this XML document in a presentable, formatted manner, see Book 3.

✦ To transform this document into HTML or a different XML structure, see Book 4.

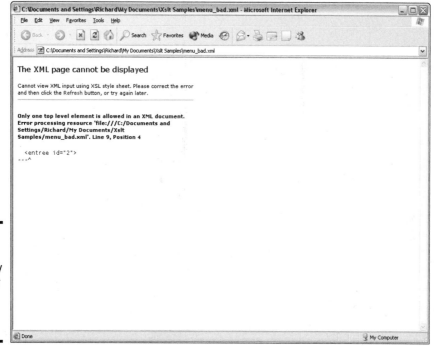

Figure 3-4:
An error is
displayed by
the browser
during
parsing of
document.

Chapter 4: Namespaces — Avoiding Naming Conflicts

In This Chapter

✔ Exploring the need for namespaces

✔ Declaring namespaces

✔ Finding out how attributes work with namespaces

✔ Using multiple namespaces

✔ Overriding namespace declarations

✔ Undeclaring namespaces

*I*n a classic *Seinfeld* episode, George Costanza becomes frantic when his girlfriend wants to meet his sidekick friends, Jerry, Kramer, and Elaine. Up until that point, his life was neatly compacted into two separate worlds, which he termed "Relationship George" and "Independent George." But if these two worlds are allowed to collide, then something earth-shattering will happen: Independent George will cease to exist. Or, in the memorable words of George, "A George divided against itself cannot stand!"

George's dilemma humorously illustrates a fundamental problem that XML has. One of XML's major advantages is that it is completely extensible, enabling you to create your own tags to describe data in a manner that works best for you. The problem becomes when you use the same name for an element as someone else used for his. Therefore, when you try to combine XML elements together from different worlds, the clashing names can cause a Costanzaesque accident. After all, an XML document divided against cannot stand!

While not helping out George's condition, namespaces are the solution around naming conflicts in XML. In this chapter, you discover what namespaces are and why they're necessary. I show you how to declare namespaces in your XML documents, how to combine multiple namespaces in a single document, and how to override and undeclare namespaces.

Even if you don't plan on sharing data outside your organization, you still need to know how to work with namespaces because many XML technologies (such as XML Schemas, XSLT, XLink, and XForms) make heavy use of them. Without namespaces being used, for example, it would be impossible to tell if you wanted to use `<element>` to describe an XML element in an XML schema or refer to an element in a chemistry periodic table.

Keeping Your Distance with Namespaces

XML uses *namespaces* to distinguish a set of element names from another group of names. The need for namespaces becomes obvious when you consider the flexibility of the XML language. Unlike HTML, XML has no pre-defined set of element names. As a result, the naming of elements and attributes is left entirely up to the one writing the XML documents. While the flexibility is critical to meeting the purposes of XML, it does leave open one potential problem: the possibility of two or more developers using an identical element name.

Consider, for example, DirecTV develops an XML vocabulary using `dish` as an element to describe those space-age ornaments that hug houses in suburbia. For example:

```
<dish>
  <model>A32201-WZ-TURBO</model>
  <size>2.0 x 2.0 x .75</size>
  <weight>27 lbs.</weight>
</dish>
```

Meanwhile, suppose Pfaltzgraff has their own `dish` element to describe those round things that you eat off of:

```
<dish>
  <model>Ashton</model>
  <shape>Hexagon</shape>
  <weight>14 ounces</weight>
</dish>
```

If DirecTV and Pfaltzgraff never exchange data outside of their respective companies, then they could use their XML vocabulary as is. But suppose they both wish to share data with outside suppliers and retailers, who in turn tried to combine them into a common data pool. If this were to happen, the chances of a DirecTV `dish` colliding with a Pfaltzgraff `dish` is very high:

```
<!-- dish elements below have differing structures -->
<supplierorder>
  <dish>
    <model>A32201-WZ-TURBO</model>
    <size>2.0 x 2.0 x .75</size>
    <weight>27 lbs.</weight>
  </dish>
  <dish>
    <model>Ashton</model>
    <shape>Hexagon</shape>
    <weight>14 ounces</weight>
  </dish>
</supplierorder>
```

The end result of this collision is that a customer gets a dinner plate hung on their roof or that a satellite dish becomes the new avant-garde way to serve pizza.

Namespaces were introduced as a way to avoid this name collision by linking a collection of names with a URI (Uniform Resource Identifier). A *URI* is the method in which resources on the Web are named, the most widespread form being URLs (Uniform Resource Locator) or Web addresses (for example, `http://www.dummies.com`). Because URIs are unique, you can be sure that the namespace associated with the URI is one of a kind.

When you define a namespace, you usually declare a URI once in a document and then refer to it elsewhere in the document by using a *namespace prefix* (also known as *namespace identifier* or *abbreviation*), as shown in Figure 4-1. This namespace identifier is used as a prefix onto element and/or attribute names.

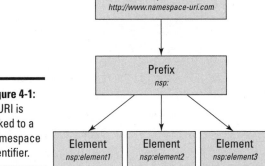

Figure 4-1:
A URI is linked to a namespace identifier.

Understanding URIs

While URI sounds like the name of a former Soviet leader in the early 1980s, the acronym actually is a common term used for all types of names and addresses that access the resources on the Web. URI (pronounced *you-are-I*) is a superset of two types of identifiers:

✔ **Uniform Resource Locator (URL).** URL identifies the location of a resource. An example of a URL is `http://www.dummies.com`.

✔ **Uniform Resource Name (URN).** You can also use a URN to identify the location of a resource and retrieve the resource. A URN is more robust than a URL, and it can refer to more than one URL. A URN is written in the form `urn:unique-string`. For example, you can specify a URN as `urn:dummies.xml.allinone.2003` and use it as a namespace URI for all documents relating to this book.

(continued)

(continued)

A namespace uses a URI as a *string* to uniquely identify a group of elements and attributes. However, even though they look the same, don't confuse a namespace URI with a Web address that you can actually visit with your browser. A namespace URI doesn't actually point to a resource on the Internet. It is just a unique identifier that's used to resolve conflicts between elements that have the same name.

For example, XSLT (discussed in Book IV) uses the `http://www.w3.org/1999/XSL/Transform` URI to identify its namespace, as shown in the following code:

```
<xsl:stylesheet
    xmlns:xsl="http://www.w3.
    org/1999/XSL/Transform"
    version="1.0">
</xsl:stylesheet>
```

During processing, the XSLT processor doesn't try to look up a data definition resource at `http://www.w3.org/1999/XSL/Transform`. Instead, an XSLT-enabled parser knows that this unique string identifies a namespace reserved for XSLT.

You can assign any name or string as a URI so long as it conforms to the URL or URN syntax requirements. However, referring to the following guidelines helps you to ensure uniqueness of the URI:

✔ **Use a URI that you control.** In order to ensure the uniqueness of the URI, the recommended strategy is to use a domain name that is under the developer's control. For example, if `www.notathing.com` is your Web address, you can feel confident that using a namespace URI, such as `http://www.notathing.com/spec/2003`, ensures that the specified URI is unique.

✔ **Avoid using a relative URI.** A relative URI is one that refers to a location that is relative to the current location or directory. Although there is no restriction on the use of relative URIs, it is recommended you use a *fully qualified name* (complete address of the resource) to specify a URI.

Declaring Namespaces

Namespaces are declared by adding an `xmlns` attribute (or another name that uses an `xmlns:` prefix) to the outermost element in which you want to use the namespace. The syntax for explicitly declaring a namespace is:

```
<myelement xmlns:prefix="URI">
</myelement>
```

In the preceding syntax,

✦ `xmlns` is a reserved attribute or prefix used to declare namespaces.

✦ `prefix` is the optional alias for the namespace.

✦ `URI` is a unique string used to identify a namespace.

What's in a name?

When you are adding your own namespace prefix, keep in mind the following naming do's and don'ts:

✔ DO use any legal XML name. A legal XML name must begin with a letter or an underscore (_). Subsequent letters may include letters, digits, underscores, or periods (.).

✔ DO NOT use any name that uses `xml` or `xmlns` in it. These are reserved for XML-related namespaces.

✔ DO NOT use any name that resembles any of the existing XML-related namespace prefixes, such as `xsl` or `xlink`. See the "XML world loves namespaces" sidebar later in the chapter for a list of these prefix conventions.

You can also define a namespace without using the optional prefix. To do so, see the "Declaring a Default Namespaces" section.

For example, suppose I want to add namespaces to the two `dish` structures described in the previous section to ensure that they were treated as separate element types. For the DirecTV dish element, I use the following namespace declaration:

```
xmlns:dtv="http://www.directv.com/2003/dish"
```

The `dtv` is the namespace prefix that is bound to the `http://www.directv.com/2003/dish` URI. I add this declaration to the dish element and then prefix each element name with the prefix to associate these elements with the declared namespace:

```
<dtv:dish xmlns:dtv="http://www.directv.com/2003/dish">
  <dtv:model>A32201-WZ-TURBO</dtv:model>
  <dtv:size>2.0 x 2.0 x .75</dtv:size>
  <dtv:weight>27 lbs.</dtv:weight>
</dtv:dish>
```

For the Pfaltzgraff `dish` element, I use a different namespace declaration and add it to the structure:

```
<pf:dish xmlns:pf="http://www.pfaltzgraf.com/dish">
  <pf:model>Ashton</pf:model>
  <pf:shape>Hexagon</pf:shape>
  <pf:weight>14 ounces</pf:weight>
</pf:dish>
```

When you declare a namespace, the element in which you define it dictates the namespace's scope. A namespace can be declared at the root level of a document or it can be declared inside any element of the XML structure.

The XML world loves namespaces

When you venture beyond basic XML and begin working with its related technologies, such as XSLT, XLink, and XForms, you'll see the widespread usage of common namespace prefixes. Here are the common namespace prefixes for XML technologies.

Technology	Common Prefix	Namespace URI
XSLT	`Xsl`	`http://www.w3.org/1999/XSL/Transform`
XLink	`Xlink`	`http://www.w3.org/1999/xlink`
XForms	`Xforms`	`http://www.w3.org/2002/xforms/cr`
XHTML	`Xhtml`	`http://www.w3.org/2002/06/xhtml2`
XML Schema	`xs` or `xsd`	`http://www.w3.org/2001/XMLSchema`
XML Events	`Ev`	`http://www.w3.org/2001/xml-events`

However, a namespace is visible to only the element in which it is declared and all of the child elements of that container element. Therefore, in the examples above, the `dtv` namespace is available by DirecTV's `dish` element and its child elements, while the `pf` namespace is available by Pfatzgraff's `dish` element and its children.

The binding of the namespace prefix to the URI is what is important, not the literal namespace prefix. The prefix can actually be any label you choose. For example, the following code snippet shows another valid namespace option:

```
<!-- awesomedishnamespace used as namespace prefix -->
<awesomedishnamespace:dish
   xmlns:awesomedishnamespace="http://www.directv.com/2003/d
   ish" >
  <awesomedishnamespace:model>A32201-WZ-
  TURBO</awesomedishnamespace:model>
  <awesomedishnamespace:size>2.0 x 2.0 x
  .75</awesomedishnamespace:size>
  <awesomedishnamespace:weight>27
  lbs.</awesomedishnamespace:weight>
</awesomedishnamespace:dish>
```

Declaring a Default Namespace

In addition to binding a prefix to a namespace, you can declare a default namespace as well. A *default namespace* applies a namespace to the element in which it is declared and all of its child elements and does so without adding a prefix before the element name.

To declare a default namespace, add a `xmlns` attribute to your element rather than a `xmlns:prefix` attribute:

```
<myelement xmlns="URI">
</myelement>
```

For example, the following code snippet defines `http://www.directv.com/2003/dish` as the namespace for `dish` and all of its child elements.

```
<dish xmlns="http://www.directv.com/2003/dish">
  <model>A32201-WZ-TURBO</model>
  <size>2.0 x 2.0 x .75</size>
  <weight>27 lbs.</weight>
</dish>
```

Default namespaces don't apply directly to attributes. See the "How Namespaces Apply to Attributes" section for details.

The default namespace doesn't override namespace prefixes inside its scope. Elements with existing prefix namespaces preserve their namespaces. For example, consider the following `dish` element:

```
<dish xmlns="http://www.directv.com/2003/dish"
      xmlns:pic="http://www.directv.com/pics">
  <model>A32201-WZ-TURBO</model>
  <size>2.0 x 2.0 x .75</size>
  <weight>27 lbs.</weight>
  <pic:graphic>turbo.jpg</pic:graphic>
</dish>
```

As you can see, both a default namespace and an explicitly named namespace were defined in the `dish` element. Because `model`, `size`, and `weight` have no prefix, they are bound to the default namespace(`http://www.directv.com/2003/dish`), while the `pic:graphic` element is bound to the `http://www.directv.com/pics` namespace.

Default declarations are useful for long documents that have a lot of markup. For such documents, you may find it inconvenient to add the namespace prefix with each element name.

How Namespaces Apply to Attributes

When you explicitly define a namespace and append its prefix on element names, the attributes that are contained within the element are "piggybacked" on the element, and so are automatically assigned the same namespace. For example, consider the following dish element:

```
<dtv:dish id="1029-2a"
    xmlns:dtv="http://www.directv.com/2003/dish">
  <dtv:model year="2003">A32201-WZ-TURBO</dtv:model>
  <dtv:size>2.0 x 2.0 x .75</dtv:size>
  <dtv:weight type="pounds">27 lbs.</dtv:weight>
</dtv:dish>
```

In this example, the id, year, and type attributes are all considered to be part of the http://www.directv.com/2003/dish namespace because their containing elements all have the dtv prefix. This assumption saves you from the need for adding prefixes to both the element and attribute names. While the code snippet below is functionally equivalent to that shown above, it is messier to work with, especially with complex XML structures:

```
<dtv:dish dtv:id="1029-2a"
    xmlns:dtv="http://www.directv.com/2003/dish">
  <dtv:model dtv:year="2003">A32201-WZ-TURBO</dtv:model>
  <dtv:size>2.0 x 2.0 x .75</dtv:size>
  <dtv:weight dtv:type="pounds">27 lbs.</dtv:weight>
</dtv:dish>
```

However, the "piggybacking" effect does not apply to default namespaces. Therefore, in the case below in which I declare a default namespace, the id, year, and type attributes are *not* considered to be part of the http://www. directv.com/2003/dish namespace:

```
<dish id="1029-2a"
    xmlns="http://www.directv.com/2003/dish">
  <model year="2003">A32201-WZ-TURBO</model>
  <size>2.0 x 2.0 x .75</size>
  <weight type="pounds">27 lbs.</weight>
</dish>
```

Therefore, using a default namespaces yet needing to apply a namespace to those attributes, you'd have to declare an explicit namespace and bind to the attributes:

```
<dish dtv:id="1029-2a"
    xmlns="http://www.directv.com/2003/dish"
    xmlns:dtv="http://www.directv.com/2003/dish">
  <model dtv:year="2003">A32201-WZ-TURBO</model>
  <size>2.0 x 2.0 x .75</size>
  <weight dtv:type="pounds">27 lbs.</weight>
</dish>
```

Using Multiple Namespaces

Explicitly defined namespace declarations may seem like a pain to work with because you need to add the prefix with each and every element that you want to bind to the namespace. If you are always working within the same namespace, then default namespaces are much easier to use. However, prefix usage becomes critical when you start working with multiple namespaces within the same document.

Multiple namespaces can then be combined inside a single XML document, enabling you, for example, to distinguish between the two distinct dish elements:

```
<supplierorder
    xmlns:dtv="http://www.directv.com/2003/dish"
    xmlns:pf="http://www.pfaltzgraf.com/dish">
  <dtv:dish>
    <dtv:model>A32201-WZ-TURBO</dtv:model>
    <dtv:size>2.0 x 2.0 x .75</dtv:size>
    <dtv:weight>27 lbs.</dtv:weight>
  </dtv:dish>
  <pf:dish>
    <pf:model>Ashton</pf:model>
    <pf:shape>Hexagon</pf:shape>
    <pf:weight>14 ounces</pf:weight>
  </pf:dish>
</supplierorder>
```

Because dtv and pf are declared at the root element level, they can be accessed anywhere inside of the document.

Overriding Namespace Declarations

When you are working with multiple namespaces at various levels of an XML document, you may have an element that needs to be bound to a different namespace that is the default within its scope. In XML, you can override the namespace declaration by declaring another default namespace. In this section, you find out how to override both default and explicit namespace declarations.

Overriding default namespace declarations

You can override a default namespace declaration in an XML document by simply declaring another default namespace, which automatically replaces the initial declaration within the scope of the second declaration. Consider the following example of XML code that overrides the default namespace declaration that refers to the Books.dtd with the namespace that refers to the BookOrder.dtd. In this case, the default namespace has been overridden to identify the Quantity element as belonging to the BookOrder.dtd DTD.

```
<supplierorder xmlns="http://www.supplierme.com">
  <dish xmlns="http://www.directv.com/2003/dish">
    <model>A32201-WZ-TURBO</model>
    <size>2.0 x 2.0 x .75</size>
    <weight>27 lbs.</weight>
  </dish>
  <dish xmlns="http://www.pfaltzgraf.com/dish">
    <model>Ashton</model>
    <shape>Hexagon</shape>
    <weight>14 ounces</weight>
  </dish>
</supplierorder>
```

Overriding explicit namespace declarations

While a far less common situation, you can also override an explicitly defined namespace by re-declaring the namespace prefix to a new URI. For example, the ds prefix is initially defined to the http://www.directv.com/2003/dish namespace and then when it gets to the second dish element, it is reassigned to the http://www.pfaltzgraf.com/dish namespace:

```
<supplierorder xmlns:ds="http://www.directv.com/2003/dish">
  <ds:dish>
    <ds:model>A32201-WZ-TURBO</ds:model>
    <ds:size>2.0 x 2.0 x .75</ds:size>
    <ds:weight>27 lbs.</ds:weight>
  </ds:dish>
  <ds:dish xmlns:pf="http://www.pfaltzgraf.com/dish">
    <ds:model>Ashton</ds:model>
    <ds:shape>Hexagon</ds:shape>
    <ds:weight>14 ounces</ds:weight>
  </ds:dish>
</supplierorder>
```

Undeclaring Namespaces

After you declare a namespace, the namespace declaration remains in scope until the last descendant (unless the namespace declaration is overridden) in a document. The last descendant is the inner-most child element in an XML document. However, sometimes, you may not need to bind certain descendants with the declared namespace in its scope. For example, some elements in an XML document might not be referenced to in a namespace. Therefore, you may need to *undeclare* the namespace, which means you need to remove certain elements from the scope of the namespace.

An explicit namespace cannot be undeclared. However, you can undeclare a default namespace. To undeclare a default namespace, you simply need to declare the default namespace with an empty name (zero-length URI). For example, in the code snippet below, the `http://www.directv.com/2003/dish` namespace is declared as the default namespace and would normally be in effect until the closing `dish` element. However, the size element declares an empty namespace, which makes both the size and weight elements to not be considered part of any namespace:

```
<dish xmlns="http://www.directv.com/2003/dish">
  <model>A32201-WZ-TURBO</model>
  <size xmlns="">2.0 x 2.0 x .75</size>
  <weight>27 lbs.</weight>
</dish>
```

Book II

Validating XML

The 5th Wave   By Rich Tennant

"Can't I just give you riches or something?"

Contents at a Glance

Chapter 1: Validating XML Documents

In This Chapter

✔ **Exploring DTDs and XML schemas**

✔ **Determining when to use DTDs and XML schemas**

✔ **Getting to know the various XML schema languages**

✔ **Using parsers to support XML schemas**

*A*ll sports teams have uniforms to wear when they play in a game — which is a good thing, because you don't want to imagine the alternative. Take, for example, the San Diego Chargers, an NFL football team. Suppose each team member was responsible for coming up with his own uniform and wearing it on game day. To the team, it didn't matter what the uniform looked like so long as it met two requirements: the basic parts of a NFL uniform (helmet, jersey, pants, and so on) were included, and the logo was a representation of a "Charger".

Given this flexibility, one player could paint a lightning bolt on his helmet to refer to the name of the team, while another designed a helmet with a battery on it. Still another member, who had shopping on his mind, decided to paint a credit card as his depiction of the team's nickname. Obviously, if the San Diego Chargers took the field with 52 different Charger uniforms and a myriad of colors, they probably wouldn't work together as a team very well. What's more, the quarterback would throw the ball to the other team as much as to his own, because he would never be sure whether the person running around in the secondary was his teammate or the opposition. Therefore, one simple but essential component for the Chargers to play like a team would be to have identical looking uniforms.

In the same way, XML has a similar need for standards any time people want to share XML data with each other. Suppose a car parts supplier would like to exchange order data with its 100 resellers. It sounds well and good until you discover that the supplier and each of the resellers have radically different ideas of what an "order" should look like in XML. Without a way to agree on a standard, their attempts to exchange data would be as comical and problematic as an NFL team trying to win a game with individualized uniforms.

This chapter introduces you to the two key technologies for creating and enforcing "standards" for XML. I discuss the oldie-but-goodie solution known as *Document Type Definitions* (DTDs), the up- and-coming young turk called *XML Schemas*, and comparisons and contrasts of the two solutions.

When Nice Form Isn't Enough

As you discovered in Book 1, a well-formed XML document is one that adheres to the standard conventions of the XML specification. You know the rules by now: elements enclosed in brackets (`<order>`), attributes in the form of a name-value pair (`id="1010"`), one root element per document, and so on. Although "well-formedness" is a first step in ensuring the correctness of a particular document, it is not a sufficient check in and of itself. For example, consider the following two `order` XML structures:

```
<!-- Type A -->
<order>
  <id>1010</id>
  <item>Chain</item>
  <item>Brace</item>
</order>

<!-- Type B -->
<order id="1010">
  <items>
    <item>Chain</item>
    <item>Brace</item>
  </items>
</order>
```

Each of the preceding `order` elements is well-formed and would be parsed without problems with an XML parser. However, if an application was written to parse type A orders, feeding it a document filled with type B orders would cause it to choke. Both types use `order` as the element name, but type A has the `id` value as a child element of `order` while type B treats the `id` as an attribute instead. Additionally, type B places an `items` element to contain all of the individual `item` elements, while type A simply places them directly under the `order` element.

A second level of verification is thus needed beyond well-formedness.

Trust but verify

Back in the 1980s when the United States and the Soviet Union started to melt the icy relations of the Cold War, Ronald Reagan and Mikhail Gorbachev employed a famous Russian proverb when it came to arms control: "Doveryay, no proveryay" ("Trust but verify"). In other words, both countries would trust each other to comply to the arms control agreements, but they'd back that up with periodic inspections to ensure that both countries adhered to the treaty. Similarly, in order to use XML effectively in heterogeneous environments, you need to have a similar "trust but verify" mantra.

However, by itself, XML provides just the "trust" part of the proverb, and it doesn't have any power or means to verify. Instead, for verification, you need to look beyond XML and turn to DTDs and XML schemas.

DTDs and XML schemas function as models or blueprints for describing the structure of XML documents, including the following:

✦ The *sequence* in which elements appear in an XML document.

✦ The *interrelationships* between different elements, including parent and child relationships and nesting levels.

✦ The *types of data* that are contained in elements or attributes.

DTDs and XML schemas, therefore, ensure that different XML documents adhere to a common, agreed-upon structure and consist of valid elements and attributes. They serve as a standard that explains how the data in a particular document is stored and formatted. Therefore, if two parties exchanging data follow the formula, they can clearly and easily exchange data between each other. They also enable an application written for a specific structure to know for certain that any XML document that is validated by a parser is of a very specific, rigid structure.

A *validating XML parser* (see "I Beg Your Parsin'" at the end of this chapter) can then use the DTD or XML schema as a litmus test when it parses through an XML document. If all the elements and the attributes that are included in the document exist and are defined and in the order specified by the validating technology, everything is hunky dory. But if the document includes extraneous elements or attributes or changes the order of them, the parser will declare the document invalid and cry foul.

Therefore, consider the parts supplier and its retailers that I discussed earlier. Suppose the parts supplier published a DTD or XML schema that specified the exact way in which an order must appear to work within its system. The individual retailers can then use the schema and make sure that its data conformed to the standard set by the supplier. If so, the parts supplier can ensure that any retailer that transmits electronic data complies to the standard or, if not, its order will be thrown out by the system.

Why use DTDs and XML schemas?

Utilizing a DTD or XML schema provides a number of benefits, including the following:

Book II
Chapter 1

Validating XML
Documents

✦ **A DTD or XML schema provides a blueprint for constructing XML documents.** A DTD or XML schema is similar to a blueprint used when building a house. In order to create a valid house that matches the required specifications, the builder constantly refers to the blueprint during construction. In the same way, a DTD or XML schema provides a plan that you can refer to in order to understand how to construct an XML document. It tells you what you can include and how to include it.

✦ **A DTD or XML schema serves as a contract between users of a given XML structure.** Both allow different users of the same XML data to have a written agreement that defines what information they will share and how it must be written so that everyone can understand the information.

✦ **A DTD or XML schema serves as a standard to verify the data that's generated and received by your application.** When developing applications that consume as well as generate XML data, developers have to make certain assumptions in their code, such as the order and placement of attributes and elements. You know that any XML document that is successfully parsed by the validating parser is reliable and your application will process the XML successfully. You can design a solution around that fact.

A Veritable Schemasbord of Validating Solutions

The issue of XML validation continues to be something of a moving target since the W3C approved the initial XML 1.0 recommendation several years ago. The 1.0 recommendation focused on the Document Type Definition (DTD), which became the standard means of validating XML data. Although DTDs have been around for years for use with SGML (Standard Generalized Markup Language) — the ancestor of HTML and XML — they weren't the perfect solution, leaving the door open for other technologies to spring up.

XML schema solutions were developed by various parties as a way to overcome the limitations of DTDs, with such names as XML-Data, XML-Data-Reduced (XDR), and SOX. These solutions were submitted to the W3C in various forms and implemented in a few software products. Perhaps most notably, XDR was implemented in Microsoft BizTalk servers (see the "XDR: An Intermediate Solution" sidebar). The W3C took the best from these different solutions and made compromises on other parts to develop the W3C XML Schema, which was finally made official as a Recommendation in 2001. Most of these earlier technologies are now being phased out to support the W3C XML Schema. There are alternative XML schema technologies, such as RELAX and Schematron, but these have a more niche focus rather than being general purpose validations. Overall, the W3C XML Schema has the greatest industry backing and looks certain to overtake DTDs as the *de facto* standard.

XDR: An intermediate solution

XML Data Reduced (XDR) was an XML schema language developed primarily by Microsoft as an immediate schema solution while the W3C went through the process of standardizing XML schemas. It is similar but not identical to the W3C XML Schema standard recommendation and has been implemented in such products as the Microsoft BizTalk framework. However, although Microsoft continues to support XDR, it has signed onto the W3C XML Schema solution, so look for XDR to be phased out as time goes on. For the complete XDR syntax, check out `www.w3.org/TR/1998/NOTE-XML-data-0105/`.

The following sections look at the two major validating solutions — DTDs and XML Schemas — and discuss their strengths and weaknesses.

"I want my, I want my, I want my DTD"

As the original means of verifying XML documents, DTDs remain the most widely used and supported validation solution. DTD's strengths, which follow below, are largely based on its front-runner status:

+ **Widespread expertise for DTDs.** DTDs have been in practical implementation for many years.

+ **Extensive parser support.** Nearly all validating parsers provide DTD support.

+ **Real-world deployment.** Multiple DTDs have been deployed in a wide ranging number of industries.

+ **Relatively low learning curve.** XML developers may find its syntax arcane, but DTDs are relatively straightforward to learn how to use.

However, despite these strong points, it is becoming increasingly clear that the days of the DTD as the *de facto* standard for XML validation are numbered because of some inherent limitations, including the following:

+ **Non-XML syntax.** DTD uses a syntax that kinda looks like XML, but isn't exactly it. As a result, DTDs can be confusing for XML developers to learn how to code.

+ **Limited data types.** Although XML documents are written using a common data type (text), you may often want to classify different pieces of data as a different data type, such as a number or date. DTDs offer only limited number of data types, forcing application developers who use XML to convert textual data into different data types before using in their applications.

✦ **No support for namespaces.** The DTD, as part of the XML 1.0 specification, was developed before the concept of namespaces existed. Therefore, DTDs don't support namespaces.

✦ **A closed system.** DTDs have no support for extensibility or inheritance, which can make large DTDs difficult to maintain.

Scheming with XML schemas

XML schemas were designed from the ground up as a solution to bypass the limitations of DTDs. The strengths of schemas include the following:

✦ **XML syntax.** XML schemas are created using XML. As a result, XML developers won't need to learn a new syntax in order to be productive with this validation solution.

✦ **Rich data types.** XML schemas provide a richer set of built-in data types, including real numbers, integers, decimal numbers, date/time, and boolean.

✦ **User-defined data types.** In addition to simple, predefined data types, XML schemas enable you to create your own data types.

✦ **Support for namespaces.** XML schemas provide native support for namespaces.

✦ **Inheritable types.** XML schemas support the inheritance of types. Therefore, you can define a more general type and then refine the type to more specific types for different elements. This feature allows you to reuse the types and thus extend elements.

However, in spite of these definite strengths, you should also consider the following cautionary issues before jumping into XML schemas:

✦ **Limited support.** The biggest limiting factor for XML schemas are their newness. Because it is a new technology, there is less support by software providers of XML schemas compared to DTDs. Therefore, you'll find less support of XML schemas today in parsers and other XML-related tools than you will find for DTDs. However, as time goes on, expect this issue to decrease in importance.

✦ **Greater learning curve.** Because XML schemas provide so much additional capability compared to DTDs, it shouldn't be surprising that they have a greater learning curve than DTDs.

Table 1-1 provides a comparison of DTDs and XML schemas.

Table 1-1	Comparison of DTDs and XML Schemas	
Feature	*DTD*	*XML Schemas*
XML syntax	No	Yes
Support for namespaces	No	Yes
Number of built-in data types	10	37
Support for user-defined data types	No	Yes
Content model to define sequence and nesting of elements	Yes	Yes
Inheritance	No	Yes

DTD or XML Schema: Which Should You Use?

Both DTD and XML schemas are viable validation solutions, but exactly which solution you use depends on your needs. Here are some issues to consider as you seek to make a decision:

+ **How simple or complex are your needs?** If the XML structure you are working with is fairly limited and straightforward, a DTD may be easier and quicker to implement than an XML schema. However, if you have complex data structures and have more advanced needs, such as namespaces, XML schemas are obviously the best solution.

+ **What kind of data are you working with?** If your data is text-based, a DTD may provide the level of power you need. But if you need to work with multiple data types and even need to define your own data types, you should consider XML schemas.

+ **How soon do you deploy?** Because tools and parsers that support DTDs have been around much longer than ones that support XML schemas, timing may be a major factor in your decision. If your needs are in the near term timeframe, DTD may be the best option. But if your timeframe extends farther into the future, the schema-supported tools and parsers may catch up in that interim period.

I Beg Your Parsin'

If you read Book I, you know that XML parsers are software tools that check XML documents for accuracy and integrity. There are two main classes of XML parsers:

+ A *non-validating parser* checks to see if a document is well-formed, but it does not attempt to validate a document structure. Some examples of non-validating parsers are Lark, XP, HEX, and expat.

✦ A *validating parser*, on the other hand, checks the well-formedness of a document as well as validates it if a DTD or XML schema is referenced. Most validating parsers support DTDs because the technology has been around the longest, but a growing number are beginning to support XML schemas as well. Some examples of validating parsers are MSXML, Xerces, XMLBooster, and Larval.

You can access an up-to-date list of XML schema validating parsers at `http://www.w3.org/XML/Schema`.

Most validating parsers support DTDs, such as MSXML, DTD Parser, CL-XML, PXP, and so on. However, many parsers don't support XML schemas because XML schemas are such a recent recommendation. But schemas are gaining support in the latest releases of most parsers. Table 1-2 lists some of the popular parsers that support schemas. Keep in mind, however, that this isn't an exhaustive list of parsers that support schemas.

Table 1-2	Parsers That Support XML Schemas	
Parser	*Description*	*Web Reference*
MSXML 4.0	A product from Microsoft that fully supports the final XML Schema a recommendation.	`www.microsoft.com/downloads`
Xerces Java	Developed by the Apache XML Project and fully supports the final XML schema recommendation.	`http://xml.apache.org/xerces-j/`
XML Schema Quality Checker (SQC)	A tool from IBM that fully supports the final XML schema a recommendation.	`www.alphaworks.ibm.com/tech/xmlsqc`
Schematron Validator	Primarily a Schematron tool that also provides support for DTD, XSD, and Schematron.	`www.topologi.com/`

Chapter 2: Creating Document Type Definitions

In This Chapter

✔ Discovering what DTDs are

✔ Finding out how to declare elements in a DTD

✔ Exploring how to declare attributes in a DTD

✔ Knowing how to work with entities

The Document Type Definition (DTD) was the original XML schema language for validating XML documents and, despite more recent schema language innovations, remains the most widely used validation solution for XML developers today. I know, a DTD sounds ominous, something like a pesticide that was outlawed in the 1950s, but you'll discover that it actually is an incredibly useful tool.

This chapter shows you how to create DTDs that represent the XML document you want to validate. It also shows you how you can use *entities*, the XML equivalent to *constants*, within your XML data. And, rest assured that DTDs are 100 percent environmentally safe and don't harm wildlife (although if you are still unsure, feel free to don a mask and gloves before creating your first one).

See Book II, Chapter 1 for an exploration of XML validation and DTDs compared with other XML schema languages.

Document Type Declaration: A Habitat for DTDs

The W3C XML 1.0 specification defined a *Document Type Definition* (DTD) as a way to ensure that the XML documents you work with adhere to a common, agreed-upon structure of your choosing. A DTD serves as a standard that details how the data in a particular document is stored and formatted.

XML is a dog-eat-dog world and can be an intimidating place for a validation schema like a DTD. The *Document Type Declaration*, not to be confused with the broader Document Type Definition concept, is the construct that safely houses the DTD, protecting it from those nasty XML elements. The `!DOCTYPE` keyword is used to reference a DTD that you are going to use for an XML document and is placed at the start of an XML document.

If the DTD is contained in an external file, the Document Type Declaration is as follows:

```
<!DOCTYPE root-element SYSTEM "filename.dtd">
```

For example, the following definition references the films.dtd and defines film as the root element:

```
<!DOCTYPE film SYSTEM "film.dtd">
```

Alternatively, if the DTD is embedded inside of the XML document, the Document Type Declaration uses the following syntax:

```
<!DOCTYPE root-element [element-declarations]>
```

For example, the following definition is supplied at the top of an XML document:

```
<?xml version="1.0"?>
<!DOCTYPE film [
  <!ELEMENT film (director, writer, year, runtime, special)>
  <!ATTLIST film name CDATA #REQUIRED>
  <!ELEMENT director (#PCDATA)>
  <!ELEMENT writer  (#PCDATA)>
  <!ELEMENT year         (#PCDATA)>
  <!ELEMENT runtime (#PCDATA)>
  <!ELEMENT special  EMPTY>
]>
<film name="Henry V">
  <director>Kenneth Branagh</director>
  <writer>Kenneth Branagh, William Shakespeare</writer>
  <year>1989</year>
  <runtime>137</runtime>
  <special/>
</film>
```

The Document Type Declaration references a DTD, but it's the stuff inside that counts. It uses markup declarations to define the rules that the XML documents must follow, which indicate the elements, the sequence of elements, attributes, and entities that an XML document can contain.

A DTD can be defined as a separate .dtd file or embedded inside of an XML document.

THINK UPPERCASE when writing DTD keywords. All of the DTD keywords must be written in uppercase, such as !DOCTYPE, !ELEMENT, !ENTITY, and !NOTATION. The rules for declaring DTDs are as persnickety as the rules for creating well-formed XML.

Declaring Elements

If you've read Book I, you know that *elements* are the basic building blocks of XML documents. When you declare elements in a DTD, you define rules that specify the elements that are allowed in XML documents. Element declaration in a DTD determines the name of the element, its type, and its content. Using the !ELEMENT keyword, the general syntax of an element declaration is as follows:

```
<!ELEMENT element-name (content-type)>
```

Or:

```
<!ELEMENT element-name (child-element-set)>
```

Book II
Chapter 2

Creating Document Type Definitions

The element-name defines the XML element and parentheses contain either its content type or a listing of its child elements.

Note these facts about the preceding syntax:

✦ The < and > brackets are used for declaring tags.

✦ !ELEMENT indicates that an element is declared. All elements are declared using the !ELEMENT keyword.

✦ element-name is the name of the element being declared. A valid XML document must contain the declared element.

✦ content-type or child-element-set specifies whether the element contains textual data or other elements.

Elements can contain nothing at all, character data, other elements, or they can be open to all of the above. These are discussed in the sections that follow.

Declaring empty elements

Empty elements don't contain any content. For example, the special element shown in the following code is an empty element:

```
<film name="Henry V">
  <director>Kenneth Branagh</director>
  <writer>Kenneth Branagh, William Shakespeare</writer>
  <year>1989</year>
  <runtime>137</runtime>
  <special/>
</film>
```

If you're familiar with HTML, you know that hr, br, and img are empty elements. These tags do not contain any data, although they may contain attributes.

If an XML document contains an empty element, the element must be declared in the associated DTD. To declare an element as an empty element, use the following element declaration:

```
<!ELEMENT element-name EMPTY/>
```

Therefore, to define the special element, you would write the following statement:

```
<!ELEMENT special EMPTY/>
```

Declaring elements with character data

A typical element in an XML document contains *character data* — data that is represented by typed characters. You can determine whether or not the character data should be parsed by the XML parser. Character data that is parsed is represented as PCDATA; character data that isn't parsed is represented as CDATA.

Parseable data (PCDATA) is processed by the XML parser. When the data is processed, all XML tags contained in the data are processed as XML tags.

However, there may be instances when you do not want data to be parsed before it is displayed. For example, suppose you want to display the < symbol as content in an element. In a PCDATA element, whenever the parser sees a <, it thinks a new tag is starting. To "fake out" the parser, you need to replace it with a "built-in" entity (see the "Free Inside: Built-in Entities" sidebar later in the chapter), in this case <. However, if you do this bait-and-switch procedure, something has to convert the < to < and later, when it is displayed, from < back to <.

Non-parseable data (CDATA) is treated differently. If the data is in a CDATA element, the parser does not examine its contents, so you can keep your < as a <.

Hands on, hands off policy

An XML parser is hands on with PCDATA elements and parses through them like there is no tomorrow. In contrast, CDATA elements are treated with kid gloves by the XML parser, and it promises to keep its hands off CDATA contents.

Therefore, to specify the type of character data that an element in an XML document can contain, you need to declare the element in a DTD specifying the data type as PCDATA or CDATA. For example, to specify that the direc-tor element can contain character data of type PCDATA, use the following declaration:

```
<!ELEMENT director (#PCDATA)>
```

The # sign precedes the PCDATA and CDATA definition.

For example, the following XML code snippet is valid:

```
<director>Kenneth Branagh</director>
```

Now, suppose you wanted to add a bold <b> HTML tag to the contents of the director element, so that its content looked like this:

```
<b>Kenneth Branagh</b>
```

Using a PCDATA element definition, as shown previously, you'd have to convert the special characters to entity references or else the XML parser would treat the <b> element as part of your XML structure. Therefore, the converted code would be as follows:

```
<director>&ltb&gtKenneth Branagh&lt/b&gt</director>
```

Alternatively, if you defined the director element using the CDATA definition:

```
<!ELEMENT director (#CDATA)>
```

You can then simply keep the <b> tag as is without any conversion:

```
<director><b>Kenneth Branagh</b></director>
```

Declaring elements with a single child

After some married couples have an exhausting experience with their first child, they decide to stop before they have any more. XML elements have feelings too, and sometimes they prefer to have but a single child, rather than a big XML family. (Those large XML family reunions can be quite boisterous, after all!)

When a container element contains only one occurrence of a child element, use the following declaration syntax:

```
<!ELEMENT element-name (child-element-name)>
```

Suppose that the film element contains a single child element called title. To declare this element in a DTD, use the following code:

```
<!ELEMENT film (title)>
```

The XML code would look like this:

```
<film>
  <title>Band of Brothers</title>
</film>
```

The preceding declaration specifies that the title element can occur only once within the film element. Because the code names only one film title, it's valid.

However, the following XML code, which names two titles is invalid, because the DTD declaration limits the number of title children to one:

```
<! -- Invalid (too many title elements)-->
<film>
  <title>Band of Brothers</title>
  <title>The Great Escape</title>
</film>
```

Declaring elements with sequential children

When parsing an XML document, you may often rely on elements being in a particular order. Therefore, if two XML documents contain the same elements but in different sequence, the misordered document won't be read correctly by your application. DTDs allow you to specify the sequence of child elements within a container element.

When a container element needs to contain certain child elements in a specific sequence, use the following declaration syntax:

```
<!ELEMENT element-name (child-element-name, child-element-
    name2, child-element-name3,...)
```

Child elements are separated by a comma (,).

For example, suppose you would like the film element to contain the following child elements in the specified sequence: director, writer, year, runtime, special. To do so, you would use the following code:

```
<!ELEMENT film (director, writer, year, runtime, special)>
```

The preceding declaration indicates that each film element must contain one director element, one writer element, one year element, one runtime element, and one `special` element. Apart from these child elements (in the specified sequence), the `film` element cannot contain any other content.

After you've named the children in the container element's definition, you need to declare the child elements as well in the DTD. For example:

```
<!ELEMENT film (director, writer, year, runtime, special)>
<!ELEMENT director  (#PCDATA)>
<!ELEMENT writer    (#PCDATA)>
<!ELEMENT year          (#PCDATA)>
<!ELEMENT runtime   (#PCDATA)>
<!ELEMENT special   EMPTY>
```

Use parentheses ( ) to enclose the content declaration for child elements and character data, but not for the empty elements, such as the `special` element shown in the preceding code. (Empty elements are loners and, rumor has it, have a hard time getting along with parentheses.)

**Book II
Chapter 2**

**Creating Document
Type Definitions**

Remember that the sequence of the child elements in the `film` element definition is not a suggestion, but a requirement. Therefore, the following code listing shows a valid and an invalid XML structure (the bolded elements are out of sequence):

```
<! -- Valid structure -->
<film name="Henry V">
  <director>Kenneth Branagh</director>
  <writer>Kenneth Branagh, William Shakespeare</writer>
  <year>1989</year>
  <runtime>137</runtime>
  <special/>
</film>

<! -- Invalid structure -->
<film name="Henry V">
  <year>1989</year>
  <writer>Kenneth Branagh, William Shakespeare</writer>
  <director>Kenneth Branagh</director>
  <runtime>137</runtime>
  <special/>
</film>
```

Declaring elements with multiple occurrences of a child

When you use an XML document to list multiple items of information, you need to have multiple occurrences of the same element within the same container element. For example, suppose you have a `films` structure that lists multiple `film` elements:

```
<films>
  <film>Beauty and the Beast</film>
  <film>Casablanca</film>
  <film>It's a Wonderful Life</film>
  <film>Groundhog Day</film>
  <film>Treasure of the Sierra Madre</film>
  <film>Vertigo</film>
</films>
```

When you would like a container element to contain one or more occurrences of a child element, use the following declaration syntax:

```
<!ELEMENT element-name (child-element-name+)>
```

In this declaration, the plus (+) sign specifies that the container element can contain one or more instances of this child element.

In addition to using it with a single child element, you can use the plus sign in a listing of children as well. For example, suppose you'd like to change the following XML structure to account for multiple writers within the `writer` element:

```
<film name="Henry V">
  <director>Kenneth Branagh</director>
  <writer>Kenneth Branagh, William Shakespeare</writer>
  <year>1989</year>
  <runtime>137</runtime>
  <special/>
</film>
```

Using the following element definition:

```
<!ELEMENT film (director, writer+, year, runtime, special)>
```

I can now transform the XML code into the following structure that better supports the data:

```
<film name="Henry V">
  <director>Kenneth Branagh</director>
  <writer>Kenneth Branagh</writer>
  <writer>William Shakespeare</writer>
  <year>1989</year>
  <runtime>137</runtime>
  <special/>
</film>
```

Declaring elements with varying occurrences of a child

You can also use wildcards in creating DTDs to specify a varying range of occurrences of a child. You've seen the + character already used in the previous section to specify one or more occurrences of a child element. You can also use the * and ? wildcards to specify a varying number of occurrences.

Zero or more occurrences of a child element

When a container element contains none, one, or many occurrences of a child element, use the following declaration syntax:

```
<!ELEMENT element-name (child-element-name*)
```

In the preceding syntax, the * wildcard denotes that the element can have zero, one, or multiple occurrences within a parent element.

For example, suppose a homerelease element is added as a child element to the film container element. Its purpose is to denote the type of home viewing releases for the film title (DVD and/or VHS). The declaration code is as follows:

```
<!ELEMENT film (director, writer+, year, runtime, special,
    homerelease*)>
```

Given this element declaration, each of the following film elements are valid:

```
<!-- Valid structure (No homerelease elements) -->
<film name="Henry V">
  <director>Kenneth Branagh</director>
  <writer>Kenneth Branagh, William Shakespeare</writer>
  <year>1989</year>
  <runtime>137</runtime>
  <special/>
</film>

<!-- Valid structure (One homerelease element) -->
<film name="Henry V">
  <director>Kenneth Branagh</director>
  <writer>Kenneth Branagh, William Shakespeare</writer>
  <year>1989</year>
  <runtime>137</runtime>
  <special/>
  <homerelease type="VHS"/>
</film>
```

```
<!-- Valid structure (Two homerelease elements) -->
<film name="Henry V">
  <director>Kenneth Branagh</director>
  <writer>Kenneth Branagh, William Shakespeare</writer>
  <year>1989</year>
  <runtime>137</runtime>
  <special/>
  <homerelease type="DVD"/>
  <homerelease type="VHS"/>
</film>
```

Zero or one occurrence of a child element

When a container element contains either none or just one occurrence of a child element, use the following declaration syntax:

```
<!ELEMENT element-name (child-element-name?)
```

For example, a `current` element could be added as an optional child element to the `film` container to denote films that are currently running in theaters. The `current` element is provided for all current releases and withheld for each film element that contains a film that is no longer in a theatrical release. The declaration would look like this:

```
<!ELEMENT film (director, writer+, year, runtime, special,
  homerelease*, current?)>
```

In the preceding code snippet, the `?` symbol (see Table 2-1) denotes that a maximum of one `current` element can be added to the `film` container. Therefore, each of the following two film elements are valid, based on this element definition:

```
<!-- Valid structure (No current element) -->
<film name="Henry V">
  <director>Kenneth Branagh</director>
  <writer>Kenneth Branagh</writer>
  <writer>William Shakespeare</writer>
  <year>1989</year>
  <runtime>137</runtime>
  <special/>
</film>

<!-- Valid structure (current element) -->
<film name="Henry V">
  <director>Kenneth Branagh</director>
  <writer>Kenneth Branagh</writer>
  <writer>William Shakespeare</writer>
  <year>1989</year>
  <runtime>137</runtime>
  <special/>
```

```
<homerelease type="VHS"/>
<current/>
</film>
```

Table 2-1	DTD Wildcards
Wildcard	*Definition*
?	The ? wildcard is used when an element occurs zero or one times in the parent element.
*	The * wildcard is used when an element occurs zero, one, or more than one times in the parent element.
+	The + wildcard is used when an element occurs one or more times in the parent element.

Defining elements with mutually exclusive children

Sometimes a declared element can contain only one child element out of several possible ones per element. When an element contains only one of several possible child elements, you specify those child elements within the parentheses, like this:

```
<!ELEMENT element-name (child-element-name | child-element-
    name2 | child-element-name3 | ...)
```

The vertical bars that fall between each child element denote an OR operator, so that only one of them can be contained within the parent element at any time.

If you liked multiple choice tests back in school compared to essay questions, you'll like this method of defining element content.

To demonstrate, suppose you have a `release` container element and a set of possible child elements that denote where the initial release of the film occurred. The declaration looks like this:

```
<!ELEMENT release (us|uk|fr|au)>
<!ELEMENT us EMPTY>
<!ELEMENT uk EMPTY>
<!ELEMENT fr EMPTY>
<!ELEMENT au EMPTY>
```

The following code shows both valid and invalid `release` elements:

```
<!-- Valid structure -->
<release>
  <uk/>
```

```
</release>

<! -- Invalid structure -->
<release>
  <uk/>
  <us/>
</release>
```

I've been focusing on child elements within the vertical bars, but you can also incorporate character data definitions in the same declaration:

```
<!ELEMENT release (#PCDATA|us|uk|fr|au)>
```

In this example, character data can be inside of the `release` element or inside one of the country identifier children, but not both.

Grouping child elements to apply common rules

When creating a DTD, you may have two or more child elements that have a common rule. You can group these elements together using parentheses and apply the rule to the combined group of elements at the same time. For example, look at this code:

```
<!ELEMENT element-name (child-element-name, child-element-
    name2, child-element-name3)*>
```

It is functionally the same as the following code:

```
<!ELEMENT element-name (child-element-name*, child-element-
    name2*, child-element-name3*)>
```

You can also include more than one grouping within your declaration. For example, suppose that in the `film` element you want to optionally allow one or more `director` and `writer` elements and zero or one `year` and `runtime` elements. The declaration would look like the following:

```
<!ELEMENT film ( (director, writer )+, (year, runtime)?,
    special)>
```

Each group of child elements is separated with a comma (,).

Declaring unrestricted elements

Unrestricted elements are the elements that can contain any content you can think of, including `<kitchensink/>`, so long as it doesn't violate the rules of XML. To declare unrestricted elements, the ANY keyword is used, as shown in the following declaration:

```
<!ELEMENT element-name ANY>
```

The preceding declaration indicates that the element can contain any combination of parseable data — all possible elements as well as PCDATA text.

The ANY keyword is sometimes used with an element in an XML document to allow for maximum flexibility inside of it for child elements, text, and their order. However, make prudent use of the ANY keyword, because the moment you use it, you lose the control over the XML structure inside of the container element when you use it too liberally. And in doing so, you start to forget the very reasons for having a DTD in the first place: control and reliability.

Declaring Attributes

If you read Book I, you know that *attributes* provide additional information about an element and are structured as name-value pairs separated by an equals (=) sign. For example, the film element below contains two elements, id and name:

```
<film id="102" name="Henry V" ></film>
```

However, in order for an element to utilize an attribute, you need to define it within the DTD using the !ATTLIST definition. The general syntax to declare an attribute of an element is as follows:

```
<!ATTLIST element-name attribute-name attribute-type default-
    value>
```

Notice these facts about the preceding syntax:

✦ <!ATTLIST> is the markup tag used for declaring an attribute.

✦ element-name is the name of the element whose attribute is being declared.

✦ attribute-name is the name of the attribute being declared.

✦ attribute-type is the type of the attribute (see Table 2-2 for a listing of valid types).

✦ default-value is the value that the attribute takes if no value is specified for the attribute in the XML document. The default value can take any one of the following four defaults: #REQUIRED, #IMPLIED, #FIXED, or a default character data value. You learn about these defaults in the section "Declaring default values for attributes," later in this chapter.

For example, to declare the name attribute of the film element, use the following declaration code:

```
<!ATTLIST film name CDATA #REQUIRED>
```

The preceding code breaks down as follows:

+ `film` is the name of the element whose attribute is being declared.

+ `name` is the name of the attribute.

+ The attribute type of the `name` attribute is `CDATA`, indicating that the attribute contains any character data.

+ The default value is set to `#REQUIRED`, which indicates that the value of the `name` attribute must be supplied in the XML document or else the XML parser will flag it as an invalid element.

When you have multiple attributes for an element, enter them successively within the `!ATTLIST` declaration, as in the following example:

```
<!ATTLIST  film  name         CDATA   #REQUIRED
                 studio       CDATA   #REQUIRED
                 distributor  CDATA   #REQUIRED>
```

Declaring the type of an attribute

Although the value of every attribute fits into the quotes of a name-value pair, it can have one of several different data types. You can specify the *attribute type* in the DTD.

You can use 10 attribute types for declaring attributes in a DTD, as shown in Table 2-2 and discussed in the sections that follow.

Table 2-2	Valid Attribute Types
Type	*Description*
CDATA	Character data without markup.
Enumerated	A list of values from which only one value can be chosen.
ID	A unique identifying name for the attribute. The value for the ID type attributes must follow the rules for names in XML.
IDREF	Value of some ID attribute within a document. IDREF type attributes are used to create links and cross-reference with documents.
IDREFS	Values of multiple ID attributes separated by whitespace. IDREFS type attributes are used to link one element to multiple other elements.
ENTITY	Name of an entity declared in the DTD.
ENTITIES	Names of multiple entities declared in the DTD separated by white-space.
NMTOKEN	An XML name.
NMTOKENS	Multiple XML names separated by whitespace.
NOTATION	Name of a notation declared in the DTD.

Defining normal text attributes

When you have an attribute that takes an ordinary text value, declare the attribute as CDATA. For example, declare the name attribute of the film element as follows:

```
<!ATTLIST film name CDATA #REQUIRED>
```

A valid film element will appear like this:

```
<film name="Field of Dreams">
```

CDATA type attributes can take character strings of any length but cannot contain markup tags. For example, the following definition is not allowed:

```
<!-- Invalid attribute value -->
<film name="<i>Field of Dreams</i>">
```

Instead, if I wanted to include that information, I'd need to convert the tags using the built-in entities:

```
<film name="&lt;I&gt;Field of Dreams&lt;/I&gt;">
```

Defining enumerated type attributes

When you have an attribute that can take one value from a given set of values, declare the attribute as an enumerated type. To do so, place all of the possible values inside of parentheses and separate them using vertical bars (|).

For example, suppose you have an aspectratio attribute for the homerelease element, in which you can have three valid types: 1.33, 1.85, and 2.35. The declaration code for the attribute would be as follows:

```
<!ATTLIST homerelease aspectratio (1.33 | 1.85 | 2.35)
    #REQUIRED>
```

The preceding declaration indicates that the aspectratio attribute can take one of these values: 1.33, 1.85, or 2.25. The following code shows valid and invalid homerelease element definitions:

```
<!-- Valid attribute value -->
<homerelease aspectratio="1.85"/>

<!-- Invalid attribute values -->
<homerelease aspectratio="1.85:1"/>
<homerelease/>
```

Defining unique values with ID

Just like when you work with traditional database records, you may want to uniquely identify each XML element so that you can work with it individually. To require that an attribute value be unique, use the ID type. For instance, suppose that you want the id attribute of the film element to be an identifier. You would define the attribute as follows:

```
<!ATTLIST film id ID #REQUIRED>
```

In an XML document, the following code shows a valid and invalid structure:

```
<!-- Invalid attribute value -->
<films>
  <film id="102"></film>
  <film id="104"></film>
  <film id="123"></film>
</films>

<!-- Invalid attribute value -->
<films>
  <film id="102"></film>
  <film id="104"></film>
  <film id="123"></film>
  <film id="102"></film>
</films>
```

The bolded element is considered invalid because it has the same id value as the first film element in the list.

You can define only one attribute per element as an ID type. Therefore, the following element declaration is invalid and would generate an error, because the bolded line defines a second ID type for the film element:

```
<!ELEMENT film (rating)>
<!ATTLIST film id ID #REQUIRED>
<!ATTLIST film name ID #REQUIRED>
```

Referencing ID values from other elements

An element that is uniquely identified by an ID type attribute may be referenced from other elements. In this manner, you can create links and cross-references within documents. To refer to one element that has an ID type attribute from another element, the other element must have an attribute of type IDREF.

For example, suppose you want to link a `film` element with a `digitalbill-board` element. The `digitalbillboard` element incorporates film information obtained from a `film` element and uses it for a computerized billboard on a Web site. Because the `film` element is uniquely identified by the `id` attribute, the `digitalbillboard` element can reference the `film` element using an `IDREF` type attribute:

```
<!ATTLIST digitalbillboard filmref IDREF #REQUIRED>
```

In an XML document, you could then reference the *Henry V* film by placing its identifier value in the `filmref` attribute:

```
<digitalbillboard filmref="102">
</digitalbillboard>

<!-- filmref attribute above references the film element
    below -->
<film id="102" name="Henry V" ></film>
```

The `IDREF` provides a one-to-one link between elements, but you may want to define a one-to-many link as well, in which one element references multiple other elements. In such situations, declare an attribute of type `IDREFS` that will house the multiple element references.

Suppose that the `digitalbillboard` element needs to reference multiple `film` elements instead of a single one. If so, you need to modify the declaration to use `IDREFS`:

```
<!ATTLIST digitalbillboard filmref IDREFS #REQUIRED>
```

The values of film IDs would then be placed inside of the `filmref` attribute value, separated by a space:

```
<digitalbillboard filmref="102 103 292 302">
</digitalbillboard>
```

The preceding code indicates that the `digitalbillboard` element refers to four `film` elements, which are uniquely identified by the following `id` numbers: 102, 103, 292, and 302.

**Book II
Chapter 2**

**Creating Document
Type Definitions**

Don't leave them hanging

IDREF and IDREFS values must reference a matching ID element elsewhere in the XML document. If the parser fails to find a match, it will generate an error.

Referencing entities in an attribute

An *entity* is something like an alias provided to the parser that says when you encounter it, replace it with some other text. Entities enable you to reuse common content at several places efficiently. (For more information on what entities are and how to use them, see the "Declaring Entities" section, later in the chapter.)

You can reference entities inside of an attribute using the ENTITY or ENTITIES attribute type. Suppose, for example, that you need to plug in descriptive text in the homerelease element. To begin, you define two entities that provide aliases to the descriptive text:

```
<!ENTITY fullscreennote "This film has been modified from its
    original version. It has been reformatted to fit your
    screen.">
<!ENTITY widescreennote "If you see black bars on the top and
    bottom of your screen, it means you've got an old style
    TV. Upgrade now!">
```

Now, to plug those into a disclaimer attribute value, you need to account for that in the DTD declaration for the homerelease element:

```
<!ATTLIST homerelease
        type ( DVD | VHS ) #REQUIRED
        aspectratio (1.33 | 1.85 | 2.35) #REQUIRED
        disclaimer ENTITY #REQUIRED>
```

Then, in your XML document, you can add entities as appropriate as the values of the disclaimer attribute:

```
<homerelease type="DVD" aspectratio="1.85"
    disclaimer="widescreennote"/>
<homerelease type="VHS" aspectratio="1.33"
    disclaimer="fullscreennote"/>
```

When the XML parser processes the document, the entities will be replaced with the full text for use in your application.

Alternatively, if you wanted to reference multiple entities within the same attribute value, you'd use the ENTITIES type.

Defining name tokens in an attribute

In "XMLSpeak," an *nmtoken* (or *name token*) is a mixture of name characters that starts with a letter or underscore (_) and has subsequent characters consisting of letters, digits, underscores, hyphens (-), periods (.), and colons (:). A space character is not permitted in an nmtoken.

To require an attribute value to be a valid nmtoken, use the `NMTOKEN` attribute type. For example, consider the following declaration for a `class` attribute:

```
<!ATTLIST film class NMTOKEN #REQUIRED>
```

The following code shows valid and invalid values:

```
<!-- Valid nmtoken values -->
<film class="Drama"/>
<film class="Action1"/>
<film class="Romantic_Comedy"/>

<!-- Invalid nmtoken values -->
<film class="1Action"/>
<film class="Romantic Comedy"/>
```

Using `NMTOKEN` is especially useful in cases in which you don't want whitespace to be permitted as part of the value.

When an attribute can take multiple nmtoken values, declare the attribute as `NMTOKENS`.

```
<!ATTLIST film classes NMTOKENS #REQUIRED>
```

Whitespace is then used to separate each nmtoken value:

```
<film class="Drama Romantic_Comedy Jimmy_Stewart"/>
```

Using foreign data in an attribute

An XML parser deals with processing character text data that conforms to the XML standard. It's not an all-purpose parser designed to know how to process other formats, such as JPG, PDF, or XLS files. However, suppose you need to reference foreign data, such as a JPG graphic, inside of an attribute value. A helper application will need to actually process this data, apart from the XML parser, but the DTD can label this data's type to make it easy for the helper application to identify. You can use the `NOTATION` attribute type for this purpose in your DTD.

To use the `NOTATION` attribute type, you first need to have a `!NOTATION` defined in the DTD:

```
<!NOTATION JPG PUBLIC "-//NCALS//NOTATION Photographic
    Codings(jpeg)//EN">
```

Then, define the attribute, specifying the type in parentheses after the `NOTATION` keyword:

```
<!ATTLIST film icon NOTATION (JPG) #REQUIRED>
```

Specifying default values for attributes

After you have declared an attribute in your DTD, you can also declare a default value for it in case the attribute isn't provided in the XML document. You can also stipulate whether or not the attribute must be included in the XML document. Table 2-3 shows the valid default values and the following sections explain their uses.

Table 2-3	Default Values for Attributes
Type	*Description*
"value"	When you explicitly specify a default character text value, the attribute assumes that value if the XML document doesn't supply one.
#REQUIRED	When you use the #REQUIRED directive while defining an attribute, it is mandatory for the user to specify a value for the attribute.
#IMPLIED	The #IMPLIED directive makes it optional for a user to specify a value for the attribute.
#FIXED	The #FIXED directive is used for specifying a default value for an attribute that cannot be changed in the XML document.

Default values

A default value can be specified by declaring it inside quotation marks after the attribute type in the !ATTLIST definition. You can declare a default value for any type that makes sense to do so, such as CDATA or enumerated attributes:

```
<!ATTLIST film
          rating  (G|PG|PG-13|R)  "PG"
          adline  CDATA "Come, watch, and enjoy">
```

Therefore, when an XML parser uses this DTD and encounters the following two elements, they are treated as identical:

```
<film/>
<film rating="PG" adline="Come, watch, and enjoy"/>
```

When the XML parser gives the parsed XML document to an application, the elements will output as follows:

```
<film rating="PG" adline="Come, watch, and enjoy"/>
<film rating="PG" adline="Come, watch, and enjoy"/>
```

Required values

You can also make an attribute value mandatory to your XML document. This ensures that a value is specified for each element, or else an error is generated by the validating parser. Requiring a value is especially useful when you have used an ID attribute type so that you can be certain that a unique value is supplied for each element.

To enforce this rule, you can declare the attribute with the #REQUIRED directive. For example, the id attribute of the film element is declared with the #REQUIRED attribute as follows:

```
<!ATTLIST film id ID #REQUIRED>
```

The following code shows a valid and an invalid film entry:

```
<!-- Valid element -->
<film id="978"/>

<!-- Invalid elements -->
<film id=""/>
<film/>
```

By using the #REQUIRED attribute, you simplify the job of the application that actually uses the XML data processed by the XML parser. The application can be sure that any XML document that makes it through the validating parser has the required attributes and can code the application logic accordingly.

Optional values

If an attribute provides supplementary information about an element but is not essential, you can designate in the DTD that this attribute is optional using the #IMPLIED directive. For example, suppose a url attribute is used to provide a Web site address for films. Not all films have companion Web sites, so you wouldn't want to require this attribute to be in the film element. Therefore, the appropriate declaration is as follows:

```
<!ATTLIST film
          name  DATA   #REQUIRED
          url   CDATA  #IMPLIED>
```

Using this DTD directive, the following elements are all valid:

```
<film name="Field of Dreams" url="www.ifyoubuildit.com"/>
<film name="Casablanca"/>
<film name="The Princess Bride" url="www.asyouwish.com"/>
```

Hardcoded values

If you would like the DTD to hardcode a value into an XML document, you can use the #FIXED directive and then supply the fixed value as part of the !ATTLIST declaration:

```
<!ATTLIST film approvedby #FIXED "Inspector9">
```

Therefore, each film element that is processed by the validating parser will contain the approvedby attribute with the value of Inspector9. If another different value in the XML is supplied, an error is flagged. The following XML code shows valid and invalid elements:

```
<!-- Valid elements -->
<film/>
<film approvedby="Inspector9"/>

<!-- Invalid elements -->
<film approvedby="inspector 9"/>
<film approvedby="Rejected"/>
```

Declaring Entities

If you've programmed in a traditional programming language before, such as Java, C, or Visual Basic, you know that a constant is a declared identifier whose value doesn't change. For example, the following is a constant:

```
Max=100;
```

After you've defined Max, this identifier can be used throughout your code to signify the numeric value of 100. Then, if you need to change Max to be 200, you can change it at one location in your code, and the entire codebase will be updated instantly as a result.

Free inside: Built-in entities

One of my favorite expressions to read as a child was "free inside" on the front of a cereal box, because I knew somewhere deep inside the box would be a toy awaiting me. Not to be outdone, XML provides some *predefined entities* that are "free inside" — provided without needing to define them yourself. These are shown in Table 2-4. These entities are used in places that require you to substitute special XML characters, such as brackets or quotation marks, so they aren't confused with being XML.

XML has its own equivalent to the traditional programming constant called an *entity*. You can create an entity in your DTD and use it either inside of your DTD or inside of your XML documents. When an entity is encountered by the parser during processing, it substitutes the entity for the text it represents.

Table 2-4	Predefined Entities
Entity	*Represents*
<	<
>	>
&	&
'	'
"	"

You can declare two types of entities in a DTD:

+ *General entities* are used both in the DTD and anywhere inside the root element of the XML document.

+ *Parameter entities* are used only within the DTD itself.

These two types are explored in the following two sections.

Declaring general entities

General entities are the most popular type of entities because they can be used inside of the XML document. The general syntax to declare a general entity is as follows:

```
<!ENTITY entity-name "replacement content">
```

Here is an explanation of the preceding syntax:

+ !ENTITY is the keyword that is used to declare an entity.

+ entity-name is the name of the entity being declared.

+ replacement content is the content that the entity refers to. This content needs to be enclosed in quotation marks so that the parser can identify that this is the content that needs to be replaced.

To reference the entity within the XML document, you use the entity-name, adding an ampersand (&) as a prefix and a semicolon (;) as a suffix:

```
&entity-name;
```

Remember to include the ampersand (&) and semi-colon (;) because these symbols help the parser recognize that the reference should be replaced with the content defined in the DTD.

For example, suppose that you'd like to add a copyright blurb at the end of each section of an XML document. Rather than copying and pasting the text everywhere, you can define an entity reference in your DTD:

```
<!ENTITY blurb "Copyright (c)2003, Gildor Industries. All
    Rights Reserved.">
```

In your XML document, you can then reference the entity:

```
<doc urc="TCI-KKL">
  <p>The animals were lost due to the compass glitch.</p>
  <i>&blurb;</i>
</doc>
```

After the XML parser processes the document, the output is as follows:

```
<doc urc="TCI-KKL">
  <p>The animals were lost due to the compass glitch.</p>
  <i>Copyright (c)2003, Gildor Industries. All Rights
    Reserved.</i>
</doc>
```

Declaring parameter entities

Parameter entities have a narrower scope than general entities. They are used only within the DTD itself, not within the XML document. The general syntax to declare a parameter entity is as follows:

```
<!ENTITY %entity-name "replacement content">
```

Notice that a percentage sign (%) precedes the entity-name. This symbol differentiates a parameter entity from a general entity. You use the % when you reference a parameter entity rather than an ampersand (&):

```
%entity-name;
```

Suppose you use a similar ID and State attribute definitions for multiple elements in your document. You could define a parameter entity as follows:

```
<!ENTITY %idtype "ID #REQUIRED">
<!ENTITY %state "( MA | RI | NH | ME | VT | CT ) 'MA'">
```

Then, in the rest of the DTD, you could use these as needed to define attributes for both the customer and supplier elements:

```
<!ELEMENT customer #CDATA>
<!ELEMENT supplier #CDATA>
<!ATTLIST customer %id;
                   %state;>
<!ATTLIST supplier %id;
                   %state;>
```

Declaring external entities

In the preceding sections, you saw how to define general and parameter entities that were defined wholly inside of the DTD. You can also utilize *external* general and parameter entities, those that have information defined outside of the DTD.

Book II
Chapter 2

The general syntax to declare an external entity is as follows:

```
<-- External general entity -->
<!ENTITY entity-name SYSTEM "URI">
<-- External parameter entity -->
<!ENTITY %entity-name SYSTEM "URI">
```

Here is an explanation of the preceding syntax:

✦ entity-name is the name of the general entity being declared (add a % for a parameter entity).

✦ SYSTEM is the keyword that indicates that the entity is an external entity and refers to that external content.

✦ URI is the URI (Uniform Resource Identifier) of the external content that the entity refers to.

To reference the entity, the following syntax is used:

```
<-- External general entity -->
&entity-name;
<-- External parameter entity -->
%entity-name;
```

To demonstrate how an external entity can be used, suppose you are storing film elements in separate .xml files depending on the date of the film's release: pre-1950.xml, 1950-79.xml, 1980-95.xml, and recent.xml. You'd then like to combine them together into a single XML document for use in your application. Entities allow you to do this quickly.

To do so, create general entities for each of these files in the DTD:

```
<!ENTITY filmera_1 SYSTEM "pre-1950.xml">
<!ENTITY filmera_2 SYSTEM "1950-79.xml">
<!ENTITY filmera_3 SYSTEM "1980-95.xml">
<!ENTITY filmera_4 SYSTEM "recent.xml">
```

Next, in the XML document, reference each external entity:

```
<?xml version="1.0"?>
<films>
   &filmera_1;
   &filmera_2;
   &filmera_3;
   &filmera_4;
</films>
```

During processing, the parser will insert the contents of the specified .xml files in place of the entity names.

Chapter 3: Creating XML Schemas

In This Chapter

✔ Creating an .xsd file

✔ Exploring simple and complex elements

✔ Discovering how to declare elements and attributes

✔ Grouping and ordering elements

✔ Extending XML documents

✔ Setting restrictions on data input

XML schemas are the "new kids on the block" in the world of XML validation. Don't fear, though: You don't have to listen to '80s teen pop music in order to use them. Instead, these new kids on the block aim to carry on the torch started by DTDs, but they allow for far more power and reuse as you blueprint the structure of XML documents.

In this chapter, you discover how to create XML schemas to validate your XML documents. You focus on the basics of schemas, including the schema document structure and how to declare elements and attributes. You close out the chapter by examining how to place restrictions on the data that is contained in an XML document.

This chapter is the first of three on XML schemas. See Book II, Chapter 5 for more on XML schema data types and Book II, Chapter 6 for best practices when designing XML schemas.

Creating an XML Schema Document

If you read Book II, Chapter 1, you already know that one of the benefits of XML schemas over DTDs (explored in Book II, Chapter 2) is that they can be created using XML, not some other esoteric markup syntax. That's right. You write the validation rules for your XML documents in XML. (If that sounds like circular reasoning and is making your head spin, don't worry about it. It really does work, as you'll see in this chapter.)

XML schema files use an .xsd file extension by convention. Within this file, an xs:schema element serves as the root element of the schema document. Its basic structure is as follows:

```
<?xml version = "1.0" ?>
<xs:schema xmlns:xsd="http://www.w3.org/2001/XMLSchema">

  <!-- XML schema code goes here -->

</xs:schema>
```

Looking at the declaration, you can see that an xs:schema element uses the URI http://www.w3.org/2001/XMLSchema and, by convention, assigns it to an xs: namespace identifier. This namespace information is used by the schema validating parser to help it know how to process the document.

If you read Book I, Chapter 3, you discovered that mapping from the namespace identifier to the URI is what is important, not the literal namespace identifier xs:. So, although the xs: identifier can be any label you desire, I recommend sticking with xs: or xsd: because these prefixes are what you'll see predominately throughout the industry. A different prefix could lead to potential misunderstanding.

Declaring Elements and Attributes

As the basic building block of an XML document, you won't be surprised that an *element* is also the key raw material used to create an XML schema. To declare a basic element in an XML schema, you use the xs:element element:

```
<xs:element name="element-name" type="element-type">
<!-- content -->
</xs:element>
```

Or, if the element contains no content, you can simplify it to the following:

```
<xs:element name="element-name" type="element-type"/>
```

The name attribute specifies the element name, and the type indicates the data type of the element.

XML schemas have the concept of simple and complex elements, which are explained in the following two sections.

Declaring simple elements

In XML schemas, a *simple element* is an element that contains no attributes or child elements, just textual content. For instance, consider the following film element:

```
<film>Henry V</film>
```

Using the `xs:element`, you can define the element in your XML schema as follows:

```
<xs:element name="film" type="xs:string"/>
```

The `xs:string` is a built-in data type for XML schemas that indicates that the element named `film` has a string as its type.

Simple elements can only contain textual content, but the content can be one of several different built-in datatypes, such as boolean, date, time, string, decimal, and integer. For example, consider the following XML elements:

```
<film>Henry V</film>
<runningTime>129<runningTime>
<dateOpened>03-31-1989</dateOpened>
<nominated>true</nominated>
```

Each of the four are simple elements, but they each have a different datatype, as can be described in a schema:

```
<xs:element name="film" type="xs:string"/>
<xs:element name="runningTime" type="xs:integer"/>
<xs:element name="dateOpened" type="xs:date"/>
<xs:element name="nominated" type="xs:boolean"/>
```

In addition to the `name` and `type` attributes, the `element` element can take many other attributes. Some of these attributes are described in Table 3-1.

Table 3-1	Attributes of the element Element	
Attribute	*Example*	*Description*
default	`<element name= "Publisher" type= "xsd:string" default ="Dream Publishers" />`	It specifies the default value of the element if you don't provide any value to the element in an instance XML document. However, the default attribute can be used only with elements that are defined as simple or text-only types.
fixed	`<element name= "Publisher" type="xsd: string" fixed="Dream Publishers" />`	It specifies a fixed value that an element takes. This value is predetermined and cannot be changed. The `fixed` attribute, just like the `default` attribute, applies only to elements that are defined as simple type or text only.

(continued)

Table 3-1 *(continued)*

Attribute	Example	Description

maxOccurs	`<element name="Author"`
	`type="xsd:string"`
	`maxOccurs="4" />`
		It is an integer value greater than or equal to zero and determines the maximum number of times the element can occur within the containing element. When there is no fixed limit on the number of occurrences of an element, set this attribute to unbounded.

minOccurs	`<element name="Author"`
	`type="xsd:string"`
	`minOccurs="1" />`
		It is an integer value greater than or equal to zero and determines the minimum number of times the element can occur within the containing element. When you want to define the element as optional, set this attribute to 0.

ref	`<element ref="City" />`	It specifies the name of another element you want to refer from the element being declared. For example, if you want to refer to the element named City from within the element named Address, set the ref attribute to City.

Declaring complex elements

A *complex element* is an element that contains attributes, other elements, or a mixture of them. Although you use the xs:element instruction to define a complex element, you also use a xs:complexType instruction to declare the contents of the element.

For example, consider the following film element:

```
<film>
  <title>Henry V</title>
  <director>Kenneth Branagh</director>
  <writer>Kenneth Branagh, William Shakespeare</writer>
  <year>1989</year>
  <runtime>137</runtime>
</film>
```

The film element contains five child elements that are listed in a particular order. In order to represent that structure in an XML schema, you define the following construct:

```
<xs:element name="film" type= "xs:string">
  <xs:complexType>
```

```
    <xs:sequence>
       <xs:element name="title" type="xs:string"/>
    <xs:element name="director" type="xs:string"/>
    <xs:element name="year" type="xs:integer"/>
    <xs:element name="runtime" type="xs:integer"/>
  </xs:sequence>
   </xs:complexType>
</xs:element>
```

Inside the film element, you use xs:complexType to denote that it is a complex element. Next, the xs:sequence element is used to specify the sequence of child elements, so that the elements inside of it must appear in that specified order. I then define the child elements, all of which are simple elements and can be defined with the xs:element instruction alone.

Book II
Chapter 3

Creating XML
Schemas

Declaring attributes

Attributes in an XML schema are declared with the xs:attribute element and, at their most basic form, follow a similar form to simple elements:

```
<xs:attribute name="attribute-name" type="attribute-type"/>
```

For example, suppose that you want to develop a schema for the following film element:

```
<film title="Henry V"/>
```

Even though the film element has an uncomplicated structure, it is still by definition a complex element because it has an attribute. Therefore, you need to use the xs:complexType element in your definition:

```
<xs:element name="film" type= "xs:string">
  <xs:complexType>
    <xs:attribute name="title" type= "xs:string"/>
  </xs:complexType>
</xs:element>
```

Consider a second code snippet:

```
<film title="Henry V">
  <writer>Kenneth Branagh</writer>
  <director>Kenneth Branagh</director>
</film>
```

In this case, you need to define the child elements writer and director as well as the title attribute. You can declare them both in the same xs:complexType element, but the attributes must be listed last, after the elements:

```
<xs:element name="film" type= "xs:string">
  <xs:complexType>
    <xs:sequence>
      <xs:element name="writer" type="xs:string"/>
      <xs:element name="director" type="xs:string"/>
    </xs:sequence>
    <xs:attribute name="title" type= "xs:string"/>
  </xs:complexType>
</xs:element>
```

Assigning Default and Fixed Values

You can assign either a default or a fixed value to a simple element using the `default` or `fixed` attribute:

A *default value* is used as the value when no other value is specified in the document. For example, if you'd like to specify 90 minutes as the default running time, you could use the `default` attribute as follows:

```
<xs:element name="runningTime" type="xs:integer"
  default="90"/>
```

A *fixed value* can be assigned to an element. When you do this, the value cannot be changed in the XML document. For example, if you have a `log-file` element included in an XML document that always needs to have the value of `syslog.txt`, you could define the element as follows:

```
<xs:element name="logfile" type="xs:string"
  fixed="syslog.txt"/>
```

Assigning Number of Occurrences

Both `xs:element` and `xs:attribute` elements allow you to specify the range of occurrences that the element or attribute can appear in its parent element. You can specify this information using one or both of the following attributes:

✦ `minOccurs` specifies the minimum number of times that the element or attribute can occur in the parent element. The default value is 1, but you can set it to be any number 0 or higher.

✦ `maxOccurs` provides the maximum number of occurrences that the element or attribute can appear in the parent element. The default value is also 1, but you can set it to be any number 0 or higher. Additionally, if you don't want to set a specific limit, you can set the value to `unbounded`.

You cannot set `minOccurs` or `maxOccurs` if the `xs:schema` element is the parent element.

For example, suppose you want to create a schema for the following structure, which requires at least one `writer` element inside of the `film` element, but allows for as many as needed. Additionally, the `award` element needs to have the flexibility of being included as many times as needed or not included at all. The code snippet is as follows:

```
<film title="Henry V">
  <writer>Kenneth Branagh</writer>
  <writer>William Shakespeare</writer>
   <award>1989 Best Film nomination</award>
</film>
```

Using the `minOccurs` and `maxOccurs` attributes, you can provide the range of occurrences that you need for this structure to work:

```
<xs:element name="film" type= "xs:string">
  <xs:complexType>
    <xs:attribute name="title" type= "xs:string"/>
    <xs:element name="writer" type="xs:string"
  maxOccurs="unbounded"/>
    <xs:element name="award" type="xs:string" minOccurs="0"
  maxOccurs="unbounded"/>
  </xs:complexType>
</xs:element>
```

Ordering Elements

The order in which elements occur inside of a parent element can be critically important in some situations or a "who cares" in other cases. What's more, you might have situations in which you have an either/or situation, so that if one element is present, the other can't be there. XML schemas support all of these options of order through the use of three elements: `xs:sequence`, `xs:all`, and `xs:choice`.

xs:sequence

`xs:sequence` declares that the child elements need to appear in a specific order in order for the structure to be valid. To illustrate, consider the following `film` element:

```
<film>
  <title>Henry V</title>
  <director>Kenneth Branagh</director>
  <runtime>137</runtime>
</film>
```

By adding an `xs:sequence` inside of the `xs:complexType` and then adding the child element declaration inside of it, I define the precise order of the `film` element's children:

```
<xs:element name="film" type= "xs:string">
  <xs:complexType>
   <xs:sequence>
     <xs:element name="title" type="xs:string"/>
   <xs:element name="director" type="xs:string"/>
   <xs:element name="runtime" type="xs:integer"/>
 </xs:sequence>
  </xs:complexType>
</xs:element>
```

xs:all

`xs:all` declares that the child elements can appear in any order they jolly well choose and that each child element can occur one time only. For example, suppose you would like to allow for the following two XML structures to be valid, even though the child elements are in different order:

```
<film>
  <title>Henry V</title>
  <director>Kenneth Branagh</director>
  <writer>Kenneth Branagh, William Shakespeare</writer>
  <year>1989</year>
  <runtime>137</runtime>
</film>
<film>
  <director>Harold Ramis</director>
  <title>Groundhog Day</title>
  <writer>Danny Rubin</writer>
  <runtime>101</runtime>
  <year>1993</year>
</film>
```

Adding the `xs:all` element inside of `xs:complexType`, the XML schema would look like this:

```
<xs:element name="film" type= "xs:string">
  <xs:complexType>
   <xs:all>
     <xs:element name="title" type="xs:string"/>
   <xs:element name="director" type="xs:string"/>
   <xs:element name="writer" type="xs:string"/>
   <xs:element name="year" type="xs:integer"/>
   <xs:element name="runtime" type="xs:integer"/>
 </xs:all>
  </xs:complexType>
</xs:element>
```

xs:all places restrictions on the usage of maxOccurs and minOccurs attributes described earlier in this chapter. minOccurs can only be 0 or 1, while maxOccurs can only be set to 1.

xs:choice

xs:choice specifies that one child can appear or the other can appear, not both. For example, in the following XML structure, either the cinemaRelease or tvRelease element needs to be in film, but not both:

```
<film title="Henry V">
  <cinemaRelease>U.K.</cinemaRelease/>
</film>
<film title="Pride and Prejudice">
  <tvRelease>A&E</tvRelease/>
</film>
```

Using xs:choice inside of the xs:complexType element, you define the schema as follows:

```
<xs:element name="film" type= "xs:string">
  <xs:complexType>
    <xs:choice>
    <xs:element name="cinemaRelease" type="xs:string"/>
    <xs:element name="tvRelease" type="string"/>
  </xs:choice>
  <xs:attribute name="title type="xs:string"/>
  </xs:complexType>
</xs:element>
```

Grouping Elements and Attributes

One of the key mantras of XML schemas is reuse. XML schemas provide considerable functionality to be able to define a schema once and reuse it across one or more XML schemas. One example of this reusability is the ability to cluster a set of related elements together using the xs:group element or grouping attributes using xs:attributeGroup. By using the xs:group or xs:attributeGroup element, you can declare a group of elements or attributes, give it a name, and then use that group throughout your document.

Grouping elements

The basic syntax of the element is as follows:

```
<xs:group name="groupname">
<!-- Elements -->
</xs:group>
```

Inside of the xs:group container, the elements of a group must be declared with a xs:sequence, xs:all, or xs:choice. To illustrate the usefulness of the xs:group element, consider the following XML code snippet:

```
<film>
  <title>Henry V</title>
  <director>
    <salutation>Mr.</salutation>
    <firstname>Kenneth</firstname>
    <lastname>Branagh</lastname>
  </director>
  <writer>
    <salutation>Mr.</salutation>
    <firstname>Kenneth</firstname>
    <lastname>Branagh</lastname>
  </writer>
  <writer>
    <salutation>Sir</salutation>
    <firstname>William</firstname>
    <lastname>Shakespeare</lastname>
  </writer>
  <year>1989</year>
  <runtime>137</runtime>
</film>
```

Notice that the salutation, firstname, and lastname elements are a set of child elements that appear in both the director and writer elements. Instead of defining this same trio inside both parent elements, you can define them once as a group and then reference them in the director and writer element declarations.

To define the schema, you first create a group called fullname, in which you use the xs:sequence element to ensure that the elements appear in the precise order specified in the schema. The group is then referenced inside the director and writer schema declarations giving the xs:group's ref attribute the fullname value:

```
<xs:group name="fullname">
  <xs:sequence>
    <xs:element name="salutation" type="xs:string"/>
    <xs:element name="firstname" type="xs:string"/>
    <xs:element name="lastname" type="xs:string"/>
  </xs:sequence>
</xs:group>

<xs:element name="film" type= "xs:string">
  <xs:complexType>
    <xs:sequence>
      <xs:element name="title" type="xs:string"/>
    <xs:element name="director" type="xs:string">
        <xs:complexType>
```

```
            <xs:group ref="fullname"/>
        </xs:complexType>
    <xs:element name="writer" type="xs:string"
    maxOccurs="unbounded"/>
        <xs:complexType>
            <xs:group ref="fullname"/>
        </xs:complexType>
    <xs:element name="year" type="xs:integer"/>
    <xs:element name="runtime" type="xs:integer"/>
 </xs:sequence>
    </xs:complexType>
</xs:element>
```

Grouping attributes

Attributes can be grouped together in the same fashion as elements, except that you use the xs:attributeGroup element. For example, suppose the XML code sample used in the previous section was based on attributes inside of the director and writer elements instead of being child elements:

```
<film>
    <title>Henry V</title>
    <director salutation="Mr." firstname="Kenneth"
      lastname="Branagh"/>
    <writer salutation="Mr." firstname="Kenneth"
      lastname="Branagh"/>
    <writer salutation="Sir" firstname="William"
      lastname="Shakespeare"/>
    </writer>
    <year>1989</year>
    <runtime>137</runtime>
</film>
```

If you want to group together the salutation, firstname, and lastname attributes, you can use the xs:attributeGroup element and then reference this group when you declare the director and writer elements in the schema:

```
<xs:attributeGroup name="fullname">
    <xs:attribute name="salutation" type="xs:string"/>
    <xs:attribute name="firstname" type="xs:string"/>
    <xs:attribute name="lastname" type="xs:string"/>
</xs:group>

<xs:element name="film" type= "xs:string">
    <xs:complexType>
      <xs:sequence>
        <xs:element name="title" type="xs:string"/>
      <xs:element name="director" type="xs:string">
          <xs:complexType>
            <xs:attributeGroup ref="fullname"/>
```

```
          </xs:complexType>
        <xs:element name="writer" type="xs:string"
        maxOccurs="unbounded"/>
          <xs:complexType>
            <xs:attributeGroup ref="fullname"/>
          </xs:complexType>
        <xs:element name="year" type="xs:integer"/>
        <xs:element name="runtime" type="xs:integer"/>
      </xs:sequence>
      </xs:complexType>
</xs:element>
```

Extending the Document Structure

The entire reason for defining DTDs and XML schemas is to ensure that the XML document has a reliable structure. However, within this framework, you still may have occasional need for being flexible and allowing for elements or attributes that are not declared in the schema.

As an illustration, suppose you want to create a schema for the following core film element structure, but you have two different purposes for it. In one case, you need to add an id attribute and a stocknumber child element to the film element. For a second case, you need to add a sequence attribute and a theaterid child element to film. The two cases are shown in the following code:

```
<!-- film element for use #1 -->
<film id="101-01">
  <title>Henry V</title>
  <director>Kenneth Branagh</director>
  <writer>Kenneth Branagh, William Shakespeare</writer>
  <year>1989</year>
  <runtime>137</runtime>
  <stocknumber>403D2</stocknumber>
</film>

<!-- film element for use #2 -->
<film sequence="0">
  <title>Groundhog Day</title>
  <director>Harold Ramis</director>
  <writer>Danny Rubin</writer>
  <year>1993</year>
  <runtime>101</runtime>
  <theaterid>19-92</theaterid>
</film>
```

With a DTD, you'd have to throw up your hands and punt, but XML schemas allow for the ability to extend XML documents using the xs:any and xs:anyAttribute elements. Therefore, to allow for the needed flexibility, you define the schema as follows:

```
<xs:element name="film" type= "xs:string">
  <xs:complexType>
    <xs:sequence>
      <xs:element name="title" type="xs:string"/>
    <xs:element name="director" type="xs:string"/>
    <xs:element name="writer" type="xs:string"/>
    <xs:element name="year" type="xs:integer"/>
    <xs:element name="runtime" type="xs:integer"/>
    <xs:any minOccurs="0"/>
  </xs:sequence>
  <xs:anyAttribute/>
</xs:complexType>
</xs:element>
```

Placing Restrictions on Values

You can place constraints on what the data looks like that goes into XML elements. The xs:restriction element is used to define a restriction on the values that an element can take. An attribute called base declares the base data type on which the restriction is to be applied. Inside of the xs:restriction element, you can define one of several facets for specifying the content structure. A *facet* defines the set of valid values that are permissible within a restriction. Table 3-2 lists the facets available for defining schemas.

Book II
Chapter 3

Creating XML
Schemas

Table 3-2	XML Schema Facets	
Facet	*Description*	*Example*
xs:enumeration	A set of these elements declares a list of acceptable values	`<xs:enumeration value="PG"/>`
xs:fractionDigits	Declares the maximum number of decimal places permitted. (Value must be greater than or equal to zero.)	`<xs:fractionDigits value="2"/>`
xs:length	Specifies the exact number of characters or list items permitted. (Value must be greater than or equal to zero.)	`<xs:length value="4"/>`
xs:maxExclusive	Declares the highest acceptable number for a numeric value. (Value must be less than this specified value.)	`<xs:maxExclusive value="400"/>`

(continued)

Table 3-2 *(continued)*

Facet	Description	Example
xs:maxInclusive	Specifies the highest acceptable number for a numeric value. (Value must be less than or equal to this specified value.)	`<xs:maxInclusive value="400"/>`
xs:maxLength	Defines the maximum number of characters or list items allowed. (Value must be equal to or greater than zero.)	`<xs:maxLength value="3"/>`
xs:minExclusive	Declares the lowest acceptable number for a numeric value. (Value must be greater than this specified value.)	`<xs:minExclusive value="12"/>`
xs:minInclusive	Specifies the lowest acceptable number for a numeric value. (Value must be greater than or equal to this specified value.)	`<xs:minInclusive value="12"/>`
xs:minLength	Defines the minimum number of characters or list items permitted. (Value must be equal to or greater than zero.)	`<xs:minLength value="5"/>`
xs:pattern	Declares the exact sequence of characters that are permitted.	`<xs:pattern value="[a-z]"/>`
xs:totalDigits	Specifies the exact number of digits permitted. (Value must be greater than zero.)	`<xs:totalDigits value="5"/>`
xs:whiteSpace	Determines how white space (line feeds, tabs, spaces, and carriage returns) are handled.	`<xs:whiteSpace value="preserve"/>`

For example, suppose you want to define a rule for the year element so that the values that this element takes must fall within the range 1902 through 2002. You can declare the element with the restriction as follows:

```
<xs:element name="year">
  <xs:simpleType>
    <xs:restriction base="xs:integer">
      <xs:minInclusive value="1902"/>
      <xs:maxInclusive value="2002"/>
    </xs:restriction>
  </xs:simpleType>
</xs:element>
```

There are several new schema elements to discover in this example:

✦ xs:simpleType. The xs:restriction element needs to be inside of a container. The xs:simpleType element, which is discussed fully in Book II, Chapter 5, is used as the container in this instance, because the year element contains only textual data. If the year element contained attributes or child elements, you would have to use the xs:complexType element.

✦ xs:restriction. The xs:restriction element is set to be an integer type and encloses the exact constraints for the year element.

✦ xs:minInclusive and xs:maxInclusive. The elements maxInclusive and minInclusive are the facets that define the upper and lower limit of the simple type.

This example shows you how to set a value range for your element.

By using this schema, you can apply it to determine valid and invalid year entries. The following sample elements show which elements would pass the test and which would not:

```
<!-- Valid -->
<year>1936</year>
<year>2000</year>

<!-- Invalid -->
<year>1900</year>
<year>2003</year>
```

Declaring a list of values

You can declare that an element must have a value taken from a set of enumerated values specified in an xs:restriction element using xs:enumeration. For example, suppose an mpaa element is used to provide the U.S. standard MPAA rating of a film. The possible ratings are G, PG, PG-13, R, NC-17, and X. The following shows the use of xs:enumeration to declare each of the following valid values for mpaa:

```
<xs:element name="mpaa">
  <xs:simpleType>
    <xs:restriction base="xs:string">
      <xs:enumeration value="G"/>
      <xs:enumeration value="PG"/>
      <xs:enumeration value="PG-13"/>
      <xs:enumeration value="R"/>
      <xs:enumeration value="NC-17"/>
      <xs:enumeration value="X"/>
    </xs:restriction>
  </xs:simpleType>
</xs:element>
```

Using this schema, the following code snippet lists valid and invalid mpaa elements:

```
<!-- Valid -->
<mpaa>G</mpaa>
<mpaa>PG-13</mpaa>
<mpaa>R</mpaa>

<!-- Invalid -->
<mpaa>2A</mpaa>
<mpaa>PG-12</mpaa>
<mpaa>A</mpaa>
```

Declaring length restrictions

XML schemas can enforce length restrictions for a given element using the following three facets:

✦ xs:length defines the exact size of an input value.

✦ xs:minLength defines the minimum size of an input value.

✦ xs:maxLength declares the maximum size of an input value.

To illustrate, suppose a zipcode element is used to capture five-digit U.S. ZIP codes. Using xs:length, the definition would look like this:

```
<xs:element name="mpaa">
  <xs:simpleType>
    <xs:restriction base="xs:string">
      <xs:length value="5"/>
      <xs:pattern value="[0-9][0-9][0-9][0-9][0-9]"/>
    </xs:restriction>
  </xs:simpleType>
</xs:element>
```

Or, suppose that the title child element of film must contain between 1 and 25 characters. To define a range of size, you could declare the following:

```
<xs:element name="mpaa">
  <xs:simpleType>
    <xs:restriction base="xs:string">
      <xs:minLength value="1"/>
      <xs:maxLength value="25"/>
    </xs:restriction>
  </xs:simpleType>
</xs:element>
```

Declaring patterns

Another common type of restriction that you'll want to place on the data for an element is a *pattern*.

Many a times, you may not define the restrictions in terms of exact limits or values. You may need a pattern to define the restrictions. For example, consider an element called localphone. This element must contain a string value, but of a specific length and in a specific format. These restrictions can be defined in the following manner:

```
<xs:element name="localphone" type="xs:string">
  <xs:simpleType>
    <xs:restriction base="xs:string">
      <xs:length value="8"/>
      <xs:pattern value="\d{3}-\d{4}"/>
    </xs:restriction>
  </xs:simpleType>
</xs:element>
```

**Book II
Chapter 3**

**Creating XML
Schemas**

The preceding code snippet defines a restriction on the localphone element in the following ways:

✦ xs:restriction element declares that the local phone can hold only string values.

✦ xs:length specifies that the string value must be eight characters long.

✦ xs:pattern defines a pattern (ddd-dddd) that the characters must adhere to. The regular expression \d represents a digit value. The angular brackets{ } are used to specify the number of digits that must appear in an expression.

The following are several example patterns:

```
<!-- String value must be a single character and be between
    an uppercase A and F -->
<xs:element name="rating" type="xs:string">
  <xs:simpleType>
    <xs:restriction base="xs:string">
      <xs:pattern value="[A-F]"/>
    </xs:restriction>
  </xs:simpleType>
</xs:element>

<!-- Alternative to the preceding example. String value must
    be a single letter and be one of the characters inside of
    the brackets -->
<xs:element name="rating" type="xs:string">
  <xs:simpleType>
    <xs:restriction base="xs:string">
```

```
      <xs:pattern value="[ABCDEF]"/>
    </xs:restriction>
  </xs:simpleType>
</xs:element>

<!-- String value is a three character string with the first
  character being between A-F, the second character being a
  number between 0-5, and the final character being between
  A and Z -->
<xs:element name="theaterid" type="xs:string">
  <xs:simpleType>
    <xs:restriction base="xs:string">
      <xs:pattern value="[A-F][0-5][A-Z]"/>
    </xs:restriction>
  </xs:simpleType>
</xs:element>

<!-- Pattern for a U.S. social security number (ddd-dd-dddd)
  -->
<xs:element name="ssn" type="xs:string">
  <xs:simpleType>
    <xs:restriction base="xs:string">
      <xs:length value="11"/>
      <xs:pattern value="\d{3}-\d{2}-\d{4}"/>
    </xs:restriction>
  </xs:simpleType>
</xs:element>

<!-- Pattern for a U.S. state abbreviation, allowing upper or
  lower case -->
<xs:element name="state" type="xs:string">
  <xs:simpleType>
    <xs:restriction base="xs:string">
      <xs:pattern value="[A-Za-z][A-Za-z]"/>
    </xs:restriction>
  </xs:simpleType>
</xs:element>

<!-- Pattern for a U.S. state abbreviation, allowing upper or
  lower case -->
<xs:element name="state" type="xs:string">
  <xs:simpleType>
    <xs:restriction base="xs:string">
      <xs:pattern value="[A-Za-z][A-Za-z]"/>
    </xs:restriction>
  </xs:simpleType>
</xs:element>
```

Declaring restrictions on white space

White space is that hidden stuff in a document that you can't see. Although it all may look the same on screen, white space actually may contain tabs, carriage return and linefeed characters, and spaces. XML schemas allow for considerable flexibility concerning how you handle white space using the xs:whiteSpace constraint. You have three options: preserve, replace, and collapse. These are discussed in the following sections.

Preserve white space

If you would like to keep the status quo and not make any changes to the white space as inputted, you can use the preserve value for the xs:whiteSpace element, as in the following example:

```
<xs:element name="summary" type="xs:string">
  <xs:simpleType>
    <xs:restriction base="xs:string">
      <xs:whiteSpace value="preserve"/>
    </xs:restriction>
  </xs:simpleType>
</xs:element>
```

Book II
Chapter 3

Creating XML
Schemas

Replace white space

When data is entered using a variety of input methods, the data is often in a messy state, with carriage returns, line feeds, and extra tabs all over the place. In order to massage this text to get it into a more storable fashion, you can use the replace value of the xs:whiteSpace. Using this option, each tab, carriage return, and linefeed is replaced with a single space, as in the following example:

```
<xs:element name="summary" type="xs:string">
  <xs:simpleType>
    <xs:restriction base="xs:string">
      <xs:whiteSpace value="replace"/>
    </xs:restriction>
  </xs:simpleType>
</xs:element>
```

Collapse white space

A final option is to collapse the white space and get rid of all unnecessary extra spaces (including multiple spaces). Using the collapse value of the xs:whiteSpace element, all tabs, carriage returns, linefeeds, and multiple spaces are condensed into a single white space. In addition, any leading or trailing spaces are deleted, as in the following example:

```
<xs:element name="summary" type="xs:string">
  <xs:simpleType>
    <xs:restriction base="xs:string">
      <xs:whiteSpace value="collapse"/>
    </xs:restriction>
  </xs:simpleType>
</xs:element>
```

Chapter 4: XML Schema Data Types

In This Chapter

✔ **Discovering XML schema built-in data types**

✔ **Exploring how to create your own data types**

✔ **Extending custom data types**

✔ **Working with list and union types**

*T*ext, text, text. If you open up an XML document in your favorite editor, you can see that XML, at its core, is always about text. You may be working with a lot of different kinds of data in your XML document, such as sales forecasts, dollars and cents, appointment times, and high and low temperatures. But in the end, all data inside of an XML document must be expressed in some way as text.

Although it is a given that XML documents must be fashioned as text, you don't have to work with all XML data as strings and then convert it to other formats in order to actually use that data. Instead, XML schemas enable you to go beyond the "everything is a string" notion by supplying 54 built-in data types that you can use to define your schemas. What's more, the extensibility of XML schemas reach a peak when working with data types, as you can create your own custom data types and reuse them across your XML schema. In this chapter, you explore both built-in and custom data types.

Working with Built-In Data Types

XML schemas come armed with an array of data types that are "built into" the schema specification. The most rudimentary types, known as *primitive data types*, include the following kinds of data:

✦ String

✦ Numeric

✦ Date and time

✦ Boolean

✦ URIs

✦ XML types

You can think of the 19 primitive types as being something akin to vowels of the English language; they are the common data types and the building blocks for defining all elements, attributes, and even other data types.

Derived data types are defined from primitive types (or from other derived types) to provide a more specific or restricted type category. For example, integer is a derived data type that originates from the decimal data type in order to describe a number more narrowly than the more general decimal type does.

Trying to make sense of the built-in data type system of XML schemas is not always an easy process. Frankly, determining why some types are primitives and others are derivatives is sometimes counterintuitive. For example, float and double are data types completely unrelated to the numeric data type of decimal, even though they all work with numbers.

In the following sections, you look at string, numeric, date/time, boolean, and URI built-in types.

Declaring string types

The string data type is used for textual data and can contain alphanumeric characters, tabs, line feeds, and carriage returns. Here is an example string type declaration:

```
<xs:element name="film" type="xs:string"/>
```

If you read Book II, Chapter 3, you saw many examples of xs:string type.

Also, two derivative string data types originating from xs:string are noteworthy:

✦ xs:normalizedString. You can declare normalized strings when you want the XML parser to replace tabs, carriage returns, and line feeds with spaces inside of the value.

✦ xs:token. You can use a token data type instead of the plain string type when you want to remove all hidden characters except single spaces. The following characters will be removed by the XML parser: tabs, carriage returns, line feeds, multiple space characters, and leading or trailing spaces.

To illustrate how an element would be processed based on these types, consider the following element:

```
<film>     Tora, Tora,
Tora    </film>
```

Because this code snippet contains hidden characters, the following expanded snippet shows these special characters (where {s}=space, {t}=tab, {cr}=carriage return, {lf}=line feed):

```
<film>{t}Tora,{s}Tora,{cr}{lf}Tora{s}{s}{s}</film>
```

Therefore, if the `film` element is declared as `xs:string`, the processed value would be as follows:

```
{t}Tora,{s}Tora,{cr}{lf}
Tora{s}{s}{s}
```

If `film` is `xs:normalizedString`, the value would be as follows:

```
{s}{s}{s}{s}{s}Tora,{s}Tora,{s}Tora{s}{s}{s}
```

But if `film` is `xs:token`, its value would be as follows:

```
Tora,{s}Tora,{s},Tora
```

Table 4-1 lists all of the data types derived from `xs:string`, many of which are XML types.

Book II
Chapter 4

XML Schema
Data Types

Table 4-1	String Types Derived from `xs:string`
Name	*Description*
ENTITIES	A whitespace separated list of ENTITY names
ENTITY	A string that represents an XML name declared as an unparsed entity in a DTD
ID	A string that represents a unique XML name among ID type attributes
IDREF	A string that references an ID type attribute used elsewhere in the document
IDREFS	A whitespace separated list of IDREF names
language	A string that represents an XML language identifier (such as `en-US`, `fr`)
Name	A string that represents a valid XML name
NCName	A string that represents a `NCName` (local name without colons)
NMTOKEN	A string that represents the `NMTOKEN` attribute in XML (attributes only)
NMTOKENS	A string that represents the `NMTOKENS` attribute in XML
normalizedString	A string that does not contain tabs, line feeds, or carriage returns
QName	A string that represents a QName (optionally prefixed name that includes a namespace qualifier)
token	A string that does not contain tabs, line feeds, carriage returns, multiple spaces, and leading/trailing spaces

Declaring numeric types

Compared to the string-based nature of DTDs, XML schemas provide considerable support for number-crunching operations. The basic number type is `xs:decimal` and is used to represent decimal values. For example, the following element needs to store decimal numbers:

```
<xs:element name="size" type="xs:decimal"/>
```

Therefore, the following elements would be valid:

```
<size>30.31020</size>
<size>3.1415926535897934</size>
<size>100.12</size>
```

XML schemas place a cap on the maximum number of decimal digits at 18.

Several numeric data types are derived from `xs:decimal`, as shown in Table 4-2. Perhaps the most commonly used is `xs:integer`, which allows you to represent a whole number by declaring the element as follows:

```
<xs:element name="turns" type="xs:integer"/>
```

Table 4-2	Numeric Data Types Derived from `xs:decimal`
Derived Data Type	*Description*
`xs:byte`	A signed 8-bit integer value
`xs:int`	A signed 32-bit integer value
`xs:integer`	Any integer value
`xs:long`	A signed 64-bit integer value
`xs:negativeInteger`	Any negative integer value
`xs:nonNegativeInteger`	Any integer that has a non-negative value (0 and higher)
`xs:nonPositiveInteger`	Any integer that has a non-positive value (0 and lower)
`xs:positiveInteger`	Any positive integer value
`xs:short`	Any signed 16-bit integer value
`xs:unsignedLong`	Any unsigned 64-bit integer value
`xs:unsignedInt`	Any unsigned 32-bit integer value
`xs:unsignedShort`	Any unsigned 16-bit integer value
`xs:unsignedByte`	Any unsigned 8-bit integer value

Although the XML schema specification does not tie them to the `xs:decimal` numeric data type, you can also use the `xs:double` and `xs:float` primitive types to express double (IEEE 754 64-bit floating point) and float (IEEE 754 32-bit floating point) values.

Declaring date and time data types

I'm late! I'm late! I'm late for a very important date. Using a DTD, in order to find out you were late for that most critical appointment, you'd have to convert string values into dates, crossing your fingers that the strings were of a structured format that would allow conversion. XML schemas, however, are much more capable in letting you store date and time data, so that you can know precisely the date, time, and even duration of your tardiness when you go off to *Wonderland*.

Dates

To work with dates, you can use the xs:date type, which accepts the date in *CCYY-MM-DD* format, where:

Book II
Chapter 4

**XML Schema
Data Types**

+ *CC* specifies the century.

+ *YY* indicates the year.

+ *MM* specifies the month.

+ *DD* denotes the day.

For example, suppose you define the following element:

```
<xs:element name="releasedate" type="xs:date"/>
```

A valid releasedate element would look like this:

```
<releasedate>2002-11-22</releasedate>
```

Each part of the date type must be included for valid dates.

XML schemas also support four additional built-in date types that are shown in Table 4-3.

Table 4-3	Additional Built-In Date Types	
Type	*Description*	*Example*
xs:gDay	A day	22
xs:gMonth	A specific month in a specific year	2004-03
xs:gMonthDay	A month and day	02-01
xs:gYear	A specific year	2005

Times

Time data is defined using the xs:time type, and it uses the *hh:mm:ss* format, where:

+ *hh* denotes the hour.

+ *mm* indicates the minute.

+ *ss* specifies the second.

For example, suppose you declare a `time` element called `showtime`:

```
<xs:element name="showtime" type="xs:time"/>
```

Valid `showtime` elements are as follows:

```
<showtime>11:30:00</showtime>
<showtime>12:57:59</showtime>
<showtime>10:00:00</showtime>
```

Each part of the `time` type must be included for valid times.

DateTime values

DateTime values can be declared using the `xs:datetime` type with a combined *CCYY-MM-DDThh:mm:ss* format, where:

+ *CC* specifies the century.

+ *YY* indicates the year.

+ *MM* specifies the month.

+ *DD* denotes the day.

+ T marks the start of the time part of the value.

+ *hh* denotes the hour.

+ *mm* indicates the minute.

+ *ss* specifies the second.

To illustrate, suppose that you define a `firstshowing` element as follows:

```
<xs:element name="firstshowing" type="xs:dateTime"/>
```

Valid entries are as follows:

```
<firstshowing>2003-12-18T12:00:00</firstshowing>
<firstshowing>2004-05-15T11:30:00</firstshowing>
<firstshowing>2005-04-30T10:59:59</firstshowing>
```

Each part of the `datetime` type must be included for valid `datetime` values.

Durations

Time intervals can be stored in XML using the `xs:duration` type by using the P*n*Y*n*M*n*DT*n*H*n*M*n*S format, where:

✦ P denotes the period (required).

✦ *n*Y specifies the number of years.

✦ *n*M indicates the number of months.

✦ *n*D specifies the number of days.

✦ T marks the start of the time part of the value (required when time is specified).

✦ *n*H specifies the number of hours.

✦ *n*M indicates the number of minutes.

✦ *n*S shows the number of seconds.

For example, suppose that you define the following `length` element:

```
<xs:element name="length" type="xs:duration"/>
```

Using the duration type format, each of the following elements are valid:

```
<!--3 hours, 30 minutes -->
<length>PT3H30M</length>
<!-- 37 years -->
<length>P37Y</length>
<!-- 1 day, 14 hours, 2 minutes, and 3 seconds -->
<length>P1DT14H02M03S</length>
```

Negative durations are permitted by prefixing the duration value with a minus sign:

```
<length>-PT5M</length>
```

Table 4-4 summarizes the formats for date and time data types:

Table 4-4   **Date and Time Data Type Formats**

Data Type	*Format*	*Example*
`xs:date`	*CCYY-MM-DD*	`<enddate>2003-09-22<enddate>`
`xs:time`	*hh:mm:ss*	`<starttime>12:00:10</starttime>`
`xs:dateTime`	*CCYY-MM-DD*T*hh:mm:ss*	`<premiere>2004-08-13T12:30:20</premiere>`
`xs:duration`	P*n*Y*n*M*n*DT*n*H*n*M*n*S	`<age>P23Y03MT12:33:30</age>`

Declaring boolean types

To be or not to be; that is the question. If Hamlet were to work with XML schemas, undoubtedly, his data type of choice would be xs:boolean, which enables you to specify boolean values. For example, to define a boolean element named current, you declare it as follows:

```
<xs:element name="current" type="xs:boolean"/>
```

Using this schema, each of the following XML elements are valid:

```
<current>true</current>
<current>1</current>
<current>false</current>
<current>0</current>
```

Declaring URI types

When storing Web addresses or other URIs (Uniform Resource Identifiers) with DTDs, you would need to store the values as strings and then test their format outside of XML. However, XML schemas provide built-in support for working with URIs with its xs:anyURI data type. To use, declare an element or attribute as follows:

```
<xs:element name="website" type="xs:anyURI"/>
```

With this schema, the following code is valid:

```
<website>http://www.lordoftherings.net</website>
```

You can include relative or absolute URIs, so the following is also valid:

```
<website>/home/index.html</website>
```

Creating Your Own Data Types

In addition to the predefined set of data types available with XML schemas that you've explored so far, you can also define your own data types. One common question you might be asking is this: "Because there are 54 built-in data types already, why would I ever need to define my own data type? After all, most people just work with the normal stuff, such as numbers, currency, or strings."

Custom data types enable you to conform an XML schema to your data and its patterns. If you have a particular ID format, why not let the schema enforce that pattern? Or, if you have a particular manner in which first and last names must be entered, why not let the schema do the validation work for you? Custom types also enable you to create your own types and reuse them across your schemas, making it much easier to write and maintain your schemas.

If you read Book II, Chapter 3, you discovered how to put restrictions on data values, enabling you to create elements or attributes that require a certain string pattern or range of acceptable values. Using restrictions, for example, you can create a phone number element that can contain data only in a xxx-xxx-xxxx pattern or a movie title element that must contain a string between 1 and 20 characters in length.

Book II, Chapter 3 shows you how to attach these types of customizations to specific elements in your schema. But suppose you want to generalize these custom restrictions and reuse them elsewhere in the schema as well as in other schemas. Consider, for example, that you've got three XML structures you work with regularly (supplier, customer, and employee), each of which has a phone number element. Instead of defining the phone number restriction three separate times, you can declare a new data type called `xs:phoneNumber` and then assign that type to the three instances where it is used in the schemas.

If you read Book II, Chapter 3, you discovered that there are two kinds of elements — simple and complex. In the same way, there are two types of custom data types:

Book II
Chapter 4

**XML Schema
Data Types**

+ **Simple.** *Simple data types* contain only values and use the `xs:simpleType` element declaration.

+ **Complex.** *Complex data types* contain child elements, attributes, or a mixture of these and use the `xs:complexType` declaration.

Declaring simple data types

You can create new simple data types from existing data types by limiting the new type to be a more targeted subset of the original base type values. The `xs:simpleType` element is used to declare the restricted data type and has a basic structure as follows:

```
<xs:simpleType name="yourDataTypeName">
  <!-- Value declaration goes here -->
</xs:simpleType>
```

Within the `xs:simpleType` construct, you specify what the makeup of the data type should be, making use of `xs:restriction` and other facets as needed. (See the "Placing Restrictions on Values" section of Chapter 3 for more information on facets.) If you read Chapter 3, you saw the use of `xs:simpleType`, but the optional `name` attribute enables you to assign a name to the type and then reuse it by calling that name.

Because this data type is referenced by a name, it is called a *named data type*. A named data type is the one in which a set of elements and attributes are referenced by a single name. At the time of declaring an element, this data type is referenced by the type identifier. Named data types can be identified by the type identifier in the element declaration statement. Named data types can be reused in any part of the schema.

Here's an illustration. To create that xs:phoneNumber type that was discussed earlier, use the following xs:simpleType structure:

```
<xs:simpleType name="phoneNumber">
  <xs:restriction base="xs:string">
    <xs:length value="12"/>
    <xs:pattern value="\d{3}-\d{3}-\d{4}"/>
  </xs:restriction>
</xs:simpleType>
```

Or, consider a second example:

```
<xs:simpleType name="usState">
  <xs:restriction base="xs:string/>
    <xs:length value="2"/>
    <xs:pattern value="[A-Z][A-Z]"/>
  </xs:restriction>
</xs:simpleType>
```

Because you have assigned a name to those custom types, you can then assign them to one or more elements in your schema, like this:

```
<xs:element name="customer">
  <xs:complexType>
    <xs:sequence>
      <xs:element name="customer_name" type="xs:string"/>
      <xs:element name="customer_phone"
    type="xs:phoneNumber"/>
      <xs:element name="customer_state" type="xs:usState"/>
    </xs:sequence>
  </xs:complexType>
</xs:element>
```

Declaring complex data types

The xs:complexType element is used to declare custom data types that contain child elements, attributes, or both. You can define a complex data type by using the following syntax:

```
<xs:complexType name="yourDataTypeName">
  <!-- Content model declaration goes here -->
</xs:complexType>
```

In the preceding syntax, the `complexType` element is used to declare a new complex data type. The `name` attribute specifies the name of the new complex data type. The content model declaration contains the declaration for the elements and attributes that make up the content of the complex type.

Consider, for example, a generic personal information structure that is used to store basic name and address for individuals. The complex data type could be defined as follows:

```
<xs:complexType name="personInfo">
  <xs:sequence>
    <xs:element name="first_name" type="xs:string"/>
    <xs:element name="last_name" type="xs:string"/>
    <xs:element name="address" type="xs:string"/>
    <xs:element name="city" type="xs:string"/>
    <xs:element name="state" type="xs:usState"/>
    <xs:element name="phone" type="xs:phoneNumber"/>
  </xs:sequence>
</xs:complexType>
```

Book II
Chapter 4

XML Schema
Data Types

After this custom data type is defined, you can use the `xs:personInfo` type as many times as you want in your schema:

```
<xs:element name="invoice">
  <xs:complexType>
    <xs:sequence>
      <xs:element name="ID" type="xs:integer"/>
      <xs:element name="customer" type="xs:personInfo"/>
      <xs:element name="supplier" type="xs:personInfo"/>
      <xs:element name="sales_employee"
   type="xs:personInfo"/>
    </xs:sequence>
  </xs:complexType>
</xs:element>
```

Extending custom data types

You can also base new data types on existing custom simple and complex data types, extending them by adding new elements or attributes. For example, suppose you have a custom complex data type named `xs:coreProduct`:

```
<!-- Core Product type -->
<xs:complexType name="coreProduct">
  <xs:sequence>
    <xs:element name="product_id" type="xs:prodID"/>
    <xs:element name="name" type="xs:string"/>
    <xs:element name="description" type="xs:string"/>
  </xs:sequence>
```

```
</xs:complexType>

<!-- Custom ID type -->
<xs:simpleType name="prodID">
   <xs:restriction base="xs:string">
     <xs:pattern value="[A-F]-[0-9][0-9][0-9][A-Z]"/>
   </xs:restriction>
</xs:simpleType>
```

If you want to extend the xs:coreProduct base type and add some new inventory-related information, you could use the xs:extension element:

```
<!-- Extended Product type -->
<xs:complexType name="extendedProduct">
  <xs:complexContent>
    <xs:extension base="coreProduct">
      <xs:sequence>
        <xs:element name="factory_location"
  type="xs:string"/>
        <xs:element name="wholesale_price"
  type="xs:decimal"/>
      </xs:sequence>
    </xs:extension>
  </xs:complexContent>
</xs:complexType>
```

This declaration creates a new xs:extendedProduct type that includes the product_id, name, and description elements from the base type and adds new factory_location and wholesale_price elements. The xs:complexContent element is used when you define extensions or restrictions on a complex type. Inside of it, xs:extension is used to extend an existing simple or complex type.

Declaring list data types

You can use the xs:list data type to create a new type that contains a set of whitespace-separated values of base data types. For example, suppose that you want to create a data type that has a list of U.S. states. To do so, create a new simple type:

```
<xs:simpleType name="usStates">
   <xs:list itemType="xs:usState" />
</xs:simpleType>

<xs:simpleType name="usState">
  <xs:restriction base="xs:string/>
    <xs:length value="2"/>
    <xs:pattern value="[A-Z][A-Z]"/>
  </xs:restriction>
</xs:simpleType>
```

The preceding code declares the simple type called xs:usStates. The list element takes an attribute called itemType. This attribute references a built-in or simple data type, which in this case is the custom xs:usState type.

Declaring union data types

The xs:union element can be used to derive new data types from multiple base types. For example, suppose that you have an element named stockDetails that describes the stock details in words or numbers. Therefore, define a simple type that is a union of integer and string data types as follows.

```
<xs:simpleType name="stockDetails">
    <xs:union memberTypes="xs:string integer" />
</xs:simpleType>
```

In the preceding declaration, notice that the union element takes an attribute called memberTypes. This attribute is set to a list of names of built-in data types or simpleType elements defined in the schema.

Chapter 5: Designing XML Schemas

In This Chapter

✔ Exploring XML schema design techniques

✔ Discovering the Mirror (Russian Doll) design model

✔ Working with the Salami Slice design model

✔ Exploring the Venetian Blind design model

✔ Using the Green design model

The task of creating a Document Type Definition (DTD) doesn't require much design work. If you read Book II, Chapter 2, you discovered that writing a DTD generally involves adding a declaration in the DTD to correspond with each element and attribute that you want to appear in an XML *instance document*. In other words, you focus on defining the structure of the XML document and then replicating that structure accordingly in the DTD.

In contrast, XML schemas are far more flexible in how they can be created. As a result, you actually have to think about how to best design them to suit your needs. Yes, you can create a schema that closely mirrors the structure of the XML document much like the DTD does. But you can also organize your schema in other ways that can make your schemas easier to reuse and maintain.

In this chapter, you explore four design models for constructing XML schemas, which I call the Mirror, Assembly Line, Venetian Blind, and Green approaches. As you explore each of these models for schema development, the schemas you create will be written to support the XML structure shown in Listing 5-1.

Listing 5-1   media.xml

```
<media>
  <book title="The Once and Future King">
    <isbn>0-441-62740-4</isbn>
    <writer>T.H. White</writer>
    <year>1939</year>
    <stock num="1020-20" location="N0110"/>
```

(continued)

Listing 5-1 *(continued)*

```
  </book>
  <cd title="Symphony No. 3">
    <artist>Henryk Gorecki</artist>
    <year>1992</year>
    <runtime>PT52M</runtime>
    <stock num="1330-39" location="S2292"/>
  </cd>
  <film title="Henry V">
    <director>Kenneth Branagh</director>
    <writer>William Shakespeare</writer>
    <year>1989</year>
    <runtime>PT2H17M</runtime>
    <stock num="9820-76" location="E2129"/>
  </film>
</media>
```

Using the Mirror Design Model

Mirror, mirror on the wall. Which is the fairest XML document structure of all? Unless you are an evil queen, jealous of the XML schemas of Snow White, you probably won't be asking your bathroom mirror for schema modeling advice. Nonetheless, the first method of designing an XML schema does act something like that mirror on the wall, as it involves creating a schema that closely emulates structure of the XML instance document (much in the same way that you naturally do when creating a DTD). It can be helpful to think of this technique as the *Mirror design model* because your goal is to essentially hold a "looking glass" up to an XML structure and represent that same structure in the schema that is created.

Because an XML document structure typically consists of nested elements each inside of the other, this schema design approach is often called the *Russian Doll design model*, referring to the nesting nature of Russian dolls inside of each other.

Using the Mirror design model, the XML schema for the media.xml document would look like the schema shown in Listing 5-2.

Listing 5-2 Mirror Schema

```
<?xml version = "1.0" ?>
<xs:schema xmlns:xs="http://www.w3.org/2001/XMLSchema">
  <xs:element name="media">
    <xs:complexType>
      <xs:sequence>
        <xs:element name="book">
          <xs:complexType>
```

```
        <xs:sequence>
          <xs:element name="isbn">
            <xs:simpleType>
              <xs:restriction base="xs:string">
                <xs:length value="14"/>
                <xs:pattern value="\d{1}-\d{3}-\d{5}-
\d{1}"/>
              </xs:restriction>
            </xs:simpleType>
          </xs:element>
          <xs:element name="writer">
            <xs:simpleType>
              <xs:restriction base="xs:string">
                <xs:minLength value="1"/>
                <xs:maxLength value="25"/>
              </xs:restriction>
            </xs:simpleType>
          </xs:element>
          <xs:element name="year" type="xs:gYear"/>
          <xs:element name="stock">
            <xs:complexType>
              <xs:attribute name="num">
                <xs:simpleType>
                  <xs:restriction base="xs:string">
                    <xs:length value="7"/>
                    <xs:pattern value="\d{4}-\d{2}"/>
                  </xs:restriction>
                </xs:simpleType>
              </xs:attribute>
              <xs:attribute name="location">
                <xs:simpleType>
                  <xs:restriction base="xs:string">
                    <xs:length value="7"/>
                    <xs:pattern value="[NSEW]\d{4}"/>
                  </xs:restriction>
                </xs:simpleType>
              </xs:attribute>
            </xs:complexType>
          </xs:element>
        </xs:sequence>
        <xs:attribute name="title" type="xs:string"/>
      </xs:complexType>
    </xs:element>

    <xs:element name="cd">
      <xs:complexType>
        <xs:sequence>
          <xs:element name="artist">
            <xs:simpleType>
              <xs:restriction base="xs:string">
                <xs:minLength value="1"/>
```

(continued)

Listing 5-2 *(continued)*

```
                      <xs:maxLength value="25"/>
                  </xs:restriction>
              </xs:simpleType>
          </xs:element>
          <xs:element name="year" type="xs:gYear"/>
          <xs:element name="runtime" type="xs:duration"/>
          <xs:element name="stock">
            <xs:complexType>
              <xs:attribute name="num">
                <xs:simpleType>
                  <xs:restriction base="xs:string">
                    <xs:length value="7"/>
                    <xs:pattern value="\d{4}-\d{2}"/>
                  </xs:restriction>
                </xs:simpleType>
              </xs:attribute>
              <xs:attribute name="location">
                <xs:simpleType>
                  <xs:restriction base="xs:string">
                    <xs:length value="7"/>
                    <xs:pattern value="[NSEW]\d{4}"/>
                  </xs:restriction>
                </xs:simpleType>
              </xs:attribute>
            </xs:complexType>
          </xs:element>
        </xs:sequence>
        <xs:attribute name="title" type="xs:string"/>
      </xs:complexType>
  </xs:element>

  <xs:element name="film">
    <xs:complexType>
      <xs:sequence>
        <xs:element name="director">
          <xs:simpleType>
            <xs:restriction base="xs:string">
              <xs:minLength value="1"/>
              <xs:maxLength value="25"/>
            </xs:restriction>
          </xs:simpleType>
        </xs:element>
        <xs:element name="writer">
          <xs:simpleType>
            <xs:restriction base="xs:string">
              <xs:minLength value="1"/>
              <xs:maxLength value="25"/>
            </xs:restriction>
          </xs:simpleType>
        </xs:element>
        <xs:element name="year" type="xs:gYear"/>
```

```
        <xs:element name="runtime" type="xs:duration"/>
        <xs:element name="stock">
          <xs:complexType>
            <xs:attribute name="num">
              <xs:simpleType>
                <xs:restriction base="xs:string">
                  <xs:length value="7"/>
                  <xs:pattern value="\d{4}-\d{2}"/>
                </xs:restriction>
              </xs:simpleType>
            </xs:attribute>
            <xs:attribute name="location">
              <xs:simpleType>
                <xs:restriction base="xs:string">
                  <xs:length value="7"/>
                  <xs:pattern value="[NSEW]\d{4}"/>
                </xs:restriction>
              </xs:simpleType>
            </xs:attribute>
          </xs:complexType>
        </xs:element>
      </xs:sequence>
      <xs:attribute name="title" type="xs:string"/>
    </xs:complexType>
  </xs:element>
</xs:sequence>
</xs:complexType>
</xs:element>
</xs:schema>
```

Whew! Reading that schema line by line is dizzying given the nested levels, but you can see that it does successfully mirror the structure of the media.xml document. The media element is defined first and nested inside of it are the complex declarations of the book, cd, and film elements.

However, notice that in addition to the fact that the nested levels of elements make it hard to work with and manage, an awful lot of redundancy is also included. The book, cd, and film elements have common title attributes, year and stock elements, and several identical data types that have to be entered multiple times.

The Mirror design is perhaps the easiest way to learn how to initially create an XML schema and does work well for small data structures. However, this approach is not recommended except in these limited cases.

Using the Salami Slice Design Model

While the Mirror approach follows the hierarchy of the XML document you are modeling after, the *Salami Slice design model* does exactly the opposite.

Stripping the hierarchy altogether, this approach removes the various elements of the XML document from their original location and declares all elements directly under the xs:schema element. You can think of this approach as similar to the way you would make a salami sandwich: You'd stack individual salami slices on top of a piece of bread and throw a bread slice on top of the pile to form a sandwich.

Using this Salami Slice approach, the schema would look like the one shown in Listing 5-3.

Listing 5-3 Salami Slice Schema

```
<?xml version = "1.0" ?>
<xs:schema xmlns:xs="http://www.w3.org/2001/XMLSchema">

  <xs:element name="media">
    <xs:complexType>
      <xs:sequence>
        <xs:element ref="book"/>
        <xs:element ref="cd"/>
        <xs:element ref="film"/>
      </xs:sequence>
    </xs:complexType>
  </xs:element>

  <xs:element name="book">
    <xs:complexType>
      <xs:sequence>
        <xs:element ref="isbn"/>
        <xs:element ref="writer"/>
        <xs:element ref="year"/>
        <xs:element ref="stock"/>
      </xs:sequence>
      <xs:attribute ref="title"/>
    </xs:complexType>
  </xs:element>

  <xs:element name="cd">
    <xs:complexType>
      <xs:sequence>
        <xs:element ref="artist"/>
        <xs:element ref="year"/>
        <xs:element ref="runtime"/>
        <xs:element ref="stock"/>
      </xs:sequence>
      <xs:attribute ref="title"/>
    </xs:complexType>
  </xs:element>

  <xs:element name="film">
    <xs:complexType>
```

```
      <xs:sequence>
        <xs:element ref="director"/>
        <xs:element ref="writer"/>
        <xs:element ref="year"/>
        <xs:element ref="runtime"/>
        <xs:element ref="stock"/>
      </xs:sequence>
      <xs:attribute ref="title"/>
    </xs:complexType>
</xs:element>

<xs:element name="isbn">
  <xs:restriction base="xs:string">
    <xs:length value="14"/>
    <xs:pattern value="\d{1}-\d{3}-\d{5}-\d{1}"/>
  </xs:restriction>
</xs:element>

<xs:element name="author" type="xs:personType"/>

<xs:element name="artist" type="xs:personType"/>

<xs:element name="writer" type="xs:personType"/>

<xs:element name="director" type="xs:personType"/>

<xs:element name="year" type="xs:gYear"/>

<xs:element name="runtime" type="xs:duration"/>

<xs:element name="stock" type="xs:stockType"/>

<xs:attribute name="title" type="xs:string"/>

<xs:simpleType name="personType">
  <xs:restriction base="xs:string">
    <xs:minLength value="1"/>
    <xs:maxLength value="25"/>
  </xs:restriction>
</xs:simpleType>

<xs:complexType name="stockType">
  <xs:attribute name="num">
    <xs:simpleType>
      <xs:restriction base="xs:string">
        <xs:length value="7"/>
        <xs:pattern value="\d{4}-\d{2}"/>
      </xs:restriction>
    </xs:simpleType>
  </xs:attribute>
  <xs:attribute name="location">
```

**Book II
Chapter 5**

Designing
XML Schemas

(continued)

Listing 5-3 *(continued)*

```
<xs:simpleType>
  <xs:restriction base="xs:string">
    <xs:length value="7"/>
    <xs:pattern value="[NSEW]\d{4}"/>
  </xs:restriction>
</xs:simpleType>
</xs:attribute>
</xs:complexType>

</xs:schema>
```

As you can see, the structure of the schema is completely flat, with the media element serving as the bread that groups all of the salami slices together. Using this approach, whenever you encounter a place in which you need to reference an element or attribute, you use the ref attribute to link the declaration to that element instance. For example, the following xs:element lines inside of media serve as placeholders for the globally defined book, cd, and film elements, which are defined elsewhere in the schema:

```
<xs:element name="media">
  <xs:complexType>
    <xs:sequence>
      <xs:element ref="book"/>
      <xs:element ref="cd"/>
      <xs:element ref="film"/>
    </xs:sequence>
  </xs:complexType>
</xs:element>
```

When you define an element or attribute just under the xs:schema element like I did here, you create a *global* (or *top-level*) element or attribute. They are visible throughout the schema, enabling them to be referenced anywhere inside of the schema document, regardless of hierarchical level.

Each of the various elements is defined globally, making it possible to reuse them as needed. However, they are also closely interconnected, so that elements depend on other elements being present in order to work. You will probably find that schemas following the Salami Slice approach can be more difficult to read, given the flat nature of the schema.

In addition to the global elements and attributes, you can see that there are two custom data types called PersonType and StockType. The PersonType type is used in various parts of the XML document, anytime a person's name is going to be stored as a value, such as the author, artist, or director elements. The StockType is a type that is used by the book, cd, and film elements. Declaring them as a named type saves you from redefining the same type over in the schema.

Best practice: Naming custom data types

When you create a custom data type, you name it anything you wish. For example, suppose you have a type that describes a customer. You could create a named `complexType` called `customer`:

```
<xs:customType name="cus-
    tomer">
  <xs:sequence>
    <xs:element name="name"
type="xs:string"/>
    <xs:element name="address"
type="xs:string"/>
    <xs:element name="city"
type="xs:string"/>
    <xs:element name="state"
type="xs:string"/>
    <xs:element name="zipcode"
type="xs:string"/>
  </xs:sequence>
</xs:customType>
```

Therefore, when you create an instance of that type in your code, you could create an element called `customer` as well:

```
<xs:element name="customer"
    type="xs:customer"/>
```

Because elements and types are in different *symbol spaces*, you can have elements and types with identical names. Although that may be permissible for the schema parser, that practice can make for confusing and hard-to-read code.

Therefore, I recommend using a standard notation for naming custom data types, so that it is always clear what declaration is a type and an element instance of that type. For example, my preference is to tack on `Type` suffix to the end of a type name. Using this convention, the following code avoids the possible naming confusion shown in the preceding code example:

```
<xs:customType
    name="customerType">
  <xs:sequence>
    <xs:element name="name"
type="xs:string"/>
    <xs:element name="address"
type="xs:string"/>
    <xs:element name="city"
type="xs:string"/>
    <xs:element name="state"
type="xs:string"/>
    <xs:element name="zipcode"
type="xs:string"/>
  </xs:sequence>
</xs:customType>
<xs:element name="customer"
    type="xs:customerType"/>
```

Declaring everything globally using the Salami Slice approach means that the scope of elements and attributes differs greatly compared to the Mirror approach. Using the Mirror model, for example, the `isbn` and `writer` elements have a local scope, visible only inside the `book` element. Not only does this have implications in terms of reuse, but it also has an impact when you work with namespaces. (See Book I, Chapter 4 for more on namespaces.)

The `xs:schema` element allows you to define how you work with namespaces in your XML instance documents through the `elementFormDefault` and `attributeFormDefault` attributes. When set to `unqualified` (the default), you don't need to add the namespace prefix for local elements or attributes (those elements or attributes that are not declared at the global level) from the target namespace. But when set to qualified, you must add the namespace prefix for local elements or attributes from the target namespace.

Therefore, in the media.xml example, using the Mirror approach, if the xs:schema element has the elementFormDefault attribute set to unqualified, the namespace prefixes of isbn and writer don't need to be present in the instance document. In contrast, using the Salami Slice approach, the value of the elementFormDefault attribute doesn't matter, because the namespace prefix of isbn and writer must always be visible in the XML instance document, because they are global elements.

Given the different ways that these two approaches deal with namespaces, you can see that another key distinction between Mirror and Salami Slice design models is that the Mirror design promotes hiding namespace complexities, whereas the Salami Slice approach does not.

Using the Venetian Blind Design Model

A third approach, called the *Venetian Blind design model*, enables you to combine the best of both worlds by combining the Mirror approach's ability to hide namespace complexities with the Salami Slice approach's ability to reuse schema components. The Venetian Blind approach involves declaring most everything in your schema as a named data type and then declaring elements within these types. This design maximizes reuse, because components are declared globally, but it also maintains the ability to hide namespaces, because elements are defined locally (inside the type declarations).

The curious name for this design model relates to its ability to easily switch off and on namespace qualifiers. In the real world, Venetian blinds allow or mask light coming into a window, depending on whether its blinds are opened or shut. In the same way, the Venetian Blind model hides or exposes namespaces of nested elements based on the setting of the xs:schema element's elementFormDefault attribute. The elementFormDefault attribute, thus, serves as a switch for managing namespace exposure: Set its value to qualified when you want to expose namespaces, or set its value to unqualified when you want to hide namespaces.

Using the Venetian Blind approach, the schema would look like the one shown in Listing 5-4.

Listing 5-4   Venetian Blind Schema

```
<?xml version = "1.0" ?>
<xs:schema xmlns:xs="http://www.w3.org/2001/XMLSchema">

  <xs:complexType name="mediaType">
    <xs:sequence>
      <xs:element name="book" type="xs:bookType"/>
      <xs:element name="cd" type="xs:cdType"/>
      <xs:element name="film" type="xs:filmType"/>
    </xs:sequence>
  </xs:complexType>

  <xs:complexType name="bookType">
    <xs:sequence>
      <xs:element name="isbn">
        <xs:simpleType>
          <xs:restriction base="xs:string">
            <xs:length value="14"/>
            <xs:pattern value="\d{1}-\d{3}-\d{5}-\d{1}"/>
          </xs:restriction>
        </xs:simpleType>
      </xs:element>
      <xs:element name="writer" type="xs:personType"/>
      <xs:element name="year" type="xs:gYear"/>
      <xs:element name="stock" type="xs:stockType"/>
    </xs:sequence>
    <xs:attribute name="title" type="xs:string"/>
  </xs:complexType>

  <xs:complexType name="cdType">
    <xs:sequence>
      <xs:element name="artist" type="xs:personType"/>
      <xs:element name="year" type="xs:gYear"/>
      <xs:element name="runtime" type="xs:duration"/>
      <xs:element name="stock" type="xs:stockType"/>
    </xs:sequence>
    <xs:attribute name="title" type="xs:string"/>
  </xs:complexType>

  <xs:complexType name="filmType">
    <xs:sequence>
      <xs:element name="director" type="xs:personType"/>
      <xs:element name="writer" type="xs:personType"/>
      <xs:element name="year" type="xs:gYear"/>
      <xs:element name="runtime" type="xs:duration"/>
```

(continued)

**Book II
Chapter 5**

**Designing
XML Schemas**

Listing 5-4 *(continued)*

```
        <xs:element name="stock" type="xs:stockType"/>
    </xs:sequence>
    <xs:attribute name="title" type="xs:string"/>
</xs:complexType>

<xs:simpleType name="personType">
    <xs:restriction base="xs:string">
        <xs:minLength value="1"/>
        <xs:maxLength value="25"/>
    </xs:restriction>
</xs:simpleType>

<xs:complexType name="stockType">
    <xs:attribute name="num">
        <xs:simpleType>
            <xs:restriction base="xs:string">
                <xs:length value="7"/>
                <xs:pattern value="\d{4}-\d{2}"/>
            </xs:restriction>
        </xs:simpleType>
    </xs:attribute>
    <xs:attribute name="location">
    <xs:simpleType>
        <xs:restriction base="xs:string">
            <xs:length value="7"/>
            <xs:pattern value="[NSEW]\d{4}"/>
        </xs:restriction>
    </xs:simpleType>
    </xs:attribute>
</xs:complexType>

<xs:element name="media" type="xs:mediaType"/>

</xs:schema>
```

As you can see, this approach involves defining everything but the top-level element as a `simpleType` or `complexType` and then declaring the elements or attributes inside of these constructs. The one global element is `media` and is assigned the `xs:mediaType`, which encapsulates the rest of the document structure.

The Venetian Blind model supports reuse and namespace flexibility, but one of the potential downsides is that it blends custom data types and element declarations together into a flat schema structure. As a result, schemas following this approach can be difficult to read and work with, especially for beginners.

Using the Green Design Model

A final approach to schema development, which I dub the *Green design model*, maintains the advantages of the Venetian Blind model, but allows for greater separation of reusable components from the declaration of the elements. The Green approach involves a three step process:

1. Looking at the entire document structure at once and identifying the basic building blocks (data types) that you want to reuse.
2. Declaring each of these building blocks as a named type.
3. Forming the document structure, utilizing named types as needed.

TIP

The "Green" moniker stems from those environmentally friendly "Think Global, Act Local" bumper stickers you've probably seen on that VW bus in front of you while stuck in traffic. This approach follows that motto: Your first responsibility is to *think globally* and determine what parts of the document should be available for reuse. Next, after defining those global components, you *act locally* by constructing the document structure that works for your local, specific context.

Using this approach, you could create a schema for the media.xml file as shown in Listing 5-5.

**Book II
Chapter 5**

**Designing
XML Schemas**

Listing 5-5   Green Schema

```
<?xml version = "1.0" ?>
<xs:schema xmlns:xs="http://www.w3.org/2001/XMLSchema">

  <!-- Reusable parts -->

  <xs:simpleType name="personType">
    <xs:restriction base="xs:string">
      <xs:minLength value="1"/>
      <xs:maxLength value="25"/>
    </xs:restriction>
  </xs:simpleType>

  <xs:complexType name="stockType">
    <xs:attribute name="num">
      <xs:simpleType>
        <xs:restriction base="xs:string">
          <xs:length value="7"/>
          <xs:pattern value="\d{4}-\d{2}"/>
```

(continued)

Listing 5-5 *(continued)*

```
        </xs:restriction>
      </xs:simpleType>
    </xs:attribute>
    <xs:attribute name="location">
    <xs:simpleType>
      <xs:restriction base="xs:string">
        <xs:length value="7"/>
        <xs:pattern value="[NSEW]\d{4}"/>
      </xs:restriction>
    </xs:simpleType>
    </xs:attribute>
</xs:complexType>

<xs:simpleType name="isbnType">
  <xs:restriction base="xs:string">
    <xs:length value="14"/>
    <xs:pattern value="\d{1}-\d{3}-\d{5}-\d{1}"/>
  </xs:restriction>
</xs:simpleType>

<!-- Instance Document Structure -->

<xs:element name="media">
  <xs:complexType>
    <xs:sequence>

      <xs:element name="book">
        <xs:complexType>
          <xs:sequence>
            <xs:element name="isbn" type="xs:isbnType"/>
            <xs:element name="writer"
  type="xs:personType"/>
            <xs:element name="year" type="xs:gYear"/>
            <xs:element name="stock" type="xs:stockType"/>
          </xs:sequence>
          <xs:attribute name="title" type="xs:string"/>
        </xs:complexType>
      </xs:element>

      <xs:element name="cd">
        <xs:complexType>
          <xs:sequence>
            <xs:element name="artist"
  type="xs:personType"/>
            <xs:element name="year" type="xs:gYear"/>
            <xs:element name="runtime" type="xs:duration"/>
            <xs:element name="stock" type="xs:stockType"/>
          </xs:sequence>
          <xs:attribute name="title" type="xs:string"/>
        </xs:complexType>
      </xs:element>
```

```
         <xs:element name="film">
            <xs:complexType>
               <xs:sequence>
                  <xs:element name="director"
type="xs:personType"/>
                  <xs:element name="writer"
type="xs:personType"/>
                  <xs:element name="year" type="xs:gYear"/>
                  <xs:element name="runtime" type="xs:duration"/>
                  <xs:element name="stock" type="xs:stockType"/>
               </xs:sequence>
               <xs:attribute name="title" type="xs:string"/>
            </xs:complexType>
         </xs:element>

      </xs:sequence>
   </xs:complexType>
</xs:element>

</xs:schema>
```

In looking at this code listing, you can see that the custom named data types are called `personType`, `stockType`, and `isbnType`. The `personType` type is used in various parts of the XML structure, anytime a person's name is going to be stored as a value, such as the `author`, `artist`, or `director` elements. The `stockType` is a type that is used by the `book`, `cd`, and `film` elements. Finally, the `isbnType`, even though it is used only once (by the `book` element) in the assembled structure, is still defined here so that you can separate your custom type definitions from your assembly code.

The rest of the schema definition puts these building blocks together in a manner that emulates the structure of the XML document you wish to validate. When you encounter an element, such as `isbn` or `writer`, that is the same data type as the ones you defined earlier in the schema, you assign the custom type name to that element, like this:

```
<xs:element name="isbn" type="xs:isbnType"/>
```

The Green design model enables your schemas to be highly manageable, allowing you to work with reusable components and the assembled document structure separately. This technique also tends to produce packages that have fewer dependencies compared to the Salami Slice and Venetian Blind approaches.

If you've done any object-oriented programming (OOP) before, you'll find that this approach to schema development has many similarities to OOP. When you work with an OOP language, such as Java or C++, you typically create objects first and then assemble them in such a way that works for a specific solution. In the same way, you create the global types and declarations first and then assemble them for the specific XML structure you wish to validate.

Now that you've explored each of the design models, Table 5-1 provides a summary comparison of them, highlighting their advantages and disadvantages.

Table 5-1	Comparison of XML Schema Design Models		
Model	*Advantages*	*Disadvantages*	*Motto*
Mirror (Russian Doll)	Easiest to read for beginners. Intuitive design, simply mirroring what the XML document structure looks like. Self-contained package. No interdependences apart from schema hierarchy. Can hide namespaces.	Nested structure is harder to maintain, especially in large XML structures. No reuse of schema declarations is possible. Less efficient.	*Be like Mike!*
Salami Slice (Flat Catalog)	Enables you to work with custom types, common declarations, and the document hierarchy separately. Facilitates reuse of data types and common elements. Even highly complex schemas can be manageable to work with. For experienced programmers, method is similar to object-oriented programming techniques.	Cannot hide namespaces. Harder to read and less intuitive for beginners. Can be overkill on simple document structures.	*Go global!*
Venetian Blind	Facilitates reuse of data types and common elements. Can hide namespaces.	Harder to read and less intuitive for beginners. Can be overkill on simple document structures.	*Stereotype everything!*

Model	Advantages	Disadvantages	Motto
Green	Facilitates reuse of data types and common elements.	For highly complex structures, the nesting can make the schema harder to maintain.	*Think global, act local.*
	Can hide namespaces.		
	Schemas are easy to read and manage, because schema structure emulates instance document structure.		
	Fewer interdependences compared to the Salami Slice and Venetian Blind models.		
	Similar methodology as object-oriented programming.		

Chapter 6: Validating Documents Using DTDs and XML Schemas

In This Chapter

✔ **Knowing the difference between validating and non-validating parsers**

✔ **Validating an XML document with a DTD**

✔ **Connecting a DTD to an XML document**

✔ **Validating an XML document with an XML schema**

*E*ver hear of a U.S. Congressman "walking the beat"? Oh, a congressman may do a lot of walking around town during re-election time, but I've never heard of one capping on a police uniform and walking the streets enforcing the laws that Congress makes in Washington. Instead, a congressman's job is to pass the laws, while enforcement is done by the men and women "in blue."

Similarly, Document Type Definitions (DTDs) and XML schemas define the syntax rules that an XML document must live by, but it's the job of the XML parser to actually enforce these validity checks.

If you've read Chapters 1 through 5 of Book II, you discovered all about how to create DTDs and XML Schemas to validate your documents. Now, it is time to test drive these validation methods using a validating parser that supports DTDs and XML Schemas. This chapter starts off by discussing the two types of XML parsers — non-validating and validating — and then proceeds to show you the process of validating using DTDs and XML schemas.

Exploring XML Parsers

XML parsers are the engines behind any XML process. Their job is to analyze the XML document, making sure it is structured appropriately, and then typically send documents that pass the test off to another application for processing of the data. XML parsers come in two flavors:

✦ **Non-validating:** A non-validating parser checks an XML document for well-formedness but doesn't check the document against a DTD or an XML schema.

✦ **Validating:** A validating parser checks an XML document for well-formedness as well as ensuring that the structure conforms to a specific structure specified by the DTD or XML Schema.

A document that passes the test of the non-validating parser is considered *well-formed*. A document that passes the test of a validating parser is considered *valid*.

You typically work with XML parsers in one of three ways:

✦ **Command-line interface:** When you work with parsers by themselves, they're not much to look at. In fact, because they are command-line utilities, they are eerily similar to those old DOS programs from the Dark Ages of the 1980s. While command-line tools are harder to work with in this Windows age of ours, they can still be an efficient way to get the job done quickly.

✦ **Browser-based interface:** Many parsers have a browser-based way to interact with the tool, making it easier to work with. The typical way of working with these parsers is to enter the filename of the XML file in the Web form, and then the Web page calls the processor to parse the specified XML document.

In this chapter, you use a browser-based interface called XValidator, which is a simple way to interact with Microsoft's core XML parser.

✦ **Integrated into an application:** While validating can be done interactively using the command-line or browser-based methods, parsers are commonly integrated into another software application and called on demand for processing of data. When a problem occurs, the application is notified by the parser.

There are a ton of XML parsers to choose from on the Web, many of which are completely free of charge. Check out the following links to see what's available:

✦ Non-validating and validating XML parsers: `www.garshol.priv.no/download/xmltools/cat_ix.html#SC_XML`

✦ Browser-based parser: `www.oasis-open.org/cover/check-xml.html`

✦ XML Schema parsers: `www.w3.org/XML/Schema#Tools`

In this chapter, I focus on a browser-based solution called XValidator, which is a simple, front-end to the Microsoft XML parser, which is part of its XML Core Services module.

To use XValidator, follow these instructions:

1. **Download XValidator from the *XML All-in-One Desk Reference For Dummies* Web site at** `www.dummies.com/extras`.

   XValidator is included as part of the code samples and can be found in the Book 2\Chapter 6 folder.

2. **Download Microsoft XML Core Services 4.01 or higher from the Microsoft Web site.**

   The URL is: `msdn.microsoft.com/downloads/default.asp?url=/downloads/sample.asp?url=/msdn-files/027/001/766/msdncompositedoc.xml`.

3. **After downloading the Microsoft XML Core Services setup file (named msxml.msi), launch the file to install the parser to your hard drive.**

4. **Open XValidator.html in Microsoft Internet Explorer 6.0 or higher.**

Figure 6-1 displays the Web page interface of XValidator.

Book II
Chapter 6

Validating
Documents Using
DTDs and XML
Schemas

Figure 6-1: XValidator enables you to validate your XML documents directly from your browser.

Validating with a DTD

If you read Book II, Chapters 1 and 2, you know how to create DTDs for validating XML documents. It's time to apply that knowledge by linking and checking against a parser.

Associating the DTD to the XML document

XML documents are validated with DTDs by either embedding the DTD into the document itself or else connecting to an external DTD. The DOCTYPE declaration is used to indicate the internal or external DTD.

Internal DTD declarations

To define an internal DTD inside an XML document, use the following syntax of the DOCTYPE declaration:

```
<!DOCTYPE root-element [declaration-of-elements]>
```

In this instruction:

+ !DOCTYPE represents a DOCTYPE declaration.

+ root-element is the root element of the XML document containing the DOCTYPE declaration.

+ [declaration-of-elements] represents the actual markup declaration of the DTD, which includes the rules that the XML document must conform to for being valid.

For example, Listing 6-1 displays a DTD embedded inside of an XML document.

Listing 6-1   film_embed.xml

```
<?xml version="1.0" ?>
<!DOCTYPE film [
  <!ELEMENT film (director, writer, year, runtime, special)>
  <!ATTLIST film name CDATA #REQUIRED>
  <!ELEMENT director  (#PCDATA)>
  <!ELEMENT writer    (#PCDATA)>
  <!ELEMENT year      (#PCDATA)>
  <!ELEMENT runtime   (#PCDATA)>
  <!ELEMENT special   EMPTY>
]>
<film name="Henry V">
  <director>Kenneth Branagh</director>
  <writer>Kenneth Branagh, William Shakespeare</writer>
  <year>1989</year>
  <runtime>137</runtime>
```

```
<special/>
</film>
```

Internal DTDs can't be shared across XML documents. Therefore, you'll generally only use internal DTDs when you don't need to apply a DTD across a number of XML documents.

External DTD declarations

To use an external DTD (a text file with a .dtd extension), you can use the following DOCTYPE declaration:

```
<!DOCTYPE root-element SYSTEM "URI">
```

In this declaration:

✦ `root-element` is the root element of the XML document that contains the `DOCTYPE` declaration.

✦ `SYSTEM` indicates that the associated DTD is an external DTD.

✦ `URI` provides the location of the .dtd file containing the markup declaration.

Listing 6-2 shows an external DTD file. Listing 6-3 provides an XML document that connects to this DTD using the DOCTYPE declaration.

Book II
Chapter 6

Validating
Documents Using
DTDs and XML
Schemas

Listing 6-2   film.dtd

```
<!ELEMENT film (director, writer, year, runtime, special)>
<!ATTLIST film name CDATA #REQUIRED>
<!ELEMENT director    (#PCDATA)>
<!ELEMENT writer      (#PCDATA)>
<!ELEMENT year        (#PCDATA)>
<!ELEMENT runtime     (#PCDATA)>
<!ELEMENT special     EMPTY>
```

Listing 6-3   film_dtd.xml

```
<?xml version="1.0" ?>
<!DOCTYPE film SYSTEM "film.dtd">
<film name="Henry V">
  <director>Kenneth Branagh</director>
  <writer>Kenneth Branagh, William Shakespeare</writer>
  <year>1989</year>
  <runtime>137</runtime>
  <special/>
</film>
```

Using a validation parser

When the DOCTYPE declaration is added to the XML document, a validating parser validates the document against the internal or external DTD when it is processed.

For example, to validate the film_embed.xml (Listing 6-1) using XValidator, follow these instructions:

1. **Open XValidator inside Internet Explorer 6.0 or higher.**

   See instructions in the "Exploring XML Parsers" section for how to open XValidator.

2. **In the DTD Validation box, type** film_embed.xml **in the XML Filename box.**

   Because film_embed.xml is in the same folder as XValidator, you're not required to specify the full path.

3. **Click the Validate button.**

XValidator validates the document based on the DTD supplied in the DOC-TYPE declaration. A message indicating a successful validation is shown in a second browser window, as shown in Figure 6-2.

Figure 6-2:
Successful
DTD
validation.

Suppose, however, that there is an inconsistency between the DTD data definition and the XML document. For example, Listing 6-4 shows an invalid document. Notice that the special element is required by the DTD to be empty, but the special element in the document contains text. Figure 6-3 displays the error message that is provided by XValidator when the document is processed.

Listing 6-4   film_invalid.xml

```
<?xml version="1.0" ?>
<!DOCTYPE film [
  <!ELEMENT film (director, writer, year, runtime, special)>
  <!ATTLIST film name CDATA #REQUIRED>
  <!ELEMENT director  (#PCDATA)>
  <!ELEMENT writer    (#PCDATA)>
  <!ELEMENT year      (#PCDATA)>
  <!ELEMENT runtime   (#PCDATA)>
  <!ELEMENT special   EMPTY>
]>
<film name="Henry V">
  <director>Kenneth Branagh</director>
  <writer>Kenneth Branagh, William Shakespeare</writer>
  <year>1989</year>
  <runtime>137</runtime>
  <special>Yes, this movie is special indeed.</special>
</film>
```

Book II
Chapter 6

Validating
Documents Using
DTDs and XML
Schemas

Figure 6-3:
Good XML
gone bad.

Validating with XML Schemas

Although XML schemas are more powerful and robust than DTDs, they perform an identical function — validating XML documents. Therefore, it's not surprising that the task of validating a document with an XML schema follows a similar path as when you validate with a DTD. However, there is one big exception. While an XML document must reference a DTD using a DOCTYPE declaration, there is no direct equivalent when using XML schemas. You can recommend a specific XML schema from the source document (see the "Referencing an XML schema" section below); quite often you'll specify the schema document to the processor at the time of processing. XValidator requires that you identify the .xml and .xsd file.

To demonstrate how to validate with an XML schema, consider media.xml (see Listing 6-5) and media.xsd (see Listing 6-6).

Listing 6-5   media.xml

```
<?xml version="1.0" ?>
<media>
  <book title="The Once and Future King">
    <isbn>0-441-62740-4</isbn>
    <writer>T.H. White</writer>
    <year>1939</year>
    <stock num="1020-20" location="N0110"/>
  </book>
  <cd title="Symphony No. 3">
    <artist>Henryk Gorecki</artist>
    <year>1992</year>
    <runtime>PT52M</runtime>
    <stock num="1330-39" location="S2292"/>
  </cd>
  <film title="Henry V">
    <director>Kenneth Branagh</director>
    <writer>William Shakespeare</writer>
    <year>1989</year>
    <runtime>PT2H17M</runtime>
    <stock num="9820-76" location="E2129"/>
  </film>
</media>
```

Listing 6-6   media.xsd

```
<?xml version = "1.0" ?>
<xs:schema xmlns:xs="http://www.w3.org/2001/XMLSchema">

  <!-- Reusable parts -->

  <xs:simpleType name="personType">
    <xs:restriction base="xs:string">
      <xs:minLength value="1"/>
      <xs:maxLength value="25"/>
    </xs:restriction>
  </xs:simpleType>
```

```
<xs:complexType name="stockType">
  <xs:attribute name="num">
    <xs:simpleType>
      <xs:restriction base="xs:string">
        <xs:length value="7"/>
        <xs:pattern value="\d{4}-\d{2}"/>
      </xs:restriction>
    </xs:simpleType>
  </xs:attribute>
  <xs:attribute name="location">
  <xs:simpleType>
    <xs:restriction base="xs:string">
      <xs:length value="5"/>
      <xs:pattern value="[NSEW]\d{4}"/>
    </xs:restriction>
  </xs:simpleType>
  </xs:attribute>
</xs:complexType>

<xs:simpleType name="isbnType">
  <xs:restriction base="xs:string">
    <xs:length value="13"/>
    <xs:pattern value="\d{1}-\d{3}-\d{5}-\d{1}"/>
  </xs:restriction>
</xs:simpleType>

<!-- Instance Document Structure -->

<xs:element name="media">
  <xs:complexType>
    <xs:sequence>

      <xs:element name="book">
        <xs:complexType>
          <xs:sequence>
            <xs:element name="isbn" type="isbnType"/>
            <xs:element name="writer" type="personType"/>
            <xs:element name="year" type="xs:gYear"/>
            <xs:element name="stock" type="stockType"/>
          </xs:sequence>
          <xs:attribute name="title" type="xs:string"/>
        </xs:complexType>
      </xs:element>

      <xs:element name="cd">
        <xs:complexType>
          <xs:sequence>
            <xs:element name="artist" type="personType"/>
            <xs:element name="year" type="xs:gYear"/>
            <xs:element name="runtime" type="xs:duration"/>
            <xs:element name="stock" type="stockType"/>
```

(continued)

Book II
Chapter 6

Validating
Documents Using
DTDs and XML
Schemas

Listing 6-6 *(continued)*

```
        </xs:sequence>
        <xs:attribute name="title" type="xs:string"/>
      </xs:complexType>
    </xs:element>

    <xs:element name="film">
      <xs:complexType>
        <xs:sequence>
          <xs:element name="director" type="personType"/>
          <xs:element name="writer" type="personType"/>
          <xs:element name="year" type="xs:gYear"/>
          <xs:element name="runtime" type="xs:duration"/>
          <xs:element name="stock" type="stockType"/>
        </xs:sequence>
        <xs:attribute name="title" type="xs:string"/>
      </xs:complexType>
    </xs:element>

    </xs:sequence>
   </xs:complexType>
  </xs:element>

</xs:schema>
```

To validate the media.xml document using the media.xsd schema, follow these steps:

1. **Open XValidator inside Internet Explorer 6.0 or higher.**

   See instructions in the "Exploring XML Parsers" section for how to open XValidator.

2. **In the XML Schema Validation box, type** media.xml **in the XML Filename box.**

   Because media.xml is in the same folder as XValidator, you're not required to specify the full path.

3. **Type** media.xsd **in the XML Schema Filename box.**

4. **Click the Validate button.**

XValidator validates media.xml based on the schema in media.xsd. A message indicating a successful validation is shown in a second browser window, identical to what is shown previously in Figure 6-2.

Book II
Chapter 6

Validating
Documents Using
DTDs and XML
Schemas

Error-free schemas

While XML schemas are used to validate XML documents, the schema has to be error-free or you'll encounter problems during the validation process. The W3C XML schema validator is a useful online tool for checking and debugging your schemas. It can be found at `www.w3.org/2001/03/webdata/xsv`.

Consider what happens when there's a problem between the schema definition and the source document. For example, Listing 6-7 displays an invalid version of the source document, changing part of the `isbn` element value to X's. Figure 6-4 displays the resulting error message from XValidator when the validation occurs.

Listing 6-7   media_invalid.xml

```
<?xml version="1.0" ?>
<media>
  <book title="The Once and Future King">
    <isbn>0-441-XXXXX-4</isbn>
    <writer>T.H. White</writer>
    <year>1939</year>
    <stock num="1020-20" location="N0110"/>
  </book>
  <cd title="Symphony No. 3">
    <artist>Henryk Gorecki</artist>
    <year>1992</year>
    <runtime>PT52M</runtime>
    <stock num="1330-39" location="S2292"/>
  </cd>
  <film title="Henry V">
    <director>Kenneth Branagh</director>
    <writer>William Shakespeare</writer>
    <year>1989</year>
    <runtime>PT2H17M</runtime>
    <stock num="9820-76" location="E2129"/>
  </film>
</media>
```

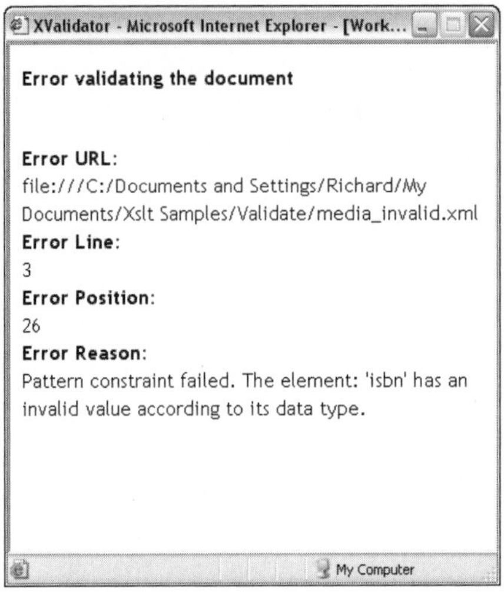

Figure 6-4:
Source XML
document
fails schema
validation.

Referencing an XML Schema

You can specify the XML schema that an XML document is associated with by adding a schemaLocation attribute to document's root element. The schemaLocation attribute indicates to the processor the URI location of the schema file for the XML document. However, unlike DTD's DOCTYPE declaration, the processor is not *required* to use the schema document specified by the schemaLocation attribute. Instead, the processor treats it something like a *recommendation*. The processor can override this schemaLocation, such as in the case of another schema document being specified at processing time.

To reference a schema document, add a schemaLocation attribute to your root element. The value of the attribute must be a set of URI pairs that the parser can turn to. However, you also need to add an xsi namespace declaration along with the schemaLocation attribute because it uses the xsi namespace. The declaration is shown below for the media element:

```
<media
  xmlns:xsi="http://www.w3.org/2001/XMLSchema-instance"

    xsi:schemaLocation="http://www.digitalwalk.net/xml/media.
    xsd media.xsd">
```

Listing 6-8 shows the complete document.

Listing 6-8   media_ref.xml

```
<media
 xmlns:xsi="http://www.w3.org/2001/XMLSchema-instance"
 xsi:schemaLocation="http://www.digitalwalk.net/xml/media.xsd
                   media.xsd">
  <book title="The Once and Future King">
    <isbn>0-441-62740-4</isbn>
    <writer>T.H. White</writer>
    <year>1939</year>
    <stock num="1020-20" location="N0110"/>
  </book>
  <cd title="Symphony No. 3">
    <artist>Henryk Gorecki</artist>
    <year>1992</year>
    <runtime>PT52M</runtime>
    <stock num="1330-39" location="S2292"/>
  </cd>
  <film title="Henry V">
    <director>Kenneth Branagh</director>
    <writer>William Shakespeare</writer>
    <year>1989</year>
    <runtime>PT2H17M</runtime>
    <stock num="9820-76" location="E2129"/>
  </film>
</media>
```

Book II
Chapter 6

Validating
Documents Using
DTDs and XML
Schemas

Chapter 7: Working with XML-Data Reduced

In This Chapter

✔ **Getting to know XML Data-Reduced (XDR)**

✔ **Grasping the basics about XDR elements**

✔ **Exploring the scope of elements**

✔ **Putting data types with elements and attributes**

✔ **Referencing XDR schemas**

✔ **Implementing XDR elements**

The names for XML technologies must be coined by engineer types, not marketing folks. Oh, maybe "XML" has a certain pizzazz to it, but terms like Extensible Stylesheet Language Transformations (XSLT) is not something that easily rolls off one's tongue. XML Data-Reduced (XDR) is another one of those technologies with a peculiar name. On first take, it sounds like a "Blue Light Special" edition of XML Data. Or perhaps it is a shrunken version of XML for cell phones. Who can tell?

I'll save the story of the name for the first section in the chapter, but rest assured that XDR is neither of these. Instead, XML Data-Reduced is a technology rolled out by Microsoft as a schema-based validation solution for XML documents before W3C XML schemas (discussed in Book II, Chapters 4 through 6) became official. And while W3C XML schemas are the long-term, vendor-independent schema solution for XML, many developers will continue to look to XDR as a capable validation solution for the foreseeable future.

In this chapter, you explore XDR syntax and how to validate XML documents based on an XDR schema. And, don't forget, you also discover exactly why "Reduced" is tacked onto the end of its name.

Getting Started with XML-Data Reduced

When the idea of a schemas-based method of validation began to surface as an alternative to DTDs (see Book II, Chapters 1 and 2), the W3C received many proposals for XML schema languages, including an early proposal from Microsoft called XML-Data. However, in its original form, this proposal was large and slow to implement. So Microsoft developed XML-Data Reduced as a subset of XML-Data and began implementing the modified specification into some of its products: BizTalk Server, SQL Server 2000, and all versions of MSXML parser — 2.0 and later — provide support for XDR. Compared to its predecessor XML-Data, XDR provides features that are carefully selected to expedite document processing and improve document management.

However, before committing to using XDR, keep in mind that non-Microsoft products typically will not support this validation technology.

Understanding XDR Elements

XDR schemas have many similarities to W3C XML schemas. It too uses XML syntax to describe the structure of XML documents, as shown in the following XDR schema sample:

```
<?xml version="1.0"?>
<Schema xmlns="urn:schemas-microsoft-com:xml-data">
  <ElementType name="BookData" />
  <ElementType name="BookTitle"/>
  <ElementType name="Author"/>
  <AttributeType name="ISBN"/>

  <ElementType name="BookData">
    <attribute type="ISBN"/>
    <element type="BookTitle"/>
    <element type="Author"/>
  </ElementType>
</Schema>
```

Note several of the XDR elements used to compose the schema:

✦ The `Schema` element declares the XDR schema. See the following section for more about this element.

✦ The `ElementType` element defines three types of elements named `BookData`, `BookTitle`, and `Author`.

✦ The `AttributeType` element defines a type of attribute named `ISBN`.

✦ The `ElementType` element also defines the type of element named `BookData` and contains child elements:

  • The `attribute` element defines an attribute of the type `ISBN`, which was defined using the `AttributeType` element.

  • `element` defines two elements of the type `BookTitle` and `Author`, which were defined using the `ElementType` element.

Following is an XML document based on the preceding schema (a valid XML document):

```
<?xml version="1.0"?>
<BookData xmlns:s="x-schema:SampleSchema.xml">
<s:Book s:ISBN="0578-7">
  <s:BookTitle>
    XML:A complete guide
  </s:BookTitle>
  <s:Author>
    James Brown
  </s:Author>
</s:Book>
</BookData>
```

In the preceding code, notice that the namespace reference to the XDR schema file (which describes the structure of the document) is specified. Also, note the s that precedes the element names: for example, s:BookTitle. This signifies that each of the elements that are prefixed by s have been referenced from the namespace.

In the following sections, you dive into each of the these XDR elements.

The Schema element

The Schema element is the root element used in a file containing the schema for an XML document. Within it, the entire structure of XML documents is defined. It uses the following basic syntax:

```
<Schema xmlns="urn:schemas-microsoft-com:xml-data">
<!-- schema declaration here -->
</Schema>
```

The XDR elements are referenced by assigning the urn:schemas-microsoft-com:xml-data namespace to the xmlns attribute.

XDR supports data types comparable to W3C XML schemas, such as string, date, char, and int. If you want to use these data types in your XDR schemas, you need to also reference the urn:schemas-microsoft-com:datatypes namespace in the Schema element.

Therefore, in most cases, the Schema element will have declarations for two namespaces, one containing the declaration for elements used in the schema itself and the other containing the declaration for data types used in the schema:

```
<Schema
        xmlns="urn:schemas-microsoft-com:xml-data"
        xmlns:dt="urn:schemas-mmicrosoft-com:datatypes">
```

```
    <!-- schema declaration here -->
</Schema>
```

The ElementType element

The `ElementType` element, similar to W3C XML schema's `complexType`, enables you to create an element type that can be reused inside the schema. Using this element, you create an element type once and then create several instances of this named element type.

For example, suppose you create an element type called `Name`. Next, to define the structure of various elements, such as `Employee` and `Department`, you can reuse the `Name` element type to describe the name of an employee or name of a department.

The syntax for the `ElementType` element is as follows:

```
<ElementType
            content= "{eltOnly | textOnly | empty | mixed} "
            dt:type= "datatype "
            model= "{open | closed} "
            name= "name "
            order= "{one | seq | many} ">

        Content Model Declaration

</ElementType>
```

`Content model declaration` specifies the elements and attributes that can be present within a specific element type. For example, if the `Name` element contains the elements `FirstName` and `LastName`, you can declare an element type called `Name`. The content model for this element type will include the declarations for the `FirstName` and `LastName` elements.

The attributes of the `ElementType` element are as follows:

✦ `content`: This attribute specifies whether the element type contains other elements, character type data, or mixed content, or whether it is an empty element type. This attribute can take one of the following values:

  • `empty`: Indicates that the element is empty — the element can't contain any content. However, empty elements can also contain attributes, which makes them quite useful.

  • `textOnly`: Indicates that the element can contain only textual data.

- eltOnly: Indicates that the element can contain only certain elements.

- mixed: Indicates that the element can contain textual data as well as other elements. This is the default value of the content attribute.

✦ dt:type: This attribute allows you to specify the data type for an element type. The type attribute belongs to the namespace containing declarations for data types, so you need to prefix this attribute with the name of the namespace declared using the xmlns keyword. This attribute is optional. If you don't specify the data type, the element type can contain any type of text.

✦ model: This attribute is used in case of an element type, which has the eltOnly content. If this attribute contains the value open, the element type can contain elements and attributes that aren't declared in the content model. If the value is closed, the element type can contain only elements declared in the content model. This attribute is optional, and open is its default value.

Book II
Chapter 7

Working with
XML-Data Reduced

✦ name: This mandatory attribute specifies the name of an element type.

✦ order: This attribute specifies whether the element type is used only once or occurs many times. The order attribute also checks for the sequence of the elements specified in the content model and can take one of the following values:

- one: Indicates that only one of the elements from the content model can be used.

- seq: Indicates that the elements should appear in the same sequence in which they're declared in the content model. For example, if you've specified the FirstName and LastName elements as the contents of the element type Name, and you set the order attribute to seq, seq ensures that the sequence of the elements used in the XML document matches the content model specified in the schema.

- many: Indicates that the elements declared in the content model can appear in any order in the XML document. The attribute also indicates that the elements can be used many times. When the content is mixed, the order must be many.

WARNING!

If you define an element type with the content attribute set to empty and the model attribute set to open, you will receive an error from the parser.

The AttributeType element

The AttributeType element allows you to declare an attribute type, which can be reused in the schema. Like ElementType, you can use the

`AttributeType` element to define a type of attribute once and then use that attribute with several elements. This enables you to reuse a type of attribute with multiple elements without describing the attribute type each time.

The syntax for the `AttributeType` element is as follows:

```
<AttributeType
          name= "name"
          dt:type= "datatype"
          dt:values= "enumerated values"
          default="default value" required= "{yes | no }"
/>
```

`AttributeType` is an empty element, denoted by the / character before the closing angle bracket. The attributes of the `AttributeType` element include the following:

✦ `name`: Specifies the name of the attribute type.

✦ `dt:type`: Specifies the data type of the values contained in the attribute type.

✦ `dt:values`: Specifies the values for enumeration types.

✦ `default`: Specifies the default value of the attribute type. This attribute can be used with any data type. However, the value used as the `default` value must be a legal value. For example, if the data type of the type is enumeration, the `default` value must appear in the value list.

✦ `required`: Specifies whether the attribute type is mandatory or optional.

In addition to the attributes discussed here, XDR also supports certain restriction attributes that enable you to restrict the values accepted in an element. These attributes are discussed later in this chapter, in the section "Constraints: Restricting data values".

The element element

The `element` element refers to an element type declared earlier in the schema by using the `ElementType` element. It is used to declare the content model for another element type. The syntax for this element looks like this:

```
<element
        type= "element type"
        minOccurs= "{0 | 1}"
        maxOccurs= "{1 | *}" />
```

The attributes of `element` are as follows:

✦ `type`: Contains a reference for an element type declared earlier in the schema. This attribute takes the value of the `name` attribute of the `ElementType` element.

✦ `minOccurs`: Allows you to specify the minimum number of times that the element should occur within the content model:

- If this attribute contains 0 as its value, the element may or may not occur in the content model.

- If this attribute contains 1, the element should occur at least once in the content model.

✦ `maxOccurs`: Enables you to specify the maximum number of times that an element can occur in the content model:

- If this attribute contains the value 1, the element can occur only once in the content model.

- If the attribute contains the value *, the element can occur multiple times in the content model.

The attribute element

The `attribute` element refers to an attribute type declared earlier in the schema by using the `AttributeType` element. The `attribute` element is used to declare the content model for an element type. The syntax for this element looks like this:

```
<attribute
        type="attribute type"
        default="default-value"
        required="{yes | no }"
/>
```

In the preceding syntax, the attributes are as follows:

✦ The `type` attribute is used to specify the name of an attribute type declared earlier in the schema.

✦ The `default` attribute is used to assign a default value to the attribute. This default value takes precedence over the default value specified in the attribute type to which the attribute refers.

✦ The `required` attribute is used to specify whether the attribute is mandatory in the content model.

The group element

When defining an element type using ElementType, you can specify a specific sequence for child elements by setting its order attribute. However, within a named element type, you can also group certain items together using the group element. With it, you can create a group and specify a sequence for the elements appearing within the group. The syntax of the group element is as follows:

```
<group
  maxOccurs="{1 | *}"
  minOccurs="{0 | 1}"
  order="{one | seq | many}" >

</group>
```

In the preceding syntax, the attributes are as follows:

✦ maxOccurs: Specifies the maximum number of times that the group can occur within an element. The value 1 indicates that the maximum number of times that the group can occur is only once. The value * indicates that the group can occur an unlimited number of times.

✦ minOccurs: Specifies the minimum number of times that the group can occur. The value 0 indicates that the group is optional — the group isn't required. The value 1 indicates that the group must occur at least once.

✦ order: Specifies the sequence of elements within the group and takes one of the following three values:

  • one: Indicates that only one instance of each element within the group can appear.

  • seq: Indicates that all the elements must appear in the sequence specified in the group definition.

  • many: Indicates that the elements specified within the group can occur in any sequence — this value doesn't restrict the sequence of elements within the group.

Scoping Out Elements

The scope of an XDR element determines which other elements in a schema can access that element. XDR elements declared within a schema can have two scopes: global and local. *Global* (top-level) scope declarations appear directly under the Schema element of the schema. Such element types or attributes can be referenced within any element of the schema to define

its content model. *Local* scope declarations appear inside a specific
ElementType structure. Such element types or attribute types can be
referenced only within the element type in which they're declared and are
hidden from the rest of the schema.

To understand how the declaration scope works, consider the following
example:

```
<?xml version="1.0"?>
<Schema
        xmlns="urn:schemas-microsoft-com:xml-data"
        xmlns:dt="urn:schemas-microsoft-com:datatypes">

<ElementType name="Name" content="textOnly" />
<AttributeType name="Publisher" dt:type="char" />

<ElementType name="Book">
    <element type="Name" />
    <attribute type="Publisher" />
</ElementType>

<ElementType name="Author">
    <element type="Name" />
    <AttributeType name="Age" dt:type="int" />
    <attribute type="Age" />
</ElementType>

</Schema>
```

Here is an explanation of the preceding schema:

✦ The element type Name and the attribute type Publisher are top-level
   or global declarations. Therefore, the Name element type is referenced
   within the element types Book and Author to define the name of a book
   and author in the schema. Similarly, the Publisher attribute type is
   referenced within the Book element.

✦ The attribute type Age is declared within the scope of the declaration of
   the Author element type. Therefore, the attribute type is referenced
   within the Author element type only.

Working with XDR Data Types

XDR provides a rich set of data types (shown in Table 7-1) that you can use
when creating XDR schemas.

Table 7-1	XDR Data Types	
Type	*Description*	*Examples*
string	PCDATA text	My name is Clancy.
char	A single character string	a
boolean	True/false value where 1 = true and 0 = false	0, 1
id	ID	id101
idref	IDREF	id101
idrefs	IDREFS	id101 id102 id103
entity	ENTITY	sample
entities	ENTITIES	sample simple
nmtoken	NMTOKEN	name1
nmtokens	NMTOKENS	name1 name2
enumeration	ENUMERATION	Whenton Warten
notation	NOTATION	JPG
number	Any number	11, 3.1459
int	A positive or negative number but no decimals, fractions, or exponents.	3, 7303, -22
fixed.14.4	Same as number type, but a maximum of 14 digits to the left of the decimal point and 4 digits on the right.	33116.3353
dateTime	A date that follows a subset ISO 8601 format, with optional time and no optional zone.	2002-03-31T13:25:12
dateTime.tz	A date that follows a subset ISO 8601 format, with optional time and optional zone.	2002-03-31T13:25:12-14:00
date	A date that follows a subset ISO 8601 format, but no time permitted.	2000-12-02
time	A time that follows a subset ISO 8601 format, but no date and no time zone permitted.	12:13:32
time.tz	A time that follows a subset ISO 8601 format, with no date but optional time zone.	05:2212-05:00
i1		
byte	A positive or negative number, but no fractions or exponents permitted.	3, -510
i2	A positive or negative number, but no fractions or exponents permitted.	-32768

Type	Description	Examples
i4, int	A positive or negative number, but no fractions or exponents permitted.	13, 233, -32768
i8	A positive or negative number, but no fractions or exponents permitted.	3, 323, -32768, 1483433434334, -1000000000000000
ui1	An unsigned number with no fractions and no exponents.	6, 233
ui2	An unsigned number with no fractions and no exponents.	3, 211, 65533
ui4	An unsigned number with no fractions and no exponents.	3, 443
ui8	An unsigned number with no fractions and no exponents.	23454663021221
r4	Float type.	
r8, float	Equivalent same as number.	
uuid	Hexadecimal digits representing octets, which may include optional embedded hyphens (ignore).	322C2BC4-445F-12D0-BC02-0082C2152A21
uri	Universal Resource Identifier.	urn:schemas-test-com:MyTest
bin.hex	Hexadecimal digits representing octets.	
bin.base64	MIME style Base64 encoded binary blob.	

Using these base types, you can apply additional restrictions on values that are supported by an element.

Constraints: Restricting data values

Data types restrict the type of values that an element or attribute can take. For example, you cannot enter a string of characters for an element that supports the integer data type. However, many times, you may need to restrict the data values further. For example, if you've defined an element, Age, as an integer, you may require the data values for the Age element to be greater than 25 years. Alternatively, you may have defined an element, Name, as a string and you may have a limit on its length; the length should be between 10 and 25. In such cases, XDR provides a way to place restrictions on these data types.

dt:min and dt:max specify the lower and upper limit of an element or an attribute as follows:

```
<s:ElementType name="Author">
   <s:AttributeType name="Age" dt:type="int" dt:min="25" />
```

```
    <s:attribute type="Age" />
</s:ElementType>
```

In the preceding example, the attribute type Age is defined as an integer. dt:min="25" further restricts the data values accepted by the attribute. Therefore, the Age attribute can accept integer values greater than or equal to 25.

For some data types, such as string, dt:minLength and dt:maxLength specify the minimum and maximum length of the data value. For example, consider the following example:

```
<s:ElementType name="Name" dt:type="string" dt:minLength="10"
    dt:maxLength="25" />
<s:ElementType name="Book">
  <s:element type="Name" />
  <s:attribute type="Publisher" />
</s:ElementType>
```

In the preceding schema, the element type Name is defined as a string. dt:minLength="10" and dt:maxLength="25" further restrict the length of the string that the Name element types can accept. Therefore, the declaration indicates that the Name element type can accept string values and the length of the string ranges between 10 and 25.

If a document violates a restriction, the parser generates an error. For example, if you have specified price as a number data type, and you specify the price as "$100.90", the parser generates an error.

Using enumerations

The enumeration data type enables you to specify a list of values that an attribute can accept. To illustrate, suppose you want the attribute type Publisher to accept only one of the following values: BenAndSons, TechPublishers, or MarkPublishers. To impose such restrictions, specify the data type as enumeration and then specify the values that the attribute can take. Consider the following example:

```
<s:ElementType name="Name" content="textOnly" />
<s:AttributeType
            name="Publisher"
            dt:type="enumeration"
            dt:values="BenAndSons TechPublishers
    MarkPublishers
/>

<s:ElementType name="Book">
  <s:element type="Name" />
  <s:attribute type="Publisher" />
</s:ElementType>
```

In the preceding schema, the attributes are as follows:

✦ The attribute type named `Publisher` is defined as an enumeration. `dt:values` specifies the enumeration values that the attribute can take.

✦ The `Publisher` attribute is defined for the `Book` element. Therefore, each `Book` element takes the `Publisher` attribute. This attribute can take any one of the values specified in the list, namely `BenAndSons`, `TechPublishers`, and `MarkPublishers`.

Calling Another XDR Schema

When creating schema documents, you may encounter situations where you would like to use element or attribute definitions that are already defined in other schemas. Rather than copying and pasting, XDR allows you to reference these schema pieces from inside another schema.

For example, suppose you're creating a schema for XML documents that store book-related data. Inside of this XDR schema called `BookSchema.xml`, you'd like to reference a structure declared in the `SalesSchema.xml` schema.

To reference the other schema, you can declare a namespace with the URI reference pointing to the other schema file. For example, consider the following element type declaration:

```
<ElementType name="BookSales"
    xmlns:ord="http://www.StarTechBooks.com/SalesSchema.xml"/>
```

In the preceding declaration, the `BookSales` element type contains the declaration for a namespace. This namespace is prefixed as `ord` and the URI points to the `SalesSchema.xml` schema that contains the definition for the `Sales` element.

Next, to use the element defined in the other schema, you need to include the namespace prefix along with that element name. For example, if the structure of the `Sales` element is defined in the schema `SalesSchema.xml`, you can use the definition in your schema as follows:

```
<ElementType name="BookSales"
    xmlns:ord="http://www.StarTechBooks.com/SalesSchema.xml">

    <element type="ord:Sales" />

</ElementType>
```

In the preceding schema code, `ord:Sales` specifies the structure of the `Sales` element as defined in the namespace `http://www.StarTechBooks.com/Sales.xml`.

The namespace declaration for another schema must be included in the scope in which the elements defined in the namespace can be used.

When you create instance documents of your schema (`BookSchema.xml`), which references another schema (`SalesSchema.xml`), you must refer to the referenced schema as follows:

```
<Booksales xmlns:ord="htp://www.StarTechBooks.com/
    SalesSchema.xml">

    <ord:Sales>

        <ord:Price> $15 </ord:Price>
        <ord:Quantity> 10 </ord:Quantity>
        <ord:Amount> $150 </ord:Amount>

    </ord:Sales>

</BookSales>
```

In the preceding code, notice that the same prefix (`ord`) is used as used in the schema `BookSchema.xml`. However, this isn't mandatory. You can use a different prefix in the XML document because the namespace prefixes are local to the document in which they're declared. Therefore, it would be acceptable if you use a different prefix (say, `sal` instead of `ord`) in the XML document as follows:

```
<Booksales xmlns:sal="http://www.StarTechBooks.com/
    SalesSchema.xml">

    <sal:Sales>

        <sal:Price> $15 </sal:Price>
        <sal:Quantity> 10 </sal:Quantity>
        <sal:Amount> $150 </sal:Amount>

    </sal:Sales>

</BookSales>
```

15

Book III

Presenting XML

The 5th Wave   By Rich Tennant

FREELANCER NED WILLIS CONSULTS
WITH A MEMBER OF HIS TECHNICAL STAFF

©RICHTENNANT

"...and that's pretty much all there is to
converting a document to an HTML file."

Contents at a Glance

Chapter 1: Styling XML with Stylesheets

In This Chapter

- Why XML isn't enough
- Essentials of CSS stylesheets
- Essentials of XSL-FO stylesheets
- Linking a stylesheet to an XML document

Sabrina is a favorite film of mine, either the original 1950s version with Audrey Hepburn or the 1990s remake with Julia Ormond. The movie tells the story of a very ordinary chauffeur's daughter who travels to Paris for a year and returns as a dazzling beauty, charming everyone around her. XML reminds me of the "plain Jane" Sabrina Fairchild at the start of the film; in spite of XML's "inner qualities" of data, the appearance of an XML document would enamor only the most die-hard of developers.

In order to make XML usable in real-world situations, more is needed besides the data itself. Instead, XML needs its own equivalent to Sabrina's trip to Paris, so it too can get a grandé makeover — preserving the data description capabilities of XML, but enabling the document to be presentable for everyday uses.

This chapter introduces you to two key technologies you can use to style XML and present it both in a browser and on the printed page.

Giving an XML Document a Makeover

Unlike HTML, which mixes data and formatting instructions into a single document, XML is all about data. An XML document contains no rules concerning how its data structure should be formatted and displayed in a browser or other software. Consider the following XML file:

```
<?xml version="1.0" encoding="utf-8" ?>

<menu>
  <entree>
    <name>Sunburnt Chicken</name>
    <fatgrams>23</fatgrams>
    <features>Salad, Vegetables, Baked Potato, and
  Dessert</features>
    <description>Chicken prepared so hot, you'll need a
  gallon of soda to wash it down. Bring
  sunscreen!</description>
  </entree>
  <entree>
    <name>Filet Mig's None</name>
    <fatgrams>0</fatgrams>
    <features>Soup, Vegetables, Baked Potato, and
  Dessert</features>
    <description>Our master chef Mig prepares a uniquely no-
  fat filet mignon. You won't believe how great it

tastes!</description>
  </entree>
  <entree>
    <name>Chicken Parmashaun</name>
    <fatgrams>20</fatgrams>
    <features>Soup, Pasta, Baked Potato, and
  Dessert</features>
    <description>Our award-winning Chicken Parmesan prepared
  especially for you by our master chef
  Shaun.</description>
  </entree>
</menu>
```

When a browser such as Internet Explorer displays this file, it can only render it by showing a generic tree-like structure to represent the data structure, as shown in Figure 1-1.

Obviously, this method of presentation is helpful only for development purposes and is not a practical way in which you'd actually want to display information in a real-world setting.

There are a multitude of mediums, formats, and devices in which people need to display or print XML documents. Some developers may opt to write their own processor to display a particular flavor of XML in a custom application. However, for most cases, you will likely want to be able to output XML in a formatted way for display in a browser or for printing purposes.

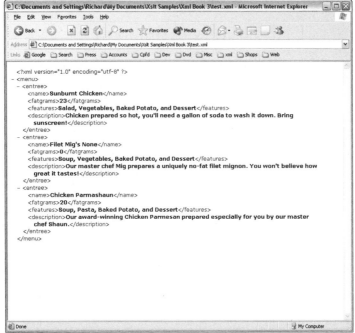

Book III
Chapter 1

Styling XML
with Stylesheets

Figure 1-1:
Display of XML document in Internet Explorer.

The following three W3C-recommended ways to apply formatting to an XML document exist:

✦ **Cascading Style Sheets (CSS)** is a standard originally developed in 1996 to augment the styling capabilities of HTML, but its role has expanded to support formatting of XML documents.

   To do so, you create a set of formatting rules in a CSS *stylesheet*, link the stylesheet into the XML document, and then open the XML document in a browser that processes XML and CSS (such as Microsoft Internet Explorer 5.0 or higher, or Netscape Navigator 5.0 or higher).

✦ **Extensible Stylesheet Language Formatting Objects (XSL-FO)** is an XML-based language that describes a formatted document and is used for print-oriented output. CSS browser-based viewing deals with formatting of a single page of infinite length, but XSL-FO is designed to deal effectively with tricky pagination issues associated with printing, such as page numbering, headers, and footers.

   The typical use of XSL-FO is trickier than CSS. You usually apply an XSLT stylesheet to an XML document to produce an XSL-FO document. This document is then processed by a formatter and produces a printed output, either directly to a printing device or as an Adobe Acrobat (PDF) file.

✦ **Extensible Stylesheet Language Transformations (XSLT)** is an XML-based language that is used to transform an XML document into another output format, be it HTML or even another XML structure. If the XML is transformed into ordinary HTML, you can view it in any browser. If it is output into an alternative XML document, you can use CSS for browser viewing or use XSL for print purposes.

To use XSLT, you define how you want to transform the document in an XSLT stylesheet, link that stylesheet to an XML document, and then run it through an XSLT processor. What you do with the output depends on whether the result document is HTML, XML, or another syntax.

XSLT is a huge topic. I mention it here so that you can understand its context relative to CSS and XSL-FO, but I deal with it fully in Book IV.

Figure 1-2 shows the various output options you have.

CSS and XSL-FO are *rendering languages* with the goal of making XML look pretty. Its instruction set focuses on tasks like assigning fonts, margin settings, or border styles. In contrast, XSLT is an *enabling language* with the purpose of changing an XML document into another form (such as HTML) that can then be displayed or processed for another purpose.

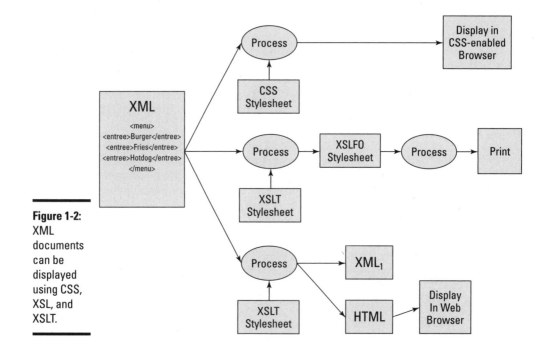

Figure 1-2:
XML documents can be displayed using CSS, XSL, and XSLT.

TECHNICAL STUFF

The XSL family: Three is enough

Although some people consider the term Extensible Stylesheet Language (XSL) as synonymous with XSL-FO, this practice has actually become a source of confusion for many. Technically, XSL is a generic term that actually consists of three different languages: XSL-FO for formatting XML documents for print mediums, XSLT for transforming XML documents from one structure to another, and XPath as an enabling technology used by XSLT and other XML technologies to navigate XML data.

Before you start working with CSS and XSL to format your XML documents in the following two chapters in this Book, use the remainder of this chapter as a primer on how these technologies operate. This information will help you understand how these technologies work.

CSS Essentials: The Least You Need To Know

Before you use CSS with your XML documents, keep in mind six essentials about the browser-based styling language:

✦ CSS syntax looks much different than XML.

✦ The rule is the primary component of a CSS stylesheet.

✦ Some CSS properties are inherited from parent to child element.

✦ CSS allows descriptive comments.

✦ How CSS handles conflicting rules.

✦ Pseudo-elements offer greater control over formatting.

These are discussed in the sections that follow.

CSS syntax isn't XML

Unlike most of the technologies that work with XML documents, such as XSLT or XLink, CSS has its own peculiar syntax quite unlike XML. The following code shows a sample stylesheet:

```
entree {
   background-color: silver;
   border-width: medium;
   border-style: solid;
```

```
      margin-bottom: .75em;
      padding: .25em;
}

name {
    color: white;
    font-weight: bold;
    background-color: red;
    border-width: thin;
    border-style: groove;
}
```

When you work with CSS, you write instructions in a document called a stylesheet. A *stylesheet* is just an ordinary text file that is read by the CSS processor, which applies the styling rules to the XML document for display. A CSS stylesheet has a .css extension.

Although case is a big deal to XML, CSS stylesheets are case-insensitive, except for the parts that reference external names. For example, in the preceding stylesheet, the `entree` and `name` words in the stylesheet reference XML elements with lowercase names of `entree` and `name`.

Rule: The basic building block for CSS

If you read Book I, you discovered that an element is the basic building block for XML. As a result, an XML document is composed of an interrelated set of elements. In CSS, the primary component of a stylesheet is a rule. A *rule* selects the elements to which you want to apply formatting and then specifies the formatting properties. It consists of two parts — the selector and the declaration:

✦ The *selector* identifies one or more XML elements that you want to format.

✦ The *declaration* consists of a property-value pair that provides instructions on how to format the elements identified by the selector.

The syntax differs, but the declaration section is similar to attributes (name-value pairs) of an XML element.

The general syntax of a rule is as follows:

```
selector { property: value }
```

You can put a rule all on one line or spread it out over multiple lines. Here is another common format:

```
selector {
    property: value
}
```

A rule can have multiple property-value pairs inside of curly brackets, so long as they are separated by a semicolon. This enables you to set multiple properties of the selector using a single statement. The syntax for this is as follows:

```
selector {
  property: value;
  property2: value;
  property3: value;
}
```

Inherit the wind (along with some properties)

When you apply CSS properties to your XML data, you should be aware of the hierarchical, tree-like nature of an XML document, as discussed in Book I, Chapter 2. The reason is that some properties are inherited by a child from its parent. For example, suppose you have the following XML code snippet:

```
<cast>
  <character>Gilligan</character>
  <character>Skipper</character>
</cast>
```

Because font properties are inherited properties, suppose you set the font family of the `cast` element:

```
cast { font-family: Courier New }
```

Because `font-family` is an inheritable property, the `character` children automatically assume this property. Therefore, if you didn't want the `character` elements to inherit this property, you'd need to explicitly set an alternative:

```
cast { font-family: Courier New }
character { font-family: Arial }
```

Most CSS properties, such as backgrounds, margins, and borders, are not inherited from parent to child. However, font and many text-related properties are passed down the hierarchy.

In addition to inherited values, properties also have *initial values*, which are the default value used when nothing is explicitly defined or inherited.

Commenting on the sheet

Like XML documents, CSS supports comments, enabling you to add descriptive information in your stylesheet. Comments are identified by a /* at the start and a */ at the end:

```
/* Add comment here */
```

Cascading through the wilderness

Ever wonder why CSS has the term *cascading* right smack dab at the front of its name? Well, another key concept to understand when working with CSS is cascading. *Cascading* refers to prioritizing property declarations when more than one applies to the same element. CSS uses a set of rules to determine the winner, as in the following example:

```
<cast>
  <character ID="1" CLASS="FearlessCrew">Gilligan</character>
  <character ID="2" CLASS="FearlessCrew">Skipper</character>
</cast>
```

The following stylesheet has a set of rules that all apply to the same `character` element (`Gilligan`):

```
/* Selected by ID */
character#ID { color: red }

/* Selected by CLASS name */
character.FearlessCrew { color: yellow }

/* Selected by hierarchy */
cast character { color: green }

/* Selected by element name*/
character { color: black }
```

The general rule of thumb for determining the winner is that selecting by ID always wins, with `CLASS` next, followed by specific hierarchical reference, and finally a general element name.

Su-su-pseudo

Rumor has it that because singer/performer Phil Collins was on the W3C committee for CSS, he successfully argued for the inclusion of su-su-psuedo elements in CSS. Well, the W3C went along with his reasoning on the feature, but changed the name to a more traditional sounding term: pseudo-element.

CSS focuses on using an element as the selector for a rule, but a *pseudo-element* enables you to select part of an element, such as the first line or first character of an element. As you'll discover in Book III, Chapter 2, pseudo-elements can come in handy in adding an increased level of control to the rendering of your XML document.

Su-su-pseudo! Just say the word!

XSL-FO Essentials: The Least You Need To Know

Before jumping off on coding XSL-FO in Book III, Chapter 3, keep in mind the following facts about XSL-FO:

+ XSL-FO is an XML vocabulary.

+ XSL-FO mirrors many properties and the formatting model of CSS.

+ XSL-FO is processed much differently than CSS is.

XSL-FO is actually XML

Unlike CSS, which has its own unique syntax, XSL-FO doesn't just look like XML; it actually is XML. For example, consider the following chunk of XSL-FO code:

```
<fo:page-sequence master-name="easy">
    <fo:flow flow-name="xsl-region-body">
        <fo:block font-family="Serif">Serif font</fo:block>
    </fo:flow>
</fo:page-sequence>
```

XSL-FO is a formatting rules language written as "XML vocabulary." You might be saying, "Wait a minute!" XSL-FO formats XML, but XML is used as the basis for XSL-FO. It may sound like circular logic, but it actually works and is used in many other XML-related technologies that you'll discover in this book, including XSLT, XForms, and more.

Because XSL-FO uses XML as the means by which you describe its instructions, you can have a much easier time becoming productive rather than dealing with the peculiarities or idiosyncrasies of yet another language syntax.

XSL-FO copycats many CSS properties

Although XSL-FO looks very different from CSS and is used for a different purpose, it actually uses many of the same properties and the general formatting model that CSS uses, making it easier to learn its syntax. For example, the font-style or font-weight attributes of XML-FO are directly identical to CSS properties bearing the same names. However, XSL-FO picks up where CSS leaves off in terms of dealing with paginated documents.

If you have a CSS stylesheet and would like to apply similar formatting rules for XSL-FO, you can often map the CSS rules to their equivalent in XSL-FO. For example, most of the display property values are mapped to an XSL-FO tag bearing the property value name, with the other properties being converted from the property-value pair (property:value) to an XML name-value pair (property="value").

XSL-FO has a different processing metaphor

The basic process of CSS is that an external CSS stylesheet is applied to an XML document and the resulting formatted document is displayed in a Web browser. In contrast, XSL-FO doesn't have a separate stylesheet that is applied to an external XML document. Instead, an XSL-FO integrates the XML data with the XSL-FO formatting instructions. This document is then processed by formatter software to generate a paginated document appropriate for the target output. Therefore, if you use XSL-FO, you often use XSLT to transform the original XML document into an XSL-FO document. Refer to Figure 1-2 for a visual look at the different processes.

Linking in a Stylesheet with an XML Document

The typical way that you link a CSS or XSL stylesheet with an XML document is to insert the xml-stylesheet processing instruction just after the XML declaration. The processing instruction syntax is shown in the following example for both CSS and XSL stylesheets:

```
<!-- CSS stylesheet -->
<?xml-stylesheet type="text/css" href="myfile.css" ?>

<!-- XSL stylesheet -->
<?xml-stylesheet type="text/xsl" href="myfile.xsl" ?>
```

The xml-stylesheet processing instruction links the document to the stylesheet that is specified by the href attribute. When this document is loaded by a browser or processor, the processor attempts to load this stylesheet and apply the formatting contained inside of it.

Chapter 2: Cascading Style Sheets — Displaying XML in a Browser

In This Chapter

✔ Exploring how XML and CSS work together

✔ Selecting elements to apply styles

✔ Applying character and paragraph styles

✔ Applying box styles

✔ Creating tables from XML documents

Cascading Style Sheets (CSS) has been something of a quirky technology since its original release in the late 1990s. Once hailed as a panacea to the formatting limitations of HTML, CSS was rather slow to gain full and consistent support inside of Web browsers. And, while support for the nuts and bolts of CSS is now commonplace across the major browsers, there are still large and noticeable gaps in support for certain features of this styling system.

In spite of these quirks, CSS remains a viable technology that you can use to easily display and style your XML documents inside of Web browsers. Some XML technologies are futuristic in terms of real-world support, but the XML+CSS solution is one that works with today's generation of browsers.

In this chapter, you explore how to effectively present XML documents in a browser by applying CSS stylesheets.

For a primer on CSS and a discussion on some of the limitations of using CSS to display XML data, please read Book III, Chapter 1.

Browser support for CSS selection and formatting features varies according to the browser maker, platform, and the version. I point out a number of major support issues in this chapter. You can also check out the following URL for the latest information: http://www.jessett.com/web_sites/css/css_browser_support.shtml.

How CSS Works with an XML Document

If you read Book III, Chapter 1, you discovered that an XML document by itself contains no formatting instructions and will therefore be displayed in a pure data structure format by a browser such as Internet Explorer. However, by applying a CSS stylesheet to the XML document, you can present the XML data in a highly tailored fashion.

When you apply a CSS stylesheet to an XML document, the browser performs two tasks:

✦ Consumes the well-formed XML document, spitting out all of the element tags and attributes but leaving the element content.

✦ Applies all stylesheet rules to the XML content.

Consider the following XML document:

```
<?xml version="1.0" encoding="utf-8" ?>
<?xml-stylesheet type="text/css" href="entree.css" ?>
<entree>
  <name>Sunburnt Chicken</name>
  <diet>false</diet>
  <fatgrams>23</fatgrams>
  <features>Salad, Vegetables, Baked Potato, and
    Dessert</features>
  <description>Chicken prepared so hot, you'll need a gallon
    of soda to wash it down. Bring sunscreen!</description>
</entree>
```

The `xml-stylesheet` processing instruction links the document to the `entree.css` stylesheet that is specified by its `href` attribute. When this document is loaded by a browser, the mere presence of the `xml-stylesheet` processing instruction causes the browser to process the XML document so that only its content is displayed.

If the `entree.css` file is not present or the stylesheet is blank, the browser will still process the XML document, except that no rules are applied. As shown in Figure 2-1, only the content is displayed with no formatting at all.

When it processes an XML document, the browser creates a rectangular box for each XML element that is rendered. As shown in Figure 2-2, this box has a *content area* for displaying the element's text. Surrounding the content area are optional *padding*, *border*, and *margin* properties.

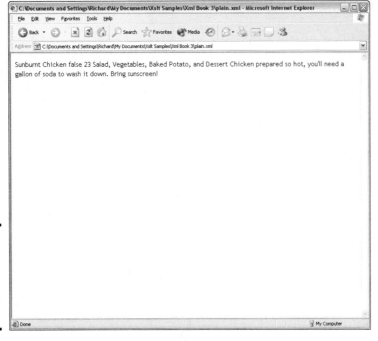

Figure 2-1:
An XML
document
displayed
with a blank
stylesheet.

Book III
Chapter 2

Cascading Style
Sheets — Displaying
XML in a Browser

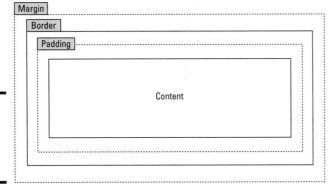

Figure 2-2:
A box
created for
an XML
element.

The rendered box of an XML element can flow in the document either inline or as a block. *Inline* formatting, such as what is shown in Figure 2-1, is used to lay out each box in a horizontal manner in the flow of the document. In contrast, *block* formatting lays out boxes vertically (top-to-bottom), with each box taking up an entire line of the document. Figures 2-3 and 2-4 show both methods. Inline display is the default setting.

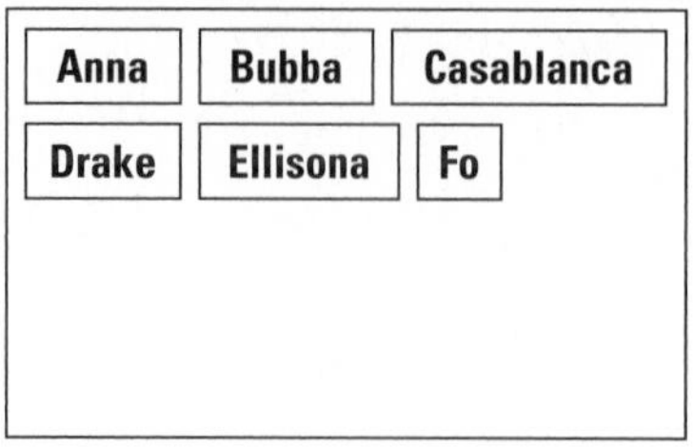

Figure 2-3:
Inline
formatting.

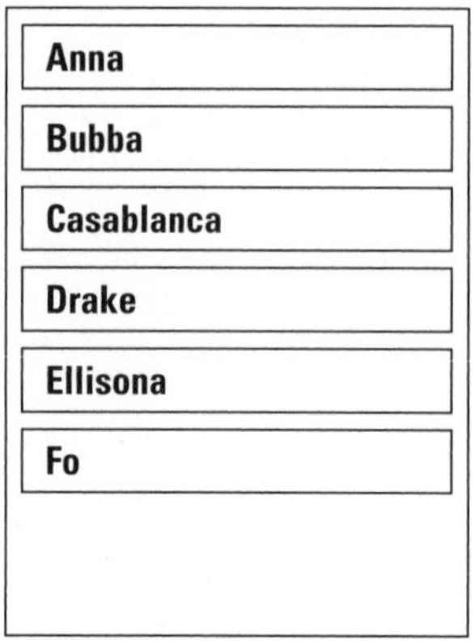

| Anna | Bubba | Casablanca |

| Drake | Ellisona | Fo |

Figure 2-4:
Block
formatting.

| Anna |
| Bubba |
| Casablanca |
| Drake |
| Ellisona |
| Fo |

Selecting Elements

CSS provides a variety of ways in which you can select the XML elements you desire for applying formatting, including the following:

+ By name
+ Multiple elements by name
+ All elements
+ By attribute or attribute value
+ By ID
+ By CLASS
+ By hierarchical position in document
+ Based on its predecessor value
+ First child of an element

These are discussed in the sections that follow.

Selecting an element by name

You can select an element by name if you use the name of the element as the selector for the CSS rule:

```
elementName {
  property: value
}
```

For example, using the following code snippet, suppose you'd like to bold the name element when it is displayed:

```
<entree>
  <name>Sunburnt Chicken</name>
</entree>
```

To do so, use the name as the selector and then assign the font-weight property a value of bold:

```
name {
  font-weight: bold
}
```

(See the "Formatting Elements" section, later in this chapter, for more on setting formatting properties.)

When the entree element is linked with the CSS stylesheet and displayed in a browser, the specified formatting instructions are applied, as shown in Figure 2-5.

Selecting multiple elements

You can select multiple elements for a rule by listing each element name in a comma-separated list:

```
elementName, elementName2, elementName3 {
  property: value
}
```

For example, suppose you'd like to display the contents of the following entree element, but you want to use block formatting to display each element on successive lines:

```
<entree>
  <name>Sunburnt Chicken</name>
  <diet>false</diet>
  <fatgrams>23</fatgrams>
```

```
<features>Salad, Vegetables, Baked Potato, and
   Dessert</features>
<description>Chicken prepared so hot, you'll need a gallon
   of soda to wash it down. Bring sunscreen!</description>
</entree>
```

To do so, you need to apply block formatting as a style for each of the elements by setting the display property to block:

```
name, diet, fatgrams, features, description {
   display: block
}

name {
   font-weight: bold
}
```

The generated display is shown in Figure 2-6. As you can see, each of the elements is block formatted, while only the name element content is bolded.

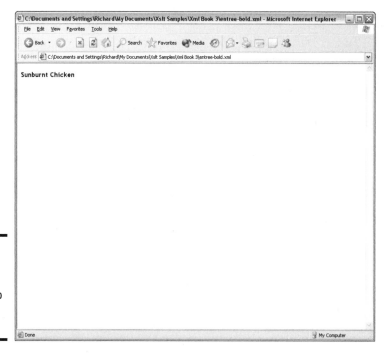

Figure 2-5:
Bold property assigned to the entrée name.

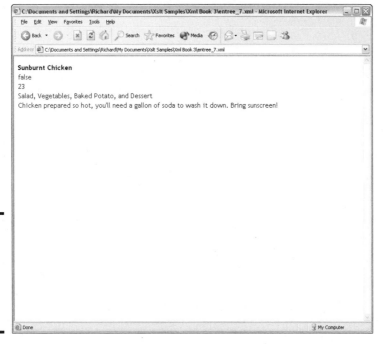

Figure 2-6:
The boxes
of each
element
have block
formatting
set.

Selecting all elements

You can select all of the elements inside of a particular scope using the wild-card character (*):

```
*  {
   property: value
}
```

For example, use the same `entree` element as before:

```
<entree>
   <name>Sunburnt Chicken</name>
   <diet>false</diet>
   <fatgrams>23</fatgrams>
   <features>Salad, Vegetables, Baked Potato, and
      Dessert</features>
   <description>Chicken prepared so hot, you'll need a gallon
      of soda to wash it down. Bring sunscreen!</description>
</entree>
```

Rather than naming each individual element by name like the previous example, suppose you simply want to assign block formatting to all of the elements. You could use the following stylesheet:

```
* {
  display: block
}

name {
  font-weight: bold
}
```

The results are identical to the ones shown in Figure 2-6.

Selecting an element by attribute

Although you can't display attributes or their values with CSS, you can select elements based on their attributes in three different ways:

✦ **Presence of an attribute.** To test an element to see if it contains an attribute, use the following syntax:

```
elementName[attributeName] {
  property: value
}
```

The name of the attribute is placed inside of square brackets and added to the end of the element.

✦ **Exact value of an attribute.** To select an element based on the value of an attribute, you add the query information to the selector:

```
elementName[attributeName="attributeValue"] {
  property: value
}
```

✦ **Partial value of an attribute.** You can also select an element based on the partial value of an attribute by using a ~= operator rather than an equal sign (=):

```
elementName[attributeName~="partialValue"] {
  property: value
}
```

For example, consider the following XML code:

```
<menu>
  <entree special="Monday" tabletent="True">
    <name>Sunburnt Chicken</name>
    <diet>false</diet>
    <fatgrams>23</fatgrams>
    <features>Salad, Vegetables, Baked Potato, and
  Dessert</features>
    <description>Chicken prepared so hot, you'll need a
  gallon of soda to wash it down. Bring
  sunscreen!</description>
```

```
  </entree>
  <entree special="Monday, Tuesday">
    <name>Filet Mig's None</name>
    <diet>true</diet>
    <fatgrams>0</fatgrams>
    <features>Soup, Vegetables, Baked Potato, and
  Dessert</features>
    <description>Our master chef Mig prepares a uniquely no-
  fat filet mignon. You won't believe how great it
  tastes!</description>
  </entree>
  <entree special="Friday">
    <name>Chicken Parmashaun</name>
    <diet>false</diet>
    <fatgrams>20</fatgrams>
    <features>Soup, Pasta, Baked Potato, and
  Dessert</features>
    <description>Our award-winning Chicken Parmesan prepared
  especially for you by our master chef
  Shaun.</description>
  </entree>
</menu>
```

Suppose that you want to apply special formatting to the entree elements in three cases: table tent entries should be in red, Friday-only specials are bold green, and entrees that are a special on Monday (even if other days as well) are bold yellow. Using the attribute syntax described earlier, the following stylesheet rules are declared:

```
/* Tabletent entrees are red */
entree[tabletent]{
  color: red
}

/* Friday only specials are green and bold */
entree[special="Friday"]{
  color: green;
  font-weight: bold;
}

/* Specials that falls on Monday are yellow and bold */
entree[special~="Monday"]{
  color: yellow;
  font-weight: bold;
}
```

The results are shown in Figure 2-7.

Microsoft Internet Explorer versions 6.0 and earlier do not support selecting elements by attributes.

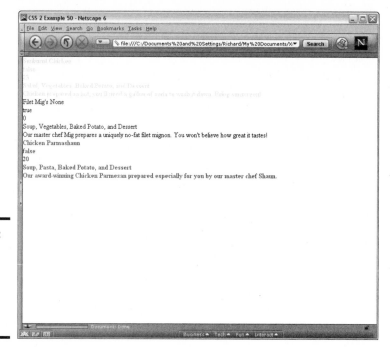

Figure 2-7:
Elements
formatted
based on
the value
of the
attributes.

Selecting an element by ID

If your XML document uses ID attributes to uniquely identify individual elements, you can use this identifier to select specific elements from your XML document. The ID value is referenced in your stylesheet rule using the following syntax:

```
elementName#IDValue {
    property: value
}
```

Consider the following XML document that uses ID values to identify the entree elements:

```
<menu>
  <entree ID="1">
    <name>Sunburnt Chicken</name>
    <diet>false</diet>
    <fatgrams>23</fatgrams>
    <features>Salad, Vegetables, Baked Potato, and
    Dessert</features>
```

```
  <description>Chicken prepared so hot, you'll need a
  gallon of soda to wash it down. Bring
  sunscreen!</description>
</entree>
<entree ID="2">
  <name>Filet Mig's None</name>
  <diet>true</diet>
  <fatgrams>0</fatgrams>
  <features>Soup, Vegetables, Baked Potato, and
  Dessert</features>
  <description>Our master chef Mig prepares a uniquely no-
  fat filet mignon. You won't believe how great it
  tastes!</description>
</entree>
</menu>
```

When I apply the following stylesheet, all element entries are italicized given the entree rule, but the entree element with an ID value of 1 is also bolded:

```
* {
  display: block;
}

entree{
  font-style: italic
}

entree#1{
  font-weight: bold
}
```

The results are shown in Figure 2-8.

The ID attribute name must be in uppercase in order to use this shortcut syntax.

Selecting an element by class

You can also select XML elements based on the value of their CLASS attribute, using a dot notation syntax in which a period and the name of the class is appended to the element name:

```
elementName.className {
  property: value
}
```

Figure 2-8:
Sunburnt
chicken
entree is
bolded
based on its
ID value.

To illustrate the use of CLASS, consider the following document that features the CLASS attribute for each entree element:

```
<menu>
  <entree CLASS="Normal">
    <name>Sunburnt Chicken</name>
    <diet>false</diet>
    <fatgrams>23</fatgrams>
    <features>Salad, Vegetables, Baked Potato, and
    Dessert</features>
    <description>Chicken prepared so hot, you'll need a
    gallon of soda to wash it
down. Bring sunscreen!</description>
  </entree>
  <entree CLASS="Lowfat">
    <name>Filet Mig's None</name>
    <diet>true</diet>
    <fatgrams>0</fatgrams>
    <features>Soup, Vegetables, Baked Potato, and
    Dessert</features>
    <description>Our master chef Mig prepares a uniquely no-
    fat filet mignon. You
won't believe how great it tastes!</description>
  </entree>
```

```
<entree CLASS="Normal">
  <name>Chicken Parmashaun</name>
  <diet>false</diet>
  <fatgrams>20</fatgrams>
  <features>Soup, Pasta, Baked Potato, and
Dessert</features>
  <description>Our award-winning Chicken Parmesan prepared
especially for you by our
master chef Shaun.</description>
  </entree>
  <entree CLASS="Lowfat">
  <name>Jerk Chicken</name>
  <diet>true</diet>
  <fatgrams>5</fatgrams>
  <features>Soup, Vegetables, and Dessert</features>
  <description>A delicious hot Jamaican dish prepared by
our most obnoxious master chef.</description>
  </entree>
  <entree CLASS="Highfat">
  <name>Gusto Spaghetti</name>
  <diet>false</diet>
  <fatgrams>55</fatgrams>
  <features>Soup, Salad, and Dessert</features>
  <description>Our famous master chef Boyd Ardee prepares a
succulent dish of spaghetti with zesty
gusto!</description>
  </entree>
</menu>
```

Suppose that you want to format this list of entrees based on the class name (Lowfat, Normal, or Highfat), with the formatting depicting the fat content of the dish. The stylesheet would be set up as follows:

```
* {
  display: block;
}

entree.Lowfat{
  font-weight: bold
}

entree.Normal{
  font-style: italic
}

entree.Highfat{
  text-decoration: line-through
}
```

When you apply this stylesheet, you get the results shown in Figure 2-9.

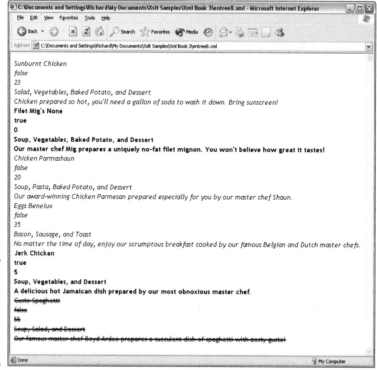

Figure 2-9:
Formatting
menu based
on the fat
content of
each entree.

Like the ID attribute, the CLASS attribute name must be in uppercase in order to use this dot notation syntax.

Selecting by an element's hierarchical position

If you'd like to select an element based on its hierarchical position within the document, you can use two syntax options:

✦ **Select based on exact hierarchy.** To provide the exact hierarchy, list each element from the root in the selector, separating each with a > symbol:

```
rootElement > level1Element > level2Element {
    property: value
}
```

Using this syntax, the right-side element must be a child of the element on the left.

✦ **Select based on indirect hierarchy.** If you'd like to indirectly reference an element, you can list one or more ancestors to the left, separating each with white space:

```
ancestor descendent {
    property: value
}
```

The names to the left of the final name simply need to appear some-where on the path from the root element to this element.

For example, consider the following XML document:

```
<menu>
  <entree>
    <name>Sunburnt Chicken</name>
    <diet>false</diet>
    <fatgrams>23</fatgrams>
    <features>
      <name>Salad, Vegetables, Baked Potato, and
    Dessert</name>
    </features>
    <description>Chicken prepared so hot, you'll need a
    gallon of soda to wash it down. Bring
    sunscreen!</description>
  </entree>
</menu>
```

The name element is used at two levels of the hierarchy (menu->entree->name and menu->entree->features->name) and describes two different name types — the name of the entree and the name of the features.

Suppose that you want to format both name elements in bold, but also italicize the name element that appears under features. To do so, you construct the following stylesheet rules:

```
* {
  display: block;
}

menu name {
  font-weight: bold
}

menu > entree > features > name {
  font-style: italic
}
```

Using this stylesheet, all `name` descendants of `menu`, regardless of the number of levels between them, are bolded. However, only the `name` elements that are in the direct lineage of `menu->entree->features` are italicized. Figure 2-10 shows the result.

Figure 2-10: Formatting the elements based on hierarchy.

Microsoft Internet Explorer versions 6.0 and earlier do not support the > operator for selecting based on exact hierarchical position.

Selecting an element by its predecessor

You can select an element in an XML document based on the element that is adjacent to it in a document. If two elements are separated with the + operator, the second element is selected only if it immediately follows the first element. The syntax is as follows:

```
elementName + elementName {
  property: value
}
```

Consider the following XML snippet:

```
<menu>
  <entree>Sunburnt Chicken</entree>
  <appetizer>Leninzella Macaroni</appetizer>
  <entree>Gusto Spaghetti</entree>
</menu>
```

To apply a formatting rule to the entree element that follows the appetizer element, use the following:

```
* {
  display: block;
}

appetizer + entree {
  font-weight: bold
}
```

The results are shown in Figure 2-11.

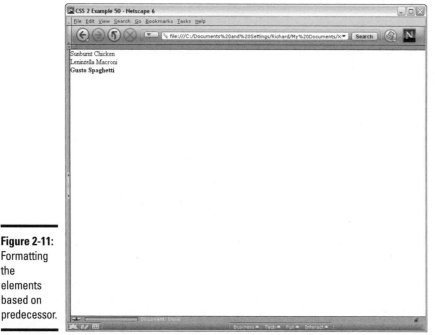

**Book III
Chapter 2**

Cascading Style
Sheets — Displaying
XML in a Browser

Figure 2-11:
Formatting
the
elements
based on
predecessor.

Microsoft Internet Explorer versions 6.0 and earlier do not support selecting elements by predecessor.

Selecting the first child of an element

The first child element of an element can be selected using the `first-child` pseudo-class selector:

```
elementName:first-child {
  property: value
}
```

To illustrate, consider the following XML document:

```
<menu>
  <entree>
    <name>Sunburnt Chicken</name>
  </entree>
  <entree>
    <name>Filet Mig's None</name>
  </entree>
  <entree>
    <name>Chicken Parmashaun</name>
  </entree>
  <entree>
    <name>Eggs Benelux</name>
  </entree>
  <entree>
    <name>Jerk Chicken</name>
  </entree>
  <entree>
    <name>Gusto Spaghetti</name>
  </entree>
</menu>
```

To apply a bold rule to the Sunburnt Chicken element, which is the first child `entree` element of the `menu` element, use the following stylesheet:

```
* {
  display: block;
}
```

```
menu:first-child {
  font-weight: bold
}
```

Microsoft Internet Explorer versions 6.0 and earlier do not support selecting the first child of an element using the `first-child` pseudo-class.

Formatting Elements

After you've selected the elements that you wish to format, you can format all aspects of the element content, including the character and paragraph parts of the text as well as its container box. Figure 2-12 shows the many properties of the element that can be manipulated with CSS.

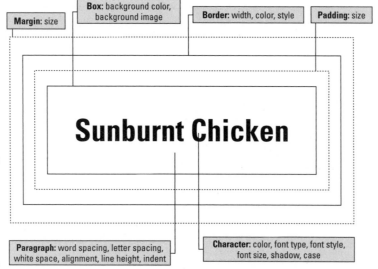

Figure 2-12:
Formatting the elements based on predecessor.

In order to practice the various aspects of formatting an XML document using CSS stylesheets, use the XML document shown in Listing 2-1 throughout to see how you can transform a data structure into a fully formatted Web page.

Listing 2-1 kingforaday.xml

```
<?xml version="1.0" encoding="utf-8" ?>
<?xml-stylesheet type="text/css" href="dw.css" ?>

<column id="6">

<title>A King For A Day</title>
<subtitle>The Lives of Three Greats Reveal the Fleeting
    Nature of Life</subtitle>
<URL>http://www.digitalwalk.net/archives/Number6/kingforaday.
    html</URL>

<section>
```

(continued)

Listing 2-1 *(continued)*

```
<para><ital>Every man dies, not every man really
    lives</ital>. These piercing words were uttered by
    Scottish hero William Wallace in the epic film
    <ital>Braveheart</ital>. Ever since hearing Mel Gibson
    deliver that line, I have been haunted by it: What does
    <emp>really lives</emp> mean? Am I living a life that
    matters? Or is my time spent on earth a &quot;ho
    hum&quot; in light of eternity?</para>

<para>As I wrestle with these matters, one way to get a fresh
    perspective is to look back in time to see if history
    provides some insight into these universally asked
    questions. In that light, consider three men, each of whom
    was considered great in their day and whose notoriety
    continues into the 21st Century. These three great men
    have long since died. But, to use Wallace&apos;s words,
    did each of them really live?</para>

</section>

<section>

<heading level="1">A Legacy of Stone</heading>

<para>On a recent trip to London, England, my wife and I had
    a chance to visit Hampton Court, a medieval castle that
    was once the summer home of Henry VIII. Walking through
    its majestically adorned rooms offered up visions of
    grandeur and regal authority. Though the stone walls were
    500 years old, I still saw traces of the power, wealth,
    and fame of one of the most powerful men in the world
    during his era.</para>

<para>The world was Henry VIII&apos;s &quot;oyster&quot; for
    quite some time -- he ruled for 38 years. But what is
    striking to me is the importance of his life as centuries
    pass. Not only was his reign &quot;15 minutes of
    fame&quot; in the span of history, but his legacy is
    little more than an encyclopedia entry, a stone castle,
    and a mention in an obscure Herman&apos;s Hermits song
    from the 1960s.</para>

</section>

<section>

<heading level="1">A Celluloid Legacy</heading>

<para>Bogie. Just hearing this nickname spurs up visions of
    Hollywood in its golden age. Hollywood stars of the 1940s
```

```
were indeed <emp>larger than life</emp>, and in the
center of the glamour stage was Humphrey Bogart. Bogie
was a superstar; he was not only adored by ladies, but he
was a man&apos;s man as well. His career had everything
an actor could ever want: over 20 major films, an Academy
award, and a starring role in arguably the greatest film
ever, <ital>Casablanca</ital>.</para>

<para>Bogie had it all for two decades before his death in
    1957. Yet, even now, in the age of Arnold Schwarzenegger
    and Adam Sandler films, his career seems oh-so distant,
    leaving us with just celluloid memories to enjoy. But
    what exactly does his legacy matter in light of eternity?
    Shouldn&apos;t it be more than mere images painted on
    strips of nitrocellulose and camphor?</para>

</section>

<!-- More... -->

<copyright>Copyright 2003, digitalwalk.net. All Rights
    Reserved.</copyright>

</column>
```

Formatting character text properties

CSS has a multitude of properties that allow you to adjust character-level formatting for the element text, including the following:

**Book III
Chapter 2**

**Cascading Style
Sheets — Displaying
XML in a Browser**

+ Color

+ Font family

+ Size

+ Styles, such as italics, bold, and underlining

These are discussed in this section.

Setting the text color

The color of the text can be adjusted using the `color` property. The value of the `color` property can be a reserved color keyword, an RGB color value, or a system color. These are described in the "Color XML Beautiful" sidebar.

In the `kingforaday.xml` example shown in Listing 2-1, if you wanted to give a bluish color to the `title`, `subtitle`, and `heading` elements, you would use the following rule:

```
title, subtitle, heading { color: #15526E }
```

Color XML beautiful

The four major types of color values you can specify in CSS are as follows:

- ✓ **Color keywords.** The 16 common keyword color names are: aqua, black, blue, fuchsia, gray, green, lime, maroon, navy, olive, purple, red, silver, teal, white, and yellow. For example:

```
title { color: lime }
```

- ✓ **RGB hexadecimal color values.** RGB is a standard color encoding scheme that encompasses the color spectrum through separate numeric values (0 to 255) for red, green, and blue colors. The format of an RGB color value in hexadecimal notation is a # symbol followed by hexadecimal value representing the color. For example:

```
title { color: #000000 }
```

HTML documents commonly use RGB values in hexadecimal notation.

- ✓ **RGB value in functional notation.** You can also select a color using the rgb(*r, g, b*) function in which r, g, and b are numbers (0 to 255) or percentages (0 to 100). For example:

```
title { color: rgb(0, 0, 125) }
```

- ✓ **System colors.** In addition to the generic color keywords specified earlier, you can also specify colors that coordinate with the graphical environment of the user. The complete list of keywords is as follows:

```
ActiveBorder
ActiveCaption
AppWorkspace
Background
ButtonFace
ButtonHighlight
ButtonShadow
ButtonText
CaptionText
GrayText
Highlight
HighlightText
InactiveBorder
InactiveCaption
InactiveCaptionText
InfoBackground
InfoText
Menu
MenuText
Scrollbar
ThreeDDarkShadow
ThreeDFace
ThreeDHighlight
ThreeDLightShadow
ThreeDShadow
Window
WindowFrame
WindowText
```

On Microsoft Windows systems, you can modify these colors for your environment through the Appearance page of the Display Properties dialog box. You can access this dialog box from the Display icon in the Control Panel.

All in the font family

Choosing a font for your display is among the most common of all formatting tasks, but it is also one of the trickiest. In order for the viewer of the document to see it in the font you chose, the desired font must first be installed on his or her computer. If that font is not available for the browser, the browser will substitute another similar style font.

Although the popularity of Windows machines have made it easier to pick fonts that most people will have on their machine, issues remain. Therefore, good forethought should go into your font decisions.

The `font-family` property is used to define the typeface of the element. It is a prioritized list of font "family" names and can be composed of specific fonts, generic font families, or both:

✦ You can include the *specific names* of a font you wish, like this:

```
para { font-family: Times New Roman }
```

✦ You can also include the names of *generic font families* (see Table 2-1), like this:

```
para { font-family: serif }
```

Table 2-1	Generic Font Family Names
Name	*Example Font*
serif	Times New Roman
sans-serif	Arial, Verdana
monospace	Courier New
cursive	Zapf-Chancery
fantasy	Andy

You will often want to use both specific and generic font family names in your list. Doing so enables the browser to try your preferred font choice first. If that choice is not available, it can continue down the list. Adding the appropriate generic name as a final entry ensures that at least the general style of the font will be used even if the desired typeface is unavailable. Suppose, for example, that you'd like to use the sans serif style `Trebuchet MS` font as your first choice for an `address` element, but you have a set of acceptable alternatives. Your rule would look something like this:

```
address { font-family: Trebuchet MS, Verdana, Tahoma, Arial,
    sans-serif }
```

In the `kingforaday.xml` example shown in Listing 2-1, you want to give the `title`, `subtitle`, `heading`, and `copyright` elements a sans serif font, the `para` element a serif font, and the URL a monospaced font. These rules would look like the following:

```
para {
  font-family: Palatino Linotype, Times New Roman, serif;
}

title, subtitle, heading, copyright {
  font-family: Trebuchet MS, Verdana, Tahoma, Arial,
   sans-serif
}

url {
  font-family: Courier New, Courier, monospace
}
```

Size that text with `font-size`

To set the font size in a CSS rule, use the `font-size` property. You can specify the size by using absolute or relative sizes as described in the following list:

✦ **Point size.** To specify a specific point size of a font, use a numeric value along with `pt` following it. For example, to specify 12 point, use this:

```
para { font-size: 12pt }
```

✦ **Absolute size keyword.** You can also specify the size based on the following keywords: `xx-small`, `x-small`, `small`, `medium`, `large`, `x-large`, and `xx-large`. For most systems, `medium` is 10pt or 12pt with the other keywords proportional to that size. For example, the following defines the title element to be extra-large:

```
title { font-size: x-large }
```

✦ **Percentage.** To declare a font size based on the relative percentage of the parent size, you can specify a percentage value, like this:

```
para3 { font-size: 40% }
```

✦ **Relative size keywords.** You can base the size of the element font relative to the size of the parent element using the `larger` and `smaller` keywords. For example, to make the size of the `para2` text smaller in proportion to its parent element, use this:

```
para2 { font-size: smaller }
```

In the `kingforaday.xml` example shown in Listing 2-1, suppose that you want to apply a point-based sizing using the following set of rules:

```
title { font-size: 18pt }
subtitle { font-size: 12pt }
heading { font-size: 12pt }
para { font-size: 10pt }
copyright, url { font-size: 8pt }
```

Display your element text in sizzlin' style

You will often need to emphasize particular parts of your text using bold or italics, or else apply a pocketful of other styling properties to the content of your XML elements. To do so, you can use several different CSS properties, including: `font-style`, `font-weight`, `font-variant`, `font-stretch`, and `text-decoration`. These are explained in this section.

Italicize with font-style

The `font-style` property is used to specify whether the text should be `normal`, `italic`, or `oblique`. For example, to set the `para` element to be normal and the `ital` and `subtitle` element to italics, the following rules would be used:

```
para { font-style: normal }
subtitle { font-style: italic }
ital { font-style: italic }
```

Though bold and italics are often grouped together in applications, such as Microsoft Word, CSS separates them in its properties. You don't set bold property with `font-style`. Instead, bolding is done using the `font-weight` property described in the next section.

Embolden your text with font-weight

The `font-weight` property is used to bold or lighten text based on its value. CSS uses a scale from 100 to 900 to specify the weight of text (100 is lightest, 900 is darkest). Possible absolute weight values are a numeric value inside the ordered sequence (100 to 900) or the `normal` or `bold` keywords, shown in Table 2-2.

Table 2-2	Absolute font-weight Values
Numeric Value	*Keyword Equivalent*
100	
200	
300	
400	normal

(continued)

Table 2-2 *(continued)*

Numeric Value	Keyword Equivalent
500	
600	
700	bold
800	
900	

You can also use the keywords `lighter` and `bolder`, which will lighten or darken the text based on the relative value of the parent.

Adding the font-weight values to the stylesheet to be applied to `kingfora-day.xml` (Listing 2-1), you would have the following set of rules:

```
title {
   font-size: 18pt;
   font-weight: bold;
}

subtitle {
   font-size: 12pt;
   font-style: italic;
   font-weight: bold;
}

heading {
   font-size: 12pt;
   font-weight: bold;
}

para {
   font-size: 10pt;
   font-style: normal;
   font-weight: normal;
}

copyright, url {
   font-size: 8pt;
   font-weight: bold;
}

ital { font-style: italic }
emp { font-weight: bold }
```

Font : The all-in-one property

The font property enables you to combine various font-related property settings into a single property. Properties include font-style, font-variant, font-weight, font-size, line-height, and font-family. The syntax is as follows:

```
elementName {
    font: fontStyle fontVariant
        fontWeight
        fontSize/lineHeight
        FontFamily
}
```

You don't have to include each of the attributes. For those that aren't specified, the initial setting for that font setting will be used. The following are sample rules with the font property:

```
para { font: 11pt/12pt Times
    New Roman, serif }
para { font: 60% sans-serif }
para { font: bold italic
    Tahoma, sans-serif }
para { font: bold small-caps
    130%/130% Arial, sans-serif
    }
```

You can also specify system fonts when using the font property, including caption, icon, menu, message-box, small-caption, and status-bar. For example:

```
def { font: message-box }
```

This rule assigns def the system-configurable font assigned to Message Boxes in the user's graphical environment.

Decorate your text with text-decoration

You can apply several line-related decorations to text using the text-decoration property. Possible values include underline, overline, line-through, and blink. For example, to cause the blue-light-special element to blink, use the following rule:

```
blue-light-special { text-decoration: blink }
```

Make it small caps with font-variant

The font-variant property allows you to specify whether or not the text should appear as small caps. The two possible values are normal and small-caps. For example, if you want to apply small caps to the copyright element, use the following rule:

```
copyright { font-variant: small-caps }
```

Condense and expand with font-stretch

The font-stretch property enables you to specify a condensed, extended, or normal typeface from a font family. The absolute keyword values are shown in Table 2-3.

Table 2-3	Absolute font-stretch Values
Values	
ultra-condensed	
extra-condensed	
condensed	
semi-condensed	
normal	
semi-expanded	
expanded	
extra-expanded	
ultra-expanded	

You can also use the relative stretch values of `wider` and `narrower`.

The `font-stretch` property is not supported on Microsoft Internet Explorer 6.0 (and earlier) and Netscape Navigator 6.0 (and earlier).

To expand an address element to the maximum possible, you could use the following rule:

```
address { font-stretch: ultra-expanded }
```

Formatting paragraph text properties

You can use CSS to format various paragraph-level properties — those formatting options that impact more than a single character or word, including the following:

✦ Alignment

✦ Indentation

✦ Line height

✦ Letter and word spacing

✦ Case

Align yourself with the text stream

For block style elements, you can set the text alignment with the `text-align` property. The possible values are `left`, `right`, `center`, and `justify`. For example, to center align the `title`, `subtitle`, and `copyright` elements, use the following rule:

```
title, subtitle, copyright { text-align: center }
```

MXPX goes styling

I'm not sure if the members of the rock band MXPX (pronounced *em-ex-p-ex*) are XML developers on the side, but their name sounds like some of the obscure units of measurement that CSS uses for some of its properties. These include the following:

- em is a relative length to the `font-size` property of the element. So, for example, to make the spacing 50 percent greater than

the font size of the `para` elements, use the following:

```
para { letter-spacing:
1.5em }
```

- ex is relative to the `x-height` of a font, so named because it is usually equal to the height of the lowercase 'x' of a font.

- px is a pixel relative to the resolution of the computer monitor.

Indenting your text, not the fender

The `text-indent` property can be used to set the indentation of text of the first line. You can use a positive or negative length (usually in em units) or a percentage value that relates to the element's parent. For example, if you want to indent the first line of the `para` element, add the following rule:

```
para { text-indent: 2% }
```

Climbing new line heights

You can set the `line-height` property to adjust the height in between lines in your element's text. You can use a number, length (usually in em units), or percentage value. When you specify a number, the line height is determined by multiplying the number by the font size. To double-space a paragraph with a 10pt font, you could use any of the following rules:

```
para { line-height: 2.0 }
para { line-height: 2.0em }
para { line-height: 200% }
```

Spacing out your text

The `letter-spacing` and `word-spacing` properties are used to apply spacing rules to your element text. The values can be either a specified length value (usually in em units, which are discussed in the "MXPX" sidebar) or the `normal` keyword. For example, to make an `address` element's `word-spacing` 80 percent of the normal spacing and its letter-spacing 120 percent of the normal, use the following rule:

```
address {
  word-spacing: .8em;
  letter-spacing: 1.2em;
}
```

Casing the sentence with text-transform

You can adjust the case of the element text using the `text-transform` property. The possible values are shown in Table 2-4. To capitalize all of the text in the address element, use the following rule:

```
address { text-transform: capitalize }
```

Table 2-4	text-transform Values
Value	*Action Performed*
capitalize	Changes the first character of each word to uppercase
lowercase	Changes all characters in the text to lowercase
uppercase	Changes all characters in the text to uppercase
none	Cancels the inherited value

Formatting box properties

An XML element contains text that is rendered on a page, but CSS places all of that text inside of a box region, which can be either invisible or formatted. This section looks at the many box-related properties you can set, including the following:

+ Background color and image

+ Border

+ Margin

+ Padding between the border and the inside text

+ Cursor style

Many of the following sections will reference the `menu.xml` file shown in Listing 2-2.

Listing 2-2   menu.xml

```
<?xml version="1.0" encoding="utf-8" ?>

<?xml-stylesheet type="text/css" href="menu.css" ?>

<menu>
```

```
<entree>
  <name>Sunburnt Chicken</name>
  <fatgrams>23</fatgrams>
  <features>Salad, Vegetables, Baked Potato, and
Dessert</features>
  <description>Chicken prepared so hot, you'll need a
  gallon of soda to wash it
down. Bring sunscreen!</description>
</entree>
<entree>
  <name>Filet Mig's None</name>
  <fatgrams>0</fatgrams>
  <features>Soup, Vegetables, Baked Potato, and
Dessert</features>
  <description>Our master chef Mig prepares a uniquely no-
  fat filet mignon. You won't believe how great it
  tastes!</description>
</entree>
<entree>
  <name>Chicken Parmashaun</name>
  <fatgrams>20</fatgrams>
  <features>Soup, Pasta, Baked Potato, and
Dessert</features>
  <description>Our award-winning Chicken Parmesan prepared
  especially for you by our master chef
  Shaun.</description>
</entree>
<entree>
  <name>Eggs Benelux</name>
  <fatgrams>35</fatgrams>
  <features>Bacon, Sausage, and Toast</features>
  <description>No matter the time of day, enjoy our
  scrumptious breakfast cooked by our famous Belgian and
  Dutch master chefs.</description>
</entree>
<entree>
  <name>Jerk Chicken</name>
  <fatgrams>5</fatgrams>
  <features>Soup, Vegetables, and Dessert</features>
  <description>A delicious hot Jamaican dish prepared by
  our most obnoxious master chef.</description>
</entree>
<entree>
  <name>Gusto Spaghetti</name>
  <fatgrams>55</fatgrams>
  <features>Soup, Salad, and Dessert</features>
  <description>Our famous master chef Boyd Ardee prepares a
  succulent dish of spaghetti with zesty
  gusto!</description>
</entree>
</menu>
```

Prettying up the background scenery

You can assign a color or image as the background of an element using either the `background-color` or `background-image` properties.

✦ The `background-color` property can take any color value (described in the "Formatting character text properties" section, earlier in this chapter) or `transparent`. For example:

```
entree { background-color: silver }
```

✦ The `background-image` property displays the specified image as background and accepts either a URL (using the `url()` function) or the `none` keyword. For example:

```
entree { background-image: url( /images/menuback.jpg ) }
```

When you use `background-image`, you can also specify how the image is repeated if space permits in the box region using the `background-repeat` property. Possible values are shown in Table 2-5. For example, to repeat the address image both horizontally and vertically, add the following line to the rule:

```
entree {
  background-image: url( /images/menu.jpg );
  background-repeat: repeat;
}
```

Table 2-5	background-repeat Values
Value	*Action Performed*
`repeat`	Image is repeated both horizontally and vertically
`repeat-x`	Image is repeated horizontally
`repeat-y`	Image is repeated vertically
`no-repeat`	Image is not repeated

To illustrate, suppose that you want to apply different background colors to the `entree` and `name` elements. The stylesheet rules you set up are as follows:

```
entree {
  color: white;
  background-color: silver;
}
```

```
name {
  font-weight: bold;
  background-color: red;
}
```

The background color will be applied to the box regardless of its inline/block formatting setting. If the formatting is inline, the results are as shown in Figure 2-13. However, suppose you add block formatting to the stylesheet:

```
* {
  display: block;
}
```

The block results are shown in Figure 2-14.

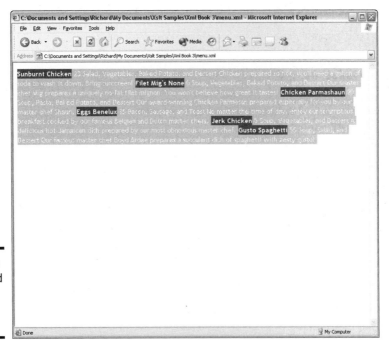

Figure 2-13:
Background color using inline formatting.

Bordering on style

You can apply styling to an element's entire border or parts of the border using the border-related properties. This set of properties can be divided into four types:

✦ **Style.** The border-style is the linchpin of the border properties, because unless you set it, other border properties (such as border-width and border-color) are ignored. There are nine border styles, as shown in Table 2-6, with the none value as the default.

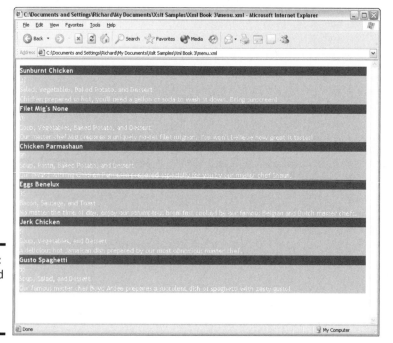

Figure 2-14:
Background color using block formatting.

Table 2-6	border-style Values
Value	*Look*
none	No border, causing the border-width and border-color values to be disregarded (default)
dotted	Dotted line
dashed	Dashed line
solid	Solid line
double	Double line (two single lines and the space between equals the border-width value)
groove	3D groove (based on color value)
ridge	3D ridge (based on color value)
inset	3D inset (based on color value)
outset	3D outset (based on color value)

You can also define the style for one of the box borders using `border-top-style`, `border-right-style`, `border-bottom-style`, or `border-left-style`.

To demonstrate the different border styles, consider the following code snippet:

```
<borderStyles>
  <none>none</none>
  <dotted>dotted</dotted>
  <dashed>dashed</dashed>
  <solid>solid</solid>
  <double>double</double>
  <groove>groove</groove>
  <ridge>ridge</ridge>
  <inset>inset</inset>
  <outset>outset</outset>
</borderStyles>
```

By applying the following stylesheet, you get the results shown in Figure 2-15:

```
* {
    display: block;
    margin: 1em;      /* Adds space between elements */
}

none    { border-style: none }
dotted  { border-style: dotted }
dashed  { border-style: none }
solid   { border-style: solid }
double  { border-style: double }
groove  { border-style: groove }
ridge   { border-style: ridge }
inset   { border-style: inset }
outset  { border-style: outset }
```

✦ **Width.** The width of a border is specified with one of the width keywords: `thin`, `medium`, or `thick` (`medium` is the default) or with a relative length (usually in em units). You can assign a width to the entire box using the `border-width` property. Or, you can specify the size of one of the box sides using the `border-top-width`, `border-right-width`, `border-bottom-width`, or `border-left-width` property.

For example, suppose you want to add a medium solid border to the `entree` element and a `groove` border to the `name` element, the stylesheet is as follows:

```
* { display: block; }

entree {
  background-color: silver;
  border-width: medium;
  border-style: solid;
}

name {
  color: white;
  font-weight: bold;
  background-color: red;
  border-width: thin;
  border-style: groove;
}
```

Figure 2-16 shows the results of this stylesheet being applied to
`menu.xml` (Listing 2-2).

To ensure consistent border widths across elements, use the width keywords. The width keywords are absolutely sized, so that `thin`, `medium`,
and `thick` are identical widths regardless of the font of the current element. In contrast, if you use `em` units, the border size varies on the size
of the element font.

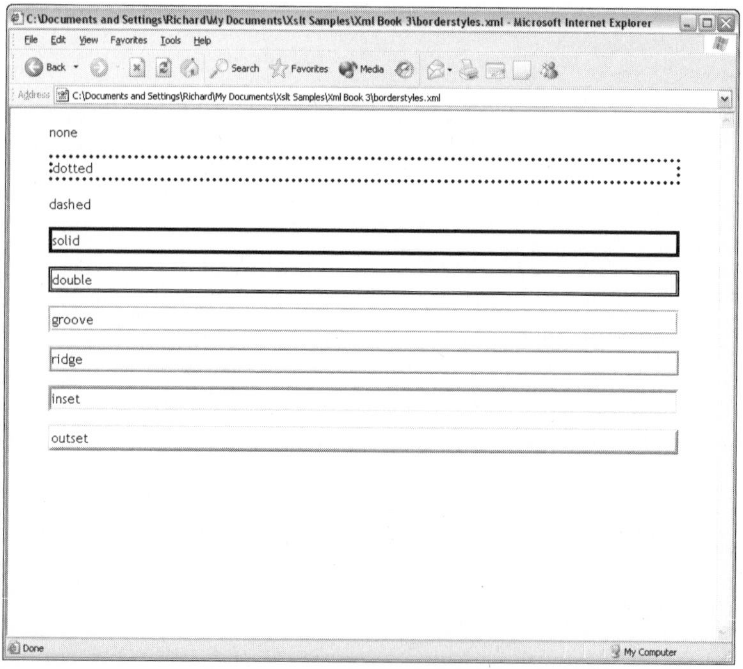

Figure 2-15:
Visual look
of the
border
styles.

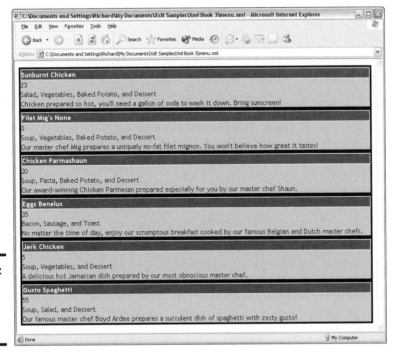

Figure 2-16:
Visual look
of the
border
styles.

✦ **Color.** The color of the border is declared using the `border-color` property and accepts the common set of CSS colors discussed in the "Color XML Beautiful" sidebar. For example, the following rule defines a solid blue thin border for the `name` element:

```
name {
    border-style: solid;
    border-width: thin;
    border-color: blue;
}
```

You can also define one of the borders using one of the following: `border-top-color`, `border-right-color`, `border-bottom-color`, or `border-left-color`.

✦ **Shorthand properties.** You can use the `border` (along with individual border sides `border-top`, `border-right`, `border-bottom`, and `border-left`) as a shortcut property to define the border width, style, and color in a single statement. The general syntax is as follows:

```
elementName { border: width style color }
```

Using the shorthand property, you could condense the three-lined property assignment of the name element (shown in the border color example) into a single statement:

```
name { border: thin solid blue }
```

Marginally speaking

The margin property allows you to set the amount of space between the element box and other elements. Acceptable values are lengths (usually in em units), percentage value, or the keyword auto.

You can also specify the margin for one side of the element using margin-top, margin-left, margin-right, and margin-bottom.

Suppose you want to add a small amount of space after each entree on the menu display document. To do so, add a bottom margin to the entree element of the menu.xml document (Listing 2-2) using the following rule:

```
entree { margin-bottom: .75em }
```

The margin is always transparent, enabling the parent color to show through.

Padding the elements

The padding of an element is the amount of filler space between element text and its border (see Figure 2-2). You can set this property using the padding property. Acceptable values are lengths (usually in em units) or percentage values. For example, to add a slight padding effect to the entree element, you could use the following stylesheet rule:

```
entree { padding: .5em }
```

You can also use padding-top, padding-right, padding-bottom, or padding-left to specify the padding on one of the box sides.

Getting mousy with the cursor

You can modify the shape of the cursor when it moves over an element with the cursor property. The list of cursor values are auto, crosshair, default, pointer, move, e-resize, ne-resize, nw-resize, n-resize, se-resize, sw-resize, s-resize, w-resize, text, wait, and help. For example, to change the mouse cursor to the hourglass shape when the name element is dragged over with the mouse, use the following rule:

```
name { cursor: wait }
```

Formatting with Special Pseudo-Elements

You can perform special formatting of certain parts of the element text based on certain pseudo-elements. These are discussed in this section.

Formatting first line and first character

You can format the first line or first character of a line using the first-line and first-letter pseudo-elements. For example, suppose you'd like to make the first character of the first paragraph of a document be a large capital. You could use the following rule:

```
/* First para element had an ID value of 1 */
para#1:first-letter { font-size: 36pt }
```

Adding text before and after text

You can add text before and after the element text using the before and after pseudo-elements. This capability is especially handy when you want to add labels to the element content that you are displaying. For example, suppose you want to label the descriptive information for each of the entree elements. Use the following rules:

```
fatgrams:before { content: 'Grams of fat: ' }
features:before { content: 'Entree includes: ' }
description:before { content: 'Description: ' }
```

When applied to the menu.xml file (see Listing 2-2), the results are displayed in Figure 2-17.

The before and after pseudo-elements are not supported in Microsoft Internet Explorer 6.0 and earlier.

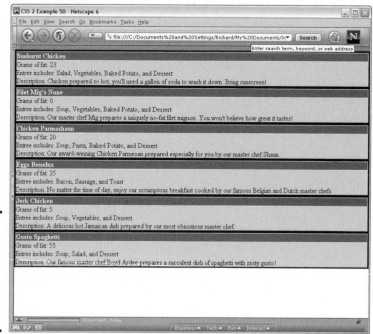

Figure 2-17:
Descriptive
labels
added to
the display
of the
document.

Formatting Tables

You can format XML documents as a table using the set of table-related properties shown in Table 2-7. For example, consider the following XML document containing a list of customers:

```
<customers>
  <caption>Customer list for Brawley, CA</caption>
  <customer>
    <id>100</id>
    <firstname>Joan</firstname>
    <lastname>Arc</lastname>
  </customer>
  <customer>
    <id>101</id>
    <firstname>Bill</firstname>
    <lastname>Shakespeare</lastname>
  </customer>
  <customer>
    <id>102</id>
    <firstname>Lane</firstname>
    <lastname>Bennett</lastname>
  </customer>
```

```
<customer>
  <id>103</id>
 <firstname>Gerald</firstname>
  <lastname>Smith</lastname>
</customer>
<customer>
  <id>104</id>
  <firstname>Rock</firstname>
  <lastname>Randels</lastname>
</customer>
<customer>
  <id>105</id>
  <firstname>Ted</firstname>
  <lastname>Narlybolyson</lastname>
</customer>
<customer>
  <id>106</id>
  <firstname>Tim</firstname>
  <lastname>Smith</lastname>
</customer>
<customer>
  <id>107</id>
  <firstname>Thomas</firstname>
  <lastname>Smith</lastname>
</customer>
</customers>
```

Table 2-7   **Table Properties**

Display Values	*Description*
display:table	Defines a block-style table
display:table-row	Defines an element as a row of cells
display:table-cell	Defines an element as a table cell
display:table-caption	Declares the caption for a table
display:table-column	Defines an element of a column of cells
display:inline-table	Specifies an inline-style table
display:table-row-group	Defines an element group of one or more rows
display:table-header-group	Defines an element group of one or more rows, and is displayed *before* all other rows and row-groups but after top captions.
display:table-footer-group	Defines an element group of one or more rows, and is displayed *after* all other rows and row-groups but before any bottom captions.
display:table-column-group	Declares an element group of one or more columns.

By default, the `display:table-caption` property value displays at the top of the table. However, you can use the `caption-side` property to move the caption to other sides of the table. Possible values include `left`, `top`, `right`, `bottom`, and `inherit`.

To create a basic table to display the customer list, create the following stylesheet:

```
customers { display: table }
customer { display: table-row }
id, firstname, lastname { display: table-cell }

caption {
  display: table-caption;
  caption-side: bottom;
  border-style: none;
}

* { border: solid black }
```

Looking at the stylesheet, first assign the `customers` element to be the `display:table` property, because it serves as the parent element, containing the data for the table. The `customer` element serves as the `display: table-row` because the table consists of a listing of customers. The `id`, `firstname`, and `lastname` elements are assigned to the `display: table-cell` to provide the cell data for each customer element. The caption element is assigned as the `display:table-caption` and is placed at the bottom using the `caption-side:bottom` property value.

Finally, a solid black border is assigned to each element, except the caption, which has a border set to `none`. The resulting table is shown in Figure 2-18.

Microsoft Internet Explorer 6.0 and earlier does not support CSS style tables.

Formatting Lists

CSS also enables you to create bulleted and numeric lists from your XML document using the `display:list-item` property value. For example, consider the following XML document:

```
<menu>
  <entree>
    <name>Sunburnt Chicken</name>
  </entree>
  <entree>
    <name>Filet Mig's None</name>
```

```
    </entree>
    <entree>
      <name>Chicken Parmashaun</name>
    </entree>
    <entree>
      <name>Eggs Benelux</name>
    </entree>
    <entree>
      <name>Jerk Chicken</name>
    </entree>
    <entree>
      <name>Gusto Spaghetti</name>
    </entree>
</menu>
```

Suppose you want to create a bulleted list of entree names. To do so, apply the following stylesheet rule:

```
name {
    display: list-item;
    margin-left: 20px;
}
```

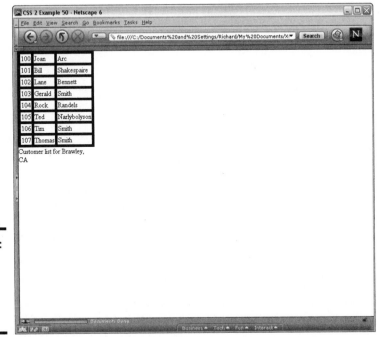

Figure 2-18:
Table
created
from an
XML
document.

The `display:list-item` property value declares the element as a list item, while the `margin-left` property allows space to display the bullet. (Without the `margin-left` adjustment, the bullet isn't visible in the browser.) Figure 2-19 displays the bulleted list.

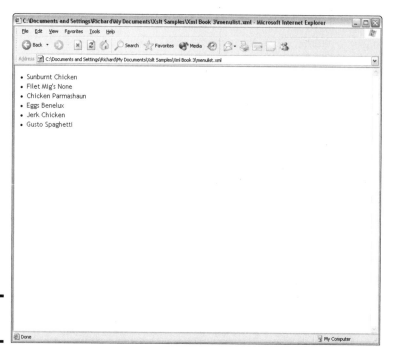

Figure 2-19:
Simple list.

However, although the default bullet is a disc-like circle, you can use the `list-style-type` property to further customize the list using other bullets or numbers. The most common list type values are shown in Table 2-8.

Table 2-8	Common list-style-type Values
Value	*Means*
disc	Rounded filled bullet
circle	Circular bullet (center not filled)
square	Square bullet
decimal	Numeric list, starting with 1
decimal-leading-zero	Numeric list, with an initial zero added to single digit numbers (1 to 9)
lower-roman	Lowercase Roman numeral list
upper-roman	Uppercase Roman numeral list
none	No leading bullet or numeric character

Putting It All Together

Throughout this chapter, Listings 2-1 and 2-2 are used multiple times to demonstrate the selection and formatting parts of applying CSS to an XML document. This section shows you how to tie all of the pieces together into a single stylesheet, and it enables you to see the end results.

Listing 2-1: Formatting an article

You can apply a series of rules to `kingforaday.xml`, the XML-based article shown in Listing 2-1 to format it like a Web-based article. The following stylesheet applies various formatting rules to achieve the article look that is shown in Figure 2-20.

```
/* Text color */

title, subtitle, heading { color: #15526E }


/* Font style */

title {
  font-size: 18pt;
  font-weight: bold;
  text-align: center;
}

subtitle {
  font-size: 12pt;
  font-style: italic;
  font-weight: bold;
  text-align: center;
}

heading {
  font-size: 12pt;
  font-weight: bold;
}

para {
  font-size: 11pt;
  font-style: normal;
  font-weight: normal;
  text-indent: 2%;
  white=space: nowrap;
}

copyright {
  font-size: 8pt;
  font-weight: bold;
```

```
    font-variant: small-caps;
    text-align: center;
  }

url {
    font-size: 8pt;
    color: blue;
    text-align: center;
    text-decoration: underline;
  }

ital { font-style: italic }
emp { font-weight: bold }


/* Font family */

para {
    font-family: Palatino Linotype, Times New Roman, serif;
  }

title, subtitle, heading, copyright {
    font-family: Trebuchet MS, Verdana, Tahoma, Arial, sans-
      serif
  }

url {
    font-family: Courier New, Courier, monospace
  }


/* Block display */
/* Note: Would not want to use block formatting for
          the ital or emp elements, which are inline
          within a paragraph. */

title, subtitle, heading, para, url, copyright { display:
    block }


/* Margin */

heading {
    margin-bottom: 0.5em;
    margin-top: 1.0em;
  }
para { margin-top: .25em }
url, copyright { margin: 1.0em; }
```

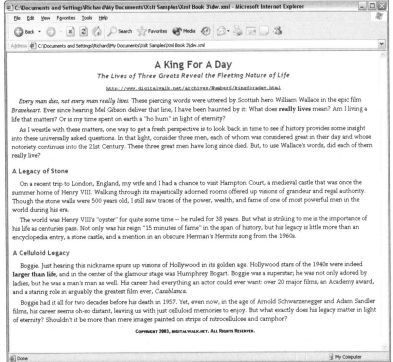

Listing 2-2: Flexible menu formatting

With the `menu.xml` file shown in Listing 2-2, suppose the source XML document was needed for multiple purposes, making multiple stylesheets a necessity. First, a basic block-based listing of the entrees is used to create a traditional style menu. Second, a table listing is used to display a summary chart of the list of meals available at the restaurant.

To create a block-based listing, I can use the following stylesheet. When applied, the results are shown in Figure 2-21.

```
/* Style #1: Block-based */

* {
  display: block;
}


/* Descriptions */
```

```
fatgrams:before { content: 'Grams of fat: ' }
features:before { content: 'Entree includes: ' }
description:before { content: 'Description: ' }


/* Box-related properties */

entree {
   background-color: silver;
   border-width: medium;
   border-style: solid;
   margin-bottom: .75em;
   padding: .25em;
}

name {
   color: white;
   font-weight: bold;
   background-color: red;
   border-width: thin;
   border-style: groove;
}
```

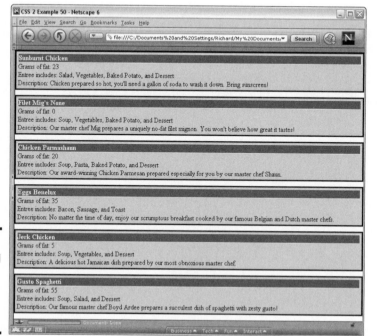

Figure 2-21:
Block-based approach to formatting the menu.xml.

As an alternative, to view the same XML document as a table structure, you can use the following CSS stylesheet:

```
*  {
   font-family: Verdana, sans serif;
   font-size: 8pt;
   border: solid black thin;
}

menu {
   display: table
   margin: .5em;
}
entree { display: table-row }
name, fatgrams, features, description { display: table-cell }
```

The results when applied to the menu.xml document are shown in Figure 2-22.

 Although the CSS capabilities of generating tables are impressive, note, for example, that there is no way to use the element name as a column header in this example. XSLT, which is discussed in Book IV, enables you to perform such additional capabilities if your needs go beyond CSS.

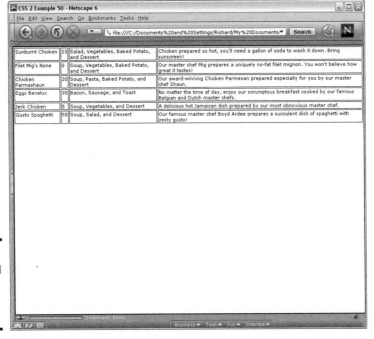

Figure 2-22:
Block-based approach to formatting
menu.xml.

Chapter 3: Printing XML Using XSL-FO

*I*f you spend half of your waking hours surfing the Net and viewing Web pages, it may come as a surprise to know that people actually have needs for printed documentation, either electronically (such as with Adobe Acrobat files) or output on printers. Although the primary purpose of XML will likely always be within the browser, in order for XML to handle all of the needs of organizations, an XML-based solution was needed for printing.

Extensible Stylesheet Language Formatting Objects (XSL-FO) is an XML-based language that was developed by the W3C as a way to describe a formatted document. XSL-FO is intended primarily for print-oriented output, so it focuses on dealing with pagination issues, such as page numbering, headers, and footers.

In this chapter, you survey XSL-FO and discover how to use it to produce paginated documents.

Before reading this chapter, be sure to read Book III, Chapter 1 for an introduction to XSL-FO and how it compares to Cascading Style Sheets (CSS) and Extensible Stylesheet Language Transformations (XSLT).

Exploring the Essential XSL-FO Elements

Many everyday applications that you work with have the concept of "master pages" or "templates" that can be applied to one or more documents and have documents assume the settings of the "master." For example, Microsoft PowerPoint has a Slide Master, and Microsoft Word and Macromedia Dreamweaver employ the concept of a template to perform a similar task.

The idea of these "master pages" is the same: Define a page or slide type once, and apply it to multiple pages. In the same way, you can think of an XSL-FO document as being part "template" and part "document." I call these two parts of the document the layout master and the content area:

✦ **Layout master:** The layout master section is used to define page masters and page sequence masters. A *page master* defines the layout details for a page. The optional *page sequence master* is used to order the sequence of multiple page masters, such as in the case of having separate masters for odd and even pages.

Some of the page settings you define in the layout master bear resemblance to the settings of the Page Setup dialog box (see Figure 3-1) in Microsoft Word (File⇨Page Setup from the menu). Although this is not a perfect analogy, this dialog box too deals with configuring different odd/even pages, margin sizes, and so on.

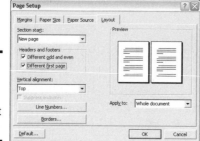

Figure 3-1:
Microsoft Word's Page Layout dialog box.

✦ **Content area:** The content area holds one or more *page sequences*, which contain the actual text to be output.

Figure 3-2 illustrates the two parts of the XSL-FO document.

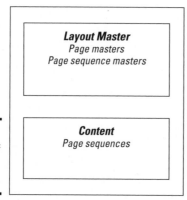

Figure 3-2:
Two parts of an XSL-FO document.

XSL-FO supports a seemingly unending number of formatting elements and properties to create a very precise layout of an outputted document.

However, each XSL-FO document must have a core set of elements that define the layout master and content area sections. Listing 3-1 shows a minimal XSL-FO document, with core elements in bold.

Listing 3-1   barebones.fo

```
<?xml version="1.0" encoding="utf-8" ?>
<fo:root xmlns:fo="http://www.w3.org/1999/XSL/Format">

  <!-- Document Layout Definition -->
  <fo:layout-master-set>
    <fo:simple-page-master master-name="basic">
      <fo:region-body margin="1in"/>
    </fo:simple-page-master>
  </fo:layout-master-set>

  <!-- Document Content -->
  <fo:page-sequence master-reference="basic">
    <fo:flow flow-name="xsl-region-body">
      <fo:block>Howdy</fo:block>
    </fo:flow>
  </fo:page-sequence>

</fo:root>
```

Consider the following core elements:

+ `fo:root` serves as the root element of an XSL-FO document and contains all FO elements.

   An XSL-FO document must declare the FO namespace in the `fo:root` element. XSLFO uses the `http://www.w3.org/1999/XSL/Format` namespace (see Book I, Chapter 4 for more on namespaces) and typically has `fo:` as the namespace prefix.

+ `fo:layout-master-set` is the container for one or more page masters and page sequence masters. For most uses, a page master is specified by `fo:simple-page-master` to define the layout details for a page. The optional `fo:page-sequence-master` element defines a sequence of page master declarations to be used by the `page-sequence` elements.

+ `fo:page-sequence` is a container element that holds a sequence of pages. You can have one or more `fo:page-sequence` elements in your document, each of which will begin a new page.

+ `fo:flow` is the container object for content. You can specify the region of the page to place the content with the `flow-name` attribute. In Listing 3-1, the main page body is specified with `xsl-region-body`.

+ `fo:block` is used as a container for normal paragraph text. Text cannot be added directly to the `fo:flow` element.

Figure 3-3 shows the result of this simple FO document when viewed in X-Smiles browser. X-Smiles is a open source browser that provides support for XSL-FO. (See `www.x-smiles.org` to download a copy.)

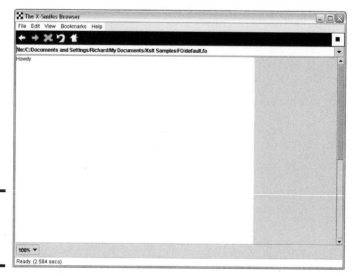

Figure 3-3:
Barebones
XSL-FO
output.

 To output XSL-FO documents to a printer or Adobe Acrobat format, you need an XSL-FO processor. Two commercially available processors are: Antenna House XSL Formatter (`http://www.antennahouse.com`) and XEP 3.0 (`www.renderx.com`). Both of these are available as an evaluation copy download.

Adding Formatting to an XSL-FO Page

As covered in Book III, Chapter 1, XSL-FO uses many of the same properties and general formatting and inheritance model that CSS uses. Therefore, you can apply CSS-like formatting to an XSL-FO document, as shown in the example XSL-FO document shown in Listing 3-2.

 See Book III, Chapter 2 for more details on CSS styles.

Listing 3-2   poem.fo

```
<?xml version="1.0" encoding="ISO-8859-1"?>
<fo:root xmlns:fo="http://www.w3.org/1999/XSL/Format"
   font-family="Palatino Linotype, Times New Roman, serif"
     font-size="12pt">
```

```
<fo:layout-master-set>
  <fo:simple-page-master master-name="poem"
    margin-bottom="25pt" margin-left="120pt" margin-
  right="120pt" margin-top="25pt">
    <fo:region-body border-style="solid" border-
  width="thin" padding="2em"/>
  </fo:simple-page-master>
</fo:layout-master-set>

<fo:page-sequence master-reference="poem">
<fo:flow flow-name="xsl-region-body" >

<fo:block font-size="16pt" font-weight="bold" text-
    align="center">Propice</fo:block>

<fo:block font-size="12pt" font-weight="bold" font-
    style="italic" text-align="center"
  space-after.maximum="2em">Robert Browning</fo:block>

<fo:block linefeed-treatment="preserve">
Fear death? to feel the fog in my throat,
The mist in my face,
When the snows begin, and the blasts denote
I am nearing the place,
The power of the night, the press of the storm,
The post of the foe:
Where he stands, the Arch Fear in a visible form,
Yet the strong man must go;
For the journey is done and the summit attained
And the barriers fall,
Though a battle's to fight ere the guerdon be gained,
The reward to it all.
I was ever a fighter, so -- one fight more,
The best and the last!
I would hate that death bandaged my eyes and forebore
And bade me creep past.
No let me taste the whole of it, fare like my peers,
The heroes of old,
Bear the brunt in a minute, pay glad life's arrears
Of pain, darkness and cold.
For sudden the worst turns the best to the brave,
The black minute's at end,
And the elements rage, the fiend-voices that rave,
Shall dwindle, shall blend,
Shall change, shall become first a peace out of pain,
Then a light, then thy breast,
O thou soul of my soul! I shall clasp thee again,
And with God be the rest!
</fo:block>

</fo:flow>
</fo:page-sequence>
</fo:root>
```

In looking over this document, keep in mind the following formatting commands that are shown in bold:

✦ The *default font* properties are specified in the `fo:root` element. Because font properties are inherited in child elements, setting these global attributes here will enable all text to assume this style unless overwritten.

✦ The *page margin* settings are declared in the `poem` page master (defined using `fo:simple-page-master`).

✦ The *border* for the body region is defined in the `fo:region-body` element, a child of `fo:simple-page-master`.

✦ Three blocks make up the content of the document. The title and subtitle blocks have special formatting, while the poem block uses the default font settings. However, notice that the poem block adds an attribute called `linefeed-treatment="preserve"` because I need to maintain the poem line structure rather than wrapping text as in a normal paragraph.

Figure 3-4 shows the output in Adobe Acrobat.

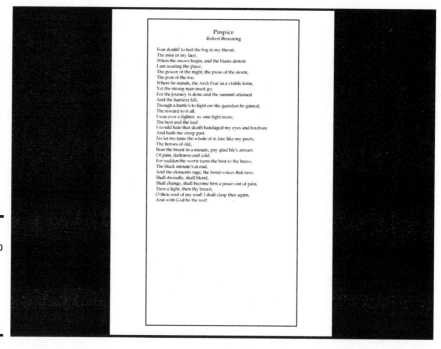

Figure 3-4:
The Poem.fo document shown in Adobe Acrobat Reader.

Producing a Paginated Document

The real power of XSL-FO lies in its ability to create paginated documents. Not only can you create page masters for different types of pages in your document (first, odd, and even), but you can also specify unique headers, footers, and footnotes.

If you read the last chapter (Book III, Chapter 2), you saw how CSS can be used to format the kingforaday.xml document (see Listing 2-1 in that chapter) as a Web page. To illustrate the power of XSL-FO, suppose that you want to output the same XML file as an Adobe Acrobat file.

To do so, you would need to transform the XML document into an XSL-FO document using XSLT. The end result of the transformation is the kingforaday.fo file shown in Listing 3-3. (See Book IV, Chapter 6 for an in-depth discussion of this transformation process for this file.)

Examine the document in Listing 3-3 and then read the explanation of the key parts of the XSL-FO document that follows.

Listing 3-3   kingforaday.fo

```xml
<?xml version="1.0" encoding="ISO-8859-1"?>
<fo:root xmlns:fo="http://www.w3.org/1999/XSL/Format"
  font-family="Palatino Linotype, Times New Roman, serif"
  font-size="15pt">

  <!-- ******* Document layout definition ******* -->
  <fo:layout-master-set>

    <!-- Page master for title page -->
    <fo:simple-page-master master-name="firstPage">
      <fo:region-body margin=".75in" margin-top="3in"
  padding="6pt"/>
    </fo:simple-page-master>

    <!-- Page master for article pages -->
    <fo:simple-page-master master-name="remainingPages">
      <fo:region-body margin="1in" padding-right="6pt"/>
      <fo:region-after extent="45pt"/>
      <fo:region-before extent="30pt" padding="10pt"/>
    </fo:simple-page-master>

    <!-- Page sequence master -->
    <fo:page-sequence-master master-name="defaultSequence">
      <fo:repeatable-page-master-alternatives>
        <fo:conditional-page-master-reference page-
  position="first" master-reference="firstPage"/>
```

(continued)

Listing 3-3 *(continued)*

```
        <fo:conditional-page-master-reference master-
    reference="remainingPages"/>
      </fo:repeatable-page-master-alternatives>
    </fo:page-sequence-master>
  </fo:layout-master-set>


<!-- ******* Document content ******* -->

<!-- Title page -->

<fo:page-sequence master-reference="defaultSequence">
  <fo:flow flow-name="xsl-region-body" font-
  family="Trebuchet MS, Verdana, Tahoma, Arial, sans-serif"
    text-align="center" color="#15526E">
    <fo:block border="thin #15526E ridge" padding="10pt">
    <fo:block font-size="30pt" font-weight="bold" >A King
For A Day</fo:block>
    <fo:block font-size="16pt" font-weight="bold" font-
style="italic" text-align="center">The Lives of Three
Greats Reveal the Fleeting Nature of Life</fo:block>
    <fo:block font-size="10pt" space-
before="8pt"><fo:basic-link external-
destination="url('http://www.digitalwalk.net/archives/Num
ber6/kingforaday.html')" text-decoration="underline"
color="blue">http://www.digitalwalk.net/archives/Number6/
kingforaday.html</fo:basic-link></fo:block>
    </fo:block>
  </fo:flow>
</fo:page-sequence>

<!-- Article pages -->

<fo:page-sequence master-reference="defaultSequence">

  <!-- Footer -->
  <fo:static-content flow-name="xsl-region-after">
    <fo:block font-size="8pt" font-weight="bold" text-
align-last="center" color="#15526E">
      Copyright 2003, digitalwalk.net. All Rights Reserved.
    </fo:block>
  </fo:static-content>

  <!-- Header -->
  <fo:static-content flow-name="xsl-region-before">
    <fo:block font-size="8pt" font-weight="bold" text-
align="end" color="#15526E">Page <fo:page-
number/></fo:block>
  </fo:static-content>
```

```
<!-- Article -->
<fo:flow flow-name="xsl-region-body"><fo:block linefeed-
treatment="preserve" line-height="1.5" intrusion-
displace="line"><fo:float float="start"><fo:block font-
size="50pt" line-height="36pt" font-weight="bold" font-
style="italic">E</fo:block></fo:float><fo:inline font-
style="italic">very man dies, not every man really
lives.</fo:inline> These piercing words were uttered by
Scottish hero William Wallace in the epic film
Braveheart. Ever since hearing Mel Gibson deliver that
line, I have been haunted by it: What does really lives
mean? Am I living a life that matters? Or is my time
spent on earth a "ho hum" in light of eternity?
```

As I wrestle with these matters, one way to get a fresh
   perspective is to look back in time to see if history
   provides some insight into these universally asked
   questions. In that light, consider three men, each of
   whom was considered great in their day and whose
   notoriety continues into the 21st Century. These three
   great men have long since died. But, to use Wallace's
   words, did each of them really live?

```
<fo:inline font-weight="bold" color="#15526E">A Legacy of
   Stone</fo:inline>
```

On a recent trip to London, England, my wife and I had a
   chance to visit Hampton Court, a medieval castle that was
   once the summer home of Henry VIII. Walking through its
   majestically adorned rooms offered up visions of grandeur
   and regal authority. Though the stone walls were 500 years
   old, I still saw traces of the power, wealth, and fame of
   one of the most powerful men in the world during his era.

The world was Henry VIII's "oyster" for quite some time -- he
   ruled for 38 years. But what is striking to me is the
   importance of his life as centuries pass. Not only was
   his reign "15 minutes of fame" in the span of history,
   but his legacy is little more than an encyclopedia entry,
   a stone castle, and a mention in an obscure Herman's
   Hermits song from the 1960s.

```
<fo:inline font-weight="bold" color="#15526E" keep-with-
   next="always">A Celluloid Legacy</fo:inline>
```

```
<fo:inline font-style="italic">Bogie.</fo:inline>Just hearing
   this nickname spurs up visions of Hollywood in its golden
   age. Hollywood stars of the 1940s were indeed larger than
   life, and in the center of the glamour stage was Humphrey
   Bogart. Bogie was a superstar; he was not only adored by
   ladies, but he was a man's man as well.
```

(continued)

Book III
Chapter 3

Printing XML Using
XSL-FO

Listing 3-3 *(continued)*

```
        His career had everything an actor could ever want: over
        20 major films, an Academy award, and a starring role in
        arguably the greatest film ever, Casablanca.

<fo:float float="left" ><fo:block color="#15526E" font-
        size="18pt" font-style="italic" padding="6pt"><fo:block
        text-align="center">Every man dies,
not every man really
        lives.</fo:block></fo:block></fo:float>Bogie had it all
        for two decades before his death in 1957. Yet, even now,
        in the age of Arnold Schwarzenegger and Adam Sandler
        films, his career seems oh-so distant, leaving us with
        just celluloid memories to enjoy. But what exactly does
        his legacy matter in light of eternity? Shouldn't it be
        more than mere images painted on strips of nitrocellulose
        and camphor?

Continued on digitalwalk.net...
</fo:block>
</fo:flow>
</fo:page-sequence>

</fo:root>
```

Multiple page masters

The XSL-FO document uses a page master for the title page and another for the remaining article pages:

```
<!-- Page master for title page -->
<fo:simple-page-master master-name="firstPage">
  <fo:region-body margin=".75in" margin-top="3in"
    padding="6pt"/>
</fo:simple-page-master>

<!-- Page master for article pages -->
<fo:simple-page-master master-name="remainingPages">
  <fo:region-body margin="1in" padding-right="6pt"/>
  <fo:region-after extent="45pt"/>
  <fo:region-before extent="30pt" padding="10pt"/>
</fo:simple-page-master>
```

Page sequence master

The document uses a fo:page-sequence-master element to define the sequence of the two page masters. The firstPage page master is specified to be used for the first page position, and the remainingPages page master is to be used for the rest of the pages:

```
<!-- Page sequence master -->
<fo:page-sequence-master master-name="defaultSequence">
  <fo:repeatable-page-master-alternatives>
    <fo:conditional-page-master-reference page-
    position="first" master-reference="firstPage"/>
    <fo:conditional-page-master-reference master-
    reference="remainingPages"/>
  </fo:repeatable-page-master-alternatives>
</fo:page-sequence-master>
```

Title page content

The title page content is defined in the first fo:page-sequence and is assigned to the defaultSequence page sequence master. Three fo:block elements are used to define the title, subtitle, and Web link.

XSL-FO allows you to define internal and external links using the fo:basic-link element. However, unlike HTML, no special formatting is given to the link, so you use normal text formatting properties to simulate the expected look of a hyperlink.

The code is as follows:

```
<fo:page-sequence master-reference="defaultSequence">
  <fo:flow flow-name="xsl-region-body" font-family="Trebuchet
  MS, Verdana, Tahoma, Arial, sans-serif"
    text-align="center" color="#15526E">
  <fo:block border="thin #15526E ridge" padding="10pt">
  <fo:block font-size="30pt" font-weight="bold" >A King For
  A Day</fo:block>
    <fo:block font-size="16pt" font-weight="bold" font-
    style="italic" text-align="center">The Lives of Three
    Greats Reveal the Fleeting Nature of Life</fo:block>
    <fo:block font-size="10pt" space-before="8pt"><fo:basic-
    link external-
    destination="url('http://www.digitalwalk.net/archives/Num
    ber6/kingforaday.html')" text-decoration="underline"
    color="blue">http://www.digitalwalk.net/archives/Number6/
    kingforaday.html</fo:basic-link></fo:block>
    </fo:block>
  </fo:flow>
</fo:page-sequence>
```

Header and footer

A header and footer were created for the article pages. The fo:static-content element is typically used to define a header or footer, and its flow-name attribute specifies the region of the page the content belongs to. Footers use the xsl-region-after value; headers use the xsl-region-before value. The code is as follows:

```
<!-- Footer -->
<fo:static-content flow-name="xsl-region-after">
  <fo:block font-size="8pt" font-weight="bold" text-align-
    last="center" color="#15526E">
    Copyright 2003, digitalwalk.net. All Rights Reserved.
  </fo:block>
</fo:static-content>

<!-- Header -->
<fo:static-content flow-name="xsl-region-before">
  <fo:block font-size="8pt" font-weight="bold" text-
    align="end" color="#15526E">Page <fo:page-
    number/></fo:block>
</fo:static-content>
```

Drop-caps and call-outs

Drop-caps and call-out boxes can be created by using the fo:float element, which is a floatable region on a page that doesn't flow with the
normal text.

The drop-cap was created with the following code:

```
<fo:flow flow-name="xsl-region-body">
  <fo:block linefeed-treatment="preserve"
    line-height="1.5" intrusion-displace="line">
    <fo:float float="start">
      <fo:block font-size="50pt" line-height="36pt" font-
    weight="bold" font-style="italic">E
      </fo:block>
    </fo:float>
  ...
```

The call-out quote box was created with the following:

```
<fo:float float="left">
  <fo:block color="#15526E" font-size="18pt" font-
    style="italic" padding="6pt">
    <fo:block text-align="center">Every man dies,
not every man really lives.
    </fo:block>
  </fo:block>
</fo:float>
```

Figures 3-5, 3-6, and 3-7 show the results when the document is output in
Adobe Acrobat format.

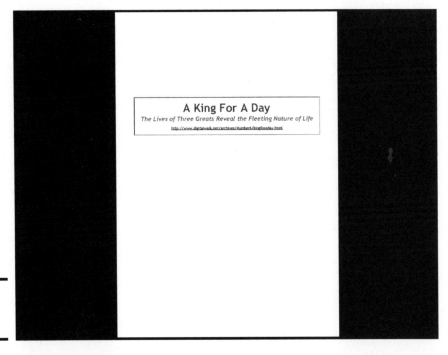

Figure 3-5:
Title page
of output.

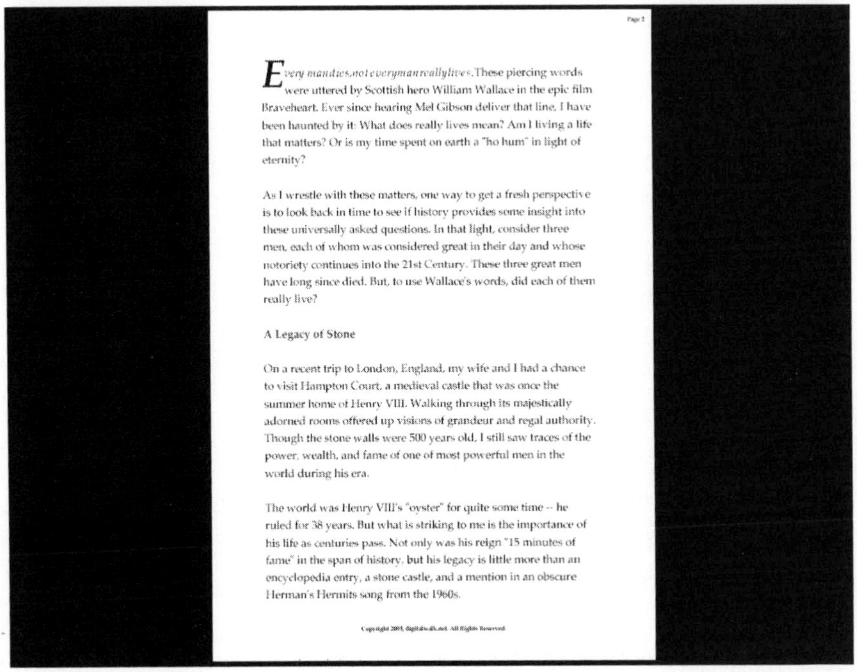

Figure 3-6:
First page
of output.

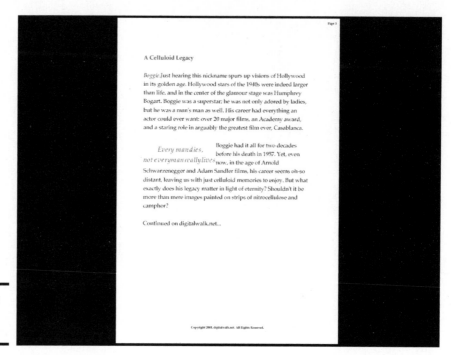

Page 3

A Celluloid Legacy

Boggie. Just hearing this nickname spurs up visions of Hollywood in its golden age. Hollywood stars of the 1940s were indeed larger than life, and in the center of the glamour stage was Humphrey Bogart. Boggie was a superstar; he was not only adored by ladies, but he was a man's man as well. His career had everything an actor could ever want: over 20 major films, an Academy award, and a staring role in arguably the greatest film ever, Casablanca.

Every man dies,
not every man really lives. Boggie had it all for two decades before his death in 1957. Yet, even now, in the age of Arnold Schwarzenegger and Adam Sandler films, his career seems oh-so distant, leaving us with just celluloid memories to enjoy. But what exactly does his legacy matter in light of eternity? Shouldn't it be more than mere images painted on strips of nitrocellulose and camphor?

Continued on digitalwalk.net...

Figure 3-7:
Last page
of output.

Book IV

Transforming XML

The 5th Wave   By Rich Tennant

Oh come on— how fatal can it be?

FATAL ERROR

Contents at a Glance

Chapter 1: XML's Swiss Army Knife — XSLT

In This Chapter

✔ **Understanding XSLT**

✔ **Dissecting an XSLT stylesheet**

✔ **Finding out the tools you need for XSLT**

✔ **Transforming an XML document**

Swiss Army knives are world-renowned for their utility, ruggedness, and general "coolness." Take a Swiss Army knife with you on a camping trip, and you've just about got everything you need, except for perhaps a sleeping bag. It's got multiple blades, pair of scissors, fork, spoon, knife, and a compass inside its red, Swiss-flag adorned wrapper.

While its name may be awkward and clumsy, Extensible Stylesheet Language Transformations (XSLT) reminds me of a Swiss Army knife. XSLT may be a small and lean language, but it's packed full of power and flexibility and can get you out of many tight situations in the vast lands of XML. Besides, XSLT is a pretty cool language to work with.

In this chapter, you explore the basics of XSLT and XSLT stylesheets and perform your first XSLT transformation.

Exploring the Basics of XSLT

The "before/after" is one of the age-old, tried-&-true advertising techniques that never goes out of style — show a "before" picture of a rounded 300-pound person and the same person in an "after" photo now weighing a trim 170 pounds. The ad proceeds to display the dietary product that caused the radical change. Whether it is a weight loss product, a fast-food restaurant, or hair loss cream, the "before/after" continues to be used for one reason: because it works!

If the World Wide Web Consortium (W3C) ever feels compelled to advertise XSLT, I recommend using the "before/after" technique to show its dramatic results:

Before

```
<customer>
  <id>101</id>
  <name>Rick Blaine</name>
  <city>Manchester</city>
  <state>NH</state>
  <zip>02522</zip>
</customer>
```

After

```
<customer id="101">
  <fullname>Rick Blaine</fullname>
  <address city="Manchester" state="NH" zipcode="02522"/>
</customer>
```

This simple example shows you how XSLT can be effectively used as a change agent to reconstruct an XML document into a completely different XML structure, HTML document, or text file.

Without XSLT's before/after magic, you'd have to write your own conversion utility in a traditional programming language. Or, if you were a glutton for punishment, you'd have to open Notepad and begin doing the migration by hand. In contrast, XSLT enables you to transform the data structure from "before" to "after" with just a few lines of code in XSLT.

XSLT is a language that allows you to transform XML documents into other XML documents or formats. Like other XML-related languages such as XML Schemas, XSLT is actually written in XML.

XSLT, however, doesn't use smoke and mirrors to get its results. Instead, as Figure 1-1 shows, an XSLT stylesheet is applied to a source XML document and fed to an XSLT processor. The processor spits out a new document based on the instructions in the stylesheet.

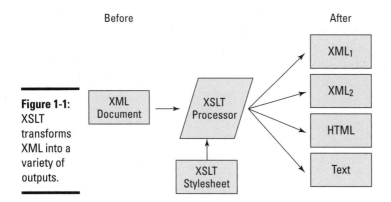

Figure 1-1:
XSLT
transforms
XML into a
variety of
outputs.

Two sides of any transformation

Just as there are two sides to any story, any XSLT transformation has two
sides to consider — the input and output. For each side, you have a basic
question to answer:

✦ **Input side.** What information from the original XML document do you
want to extract?

You answer that question by writing an XPath expression that retrieves
the information you want. XPath is the language used by XSLT to locate
nodes in a source XML document. XPath is something like a commando
charged with going into an XML document and picking out the
requested information for an XSLT stylesheet.

✦ **Output side.** How would you like that information structured in the
output document?

This question is answered by creating a "template" that expresses how
you'd like the information structured in the document that is generated
by the transformation process.

Figure 1-2 illustrates the two sides to any XSLT transformation.

Book IV
Chapter 1

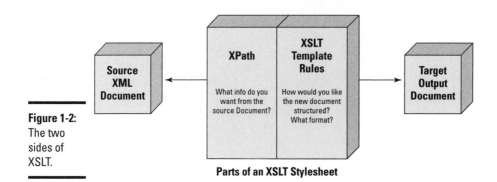

Parts of an XSLT Stylesheet

Figure 1-2:
The two
sides of
XSLT.

How XSLT views XML documents

A critical part in figuring out how XSLT works is understanding the way it views XML documents. When you first start working with XML, you may look at an XML document and see a jumbled collection of data and descriptor tags. But after you get more experience with the markup language, you begin to understand the natural hierarchy that exists between elements and see the parent, child, and sibling relationships that exist among the various parts.

An XSLT processor also sees an XML document as a hierarchical tree. But rather than staying at the element level that you and I have stayed at so far in this book, XSLT dives deeper to the node level. A *node* is a single point in the document hierarchy. Elements are the most common type of node that you work with, but there are actually six different node types: element, attribute, namespace, processing instruction, comment, and text.

Just like an element can have child elements inside of it, so too can nodes contain other nodes. Therefore, an element node has children not only when it contains other elements, but also when it contains attributes and text.

Each document has something called a *root node* that contains all other nodes. Don't confuse the root node with the root (or document) element, because the two are not the same. The root node is never visible in the document itself, but is the invisible container node for everything inside of it.

The XML snippet below contains several of these node types:

```
<?xml version="1.0" encoding="UTF-8"?>
<film name="Braveheart">
   <!-- Last modified 2/01 -->
   <storyline>William Wallace unites the 13th Century Scots in
      their battle to overthrow English rule.</storyline>

</film>
```

Figure 1-3 shows how this sample can be viewed as a hierarchy of nodes. One aspect of this hierarchy may jump out at you: the presence of all of those additional text nodes. These text nodes represent the whitespace in between the various elements. Although no actual text is between the `film` element and the comment or between the comment and the `storyline` element, invisible carriage return and linefeed characters are present to start a new code line. However, because there is no non-whitespace text around it, these whitespace characters are not added to the result document by default. (See Book IV, Chapter 6 for how to deal with whitespace in your stylesheets.)

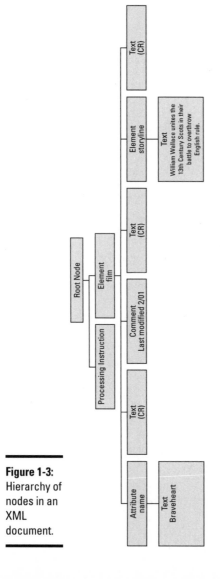

Figure 1-3:
Hierarchy of
nodes in an
XML
document.

Dissecting an XSLT Stylesheet

The heart of any XSLT transformation is a stylesheet. An *XSLT stylesheet* is a well-formed XML document that, by convention, has an .xsl file extension. It consists of five major parts, including:

✦ XML Declaration

✦ Stylesheet element

✦ Template rules

✦ Other top-level elements

✦ Comments

Listing 1-1 provides a typical stylesheet. The following sections discuss the various parts.

Listing 1-1   Sample XSLT Stylesheet

```
<?xml version="1.0" encoding="utf-8" ?>
<xsl:stylesheet
   xmlns:xsl="http://www.w3.org/1999/XSL/Transform"
   version="1.0">

 <!-- Developed by: R. Wagner -->
 <!-- Last modified: 04/22 -->

 <!-- This stylesheet will output an HTML document using
   several
      template rules, one defined in this file and the
   others from
      moretemplates.xsl -->

 <!-- Output document to HTML format -->
 <xsl:output method="html"/>

 <!-- Preserve space for chapters elements -->
 <xsl:preserve-space elements="chapters"/>

 <! --- For each book element, surround its content with
    HTML paragraph tags -->
 <xsl:template match="book">
   <p><xsl:apply-templates/></p>
 </xsl:template>

 <!-- Include more template rules, which
```

```
      are stored in a separate file -->
  <include href="moretemplates.xsl"/>

</xsl:stylesheet>
```

XML declaration

Because an XSLT stylesheet is an XML document, you should start off the stylesheet with an XML declaration:

```
<?xml version="1.0" encoding="utf-8" ?>
```

See Book I, Chapter 2 for more information on XML declarations.

xsl:stylesheet element

The `xsl:stylesheet` element serves as the topmost element (or root element) of an XSLT stylesheet. All XSLT instructions must be inside this container element. The shell of any XSLT stylesheet consists of:

```
<xsl:stylesheet
    xmlns:xsl="http://www.w3.org/1999/XSL/Transform"
    version="1.0">

</xsl:stylesheet>
```

An `xsl:stylesheet` element must have two attributes defined:

✦ **Namespace:** The XSLT namespace is set to `xmlns:xsl="http://www.w3.org/1999/XSL/Transform"` and must be declared within the `xsl:stylesheet`.

✦ **Version:** The `version` attribute defined providing the version of XSLT used in the stylesheet, which is currently `1.0`.

This information is used by the XSLT processor as it determines how to process the stylesheet.

Template rules

The heart of an XSLT stylesheet, and XSLT for that matter, is the template rule. The *template rule* specifies what information should be retrieved from the source XML document (through its `match` attribute) and how that information should be added to the result document (through its template).

A stylesheet may have one or more template rules. Each is defined with the `xsl:template` element:

```
<xsl:template match="XPathExpression">
  <!-- Template -->
</xsl:template>
```

The terms *template rule* and *template* can be easy to mix up. However, note that a template rule is the entire `xsl:template` element, while the template is the contents of the element (in other words, what's inside the start and end tags).

Don't concern yourself with how template rules work just yet. Save that meaty topic for the next chapter (Book IV, Chapter 2).

Other top-level elements

While the template rule (defined using `xsl:template`) is the basic building block of an XSLT stylesheet, there are other elements that can be defined directly underneath the `xsl:stylesheet` element. These elements are called *top-level elements* and are shown in Table 1-1.

Table 1-1	Top-Level XSLT Elements
Element	*Definition*
xsl:template	Defines a template rule.
xsl:output	Specifies the output format for the result document.
xsl:variable	Defines a variable.
xsl:param	Defines a parameter, which is a special kind of variable.
xsl:import	Loads an external stylesheet.
xsl:include	Loads an external stylesheet as part of the current stylesheet.
xsl:preserve-space	Preserves whitespace in the result document.
xsl:strip-space	Removes whitespace in the result document.
xsl:key	Defines a key that can be used to link together XML elements.
xsl:decimal-format	Defines the decimal format to use when converting numbers to strings.
xsl:namespace-alias	Maps a namespace to another namespace.
xsl:attribute-set	Defines a named set of attributes for use in the result document.

The following stylesheet provides an example using several of these top-level elements:

```
<xsl:stylesheet xmlns:xsl="http://www.w3.org/
    1999/XSL/Transform" version="1.0">
```

```
<xsl:output method="html"/>
<xsl:preserve-space elements="chapters"/>
<xsl:template match="book">
  <p><xsl:apply-templates/></p>
</xsl:template>
<xsl:include href="moretemplates.xsl"/>
</xsl:stylesheet>
```

As a general rule, you can put these top-level elements in any sequence you wish because the XSLT processor handles these instructions the same way regardless of order. For example, even if I rearrange the elements as shown below, the result document looks exactly the same as the first stylesheet:

```
<xsl:stylesheet
    xmlns:xsl="http://www.w3.org/1999/XSL/Transform"
    version="1.0">
  <xsl:include href="moretemplates.xsl"/>
  <xsl:template match="book">
    <p><xsl:apply-templates/></p>
  </xsl:template>
  <xsl:preserve-space elements="chapters"/>
  <xsl:output method="html"/>
</xsl:stylesheet>
```

(There are a couple of exceptions to this rule — notably the use of xsl:import, but these tend to occur only in advanced situations.)

While the order of top-level elements doesn't matter much, the order in which you place instructions and text *within* a template rule is critically important to the output of the result document. But more on that in the next chapter.

Take your pick

In addition to xsl:stylesheet, you can also use the xsl:transform element, which is functionally equivalent. Its syntax is:

```
<xsl:transform
    xmlns:xsl="http://www.w3.
    org/1999/XSL/Transform"
    version="1.0">
</xsl:transform>
```

While both xsl:stylesheet and xsl:transform are valid, xsl:stylesheet is usually the preferred element of the two. I use xsl:stylesheet throughout this book.

Comments

A comment is descriptive text included in your stylesheet for "behind-the-scenes" use. XSLT processor ignores these instructions during transformation and, by default, they're not carried over to the resulting document.

Comments are helpful for labeling template rules or describing the functionality of a particular construct. Because XSLT is an XML vocabulary, a comment conforms to the syntax of XML and is any text surrounded by a $<!-$ prefix and $->$ suffix. Listing 1-1 illustrates how the liberal use of comments can greatly add to the readability of a stylesheet.

Transforming an XML Document

The transformation of an XML document into a new document structure can be summed up in a six-step process:

✦ Gathering your tools

✦ Locating or creating an XML document

✦ Determining the output requirements

✦ Writing your XSLT stylesheet

✦ Applying the stylesheet to the XML document

✦ Viewing the results

The following sections explore each of these steps.

Step 1: Gathering your tools

In order to perform XSLT transformations, you need two primary software programs — a text editor and an XSLT processor:

✦ **Text editor.** Because XML and XSLT files are plain text documents, you simply need a text editor to write your transformations. If you are a Windows user, you can use Notepad. Or if you already have a favorite editor, feel free to use it.

✦ **XSLT processor.** An XSLT processer applies the rules you have defined in your stylesheet to the source XML document and outputs the results to a new file. An XSLT processor is a command-line tool without any real user interface. Table 1-2 lists several XSLT processors you can download from the Web.

Table 1-2	**XSLT Processors**	
Name	*Description*	*Web Address*
Microsoft msxsl	The msxsl.exe command line utility invokes the Microsoft XML Parser 4.0 (msxml4.dll) to perform the transformation. Now fully supports the W3C standard. Runs on Windows platforms.	`msdn.microsoft.com/ downloads`
	Available as a Windows Executable	
Saxon	Saxon is a W3C-compliant processor that comes in two forms. Full Saxon includes Java source, API documentation, and related resources. Instant Saxon is a Windows executable version (without source code). Open Source project.	`saxon.sourceforge. net`
	Available as a Windows Executable	
Sablotron	Sablotron is a W3C compliant processor that runs on multiple platforms, including Windows, Linux, FreeBSD, and more. Open Source project, so its C++ source code can optionally be downloaded.	`www.gingerall.com/ charlie/ga/xml/ p_sab.xml`
	Available as a Windows Executable	
Xalan C++	Xalan-C++ is a W3C compliant XSLT processor written in C++. Runs on multiple platforms, including Windows, Linux, and Solaris. Open Source, includes source code.	`xml.apache.org/ xalan-c`
	Available as a Windows Executable	
Xalan Java	Xalan-Java is a Java-based W3C compliant XSLT processor. It can be used from the command line, in an applet or a servlet, or as a module in other program.	`xml.apache.org/ xalan-j`
XT	Java-based XSLT processor. Includes a downloadable package as a Windows executable for easier running on Windows systems.	`www.jclark.com/xml/ xt.html`
	Available as a Windows Executable	
js.xslt	Another Java-based XSLT processor. Open Source.	`www.aztecrider.com/ xslt`

(continued)

Table 1-2 *(continued)*

Name	Description	Web Address
XML::XSLT	An XSLT processor, written in Perl that fully implements the W3C XSLT recommendation.	`sourceforge.net/ projects/perl-xslt`
libxslt	An XSLT processor written in C that works under Linux, Unix, and Windows.	`xmlsoft.org/XSLT/ intro.html`

To make the task of learning XSLT easier, I recommend you start off by using X-Factor. X-Factor is an easy-to-use software program (see Figure 1-4) that integrates a basic text editor along with the Saxon XSLT processor. It enables allows you to open up your XML source and XSLT stylesheet at the same time, perform transformations with the click of a button, and view the results of the transformation inside the X-Factor window. If you use X-Factor, since Saxon processor is included with it, you don't need to install or configure it.

X-Factor is available as a free download from the *XML All-In-One Desk Reference For Dummies* Extras page on the Web (`www.dummies.com/ extras`). To setup X-Factor, download the setup file and run setup.exe on your computer. The X-Factor setup program guides you through the installation process.

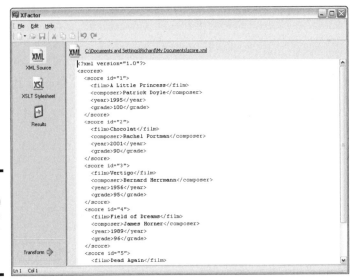

Figure 1-4:
X-Factor, an easy-to-use program for XSLT transformations.

Step 2: Locating or creating an XML document

XSLT always acts on an XML document, so when you have your tools assembled, you are ready to create a simple XML document you can use as a sample. Alternatively, you can download the sample from the *XML All-In-One Desk Reference For Dummies* Extras site on the Web (www.dummies.com/extras) and save yourself a lot time from manually typing in the code.

If you downloaded the book samples, open scores.xml in X-Factor. Or, if you are creating the XML document from scratch, open X-Factor and choose New XML Source File from the File menu. Enter the following code in the XML editor window as shown in Listing 1-2. Save the file as scores.xml.

Listing 1-2   scores.xml

```xml
<?xml version="1.0" encoding="UTF-8"?>

<scores>
  <score id="1">
    <film>A Little Princess</film>
    <composer>Patrick Doyle</composer>
    <year>1995</year>
    <grade>100</grade>
  </score>
  <score id="2">
    <film>Chocolat</film>
    <composer>Rachel Portman</composer>
    <year>2001</year>
    <grade>90</grade>
  </score>
  <score id="3">
    <film>Vertigo</film>
    <composer>Bernard Herrmann</composer>
    <year>1956</year>
    <grade>95</grade>
  </score>
  <score id="4">
    <film>Field of Dreams</film>
    <composer>James Horner</composer>
    <year>1989</year>
    <grade>96</grade>
  </score>
  <score id="5">
    <film>Dead Again</film>
    <composer>Patrick Doyle</composer>
    <year>1991</year>
    <grade>97</grade>
  </score>
</scores>
```

**Book IV
Chapter 1**

**XML's Swiss Army
Knife — XSLT**

Step 3: Determining the output requirements

XSLT transforms something "old" into something "new." But before you can write a stylesheet to do this transformation process, you need to know what that "new" something should look like.

For this example, suppose you need to create a new version of the scores. xml (Listing 1-2) document that has three changes from the original:

+ Change the children of each `score` element into attributes.

+ Remove the `grade` element.

+ Rename the `year` element to `releasedate`.

So, for example, take the first element in scores.xml:

```
<score id="1">
  <film>A Little Princess</film>
  <composer>Patrick Doyle</composer>
  <year>1995</year>
  <grade>100</grade>
</score>
```

With these changes applied, the new element in the result document will be output like:

```
<score id="1" film="A Little Princess" composer="Patrick
  Doyle" releasedate="1995"/>
```

Step 4: Writing your XSLT stylesheet

You are now ready to create an XSLT stylesheet. To do so, return to X-Factor and chose New XSLT Stylesheet from the File menu.

Alternatively, instead of typing in the stylesheet, you can save time by downloading the sample code from the *XML All-In-One Desk Reference For Dummies* Web site (www.dummies.com/extras) and opening up scores.xsl.

If you are typing the stylesheet, enter in the complete XSLT stylesheet shown in Listing 1-3. Save it as `score.xsl` in the same location as your `score.xml` file. By convention, an XSLT stylesheet has an extension of .xsl.

Listing 1-3   scores.xsl

```
<xsl:stylesheet
   xmlns:xsl="http://www.w3.org/1999/XSL/Transform"
   version="1.0">
```

```
<!-- #1 Template rule to convert child elements to attributes
     -->
<xsl:template match="score">
  <score id="{@id}" film="{film}" composer="{composer}"
    releasedate="{year}"/>
  <xsl:apply-templates/>
</xsl:template>

<!-- #2 Remove child elements from appearing as usual in the
           result document -->
<xsl:template match="grade"/>
<xsl:template match="film"/>
<xsl:template match="year"/>
<xsl:template match="composer"/>

<!-- #3 Maintain the scores element -->
<xsl:template match="scores">
  <scores>
  <xsl:apply-templates/>
  </scores>
</xsl:template>
</xsl:stylesheet>
```

Consider what the different parts of the stylesheet do:

+ `score` **template rule.** The first template rule converts the `score` element's children into attributes. It tells the processor to look for each `score` element in the document and, when the processor encounters one, to replace the `score` element's original content with this new structure. The `{@id}` plugs in the value of the `score` element's id attribute. The `{film}`, `{composer}`, and `{year}` expressions fill in the value of the child element that matches the text inside of the brackets.

+ **Empty template rules.** The "empty" template rules remove original child elements from appearing in the result document. Adding these empty template rules are important because the processor assumes by default that all element values should be included in the output document — unless you specifically tell it *not* to include them. If you didn't add these rules, the processor would include their content in the output document both as elements (their original form) and as attributes (the new form defined in the preceding `score` template rule).

+ `scores` **template rule.** The final template rule uses the `apply-templates` instruction to tell the processor to include the contents of the `scores` element in the output. However, `apply-templates` doesn't include the tags of the element — only the content that's inside the tags. Therefore, I re-add the `scores` tags to the output document by placing `apply-templates` in between the `scores` start and end tags.

Don't concern yourself with the details of the template rules just yet. You explore those fully in the next chapter (Book IV, Chapter 2).

Step 5: Processing the stylesheet

All the various pieces are now ready to go. Let the transformation begin!

If you are using X-Factor, you can apply the XSLT stylesheet to the XML source document you created by clicking the Transform button. X-Factor kicks off the Saxon processor behind-the-scenes to process the transformation and display the results in the Results view.

Step 6: Viewing the result document

After the transformation finishes in X-Factor, you have a new XML document that is shown in the Results view, as shown in Figure 1-5.

You see a lot of extra spaces in the result document. Don't worry about these now — an XML processor ignores this whitespace. However, you can get rid of this extra whitespace when you need to, as explained fully in Book IV, Chapter 6.

Figure 1-5:
X-Factor's Results view shows you the results of a transformation

Chapter 2: Powered by Template Rules

In This Chapter

✓ Understanding template rules

✓ Accounting for built-in template rules

✓ Using xsl:apply-templates to apply templates

✓ Copying nodes using xsl:copy and xsl:copy-to

✓ Generating text with xsl:text

✓ Understanding attribute value templates

✓ Exploring named templates

*I*f you were invited to see a Formula One race car up close and in person, chances are you'd probably start with a tour around the car itself and then jump into the cockpit to see what it felt like to sit in the driver's seat of a race car. However, if you really wanted to know how the vehicle achieves the speeds that it does, you'd have to "pop the hood" and look up close at the 800-horsepower engine that propels the car to blazing speeds.

In Book IV, Chapter 1, you took a tour of XSLT, even stepping into the driver's seat as you transformed your first XML document. However, in order to really understand how XSLT works, you have to dive under the hood and explore template rules, the engine that powers any XSLT transformation. This chapter gives you that turbo boost as you explore the ins and outs of template rules. Vroom!

Understanding Template Rules

At the heart of any XSLT stylesheet is one or more template rules. A *template rule* transforms a set of nodes you specify from the source XML document into a new output in the result document. It is defined using the `xsl:template` element and consists of two key parts: the match pattern and the template (see Figure 2-1).

See Book IV, Chapter 1 for a full details on *nodes*.

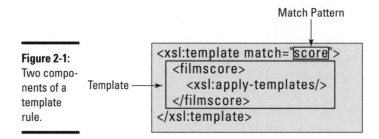

Match Pattern

Figure 2-1:
Two compo-
nents of a
template
rule.

Template

```
<xsl:template match="score">
    <filmscore>
        <xsl:apply-templates/>
    </filmscore>
</xsl:template>
```

Extracting with match patterns

A template rule uses a match pattern to define what information is taken
from the source XML document and used in the transformation. A *match
pattern* is an XPath expression that specifies the conditions that a node must
meet in order for it to be included in the result document.

A match pattern takes the form of a specific XPath expression called a
location path (see the "Express yourself with XPath" sidebar) and is placed
in the stylesheet as the value of the `match` attribute of an `xsl:template`
element.

XPath location paths are the subject of the next chapter (Book IV, Chapter 3),
but let me provide a brief overview to help you understand how location
paths are used within the match pattern to retrieve nodes for the template
rule.

Consider the XML file shown in Listing 2-1 as the source XML document.

Listing 2-1   scores.xml

```
<?xml version="1.0" encoding="utf-8"?>
<scores>
  <score id="1">
    <film>A Little Princess</film>
    <composer>Patrick Doyle</composer>
    <year>1995</year>
    <grade>100</grade>
  </score>
  <score id="2">
    <film>Chocolat</film>
    <composer>Rachel Portman</composer>
    <year>2001</year>
    <grade>90</grade>
```

```
  </score>
  <score id="3">
    <film>Vertigo</film>
    <composer>Bernard Herrmann</composer>
    <year>1956</year>
    <grade>95</grade>
  </score>
  <score id="4">
    <film>Field of Dreams</film>
    <composer>James Horner</composer>
    <year>1989</year>
    <grade>96</grade>
  </score>
  <score id="5">
    <film>Dead Again</film>
    <composer>Patrick Doyle</composer>
    <year>1991</year>
    <grade>97</grade>
  </score>
  <!-- Scores 6 to 10 added later -->
</scores>
```

Suppose I want to retrieve the film elements in my template rule. To do so, I set my match pattern to be the name of the element:

```
<xsl:template match="film">
  <!-- Do something with the film elements -->
</xsl:template>
```

When the template rule is triggered, the XSLT processor examines each of the nodes in the source document in turn, looking for a child of that node that is named *film*. When the processor finds a match, the node is added to the set of nodes that are returned to the template rule. In this example, the match pattern returns all five film element nodes to the template rule.

Express yourself with XPath

An *XPath expression* is a string of instructions that the XSLT processor evaluates to produce a result, which may be a number, string, boolean value, or a node set. However, when you work with XSLT, you focus on a more specific type of XPath expression called a location path. A *location path* is an expression that specifies what nodes to bring back to the template rule. See Book IV, Chapter 3 for complete details on XPath and location paths.

Tree hugging

Whether or not you're an environmentalist, if you transform using XSLT, you can call yourself a "tree hugger." As Book IV, Chapter 1 discusses, XML source and result documents are treated as "trees" by XSLT because they have a hierarchical structure to them. Therefore, the terms "source document" and "source tree" are interchangeable, as are "result document" and "result tree."

Outputting with templates

While the match pattern retrieves nodes, the other half of a template rule — the template — defines how the returning node set is output to the result tree. A template contains two types of information:

✦ **Literal text:** Plain text that is simply copied to the result tree as is.

✦ **XSLT instructions:** XSLT instructions that generate text or nodes for the result document. The usual XSLT instructions you'll use include `xsl:apply-templates`, `xsl:copy`, `xsl:copy-of`, and `xsl:value-of`.

For example, check out the following template rule:

```
<xsl:template match="score">
  The film: <xsl:value-of select="film"/>
</xsl:template>
```

The `film:` is literal text, and the `xsl:value-of` instruction is evaluated at processing time to generate text for the result document.

The terms *template* and *template rule* are easily confused; keep in mind that a *template rule* is the entire `xsl:template` element, while the *template* is everything inside the start and end tags of `xsl:template`.

Understanding Built-In Template Rules

Before you begin writing your own template rules, you first need to know about the default template rules that are already defined by XSLT itself. When you perform a transformation, these *built-in template rules* are applied by the XSLT processor to any node that isn't matched with an explicitly defined template rule in your stylesheet.

A solid awareness and understanding of built-in template rules is essential for working with XSLT. If you forget about them, you'll be confused as to what happened in your transformation and why.

To demonstrate how built-in templates work, I'll create a blank stylesheet:

```
<xsl:stylesheet
    xmlns:xsl="http://www.w3.org/1999/XSL/Transform"
    version="1.0">

</xsl:stylesheet>
```

When the processor applies this empty stylesheet to the scores.xml file (Listing 2-1), there are no template rules written in the stylesheet to produce any results in the output document. However, something clearly happens when the empty stylesheet is applied, as shown in the result document in Listing 2-2.

Listing 2-2   Results of built-in template transformation

```
<?xml version="1.0" encoding="utf-8"?>

A Little Princess
Patrick Doyle
1995
100

Chocolat
Rachel Portman
2001
90


Vertigo
Bernard Herrmann
1956
95


Field of Dreams
James Horner
1989
96


Dead Again
Patrick Doyle
1991
97
```

The output shown in Listing 2-2 is an illustration of the behind-the-scenes magic of built-in template rules. Because every node in a source XML document is transformed by some template rule, the processor looks for the best rule to handle that specific node. It looks first in your stylesheet, but if you didn't define one that fits the node being evaluated, then it turns to its built-in template rule.

Each node type has its own customized built-in template rule:

+ *Element nodes* have a built-in template that strips off their tags and the tags of its child elements but outputs the content of these elements into the result document. In Listing 2-2, the resulting output is actually the content of each of the elements in the scores.xml file.

+ *Text nodes* have a built-in template rule that copies their text straight into the result tree. In the example shown in Listing 2-2, the content of the element nodes are actually text nodes.

+ *Attribute nodes* have a built-in template rule that adds them to the result tree if tags of its parent element are included. For the Listing 2-2 example, because the element tags are not added to the result, the attribute nodes are not included in the result document.

+ *Processing instruction, comment, and namespace nodes* have a built-in template rule that strips them from the result document. There were no processing instructions or namespaces to speak of in Listing 2-2, although there was a comment at the end of the document that was removed during transformation.

Working with the Major XSLT Instructions

There are four main XSLT instructions that you use within the template of a template rule to generate text or nodes for the result document:

+ `xsl:apply-templates`
+ `xsl:copy`
+ `xsl:copy-of`
+ `xsl:value-of`

The following sections discuss these instructions.

Top-level XSLT elements, such as `xsl:template` or `xsl:output`, are typically referred to as *elements*. XSLT elements in the template rule that are used to generate part of the result tree are often called *instructions*.

Applying templates with xsl:apply-templates

The `xsl:apply-templates` element is the most commonly used instruction inside template rules, but arguably has the cloudiest purpose. The syntax for `xsl:apply-templates` is:

```
<xsl:apply-templates select="expression"/>
```

The `select` attribute (shown in italic) is optional.

Think of `xsl:apply-templates` as playing the role of manager in a template rule that is being processed: it doesn't get its hands dirty doing the actual work of outputting to the result document; instead it is responsible for telling other templates what to do. Listen in on a typical conversion within a template rule:

> *Andy Apply-Templates: Hey, Timmy the Template Rule! Get to that* `film` *node pronto and apply yourself!*
>
> *Timmy: Sure thing, boss.*
>
> *Andy: And you, Billy the Built-in Template Rule, Sally the Stylesheet has no defined template rules. So, you've got to handle it!*
>
> *Billy: I won't let you down.*

Rather than generating output itself, `xsl:apply-template` simply invokes the template rule most appropriate for the context. In some cases, the template rule called upon is the one that contains the `xsl:apply-templates` instruction. But in other cases, it may actually be another template rule defined in your stylesheet. Finally, if nothing else is found, then the XSLT processor applies one of XSLT's built-in template rules for the node set in question.

The `xsl:apply-templates` instruction processes all nodes and the children of those nodes within its scope. If the `select` attribute is not defined, then it processes all the nodes in the node set returned from the match pattern of the template rule it is inside of. Or, if a `select` attribute is included with the instruction, then the expression in the `select` attribute is run against the node set returned from the template rule match pattern. Only the nodes returned by this `select` expression are then processed.

To illustrate the use of `xsl:apply-templates`, I use the tv.xml shown in Listing 2-3 as the source XML document.

Listing 2-3   tv.xml

```xml
<?xml version="1.0" encoding="utf-8"?>
<tv>
    <model>1010</model>
    <type>WideScreen</type>
    <aspectratio>16x9</aspectratio>
</tv>
```

Applying all nodes inside a template rule

In stylesheet below, the lone template rule includes an `xsl:apply-tem-plates` instruction to process the `tv` element and its children (`model`, `type`, and `aspectratio`) from the tv.xml document (Listing 2-3):

```xml
<xsl:stylesheet
    xmlns:xsl="http://www.w3.org/1999/XSL/Transform"
    version="1.0">
  <xsl:template match="tv">
    <xsl:apply-templates/>
  </xsl:template>
</xsl:stylesheet>
```

Because no other template rules exist, `xsl:apply-templates` processes the `tv` node and its children using their built-in templates to send their content to the result tree. Because the `tv` element has no text content itself, no text is added to the result tree. However, because the `tv` element has three child elements that do have content (text nodes), these text nodes are transferred to the result document:

```
1010
WideScreen
16x9
```

Applying selected nodes

When I define a `select` attribute for `xsl:apply-templates`, only selected nodes are processed, not all of them within the match pattern. For example:

```xml
<xsl:stylesheet
    xmlns:xsl="http://www.w3.org/1999/XSL/Transform"
    version="1.0">
  <xsl:template match="tv">
    <xsl:apply-templates select="aspectratio"/>
  </xsl:template>
</xsl:stylesheet>
```

In this case, only the `aspectratio` element is applied by `xsl:apply-templates`; the `tv`, `model`, and `type` elements are not processed at all. The results are as follows:

```
16x9
```

Or, suppose you add two `xsl:apply-templates` instructions to get a new result:

```
<xsl:stylesheet
    xmlns:xsl="http://www.w3.org/1999/XSL/Transform"
    version="1.0">
  <xsl:template match="tv">
Model <xsl:apply-templates select="model"/> has an aspect
    ratio of <xsl:apply-templates select="aspectratio"/>
  </xsl:template>
</xsl:stylesheet>
```

The results are shown here:

```
Model 1010 has an aspect ratio of 16x9
```

Applying multiple template rules

As said before, the XSLT processor processes each node by determining which is the best template rule to use. If one hasn't been explicitly defined, then the built-in template rule is called on. Consider the following example:

```
<xsl:stylesheet
    xmlns:xsl="http://www.w3.org/1999/XSL/Transform"
    version="1.0">

<xsl:template match="tv">
    <description>Model <xsl:apply-templates select="model"/>
    has an aspect ratio of <xsl:apply-templates
    select="aspectratio"/></description>
  </xsl:template>

<xsl:template match="aspectratio">N/A</xsl:template>

</xsl:stylesheet>
```

In this stylesheet, all `tv` elements and their children are processed using the first template rule. For the first `xsl:apply-templates` instruction, no defined template rule exists for model, so its built-in template rule is called. However, when the `xsl:apply-templates` instruction is called for the `aspectratio` element, the second template rule in the stylesheet is called on. Therefore, the literal text N/A is inserted into the result document rather than the content of aspectratio. The results are:

```
<description>Model 1010 has an aspect ratio of
    N/A</description>
```

Copying nodes with xsl:copy and xsl:copy-of

Two XSLT instructions deal with copying nodes from the source to the result document: xsl:copy and xsl:copy-of. While similar in name, the behavior of each of these two is quite distinct from the other. Table 2-1 summarizes the major features of each copy instruction and helps you determine what works best for your situation.

Table 2-1	xsl:copy vs.xsl:copy-of	
Feature	*xsl:copy*	*xsl:copy-of*
select attribute	No. Copies the nodes resulting from the template rule's match pattern.	Required. Copies all nodes returned from the select expression.
Copy element tags	Yes	Yes
Copy children	No	Yes
Copy attributes	No	Yes
Copy content	Copies content only if you put an xsl:apply-templates inside the xsl:copy element. An empty xsl:copy doesn't copy content.	Yes
Copy comments and processing instructions	No	Yes

xsl:copy

The xsl:copy instruction copies the current node and has a basic syntax of:

```
<xsl:copy>
    <!-- Template body -->
</xsl:copy>
```

To illustrate how it can be used, I'll use the miniscore.xml file (Listing 2-4) as my source document.

Listing 2-4   miniscore.xml

```
<?xml version="1.0" encoding="utf-8"?>
<score id="1">
  <film>A Little Princess</film>
  <composer>Patrick Doyle</composer>
  <year>1995</year>
  <grade>100</grade>
</score>
```

By default, xsl:copy copies only the tags of an element. For example, by defining an empty `xsl:copy` instruction to the following template rule, I can copy the `composer` element tags:

```
<xsl:template match="composer">
  <xsl:copy/>
</xsl:template>
```

The output of this template is `<composer></composer>`, but the XSLT processor shortens the empty tag to the following:

```
<composer/>
```

The `xsl:copy` instruction can contain `xsl:apply-templates` to copy both the tags and its content. For example:

```
<xsl:template match="composer">
  <xsl:copy>
    <xsl:apply-templates/>
  </xsl:copy>
</xsl:template>
```

When this template rule is applied to miniscore.xml (Listing 2-4), the result is:

```
<composer>Patrick Doyle</composer>
```

If you use `xsl:copy` and `xsl:apply-templates` on a node that contains children, then the current node's tags are preserved, but the children are processed using the normal `xsl:apply-templates` rules (see the "Applying templates with xsl:apply-templates" section earlier in the chapter). For example:

```
<xsl:template match="score">
  <xsl:copy>
    <xsl:apply-templates/>
  </xsl:copy>
</xsl:template>
```

**Book IV
Chapter 2**

**Powered by
Template Rules**

Game, set, match

For each node in the source document, the XSLT processor looks at the list of available template rules and determines which is a match for the current node. However, when more than one template rule actually matches the node, the processor has to determine which is the *best* template to use.

XSLT prioritizes template rules based on a fairly complex system of weighting, but the following table shows a simplified look at the common scenarios (where Level 1 is highest priority, Level 4 is lowest).

Priority of Common Template Rules

Level	Description of Rule	Example
1 (most specific)	Element name with a filter	`<xsl:template match="score[@id='1']">`
1	Element as part of a path	`<xsl:template match="scores/score">`
2	Element name	`<xsl:template match="score">`
3	Nodetest	`<xsl:template match="node()">` or `<xsl:template match="*">`
4	Built-in template rule	`<xsl:template match="*|/">`

To illustrate, suppose I use the `score.xml` file (shown in Listing 2-1) as the source document and then want to apply the following XSLT stylesheet:

```
<xsl:stylesheet
   xmlns:xsl="http://www.w3.
   org/1999/XSL/Transform"
   version="1.0">
 <xsl:output method="xml"
   omit-xml-
   declaration="yes"/>
 <xsl:template match="score">
  Almost: <xsl:apply-
   templates select="film"/>
 </xsl:template>
 <xsl:template
   match="score[@id='1']">
  The Best: <xsl:apply-
   templates select="film"/>
 </xsl:template>
</xsl:stylesheet>
```

The first template rule returns a match when the current node has a `score` element node as a child. The second template rule returns a positive match when the current node has a `score` element node with an `id` attribute that equals 1.

When the source document is processed, the XSLT processor finds two template rules that match when the current node is found to have a `score` element node with an `id` attribute equaling 1. However, the second template rule, being more specific to this particular node, is considered higher in priority; as a result, the node is matched to the second template rule, not the first. The result document is shown below:

```
The Best: A Little Princess
Almost: Chocolat
Almost: Vertigo
Almost: Field of Dreams
Almost: Dead Again
```

This template rule generates the following results when applied to miniscore.xml:

```
<score>
  A Little Princess
  Patrick Doyle
  1995
  100
</score>
```

xsl:copy-of

As shown in Table 2-1, the behavior of xsl:copy-of is more powerful than xsl:copy and has a basic syntax of:

```
<xsl:copy-of select="expression"/>
```

Suppose I want to copy the score element from miniscore.xml (Listing 2-4) to the result document. I can set up the following template rule to do this:

```
<xsl:template match="score">
  <xsl:copy-of select="."/>
</xsl:template>
```

The match pattern of the template rule returns a score element, and the . expression inside the select attribute of the xsl:copy-to returns the context node and all of its children to generate the following output:

```
<score id="1">
  <film>A Little Princess</film>
  <composer>Patrick Doyle</composer>
  <year>1995</year>
  <grade>100</grade>
</score>
```

Suppose you want to copy just year element. You can use the following template rule to perform this action:

```
<xsl:template match="score">
  <xsl:copy-of select="year"/>
</xsl:template>
```

This template rule results in a literal copy of only the year element (both tags and content):

```
<year>1995</year>
```

**Book IV
Chapter 2**

**Powered by
Template Rules**

Outputting a string with xsl:value-of

The xsl:value-of instruction is used when you want to output text to the source document. Its syntax is:

```
<xsl:value-of select="expression"/>
```

xsl:value-of converts the result from its required select attribute to a string and adds it as a text node to the result tree. If the result is a single element, then its contents are converted to text. If the result is a node set (such as a node with children), then just the first node is converted to text and the rest are ignored.

With miniscore.xml (Listing 2-4) as the source document, suppose I use xsl:value-of on a single element (film). The template rule is shown below:

```
<xsl:template match="score">
  <xsl:value-of select="film"/>
</xsl:template>
```

When this template rule is applied, the film element contents are converted to text:

```
A Little Princess
```

xsl:value-of can also be used to convert an attribute value to a string. For example, check out the use of a special @ character in the select attribute to reference the id attribute value:

```
<xsl:template match="score">
  <xsl:value-of select="@id"/>
</xsl:template>
```

The following output is generated:

```
1
```

A common mistake many XSLT stylesheet authors make is to use a match attribute in place of the select attribute in an xsl:copy-of, xsl:apply-templates, or xsl:value-of instruction. The xsl:template element gets a match attribute while the other instructions get a select attribute.

Deciding which instruction to use

Knowing which instruction to use at a given time can seem perplexing. After all, xsl:apply-templates and xsl:value-of look like they do the same thing under certain conditions. And xsl:copy and xsl:copy-of seem to kinda do the same thing, too. Therefore, keep the following pointers in mind as you decide which instructions to use:

✦ Use xsl:apply-templates when you want to process a node and its children.

✦ Use xsl:copy to preserve the current node's start and end tags during processing, but not its child elements or attributes. An element node's content is included in the process only if you add an xsl:apply-templates instruction inside the xsl:copy instruction.

✦ Use xsl:copy-of when you want to duplicate an entire node, including its tags, content, attributes, and children.

✦ Use xsl:value-of when you want to convert the result of its select attribute to text.

Using Attribute Value Templates

Inside a template rule designed to generate XML or HTML elements, you may need to add the result of an XPath expression as the value of an attribute. However, the processor doesn't necessarily know whether the quoted text in the template is an expression to be evaluated or literal text to be copied as is to the result document. To solve this dilemma, XSLT provides an *attribute value template* that is a set of curly brackets ({ }) that tell the processor that the contents of the brackets should be treated as an expression rather than literal text.

For example, using the miniscore.xml document (Listing 2-4) as the source file, suppose I'd like to convert each of the score's child elements to attributes, causing the end result to appear as follows:

```
<score year="1995" grade="100" composer="Patrick Doyle"
    film="A Little Princess"/>
```

To perform this transformation, I create the following stylesheet:

```
<xsl:stylesheet
    xmlns:xsl="http://www.w3.org/1999/XSL/Transform"
    version="1.0">

  <xsl:template match="score">
    <score year="{year}" grade="{grade}"
    composer="{composer}" film="{film}"/>
    <xsl:apply-templates/>
  </xsl:template>
```

```
    <xsl:template match="film"/>
    <xsl:template match="composer"/>
    <xsl:template match="year"/>
    <xsl:template match="grade"/>
</xsl:stylesheet>
```

In the first template, I enclose the name of each child node in curly brackets to create attribute value templates. They flag the XSLT processor to evaluate their contents as an expression.

In addition, I define several empty template rules for the child elements of `score` to ensure that they don't appear as elements in the result tree. If I didn't explicitly define these empty template rules, they'd be added twice to the result document: once as attributes (through the attribute value templates in the first template) and a second time as element content (through `xsl:apply-templates`, which would have triggered their built-in template rules).

Working with Named Templates

A *named template* is an `xsl:template` element that has a `name` attribute but no defined `match` attribute. However, because it doesn't have a `match` attribute, in order for the template rule to be processed, another template rule or element must explicitly call it using the `xsl:call-template` instruction.

To demonstrate how named templates can be utilized, I turn again to the miniscore.xml (see Listing 2-4) as the source document. Suppose I want to add a text string to several of the template rules being processed. Instead of copying and pasting the same text string to each template rule, I can instead create a single named template that is called by each of the template rules. To that end, check out the XSLT stylesheet that follows:

```
<xsl:stylesheet
    xmlns:xsl="http://www.w3.org/1999/XSL/Transform"
    version="1.0">

  <xsl:template name="Copyright">
    <xsl:value-of select="."/>
Copyright, 2003. All Rights Reserved.
  </xsl:template>

  <xsl:template match="film">
    Film: <xsl:call-template name="Copyright"/>
  </xsl:template>
```

```
<xsl:template match="composer">
  Composer: <xsl:call-template name="Copyright"/>
</xsl:template>

<xsl:template match="year"/>
<xsl:template match="grade"/>

</xsl:stylesheet>
```

The first template rule defines the named template. If called by another template rule, the name template adds text to the result document using `xsl:value-of`.

The next two template rules make use of the `xsl:call-template` instruction to call the `Copyright` named template. The output generated is shown below:

```
Film: A Little Princess - Copyright, 2003. All Rights
  Reserved.

Composer: Patrick Doyle - Copyright, 2003. All Rights
  Reserved.
```

To find out how to use named templates in combination with parameters, see Book IV, Chapter 5.

Chapter 3: XPath — Scouting Out XML Data

*W*hether it is *Lord of the Rings, The Matrix,* or *Star Wars,* every sci-fi film always seems to have a creature or droid that is charged with being the scout that gathers information for the evil villain, usually the whereabouts of the hero you and I are rooting for. The scout doesn't usually do anything with the information, but instead passes it off to its boss to do whatever he, she, or it chooses.

XPath is the scout of the XML world and does the legwork for XSLT and other XML technologies as they work with XML documents. In this chapter, I introduce you to XPath and how to work with the most important of XPath expressions called a location step. You also discover how to work with XPath built-in functions.

XPath, the XML Scout

Programming languages are often designed for quite distinct uses. The general purpose languages like Java and C++ get much of the fame and glory, while markup languages like XML and HTML are increasingly getting their share as well. However, other languages have more targeted uses. SQL (Structured Query Language) is an example from the database world of a language designed not to create applications, but simply to get data from databases. In the XML world, XPath is much like this targeted query language.

XPath is a language employed by many XML technologies — such as XSLT, XPointer, and XForms — as a way to seek out information (or, more precisely, *nodes*) in an XML document. XPath truly is the "scout" of the XML world; it is responsible for diving into a given XML document and retrieving particular nodes that match a profile provided to it. XPath then returns that information to the technology using it, such as XSLT, for actually doing something with the nodes that are returned.

Stepping Down the Location Path

A *location step* is an XPath expression that enables you to locate a node in the source document. Location steps are the primary units you use when working with XPath expressions. A location step consists of an axis, a node test, and an optional predicate:

✦ **Axis.** The axis deals primarily with *relationships*. It defines the relationship of the nodes you are targeting with respect to the context node.

✦ **Node test.** The node test focuses on *identification*. From the pool of nodes that were selected by the axis, the node test identifies the specific nodes that can meet certain conditions.

✦ **Predicate.** The predicate is a *filter*. A predicate allows you to optionally filter out some of the unwanted nodes that are returned by the axis and node test parts.

In XPath syntax, a location step takes the following form:

```
axis::nodetest[predicate]
```

An XSLT processor uses a location step to get a result set. A given node is evaluated against the location step:

✦ Does the node match the relationship requirement that is specified by the axis?

✦ If so, does the node then pass the criteria set by the node test?

✦ If so and if there's a predicate, then does the node avoid getting sifted out by the predicate's filter?

If a node passes all three of these tests, it is included in the result set.

For example, consider the following location step:

```
child::country[@name]
```

When a source document is processed by an XSLT processor, it evaluates each node, initially using the `child::` axis to return all the context node's children as a node set. Then, using the `country` node test, the processor retrieves the child nodes that are `country` element nodes. And, as a last step, the processor runs the nodes through the `@name` predicate to filter out all `country` elements that do not have a `name` attribute defined.

A *location path* is a set of one or more location steps. A / is used to separate each step if there are multiple steps defined. For example, `continent/country` is a location path with two location steps (`continent` and `country`).

Location paths are read in a left-to-right manner and indicate the hierarchical relationship between steps. In the previous example, the `country` element is a child of the `continent` element. So, XPath goes first to the `continent` element and then looks for a child element inside of it named `country`.

Axes: It's All Relative

A location step's axis is chiefly concerned with relationships between the context node and the nodes that you want to retrieve. Table 3-1 lists the 13 axes, along with an optional abbreviated syntax you can use.

Table 3-1	XPath Axes	
Axis	*Relationship to Context Node*	*Abbreviation (if any)*
`child`	Children of context node	No axis provided implicitly means child axis
`self`	Context node	`self::node()` is same as .
`parent`	Parent of the context node (always a single node)	`parent::node()` is same as ..
`attribute`	All attributes of the context node	@

(continued)

Table 3-1 *(continued)*

Axis	Relationship to Context Node	Abbreviation *(if any)*
descendant	Children of context node, plus all descendants under them	
ancestor	Parent of the context node, plus all of its ancestors (including the root node)	
ancestor-or-self	Context node and all of its ancestor nodes (including the root node)	
following-sibling	Siblings appearing after the context node	
preceding-sibling	Siblings appearing before the context node	
following	All nodes appearing after the context node	
preceding	All nodes appearing before the context node	
namespace	All namespace nodes of the context node	
descendant-or-self	Context node and all of its descendant nodes.	descendant-or-self:: node() is the same as //

However, in addition to relationships, the axis also specifies the direction from the context node that the processor will traverse the source document. For most axes, the direction is top-to-bottom, left-to-right. But there are a few axes — ancestor, ancestor-or-self, preceding, and preceding-sibling — that navigate the source tree in reverse order.

To illustrate, using a descendant axis, the processor begins at the context node and identifies the first descendant and proceeds downward until the last descendant is reached in a downward, left-to-right fashion. On the other hand, using a preceding axis, the processor moves in a bottom-to-top, right-to-left manner, starting with the node that appears to the left or above the context node and climbing to the top of the document tree.

Using the child axis

The child axis is the most commonly used axis value and is used to identify each of the child nodes of the context node (see Figure 3-1). The order of the nodes is based on the sequence of the children in the document.

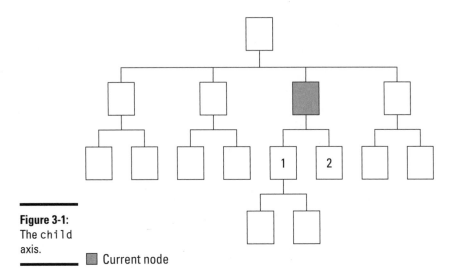

Figure 3-1:
The child
axis.

■ Current node

To illustrate, consider the following `continent` XML structure:

```
<!-- continent.xml -->
<continent name="Africa">
  <region name="Sahel">
    <country>Burkina Faso<country>
    <country>Mail<country>
    <country>Mauritania<country>
    <country>Niger<country>
  </region>
  <region name="West Africa">
    <country>Senegal<country>
    <country>Sierra Leone<country>
    <country>Liberia<country>
    <country>Nigeria<country>
    <country>Benin<country>
  </region>
  <region name="North Africa">
    <country>Morocco<country>
    <country>Tunisia<country>
    <country>Libya<country>
    <country>Algeria<country>
    <country>Egypt<country>
  </region>
</continent>
```

Suppose you wanted to get a list of African countries. To get that result set, you could define a template rule like this:

```
<xsl:template match="child::country">
 <xsl:apply-templates/>
</xsl:template>
```

The match pattern for the template rule uses the `child` axis to look for all children elements of the context node that has the name of `country`. The template rule uses the `xsl:apply-templates` instruction to return the country names, producing the following output:

```
Burkina Faso
Mail
Mauritania
Niger


Senegal
Sierra Leone
Liberia
Nigeria
Benin


Morocco
Tunisia
Libya
Algeria
Egypt
```

Interestingly, while `child` is the most common axis used, you rarely see `child` in XSLT templates. The reason is that, because `child` is the default axis for a location, you can leave it out and `child` will become the implicit axis value.

From my previous example, I can remove the `child::` from the template rule and get an identical result:

```
<xsl:template match="country">
 <xsl:apply-templates/>
</xsl:template>
```

Using the attribute axis

Another frequently used axis type is `attribute`, which selects all attributes of the context node. For example, if you would like to retrieve the `region` names from the `continent.xml` file, you could create a template rule as follows:

```
<xsl:template match="child::region">
<xsl:value-of select="attribute::name"/>
</xsl:template>
```

This template rule looks for each `region` child of the context node and then uses `xsl:value-of` to output the value of its `name` attribute. The results are:

```
Sahel
West Africa
North Africa
```

The `attribute::` axis uses the @ symbol as an abbreviation, making the following template rule equivalent to the one shown above:

```
<xsl:template match="region">
<xsl:value-of select="@name"/>
</xsl:template>
```

Using the parent axis

The `parent` axis selects the node above of the context node, as Figure 3-2 demonstrates. While `child` and other axes may refer to one or more nodes, `parent` always selects just a single node. You've heard the expression of "being an only child"; in contrast, XML has an "only parent" mentality because it is impossible to have two nodes be the parent of a child.

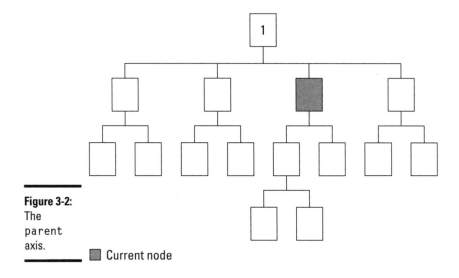

Figure 3-2: The parent axis.

■ Current node

The parent axis doesn't have an abbreviation by itself, but you can combine the parent axis and the node() node test together (parent::node()) and shorten it to double periods (..).

For example, suppose you wanted to list the name of each country listed in continents.xml and then identify the region in which that the country is located. To do so, you could set up a template rule that looks like:

```
<xsl:template match="country">
<xsl:apply-templates/> is located in the <xsl:value-of
    select="../@name"/>
</xsl:template>
```

The expression ../@name is equivalent to parent::node()/attribute::name/.

This template rule selects all the country elements and uses xsl:apply-templates to output their content. The xsl:value-of instruction uses a location path (a series of location steps separated by / characters) to traverse the tree to get the parent node's name. Specifically, the first location step .. selects the parent node of the context node, regardless of its type. Next, the second location step @name retrieves the name attribute value of the parent. Remember, the / symbol describes the hierarchical relationship between the parent element (region) and its child name attribute.

The result of this template rule is shown below:

```
Burkina Faso is located in the Sahel
Mail is located in the Sahel
Mauritania is located in the Sahel
Niger is located in the Sahel


Senegal is located in the West Africa
Sierra Leone is located in the West Africa
Liberia is located in the West Africa
Nigeria is located in the West Africa
Benin is located in the West Africa


Morocco is located in the North Africa
Tunisia is located in the North Africa
Libya is located in the North Africa
Algeria is located in the North Africa
Egypt is located in the North Africa
```

Using the self axis

If you want to select the context node itself, you can use the self axis. Like parent, self doesn't have an abbreviation by itself, but when used in combination with the node() node test, self::node() is shortened to a single period (.).

For example, you can use the . shortcut in the following template rule to return the value of the context node:

```
<xsl:template match="country">
<xsl:value-of select="."/> is located in Africa.
</xsl:template>
```

The . is the same as self::node().

The end result is:

Burkina Faso is located in Africa.

Mail is located in Africa.

Mauritania is located in Africa.

Niger is located in Africa.

Senegal is located in Africa.

Sierra Leone is located in Africa.

Liberia is located in Africa.

Nigeria is located in Africa.

Benin is located in Africa.

Morocco is located in Africa.

Tunisia is located in Africa.

Libya is located in Africa.

Algeria is located in Africa.

Egypt is located in Africa.

Using the descendant and descendant-or-self axes

The `descendant` axis selects all the nodes underneath the context node regardless of the level, including children, grandchildren, great grandchildren, and continuing on until the last node (see Figure 3-3). The `descendant-or-self` axis differs only in that it also selects the context node with all of its descendants (see Figure 3-4).

The `descendant-or-self` axis comes in handy when you are unsure of the levels between nodes.

Another common XPath abbreviation is `//`, which is short for `/descendant-or-self::node()`.

To illustrate, suppose you wanted to get the value of all the name attributes in the `continents.xml` document, regardless of the level. Using `/descendant-or-self::node()` (or `//` for short), you can create the following template rule shown that outputs the names for the `continent` element and the `region` elements:

```
<xsl:template match="continent">
<xsl:apply-templates select="//@name"/>
</xsl:template>
```

If you don't concern yourself with whitespace issues, the raw output is:

```
AfricaSahelWest AfricaNorth Africa
```

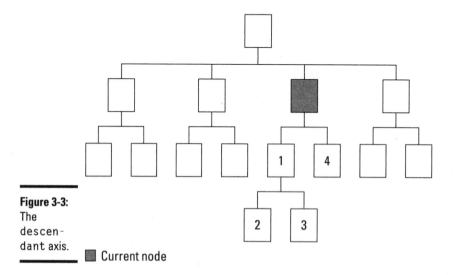

Figure 3-3:
The descendant axis.

■ Current node

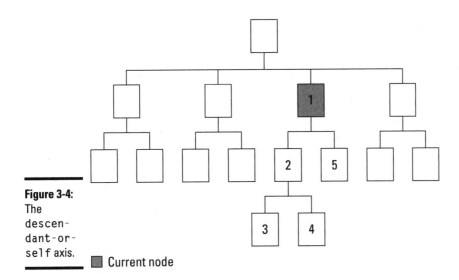

Figure 3-4:
The descendant-or-self axis.

■ Current node

As you can see, the `continent` node is selected by the template rule's match pattern. The `xsl:apply-templates` instruction then outputs all the values of the `name` attributes, regardless of their level.

Using the ancestor and ancestor-or-self axes

The `ancestor` axis selects all the nodes above of the context node, including parent, grandparent, and great-grandparent. The `ancestor-or-self` axis selects the context node along with its ancestors (see Figures 3-5 and 3-6). Both of these axes come in handy when the node you are looking for is above the context node in the hierarchy but could be one of many levels.

Abbreviations for XPath axes

XPath provides some abbreviated ways to write axes, including the following:

✔ `child::` axis does not need to be explicitly defined, so you can leave it off.

✔ `attribute::` can be shortened to `@`.

✔ `self::node()` is abbreviated to `.` (single period).

✔ `parent::node()` is shortened to `..` (double period).

✔ `/descendant-or-self::node()/` is reduced to `//`.

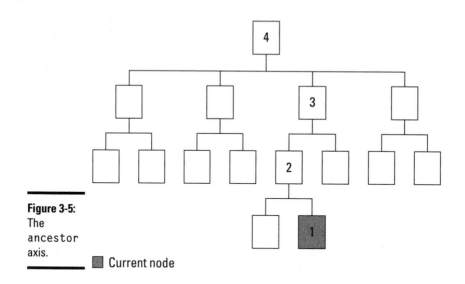

Figure 3-5:
The ancestor axis.

▫ Current node

For example, consider the following template rule:

```
<xsl:template match="country">
  <xsl:apply-templates select="ancestor::node()/@name"/>
</xsl:template>
```

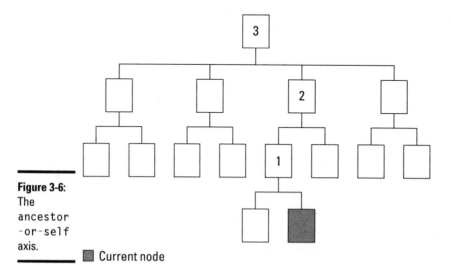

Figure 3-6:
The ancestor
-or-self
axis.

▫ Current node

For each `country` node encountered, the names of the ancestors are out-putted. Again, if you don't concern yourself with formatting issues, here's the result:

```
AfricaSahel
AfricaSahel
AfricaSahel
AfricaSahel

AfricaWest Africa
AfricaWest Africa
AfricaWest Africa
AfricaWest Africa
AfricaWest Africa

AfricaNorth Africa
AfricaNorth Africa
AfricaNorth Africa
AfricaNorth Africa
AfricaNorth Africa
```

Using the preceding-sibling and following-sibling axes

The `preceding-sibling` and `following-sibling` axes are used to select all the nodes on the same level as the context node in either forward or backward direction, as shown in Figures 3-7 and 3-8.

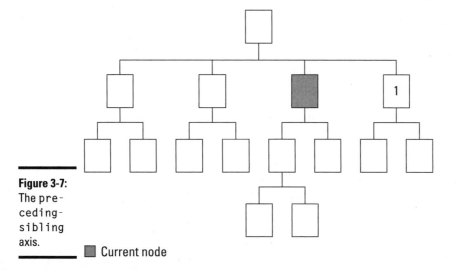

Figure 3-7: The preceding-sibling axis.

■ Current node

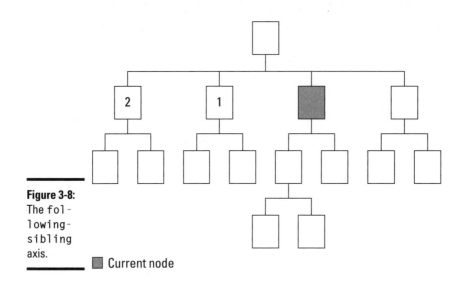

Figure 3-8:
The fol-
lowing-
sibling
axis.

■ Current node

Using the preceding and following axes

While `preceding-sibling` and `following-sibling` select only nodes on the same level as the context node, the `preceding` and `following` axes have a broader scope selecting all nodes in forward or backward direction, regardless of their level in the document. Figures 3-9 and 3-10 show these axes and their direction.

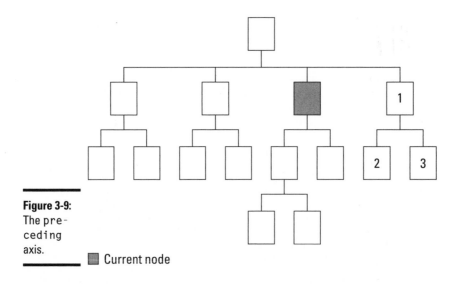

Figure 3-9:
The pre-
ceding
axis.

■ Current node

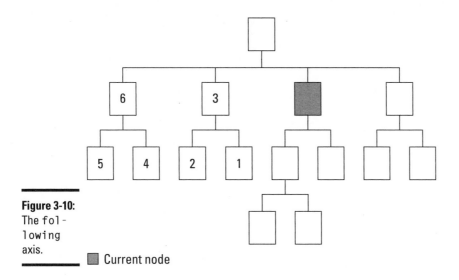

Figure 3-10:
The fol-
lowing
axis.

■ Current node

Using the namespace axis

The `namespace` axis selects all namespace nodes relevant to the current node. The `namespace` axis is typically the least used axis, but comes in handy when you need to differentiate between multiple namespaces within your source document.

Axis examples

The following list shows several examples of selecting nodes using axes:

✦ `country` or `child::country` selects all the `country` child elements of the context node.

✦ `@name` or `attribute::name` selects all the `name` attributes of the context node.

✦ `..` or `parent::node()` selects the parent of the context node.

✦ `.` or `self::node()` selects the context node, regardless of its type.

✦ `self::country` selects the context node if it is a `country` element.

✦ `descendant::country` selects all of the `country` descendants of the context node, regardless of their place in the hierarchy.

✦ `descendant-or-self::region` selects all the `region` element descendants of the context node and, if the context node is a `region` element, then it is selected as well.

**Book IV
Chapter 3**

**XPath — Scouting
Out XML Data**

- ✦ `ancestor::region` selects all the `region` element ancestors of the context node.

- ✦ `ancestor-or-self::region` selects all the `region` element ancestors of the context node and selects the context node if it is a `region` element.

- ✦ `region/descendant::country` selects the `country` descendants of the `region` element children of the context node.

Node Test: Making a Match

After the XSLT processor has selected a group of nodes based on the axis value, it uses the second part of the location step — the *node test* — to match nodes based on their name or type.

To illustrate, the following template rules selects all the child elements of the context node that have an element name of `country`:

```
<xsl:template match="country">
 <xsl:apply-templates/>
</xsl:template>
```

While element names are the most common node test, there are many more node tests, as shown in Table 3-2. Each axis has a *principal node type* to ensure the processor knows exactly what node type that the node test is referring to. Nearly all the axes have a principal node type of an element. However, the `attribute` axis has a principal node type of attribute and the `namespace` axis has a principal node type of namespace.

Table 3-2	Node Tests
Node Test	*Description*
`elementname`	Matches `<elementname>` element nodes.
`*`	Matches all nodes of the principal node type. For example, `child::*` (or simply `*`) returns all child element nodes and `attribute::*` (or `@*`) returns all attribute nodes.
`node()`	Matches all nodes, regardless of their type.
`text()`	Matches all text nodes.
`comment()`	Matches all comment nodes.
`namespace:elementname`	Matches `<elementname>` element nodes in the defined namespace.
`namespace:*`	Matches all element nodes in the defined namespace.

Node Test	Description
`processing-instruction()`	Matches processing instructions.
`processing-instruction ('target')`	Matches processing instructions with the specified target `<?target ...?>`.

The following list shows several examples of selecting nodes based on the node test:

✦ `*` or `child::*` selects all the element children of the context node.

✦ `@*` or `attribute::*` selects all the attributes of the context node.

✦ `text()` or `child::text()` selects all the text node children of the context node.

✦ `node()` or `child::node()` selects all the node children of the context node.

✦ `*/country` selects all the `country` grandchildren of the context node.

Predicates: Filtering Out the Riff-Raff

The *predicate* is the third and optional part of the location step and can be used to sift out unwanted nodes that were selected by the axis and node test. The predicate is evaluated and determined to have a true or false value. Nodes that evaluate to true are passed through to be part of the result document, while those that evaluate to false are thrown away.

To illustrate, suppose you wanted to list only those countries which are part of the Sahel region of Africa. This filtering process is easy with a predicate, as shown in the following set of template rules:

```
<!-- Output Sahel countries-->
<xsl:template match="region[@name='Sahel']">
<xsl:apply-templates/>
</xsl:template>

<!-- Don't include other region's countries -->
<xsl:template match="region"/>
```

In the first template rule, the match pattern is defined as `region[@name='Sahel']`, telling the processor to select only those `region` nodes that have a `name` attribute of `Sahel`. However, to prevent the other `region` elements from coming through with the built-in template rule, I create an empty template rule.

After looking at these rules, you may be asking yourself: "What a minute? Won't Sahel countries match both template rules and conflict with each other?" Yes, they do conflict, but because the first template rule has a predicate, it receives priority over the second template rule for any nodes that match both of them.

The result of the transformation is the list of Sahel countries:

```
Burkina Faso
Mail
Mauritania
Niger
```

A location step can have one or more predicates. Each predicate needs to be enclosed in brackets. For example, to retrieve a list of countries that have government attribute value of republic and climate attribute of tropical, you use the following template rule:

```
<xsl:template match="country[@government='republic'][@climate='tropical']">
<xsl:apply-templates/>
</xsl:template>
```

The following list shows several match patterns that use predicates to select nodes. (Some of these examples use XPath built-in functions, which are discussed later in the chapter.)

✦ country[1] or country[position()=1] selects the first country element child of the context node.

✦ country[last()] selects the last country element child of the context node.

✦ following-sibling::country[1] selects the next country element sibling of the context node.

✦ preceding-sibling::country[1] selects the previous country element sibling of the context node.

✦ country[@name] selects all the country element children of the context node that have a name attribute defined.

✦ country[not(@name)] selects all the country element children of the context node that do not have a name attribute defined.

✦ region[@name='Sahel'] selects all the region element children of the context node that have a name attribute with a value of Sahel.

✦ region[country] selects all the region element children of the context node that have one or more country element children.

+ `country[2][@name]` selects the second `country` element child of the context node if it has a `name` attribute defined.

+ `country[@name][2]` selects the second `country` element child of the current node that has a `name` attribute defined.

Working with Absolute Location Paths

Like directory/file structures on your computer, location paths can either be relative or absolute. So far, in this chapter, you've focused on *relative location paths,* which are defined by the axis relation to the current node. In contrast, an *absolute location path* begins at the root node and has specific location steps defined that navigate the tree to the desired node set.

The tell-tale sign of an absolute location path is that it begins with an / character indicating that you want to start at the root node. For example, to select all of the `country` nodes in the `continents.xml` using an absolute location path, I would use the following template rule:

```
<xsl:template match="/continent/region/country">
 <xsl:apply-templates/>
</xsl:template>
```

The match pattern of the template rule starts with / to denote an absolute location path and then looks for a `continent` element nodes just under the root node, then `region` element children, and then finally down to a `country` node set that are children of `region`. For all `country` elements selected, the node set is applied using `xsl:apply-templates`.

Some aspects of XPath notation (such as — ., .., /, and //) resemble common file system syntax. Therefore, if you are familiar with this notation when working with files and directories, you can apply the same logic to XPath.

You can also use an absolute location path when you need to work with the root node itself. For example, suppose I'd like to wrap the contents of the continent.xml file with a new `continents` element. Using an absolute location path, I can select the entire tree and then add the new element:

```
<xsl:template match="/">
  <continents>
    <xsl:copy-of select="."/>
  </continents>
  </xsl:template>
```

In this template rule, the match pattern of / selects the root node for the template and adds literal text before and after the result of the xsl:copy-of instruction.

The following list shows several example absolute location paths to select node sets:

✦ / selects the root node.

✦ /descendant::country selects all the country elements in the source document, regardless of their level in the hierarchy.

✦ /descendant::country[12] selects the 12th country element in the source document.

Using Built-in XPath Functions

XPath provides more than grammar for creating location steps. It also provides a set of built-in functions for performing specific tasks, such as calculating a sum or returning the last node of a node test selection.

XPath functions operate on different types of data, including the following:

✦ String

✦ Node-set

✦ Boolean

✦ Number

In the following sections, I identify the functions belonging to the listed categories.

String functions

String functions are used to perform string operations, such as finding the length of a string or converting a string from uppercase to lowercase. String functions can also be used to manipulate the text content of an XML element or attribute.

Table 3-3 lists the major string functions. Note that in the table, str represents a string argument, str* represents a set of zero or more strings, obj represents an object of some type, such as a node-set or number, and num represents an integer number. A question mark (?) after the argument indicates that the argument is optional.

Table 3-3	String XPath Functions	
Function	*Description*	*Example*
`string(obj?)`	This function is used to convert the argument to a string value. If you do not provide the argument, it takes the current node-set as its default parameter and returns the string value of the first node in the node-set.	`string("0001")` returns 0001 as a string value. `string()` returns the value of the first node in the current node-set.
`starts-with (str, str)`	This function accepts two arguments. It returns `true` if the first argument starts with the second. Otherwise, it returns `false`.	`starts-with ('Sahel', 'Sa')` returns `true`. `starts-with ('Sahel', 'Sh')` returns `false`.
`contains (str, str)`	This function accepts two strings as arguments and returns `true` if the first argument contains the second. Otherwise, it returns `false`.	`contains('Sahel', 'ah')` returns `true`. `contains('Sahel', 'um')` returns `false`.
`substring (str, num, num?)`	This function accepts three arguments. It extracts a portion of the first argument, starting from the position specified in the second argument, for a length of characters specified in the third argument. If you do not specify the third argument, the `substring()` function returns all characters from the specified position.	`substring ('MM/DD/YY',1,2)` returns MM. `substring ('MM/DD/YY', 2)` returns M/DD/YY.
`substring- before(str, str)`	This function accepts two strings as arguments and returns the portion of the first argument that precedes the value of the second argument.	`substring-before ('MM/DD/YYYY', '/')` returns 'MM'.
`substring- after(str, str)`	This function takes two string arguments and returns the portion of the first argument that follows the value specified in the second argument.	`substring-after ('MM/DD/YYYY','/')` returns 'DD/YYYY'.
`string- length(str?)`	This function accepts one argument and returns the number of characters in the argument. If you do not specify the argument, this function returns the length of the string-value of the current node.	`string-length ("Sahel")` returns 5.

Node-set functions

Node-set functions are used to manipulate node-sets or to return information about node-sets. Table 3-4 lists some of the node-set functions. Note that in the table, ns represents a node-set passed as an argument and obj represents an object of some type, such as a string or a node-set.

Table 3-4	Node-Set Functions	
Function	*Description*	*Example*
last()	This function returns the number of the last node in the currently selected node-set.	If the fifth node is the last node in the current node-set,the last() function returns 5.
position()	This function returns the index number of the current node within the parent node.	If the region element has three child country elements, the position() function returns the index of the child being processed.
count(ns)	This function returns the number of occurrences of the node (passed as argument) in the XML document.	count(//country) returns the number of occurrences of the country element.
id(obj)	This function returns an element with the specified unique ID. These nodes must have an attribute, which has the value type as ID. This value type can be specified with the help of a DTD.	id('0001') returns the element that has the unique ID attribute set to 0001.

Boolean functions

All boolean functions return either true or false. Table 3-5 lists some of the boolean functions. Note that in the table, obj represents an object of a type, such as a node-set or a number, and boolean represents a boolean condition.

Table 3-5	Boolean Functions	
Function	*Description*	*Example*
boolean(obj?)	This function converts the argument to a boolean expression. If obj is a node-set, the function returns true. Node sets are false if they are empty and are true if they contain at least one node. If the argument type is a string, the boolean() function returns false if the string has zero length. If the argument is not included, it converts the context node.	boolean(0) returns false; boolean(1) returns true; boolean(-100) returns true; and boolean(") returns false.

Function	Description	Example
`not(boolean)`	This function returns `true` if the argument passed to it is `false` or `false` if the argument passed to it is `true`.	`not(@id>400)` is almost always equivalent to (`@id<=400`).
`false()`	This function always returns `false`.	`false()` returns `false`.

Number functions

XPath is not a language meant for heavy duty number crunching, but it does provide number functions for various purposes, such as adding numbers, finding the nearest integer value, and converting strings to numbers. Table 3-6 lists some of the number functions. Note that in these functions, `obj` represents an object of some type, such as a node-set or a number, `ns` represents a node-set, and `num` represents an integer number. A question mark (?) with an argument indicates that the argument is optional.

Table 3-6	Number Functions	
Function	*Description*	*Example*
`number(obj?)`	This function converts the argument to a number and returns the result. If you do not specify the argument, it takes the current node-set as its argument by default. If you pass a string as an argument, the function converts the string to a number. If you pass a boolean value, this function converts `true` to 1 and `false` to 0. If you pass a node-set as an argument, this function converts the node-set to a string and then it converts the string to a numeric value.	`number('12')` returns the numeric value 12. `number('a')` returns NaN. NaN stands for *Not a Number*.
`sum(ns)`	This function returns the sum of all nodes in the node-set that is passed as an argument.	`sum(Quantity)` returns the sum of all values contained in the `Quantity` node in an XML document. `sum(Quantity * Price)` results in an error. This is because the `sum()` function expects a node-set as an argument, whereas `Quantity * Price` results in a numeric value.

(continued)

Table 3-6 *(continued)*

Function	Description	Example
floor(num)	This function returns the largest integer that is less than or equal to the argument.	floor(-1.3) returns –2.
ceiling(num)	This function returns the smallest integer that is greater than or equal to the argument.	ceiling(2.5) returns 3.
round(num)	This function rounds up the number to the nearest integer.	round(5.6) returns 6.

Built-in XPath functions are very useful when used inside of predicates. To demonstrate, consider the following XML file called continents2.xml:

```
<?xml version="1.0"?>
<continent name="Africa">
  <region name="Sahel" climate="desert">
    <country>Burkina Faso</country>
    <country>Mail</country>
    <country>Mauritania</country>
    <country>Niger</country>
  </region>
  <region name="West Africa" climate="subtropical"
   exports="Oil, Rubber">
    <country>Senegal</country>
    <country>Sierra Leone</country>
    <country>Liberia</country>
    <country>Nigeria</country>
    <country>Benin</country>
  </region>
  <region name="North Africa" climate="desert" exports="Oil">
    <country>Morocco</country>
    <country>Tunisia</country>
    <country>Libya</country>
    <country>Algeria</country>
    <country>Egypt</country>
  </region>
</continent>
```

I can select the region elements with an exports attribute defined by using a match pattern of region[@exports]. But suppose I'd like to get the region elements that don't have an exports attribute assigned. To get this result set, I can use the not() function to return the opposite value of the XPath expression inside of it. Therefore, region[not(@exports)] will return all region elements that do *not* have an exports attribute.

You can also use predicates to select a specific node based on its position in the node set. For example, if you would like to select the first country child of the context node, you could use the position() built-in function:

```
country[position()=1]
```

The position() function is implied in a predicate. When the processor sees a numeric value by itself in the predicate, it implicitly adds the position()=. Therefore, as a shortcut, you can simply leave off the position() function name and specify a position value:

```
country[1]
```

Or to select the last country child, use another built-in function, last():

```
country[last()]
```

When you use the reverse order axes (ancestor, ancestor-or-self, preceding, and preceding-sibling), keep in mind that [1] (or [position=1]) selects the first node in reverse order.

Chapter 4: Adding Logic to Your XSLT

In This Chapter

✔ **Understanding conditional and looping statements**

✔ **Testing for conditions with** `xsl:if`

✔ **Picking among a set of conditions with** `xsl:choose`

✔ **Using logical operators in your test expressions**

✔ **Cycling through a set of nodes with** `xsl:for-each`

As a parent of three growing boys, I am constantly making conditional and looping statements around the house:

If you boys don't straighten up your room, **then** *you're going to go to bed early.*

Remember kids: **when** *it's snowing out, wear your mittens;* **when** *it is raining out, wear your raincoat;* **or when** *it is really hot, wear a swimsuit.*

For each *of those Legos on the floor,* **do** *this: actually pick them up for a change!*

Indeed, your and my life in the real world is filled everyday with situations in which we use conditional and looping logic. It is not surprising then that when it comes to developing solutions in the computer world, that these same logical thought patterns are invariably an integral part of any software program. If you've programmed in a traditional programming language before, you'll recall that one of the first parts of the language you learned were those if/else and for statements. In this chapter, you explore why and how to add conditional and looping statement into your XSLT stylesheets.

Using Logical Expressions in Template Rules

While you and I may use these logical deductions on a daily basis, perhaps it's not always so clear what exactly conditional and looping statements are. For purposes of XSLT:

✦ A *conditional statement* executes parts of an XSLT template when certain conditions are met.

✦ A *looping structure* cycles through a series of nodes and performs actions on each node in the set.

In many ways, template rules implicitly pack conditional and looping logic right into their structures. For example, consider the following template rule:

```
<xsl:template match="product">
  <xsl:value-of select="name">
</xsl:template>
```

This template rule outputs the name of each product in the source document. However, notice the implicit logic built into the rule:

✦ *For each* node in the source document, evaluate against this rule.

✦ *If* the context node has a name of `product`, *then* perform the instructions inside the `xsl:template` element.

If you read Chapters 1-3 of Book IV, you already know that there is heck of a lot of things that you can do with the implicit logic of a plain vanilla template rule like the one shown above. However, as you discover in this chapter, there are certain tasks that require some added power in order to achieve the result document you are looking for. For XSLT, these turbo-charged instructions are: `xsl:if`, `xsl:choose`, and `xsl:for-each`.

Adding xsl:if Statements

XSLT sports `xsl:if` to provide "if" logic to your stylesheets. The `xsl:if` element processes the instructions contained inside of it if its `test` expression evaluates to true. The basic syntax is:

```
<xsl:if test="boolean-expression">
   do something
</xsl:if>
```

For example, consider the following sample:

```
<xsl:if test="@id">
  The id attribute exists.
</xsl:if>
```

In plain English, this `xsl:if` instruction says:

If the context node has an id attribute, then output the literal text: `The id attribute exists.`

You can only use the `xsl:if` instruction inside an `xsl:template` element. You'll get a lecture from the XSLT processor if you forget.

Consider a more in-depth example to demonstrate `xsl:if`, starting with the `students.xml` file shown in Listing 4-1 as my source document.

Listing 4-1   students.xml

```
<?xml version="1.0"?>

<school name="Elliot Academy">

  <student id="601" name="Jordan">
   <class name="Language Arts" days="5">Sentence
   diagramming</class>
   <class name="Reading" favorite="true" days="5">Lord Of
   The Rings</class>
   <class name="Writing" days="3">Colonial Times</class>
   <class name="Geography" days="2">African Sahel</class>
   <class name="Math" days="5"
   section="6.42">Decimals</class>
   <class name="Science" days="3"
   level="advanced">Volcanos</class>
   <class name="History" days="3">American
   Presidents</class>
   <class name="Art" days="1">Drawing</class>
  </student>

  <student id="401" name="Jared">
   <class name="Language Arts" days="5"
   section="4.56">Punctuation</class>
   <class name="Reading" days="5">Voyage Of The
   Dawntreader</class>
   <class name="Writing" days="3">Haiku Poetry</class>
   <class name="Geography" favorite="true" days="2">African
   Sahel</class>
   <class name="Math" days="5"
   section="4.45">Fractions</class>
   <class name="Science" days="3"
   level="basic">Insects</class>
   <class name="History" days="3">American
   Presidents</class>
   <class name="Art" days="1">Paper Mache</class>
  </student>
```

**Book IV
Chapter 4**

Adding Logic to
Your XSLT

(continued)

Listing 4-1 *(continued)*

```
<student id="301" name="Justus">
   <class name="Language Arts" days="5"
   section="3.80">Capitalization</class>
   <class name="Reading" days="5">Sherlock Holmes Solves
   Them All</class>
   <class name="Writing" days="3">Penmanship</class>
   <class name="Geography" days="2">African Sahel</class>
   <class name="Math" favorite="true" days="5"
   section="3.30">Division</class>
   <class name="Science" days="3"
   level="basic">Vertebrates</class>
   <class name="History" days="3">American
   Presidents</class>
   <class name="Art" days="1">Clay Sculptures</class>
</student>

</school>
```

Using this document as the source, suppose I'd like to create a customized report for each of the three students in the file. If I wanted uniform output, then I could use a normal template rule to achieve this result. However, for my purposes, I'd like to provide unique "hard-coded" (literal text) output for each of the students.

As a result, in order to test for a specific student, I can use xsl:if and then orient the output based on the results of this expression. For example, Jordan is the first student in the document. I'd use the xsl:if instruction provided below to generate his customized report:

```
<xsl:template match="student">
  <xsl:if test="@name='Jordan'">
    *******************************************
      Jordan is a 6th grader with an id
      of <xsl:value-of select="@id"/>

      Emphasizing:
        Reading: <xsl:value-of
    select="class[@name='Reading']"/>
        Writing: <xsl:value-of
    select="class[@name='Writing']"/>

      Comments:
       Jordan is making strong progress in all areas of
    study.

    *******************************************
  </xsl:if>
</xsl:template>
```

When this template rule is processed, it is run against each student element. The processor then evaluates each student to see if its name attribute equals Jordan. If not, then no further action is taken. But, if it is, then the generated text inside is output to the result document.

For the complete stylesheet, I want to add custom output for each of the students, as shown in Listing 4-2.

Listing 4-2 students.xsl

```
<xsl:stylesheet version="1.0"
   xmlns:xsl="http://www.w3.org/1999/XSL/Transform">

  <xsl:output method="text"/>

  <xsl:template match="student">

    <xsl:if test="@name='Jordan'">
    ******************************************
     Jordan is a 6th grader with an id
     of <xsl:value-of select="@id"/>

     Emphasizing:
      Reading: <xsl:value-of
 select="class[@name='Reading']"/>
      Writing: <xsl:value-of
 select="class[@name='Writing']"/>

     Comments:
      Jordan is making strong progress in all areas of
 study.

    ******************************************
    </xsl:if>

    <xsl:if test="@name='Jared'">
    ******************************************
     Jared is a 4th grader with an id
     of <xsl:value-of select="@id"/>

     Emphasizing:
      Language: <xsl:value-of select="class[@name='Language
 Arts']"/>
      Writing: <xsl:value-of
 select="class[@name='Writing']"/>

     Comments:
      Jared has great potential in writing!
```

(continued)

Listing 4-2 *(continued)*

```
************************************************
</xsl:if>

<xsl:if test="@name='Justus'">
************************************************
   Justus is a 3rd grader with an id
   of <xsl:value-of select="@id"/>

   Emphasizing:
    Reading: <xsl:value-of
select="class[@name='Reading']"/>
    Geography: <xsl:value-of
select="class[@name='Geography']"/>

   Comments:
    As a hobby, Justus is a wiz at nuclear physics!


************************************************
</xsl:if>

  </xsl:template>

</xsl:stylesheet>
```

The text document generated is as follows:

```
************************************************
   Jordan is a 6th grader with an id
   of 601

   Emphasizing:
    Reading: Lord Of The Rings
    Writing: Colonial Times

   Comments:
    Jordan is making strong progress in all areas of
study.

************************************************


************************************************
   Jared is a 4th grader with an id
   of 401

   Emphasizing:
    Language: Punctuation
    Writing: Haiku Poetry
    Comments:
    Jared has great potential in writing!
```

```
*****************************************

*****************************************
    Justus is a 3rd grader with an id
    of 301

    Emphasizing:
     Reading: Sherlock Holmes Solves Them All
     Geography: African Sahel

    Comments:
     As a hobby, Justus is a wiz at nuclear physics!

*****************************************
```

In most programming languages, "if" is joined at the hip with an "else" statement:

If a is true, then do this and that. Else, do that other thing.

XSLT does *not* have an xsl:else statement to go along with xsl:if. If you need that if/else logic, you should either use a set of xsl:if statements (as shown in Listing 4-2) or else the xsl:choose instruction (discussed below) instead.

Adding xsl:choose Statements

The xsl:choose instruction is the other type of conditional statement that you can add to your stylesheets. While xsl:if allows you to test a single condition, you can use xsl:choose to select among a group of alternatives or, if no conditions are met, then you can optionally default to a final alternative. An xsl:choose element contains one or more xsl:when sub-elements that test for each condition and an optional xsl:otherwise to specify a default response.

The xsl:choose syntax is as follows:

```
<xsl:choose>
  <xsl:when test="expression">
    do something
  </xsl:when>
  <xsl:when test="expression2">
    do something else
  </xsl:when>
  <xsl:when test="expression3">
    do something
```

```
  </xsl:when>
  <xsl:otherwise>
    do as a last resort
  </xsl:when>
</xsl:choose>
```

When the processor comes across an xsl:choose element, it automatically dives right into the structure because xsl:choose doesn't have any test expression at the top level. The processor then goes down the list of xsl:when statements sequentially looking for the first one that has a test expression that evaluates to true. If the processor gets a true result, then the instructions inside the xsl:when element are processed. The remaining xsl:when and xsl:otherwise statements below are ignored. However, if no xsl:when elements are found to be true, then the xsl:otherwise statement is processed if one is present.

For example, suppose the element <sheriff badge="none"/> is evaluated with the following xsl:choose statement:

```
<xsl:choose>
  <xsl:when test="@badge='gold'">
    We have gold badges.
  </xsl:when>
  <xsl:when test="@badge='silver'">
    We have silver badges.
  </xsl:when>
  <xsl:otherwise>
    Badges? We don't need no stinkin' badges.
  </xsl:when>
</xsl:if>
```

The processor jumps into the xsl:choose block and performs the first test on the badge attribute value of the sheriff element to see if it is gold. Because it isn't, the processor evaluates the second test expression. Once again, the test returns false, causing the xsl:otherwise statement to be used. As a result, the literal text — Badges? We don't need no stinkin' badges. — is output to the result document.

xsl:choose can only be used inside of an xsl:template instruction.

To illustrate how you can use xsl:choose, transform the school.xml document (see Listing 4-1) into a new structure call fallclasses.xml. The changes are as follows:

✦ For class name="Reading" elements, new schedule="9am" and priority="A" attributes are added.

✦ For `class name="Writing"` elements, new `schedule="10am"` and `priority="B"` attributes are added.

✦ For `class name="Math"` elements, new `schedule="11am"` and `priority="C"` attributes are added.

✦ For every other `class` element, new `schedule="postlunch"` and `priority="D"` attributes are added.

The stylesheet to perform this transformation is shown in Listing 4-3.

Listing 4-3   fallclasses.xsl

```
<?xml version="1.0"?>
<xsl:stylesheet version="1.0"
   xmlns:xsl="http://www.w3.org/1999/XSL/Transform">

  <xsl:output method="xml"/>

  <!-- Replace school element with fallclasses -->
  <xsl:template match="/">
  <xsl:text>
</xsl:text><fallclasses teacher="ksw">
      <xsl:apply-templates/>
    </fallclasses>
  </xsl:template>

  <!-- Transform class elements -->
  <xsl:template match="class">
    <xsl:choose>
      <xsl:when test="@name='Reading'">
        <class student="{../@name}" subject="{@name}"
 assignment="{.}" schedule="9am" priority="A"/>
      </xsl:when>
      <xsl:when test="@name='Writing'">
        <class student="{../@name}" subject="{@name}"
 assignment="{.}" schedule="10am" priority="B"/>
      </xsl:when>
      <xsl:when test="@name='Math'">
        <class student="{../@name}" subject="{@name}"
 assignment="{.}" schedule="11am" priority="C"/>
      </xsl:when>
      <xsl:otherwise>
        <class student="{../@name}" subject="{@name}"
 assignment="{.}" schedule="postlunch" priority="D"/>
      </xsl:otherwise>
    </xsl:choose>
  </xsl:template>

</xsl:stylesheet>
```

After specifying that the output is XML with the xsl:output instruction, the first template rule replaces the school element with a fallclasses element. In the second rule, I run each class element through the xsl:choose block.

Reading elements (class elements with a name attribute of Reading) are processed with the first xsl:when; Writing elements are processed with the second, and Math elements on the third. All other class elements are directed to the xsl:otherwise instruction.

By applying this stylesheet to the students.xml file (Listing 4-1), I get the following result document (Listing 4-4):

Listing 4-4   fallclasses.xml result document

```xml
<?xml version="1.0" encoding="utf-8"?>
<fallclasses teacher="ksw">

    <class student="Jordan" subject="Language Arts"
    assignment="Sentence diagramming" schedule="postlunch"
    priority="D"/>
    <class student="Jordan" subject="Reading"
    assignment="Lord Of The Rings" schedule="9am"
    priority="A"/>
    <class student="Jordan" subject="Writing"
    assignment="Colonial Times" schedule="10am"
    priority="B"/>
    <class student="Jordan" subject="Geography"
    assignment="African Sahal" schedule="postlunch"
    priority="D"/>
    <class student="Jordan" subject="Math"
    assignment="Decimals" schedule="11am" priority="C"/>
    <class student="Jordan" subject="Science"
    assignment="Volcanos" schedule="postlunch" priority="D"/>
    <class student="Jordan" subject="History"
    assignment="American Presidents" schedule="postlunch"
    priority="D"/>
    <class student="Jordan" subject="Art"
    assignment="Drawing" schedule="postlunch" priority="D"/>


    <class student="Jared" subject="Language Arts"
    assignment="Punctuation" schedule="postlunch"
    priority="D"/>
    <class student="Jared" subject="Reading"
    assignment="Voyage Of The Dawntreader" schedule="9am"
    priority="A"/>
```

```
  <class student="Jared" subject="Writing"
assignment="Haiku Poetry" schedule="10am" priority="B"/>
  <class student="Jared" subject="Geography"
assignment="African Sahal" schedule="postlunch"
priority="D"/>
  <class student="Jared" subject="Math"
assignment="Fractions" schedule="11am" priority="C"/>
  <class student="Jared" subject="Science"
assignment="Insects" schedule="postlunch" priority="D"/>
  <class student="Jared" subject="History"
assignment="American Presidents" schedule="postlunch"
priority="D"/>
  <class student="Jared" subject="Art" assignment="Paper
Mache" schedule="postlunch" priority="D"/>


  <class student="Justus" subject="Language Arts"
assignment="Capitalization" schedule="postlunch"
priority="D"/>
  <class student="Justus" subject="Reading"
assignment="Sherlock Holmes Solves Them All"
schedule="9am" priority="A"/>
  <class student="Justus" subject="Writing"
assignment="Penmanship" schedule="10am" priority="B"/>
  <class student="Justus" subject="Geography"
assignment="African Sahel" schedule="postlunch"
priority="D"/>
  <class student="Justus" subject="Math"
assignment="Division" schedule="11am" priority="C"/>
  <class student="Justus" subject="Science"
assignment="Vertebrates" schedule="postlunch"
priority="D"/>
  <class student="Justus" subject="History"
assignment="American Presidents" schedule="postlunch"
priority="D"/>
  <class student="Justus" subject="Art" assignment="Clay
Sculptures" schedule="postlunch" priority="D"/>

</fallclasses>
```

Testing 1, 2, and 3

Which kind of test did you prefer when you were in school? Chances are you hoped for true/false or multiple choice questions instead of the dreaded essay test. When it comes to XSLT, you may find it helpful to think of xsl:if as something like a true/false test while xsl:choose is reminiscent of a multiple choice test.

Getting Testy with Your Expressions

The `xsl:if` and `xsl:when` elements both have a required `test` attribute that is used to determine whether or not their instructions should be executed:

✦ Yes, if the expression inside of the `test` attribute evaluates to `true`.

✦ No, if the expression inside of the test attribute evaluates to `false`.

The logical operators (`and` and `or`) and the `not()` function come in handy inside of the test expressions depending on what exactly you are testing for. In addition, numeric expressions can be tested using the familiar comparison operators shown in Table 4-1.

Table 4-1	XPath Comparison Operators
Operator	*Means*
`>`	Greater than
`>=`	Greater than or equal to
`&lt;`	Less than
`&lt;=`	Less than or equal to
`=`	Equals
`!=`	Not equal

Note the use of the `&lt;` and `&lt;=` entities in place of the `<` and `<=` operators. The use of the `<` character is a no-no in this context because it is reserved by XML denoting the start of an element tag. (See Book II, Chapter 2 for more discussion on entities.)

Using these logical and comparison operators, there are a variety of tests you may want to perform, including typical examples shown in Table 4-2.

Table 4-2	Types of Test Expressions
Type of test	*Example*
Specific attribute value	`<xsl:if test="@id='101'">`
Not a specific attribute value	`<xsl:if test="not( @id='101')">` or `<xsl:if test="@id!='101'">`
Whether an attribute is present	`<xsl:if test="@id">`
Whether an attribute is not present	`<xsl:if test="not(@id)">`
Numerical expression	`<xsl:if test="@id &lt; 9">`

Type of test	Example
One of several expressions is true	`<xsl:if test="(@name='Language Arts') or (@name='Reading') or (@name='Writing')">`
All expressions in a set are true	`<xsl:if test="(@days='5') and (../@name='Justus')">`

To illustrate, consider the stylesheet shown in Listing 4-5, which uses a variety of logical and conditional operators to achieve a new result document.

Listing 4-5   enhancedreport.xsl

```
<?xml version="1.0"?>
<xsl:stylesheet version="1.0"
   xmlns:xsl="http://www.w3.org/1999/XSL/Transform">
  <xsl:output method="text"/>

   <!-- if favorite attribute exists -->
   <xsl:if test="@favorite">
     <xsl:value-of select="@name"/> is the favorite class of
<xsl:value-of select="../@name"/><xsl:text>
   </xsl:text>
   </xsl:if>

   <!-- if favorite attribute does not exist -->
   <xsl:if test="not(@favorite)">
     <xsl:value-of select="@name"/> is not the favorite
class of <xsl:value-of select="../@name"/><xsl:text>
   </xsl:text>
   </xsl:if>

   <!-- if name is language arts, reading, or writing -->
   <xsl:if test="(@name='Language Arts') or
(@name='Reading') or (@name='Writing')">
     <xsl:text>English class topic: </xsl:text><xsl:value-
of select="."/><xsl:text>
   </xsl:text>
   </xsl:if>

   <!-- if favorite attribute exists -->
   <xsl:if test="(@days='5') and (../@name='Justus')">
     <xsl:text>One of Justus' 5-day/week classes:
</xsl:text><xsl:value-of select="@name"/><xsl:text>
   </xsl:text>
   </xsl:if>

   <!-- if days less than 3 -->
   <xsl:if test="@days &lt; 3">
```

(continued)

Listing 4-5 *(continued)*

```
    <xsl:text>Minor subject: </xsl:text><xsl:value-of
select="@name"/><xsl:text>
</xsl:text>
</xsl:if>

<!-- if days greater than or equal to 3 -->
<xsl:if test="@days >= 3">
    <xsl:text>Major subject: </xsl:text><xsl:value-of
select="@name"/><xsl:text>
</xsl:text>
</xsl:if>

<!-- if days does not equal 5 -->
<xsl:if test="@days != 5">
    <xsl:text>Not a full-time subject: 
</xsl:text><xsl:value-of select="@name"/><xsl:text>
</xsl:text>
</xsl:if>

</xsl:template>

</xsl:stylesheet>
```

The following result document is generated when the stylesheet is applied to students.xml (Listing 4-1):

```
Language Arts is not the favorite class of Jordan
English class topic: Sentence diagramming
Major subject: Language Arts

Reading is the favorite class of Jordan
English class topic: Lord Of The Rings
Major subject: Reading

Writing is not the favorite class of Jordan
English class topic: Colonial Times
Major subject: Writing
Not a full-time subject: Writing

Geography is not the favorite class of Jordan
Minor subject: Geography
Not a full-time subject: Geography

Math is not the favorite class of Jordan
Major subject: Math

Science is not the favorite class of Jordan
Major subject: Science
Not a full-time subject: Science
```

History is not the favorite class of Jordan
Major subject: History
Not a full-time subject: History

Art is not the favorite class of Jordan
Minor subject: Art
Not a full-time subject: Art

Language Arts is not the favorite class of Jared
English class topic: Punctuation
Major subject: Language Arts

Reading is not the favorite class of Jared
English class topic: Voyage Of The Dawntreader
Major subject: Reading

Writing is not the favorite class of Jared
English class topic: Haiku Poetry
Major subject: Writing
Not a full-time subject: Writing

Geography is the favorite class of Jared
Minor subject: Geography
Not a full-time subject: Geography

Math is not the favorite class of Jared
Major subject: Math

Science is not the favorite class of Jared
Major subject: Science
Not a full-time subject: Science

History is not the favorite class of Jared
Major subject: History
Not a full-time subject: History

Art is not the favorite class of Jared
Minor subject: Art
Not a full-time subject: Art

Language Arts is not the favorite class of Justus
English class topic: Capitalization
One of Justus' 5-day/week classes: Language Arts
Major subject: Language Arts

```
Reading is not the favorite class of Justus
English class topic: Sherlock Holmes Solves Them All
One of Justus' 5-day/week classes: Reading
Major subject: Reading

Writing is not the favorite class of Justus
English class topic: Penmanship
Major subject: Writing
Not a full-time subject: Writing

Geography is not the favorite class of Justus
Minor subject: Geography
Not a full-time subject: Geography

Math is the favorite class of Justus
One of Justus' 5-day/week classes: Math
Major subject: Math

Science is not the favorite class of Justus
Major subject: Science
Not a full-time subject: Science

History is not the favorite class of Justus
Major subject: History
Not a full-time subject: History

Art is not the favorite class of Justus
Minor subject: Art
Not a full-time subject: Art
```

Adding xsl:for-each Statements

While the xsl:if and xsl:choose statements are used to test conditions, xsl:for-each has a much different purpose. It is used to perform a set of instructions on each node returned from its select attribute. The syntax is:

```
<xsl:for-each select="expression">
  do something
</xsl:for-each>
```

For example, consider the following:

```
<xsl:for-each select="name">
  The position of this element is <xsl:value-of
    select="position()"/>
</xsl:for-each>
```

This instruction tells the processor to loop through every name element and output the literal text and instruction results inside of it.

xsl:for-each can only be used inside an xsl:template element block.

By their very nature, template rules perform a similar process of iterating through all nodes and performing actions based on those identified by its match pattern. However, there are times in which you'll need an additional loop to occur *inside* of a template rule to achieve the output document you want.

To illustrate, suppose I want to create a list of classes for each student in the students.xml document (Listing 4-1). The stylesheet shown in Listing 4-6 uses xsl:for-each to accomplish this task.

Listing 4-6   classlist.xsl

```
<xsl:stylesheet version="1.0"
    xmlns:xsl="http://www.w3.org/1999/XSL/Transform">

  <xsl:output method="text"/>

  <!-- Create list of classes for each student -->
  <xsl:template match="student">
    <xsl:value-of select="@name"/>'s Classes:
    <xsl:for-each select="class">
      <xsl:value-of select="@name"/>
      <xsl:if test="position()!=last()">
        <xsl:text>, </xsl:text>
      </xsl:if>
    </xsl:for-each>
    <xsl:text>
</xsl:text>
  </xsl:template>

</xsl:stylesheet>
```

The template rule in the stylesheet returns a node set of student elements. The student's name is first written to the result document using xsl:value. The xsl:for-each instruction is then used to cycle through each class element inside the current student element and output the class name.

Notice the use of the xsl:if instruction inside of the xsl:for-each block. In the result document, each class name needs to be separated with a comma. However, if I just added <xsl:text>, <xsl:text> after the xsl:value-of instruction, I'd get a trailing comma at the end of my list.

To get around this, I add the xsl:text instruction inside of an xsl:if element that tests uses the built-in XPath functions position() and last() to determine whether the node is the last one in the given node set.

The output document from this transformation is shown below:

```
Jordan's Classes:
   Language Arts, Reading, Writing, Geography, Math,
  Science, History, Art

Jared's Classes:
   Language Arts, Reading, Writing, Geography, Math,
  Science, History, Art

Justus's Classes:
   Language Arts, Reading, Writing, Geography, Math,
  Science, History, Art
```

I talk about the xsl:for-each as being akin to a loop through each node of the returned node set. However, purists rightfully argue that such a statement is not entirely accurate. The xsl:for-each instruction technically does not loop, but *maps*. In other words, xsl:for-each adds something to the result document for each node found in the returning node set.

Chapter 5: Variables and Parameters

In This Chapter

✔ Working with variables in your stylesheets

✔ Knowing how parameters are different than variables

✔ Understanding the scope of variables and parameters

*E*verybody loves shortcuts. Why spend an hour on the jam-packed high-way into the city when you can wind through local neighborhoods and get there in half the time? Why work until 65 years of age if you can retire at 55? Or why use long terms like United States of America or North American Free Trade Agreement in your conversations when their acronyms (USA and NAFTA) roll off the tongue in comparison?

Shortcuts are also an important part of programming world, whether it is a relic COBOL program, object-oriented Java component, or an XML document. If you read Book II, Chapter 2, you discovered that you can use Document Type Definition (DTD) entities to serve as a shortcut in your XML (an *entity* serves as placeholders for a bigger piece of information — much like NAFTA serves as a placeholder for North American Free Trade Agreement).

In this chapter, you look at how XSLT uses variables and parameters as shortcuts in your stylesheets to make your life easier.

Working with Variables

In XSLT, a *variable* is used to represent something else, whether it be a string of text, number, a chunk of Hypertext Markup Language (HTML), or a collection of nodes in an XML document.

A variable is also the biggest misnomer in all of XSLT, because unlike a variable in a traditional programming language, you cannot change the value of an XSLT variable after one has been assigned. An XSLT "variable" can't vary much because its value cannot be changed after the initial declaration. Actually, if you want to draw any comparisons, a variable in XSLT is closest to a *constant* in traditional programming languages.

A variable is defined in XSLT with the `xsl:variable` element, which can be used in two ways: either as a *content variable* or a *select attribute variable*.

Content variables

The first way to declare a variable is to use the `xsl:variable` element to assign a name to the content enclosed by its tags. The basic syntax is:

```
<xsl:variable name="name">value</xsl:variable>
```

Then, when you want to use this variable inside of your stylesheet, you use reference the name prefixed with a dollar sign ($):

```
$name
```

Consider a simple example:

```
<xsl:variable name="nafta">North American Free Trade
    Agreement</xsl:variable>
```

In this code, the variable named `nafta` represents the literal text string `North American Free Trade Agreement`.

When you want to insert the text `North American Free Trade Agreement` into a template rule, you can then substitute with `$nafta` instead. For example, if you want to output the variable as text, you could use the `xsl:value-of` element:

```
<p>Canada, United States, and Mexico are part of the
    <xsl:value-of select="$nafta"/>.</p>
```

The result of this instruction would be as follows:

```
<p>Canada, United States, and Mexico are part of the North
    American Free Trade Agreement.</p>
```

See Book IV, Chapter 2 for more information on using the `xsl:value-of` instruction.

You can use variables inside of an attribute value template. (See Book IV, Chapter 1 for more information on attribute value templates.) Putting the variable inside of the curly brackets of the attribute value template, the code would look like:

```
<treaty name="{$nafta}"/>
```

When this snippet is processed, the following element is output to the result document:

```
<treaty name="North American Free Trade Agreement"/>
```

Because the content of an element is considered text, any numeric or other type values of a content variable are *always* converted to text in the result document.

Select attribute variables

The second way to define a variable is to use a `select` attribute inside the `xsl:variable` element in place of the element content. This type of variable is often referred to as a select attribute variable and has a syntax of:

```
<xsl:variable name="name" select="expression"/>
```

For example, the `nafta` variable discussed in the last section can also be declared as:

```
<xsl:variable name="nafta" select="'North American Free Trade
    Agreement'"/>
```

When used in a template rule, a select attribute variable is represented just like a content variable:

```
$nafta
```

A content variable treats all values as text, but a select attribute variable stores the result of the `select` expression. (An *expression* is an XSLT statement that represents a value or is used to calculate a value.) The expression may return a string value, but it can also return a number, boolean value, and even nodes.

As a result, notice that I placed single quotation marks around `North American Free Trade Agreement` when using it inside a `select` attribute. That's because if I didn't, the processor would attempt to evaluate `North American Free Trade Agreement` as an expression. Because it isn't one, you'd get a zero when the variable is evaluated without surrounding quotes.

Consider the following samples:

```
<!-- Numeric value of 8 -->
<xsl:variable name="sum" select="4+4"/>
```

```
<!-- Literal string of '8' -->
<xsl:variable name="sum" select="'8'"/>

<!-- Numeric value of 5 -->
<xsl:variable name="sum" select="round(5.129)"/>

<!-- Value of the total attribute of the context node-->
<xsl:variable name="sum" select="@total"/>

<!-- Boolean value of whether the total attribute
    equals 60 -->
<xsl:variable name="sum" select="@total=60"/>

<!-- Nodeset of invoices over $250 -->
<xsl:variable name="largeInvoices"
    select="invoice[@total>250]"/>
```

You can use a select attribute variable anywhere that you would use a content variable for outputting text, but its typical use is working with node sets or numbers.

Make special note of the final `xsl:variable` instruction. The `largeInvoices` variable differs from the rest in that its value is not a string, number, or Boolean value, but rather a *result tree fragment*, or a collection of nodes that meet the stated requirements (all invoices that have a `total` attribute value over 250).

Select attribute variables must not have content in between the start and end tags or you'll get an error by the processor. For example:

```
<!-- Select attribute + content = no-no! -->
<xsl:variable name="id" select="'101'">102</xsl:variable>
```

Or, if you fail to add a select attribute and content, the result of the variable is an empty string.

Using Variables

Because of the nature of XSLT, variables are not often needed when you are transforming XML documents. However, `xsl:variable` instructions remain useful devices to have in your XML toolkit when you want to reuse literal text values across your stylesheet as well as use the result of an expression in your output document.

Variable as a placeholder for literal text

Clearly the most straightforward purpose for XSLT variables is to use them as placeholders to values that you want to use across a stylesheet.

To illustrate, consider the following HTML footer that you want to place at the bottom of each result document that is generated:

```
<xsl:variable name="footer">
<p><font size="8pt">Copyright (c)2003, Variably Speaking,
    Inc.</font></p>
<p><font size="8pt">Send us email at <a
    href="mailto:feedback@variably.com">feedback@variably.com
    </a></font>
</p>
</xsl:variable>
```

To use this `footer` variable in my stylesheet, I can reference it using the `xsl:value-of` element:

```
<xsl:value-of select="$footer"/>
```

When this instruction is processed, the following HTML is generated in the result document:

```
<p><font size="8pt">Copyright (c)2001, Variably Speaking,
    Inc.</font></p>
<p><font size="8pt">Send us email at <a
    href="mailto:feedback@variably.com">feedback@variably.com
    </a>
<font></p>
```

Consider a second example with the following XML snippet:

```
<film name="Henry V">
   <director>Kenneth Branagh</director>
   <writer>Kenneth Branagh, William Shakespeare</writer>
   <year>1989</year>
   <runtime>137</runtime>
   <sound>Stereo</sound>
   <genre>Drama</genre>
   <score>10.0</score>
   <mpaa>PG-13</mpaa>
</film>
```

Suppose you'd like to generate the following HTML result document from that XML code:

```
<p>Highest movies by score:</p>
<b>
<font color="FF0000" size="2">Henry V by Kenneth
    Branagh</font>
</b>
<br/>
```

```
<i>
<font color="FF0000" size="-2">Received a score of:
    10.0</font>
</i>
<br/>
```

Looking through the resulting HTML code, you'll note that the font color is used twice. And, while the two specified font sizes are not identical, they're relative to each other. Therefore, in my XSLT stylesheet that follows, variables can be used for both the font color and size:

```
<xsl:stylesheet
    xmlns:xsl="http://www.w3.org/1999/XSL/Transform"
    version="1.0">

<!-- Define variables -->
<xsl:variable name="myfontcolor">FF0000</xsl:variable>
<xsl:variable name="myfontsize" select="2"/>

<!-- Director template  -->
<xsl:template match="director">
    <p>Highest movies by score:</p>
    <b><font size="{$myfontsize}" color="{$myfontcolor}">
    <xsl:value-of select="../@name"/>
    <xsl:text> by </xsl:text>
    <xsl:apply-templates/>
    </font></b><br/>
</xsl:template>

<!-- Score template  -->
<xsl:template match="score">
    <i><font size="{$myfontsize - 4}">
    Received a score of:
    <xsl:apply-templates/>
    </font></i><br/>
</xsl:template>

<!-- Remove these elements from our results document -->
<xsl:template match="year"/>
<xsl:template match="writer"/>
<xsl:template match="sound"/>
<xsl:template match="genre"/>
<xsl:template match="mpaa"/>
<xsl:template match="runtime"/>

</xsl:stylesheet>
```

Looking at the stylesheet, you can see that I plug in the myfontcolor and myfontsize variables using attribute value templates in the director template rule. In the `score` template rule, the `myfontcolor` variable is simply placed as is. However, because I want the font size of this text to be four increments smaller than the `myfontsize` value, I subtract one from the variable. The XSLT processor evaluates the attribute value template `{$myfontsize - 4}` and gets `-2` as the result of the expression.

Variable as a result of an expression

Select attribute variables are useful when you want to use the result of a calculation as a value. To illustrate this use, consider the films.xml file shown in Listing 5-1.

Listing 5-1   films.xml

```
<films>
  <film name="Henry V">
    <director>Kenneth Branagh</director>
    <writer>Kenneth Branagh, William Shakespeare</writer>
    <year>1989</year>
    <runtime>137</runtime>
    <sound>Stereo</sound>
    <genre>Drama</genre>
    <score>10.0</score>
    <mpaa>PG-13</mpaa>
  </film>
  <film name="Groundhog Day">
    <director>Harold Ramis</director>
    <writer>Danny Rubin</writer>
    <year>1993</year>
    <runtime>101</runtime>
    <sound>Dolby</sound>
    <genre>Romantic Comedy</genre>
    <score>9.0</score>
    <mpaa>PG</mpaa>
  </film>
  <film name="Man for All Seasons">
    <director>Fred Zinnemann</director>
    <writer>Robert Bolt</writer>
    <year>1966</year>
    <runtime>120</runtime>
    <sound>Mono</sound>
    <genre>Drama</genre>
    <score>8.0</score>
    <mpaa>PG</mpaa>
  </film>
  <film name="Field of Dreams">
    <director>Phil Alden Robinson</director>
    <writer>W.P.Kinsella, Phil Alden Robinson</writer>
    <year>1988</year>
```

**Book IV
Chapter 5**

**Variables
and Parameters**

(continued)

Listing 5-1 *(continued)*

```
        <runtime>107</runtime>
        <sound>Dolby</sound>
        <genre>Drama</genre>
        <score>9.8</score>
        <mpaa>PG</mpaa>
    </film>
    <film name="Babette's Feast">
        <director>Gabriel Axel</director>
        <writer>Gabriel Axel</writer>
        <year>1987</year>
        <runtime>102</runtime>
        <sound>Dolby</sound>
        <genre>Drama</genre>
        <score>9.5</score>
        <mpaa>PG</mpaa>
    </film>
</films>
```

For the result document, I'd like to calculate the total number of PG-rated films in the document and then assign the result of the calculation to a variable.

To get this information, I need to begin by defining a variable that returns the desired PG-films as a node set. I do this using an XPath expression in the select attribute:

```
<xsl:variable name="pgFilms" select="count(
    //film[mpaa='PG'])"/>
```

The pgFilms variable uses the //film[mpaa='PG'] expression to retrieve all of the film elements in the source document that have an mpaa child element with the value of PG.

This XPath expression, however, returns the nodes themselves, not the number of film elements being returned. As a result, the count() function is added to return the total number of nodes in the result tree fragment.

In the preceding expression, the built-in XPath count() function adds up the total number of nodes contained in the result tree fragment stored in pgFilms variable.

I'll keep the result document minimal and use the variable in the following stylesheet:

```
<xsl:stylesheet
    xmlns:xsl="http://www.w3.org/1999/XSL/Transform"
    version="1.0">
```

```
<xsl:variable name="pgFilms"
 select="count(//film[mpaa='PG')"/>

<xsl:template match="/">
   The total number of PG films: <xsl:value-of
 select="$pgFilms"/>
</xsl:template>

</xsl:stylesheet>
```
The output of the transformation is shown below:

```
The total number of PG films: 4
```

Working with Parameters

In XSLT, a very close relative to a variable is the *parameter*. Parameters have essentially the same use and purpose of variables, except that they have the added flexibility of *actually* being able to vary their value at the time that the XSLT stylesheet is processed. What a novel concept!

A parameter is declared using the xsl:param element and follows the same syntax rules of variables:

```
<!-- Content-based parameter -->
<xsl:param name="name">value</xsl:param>

<!-- Select attribute parameter -->
<xsl:param name="name" select="expression"/>
```

You can think of parameters as a *superset* of variables because they do everything that variables do and more. In fact, for any variable example shown in this chapter, you can replace xsl:param with xsl:variable and achieve the exact same results.

Even though parameters can be used in place of variables, their chief purpose is be a means of overriding a default value at the time the document is being processed. You can actually override the parameter from both from inside and outside of XSLT stylesheets.

Overriding parameters with the with-param element

The xsl:with-param element is used to update the value of a parameter *within* a stylesheet. Its syntax is:

```
<xsl:with-param name="name" select="expression"/>
```

Or:

```
<xsl:with-param name="name">value</xsl:with-param>
```

The common use of `xsl:with-param` is to override a parameter that's been defined in a named template. (A *named template* is a template rule that has a name attribute in place of a match attribute and has to be called using `xsl:call-template` See Book IV, Chapter 2 for more on named templates.)

For example, consider the following XML fragment:

```
<film name="Field of Dreams">
  <director>Phil Alden Robinson</director>
  <writer>W.P. Kinsella, Phil Alden Robinson</writer>
  <year>1988</year>
  <runtime>107</runtime>
  <sound>Dolby</sound>
  <genre>Drama</genre>
  <score>9.8</score>
  <mpaa>PG</mpaa>
</film>
```

Suppose I'd like to generate an HTML document that transforms the values of the `director`, `writer`, and `year` elements and turns them into links (a elements), giving each link a unique URL. The output would look like:

```
<p><a href="legend.html#director">Phil Alden Robinson</a></p>
  <p><a href="legend.html#writer">W.P.Kinsella, Phil Alden
  Robinson</a></p>
    <p><a href="legend.html#year">1988</a></p>
```

To achieve this output, I use the stylesheet shown in Listing 5-2 (labels.xsl).

Listing 5-2   labels.xsl

```
<xsl:stylesheet
    xmlns:xsl="http://www.w3.org/1999/XSL/Transform"
    version="1.0">

<!-- Labels named template -->
<xsl:template name="labels">
  <xsl:param name="legendUrl">legend.html#main</xsl:param>
  <a href="{$legendUrl}"><xsl:apply-templates/></a>
</xsl:template>

<!-- Director -->
<xsl:template match="director">
  <xsl:call-template name="labels">
```

```
    <xsl:with-param
    name="legendUrl">legend.html#director</xsl:with-param>
  </xsl:call-template>
</xsl:template>

<!-- Writer -->
<xsl:template match="writer">
  <xsl:call-template name="labels">
    <xsl:with-param
    name="legendUrl">legend.html#writer</xsl:with-param>
  </xsl:call-template>
</xsl:template>

<!-- Year -->
<xsl:template match="year">
  <xsl:call-template name="labels">
    <xsl:with-param
    name="legendUrl">legend.html#year</xsl:with-param>
  </xsl:call-template>
</xsl:template>

<!-- Remove these elements from our results document -->
<xsl:template match="sound"/>
<xsl:template match="genre"/>
<xsl:template match="mpaa"/>
<xsl:template match="runtime"/>
<xsl:template match="score"/>

</xsl:stylesheet>
```

In looking at this stylesheet, I create a named template called `labels` that contains a parameter value called `legendUrl`. The `labels` template is used to declare an `a` element and insert the value of the `legendUrl`.

The template rules for the `director`, `writer`, and `year` elements use a `xsl:call-template` instruction to call the `labels` template when these template rules are processed by the processor. Inside of the `xsl:call-template` is an `xsl:with-param` element that sends a new value to the `legendUrl` parameter. This value is then used as the `href` value in the resulting HTML.

Overriding parameters from the XSLT processor

Most XSLT processors also allow you override default parameter values by passing a new value into a stylesheet being processed from the processor itself. Each XSLT processor has a different way in which you can do this. For example, the SAXON processor enables you to declare a parameter name-value pair from the command line. For example:

```
saxon xmlfile.xml xslfile.xsl param=value
```

If you wanted to pass in a value for a parameter called `myfontsize`, the command line is shown below:

```
saxon films.xml param2.xsl myfontsize=2
```

The XSLT processor passes the value of `2` to the `myfontsize` parameter in the stylesheet being parsed, updating the parameter's current value.

By making use of parameters from outside of a stylesheet in this manner, you can run new transformations without changing the underlying stylesheet at all.

Understanding the Scope of Variables and Parameters

While many XSLT instructions can be used only inside of template rules, `xsl:variable` and `xsl:parameters` elements can be placed both inside `xsl:template` blocks as well as outside of them directly under the `xsl:stylesheet` container element. However, the location of the variable and parameter declaration impacts at its scope. The *scope* of a variable or parameter is the area of the stylesheet that can be used.

Variables that are defined at the top level of the stylesheet (a direct child of `xsl:stylesheet`) are considered *global variables* and are available anywhere inside of the stylesheet. Variables defined inside of a template rule are considered *local variables* and are accessible only inside that rule. The same logic applies to parameters.

For example, the global variable `thinkGlobally` can be used anywhere in the following stylesheet, while the local variable `actLocally` can only be accessed within the `film` element:

```
<xsl:stylesheet
    xmlns:xsl="http://www.w3.org/1999/XSL/Transform"
    version="1.0">

  <xsl:variable name="thinkGlobally">14pt</xsl:variable>

  <xsl:template match="film">

    <font size="{$thinkGlobally}">
      <xsl:apply-templates select="writer"/>
    </font><xsl:text>
    </xsl:text>
```

```
<xsl:variable name="actLocally">12pt</xsl:variable>
  <font size="{$actLocally}">
    <xsl:apply-templates select="director"/>
  </font>
</xsl:template>

</xsl:stylesheet>
```

The scope of a variable or parameter impacts precedence when two have identical names and are within the same "space." If, for example, a global variable and a local variable have the same name, the local variable always takes precedence over the global variable.

Chapter 6: The Output Side of XSLT

In This Chapter

✔ Tweaking the structure of an XML document

✔ Performing utility-oriented tasks for XML output

✔ Outputting to HTML format

✔ Working with whitespace

"**T**weak" is one of those curiously underrated words of the English language. I am not sure why it doesn't receive more acclaim; not only is it a fun word to speak, but consider for a moment how its usage could have improved some of the most famous speeches over the years:

✦ "That's one small tweak for man, one giant tweak for mankind."
   – Neil Armstrong

✦ "Four score and seven years ago our fathers tweaked this continent to form a new nation." – Abraham Lincoln

✦ "Ask not what your country can tweak for you, but what you can tweak for this country." – John F. Kennedy

✦ "We few, we happy few, we band of brothers. For he today that tweaks with me shall be my brother. Be he ne'er so vile, this day shall gentle his condition . . ." – Shakespeare, *Henry V*

Well, even if the word "tweaking" was not used in those famed addresses, you find that transforming XML documents using XSLT is all about tweaking. You create template rules to produce the results you are looking for, tweaking as you go to get the precise outlook you need.

In this chapter, you explore this tweaking process on the output side of transformations, highlighting how to output to various formats and how to manipulate the structure of the result document.

Declaring the Output Method

XSLT enables you to output to XML, HTML, and text formats. The `xsl:output` instruction is used to specify the type of output format you want to use by the method attribute value:

```
<xsl:output method="xml|html|text"/>
```

✦ **XML.** When XSLT outputs to XML format, the result is a well-formed XML document, although the results you generate need to obviously conform to the XML syntax rules as well (such as having one root element). XML is the default format and is assumed if no `xsl:output` instruction is provided. An XML declaration is included at the start of the result document unless you add an `omit-xml-declaration="yes"` attribute to `xsl:output`.

✦ **HTML.** When you specify the HTML method, XML generates a result document that adheres to the syntax requirements of HTML 4.0. For example, a horizontal rule element specified in your stylesheet as `<hr></hr>` or `<hr/>` is output as `<hr>`.

If you are outputting to HTML, it's wise to use the `<xsl:output method="html"/>` instruction in your stylesheet. However, if you use `html` as the name of your root element in your result document, the XSLT processor assumes that the document is meant to be HTML, so it formats the document accordingly.

✦ **Text.** Specify the text method when you want to output a plain text file, apart from markup elements associated with XML or HTML documents.

The `xsl:output` element must be declared as a top-level element, a direct child of `xsl:stylesheet`.

Outputting XML Documents

Perhaps the most common usage of XSLT is to transform an XML document into a completely new structure in the document that is output by the processor. Indeed, much of the power of XSLT lies in its ability to perform a multitude of transformation tasks at the element and attribute levels of the documents, including:

✦ Copying an element

✦ Copying all elements in a document

✦ Adding a new element

✦ Adding a new attribute

✦ Renaming an element

✦ Deleting an element

✦ Deleting an attribute

✦ Moving an attribute to another element

✦ Converting elements into attributes

✦ Converting attributes into elements

✦ Combining elements

✦ Rearranging elements in a document

These how-to tasks are demonstrated in the sections that follow using the two XML files shown in Listing 6-1 and 6-2.

Listing 6-1   coffee.xml

```xml
<?xml version="1.0"?>
<!-- coffee.xml -->
<coffees>
 <region name="Latin America">
  <coffee name="Guatemalan Express" origin="Guatemala">
    <taste>Curiously Mild And Bland</taste>
    <price>11.99</price>
    <availability>Year-round</availability>
    <bestwith>Breakfast</bestwith>
  </coffee>
  <coffee name="Costa Rican Deacon" origin="Costa Rica">
    <taste>Solid Yet Understated</taste>
    <price>12.99</price>
    <availability>Year-round</availability>
    <bestwith>Dessert</bestwith>
  </coffee>
 </region>
 <region name="Africa">
  <coffee name="Ethiopian Sunset Supremo" origin="Ethiopia">
    <taste>Exotic And Untamed</taste>
    <price>14.99</price>
    <availability>Limited</availability>
    <bestwith>Chocolate</bestwith>
  </coffee>
  <coffee name="Kenyan Elephantismo" origin="Kenya">
    <taste>Thick And Chewy</taste>
    <price>9.99</price>
    <availability>Year-round</availability>
    <bestwith>Elephant Ears</bestwith>
  </coffee>
  </region>
</coffees>
```

Listing 6-2   coffee-light.xml

```
<?xml version="1.0"?>
<!-- coffee-light.xml -->
<coffee name="Guatemalan Express" origin="Guatemala">
  <taste>Curiously Mild And Bland</taste>
  <price>11.99</price>
  <availability>Year-round</availability>
  <bestwith>Breakfast</bestwith>
</coffee>
```

Copying an element

When an XML document is fed through an XSLT processor, built-in templates automatically carry over the content of XML elements into the result document. For some purposes, that default behavior serves your needs. However, other times you may want to duplicate the element tags as well or in place of. Consider each of these options.

Content only

The xsl:apply-templates instruction applies a template for each element in the node set. It first looks for any explicitly defined template rules in the stylesheet for that element and calls it if found. If not, it uses the built-in template for an element, which strips away the tags of an element and sends the element's content to the result document.

Suppose I want to output the content of the price element in the coffee.xml document (Listing 6-1) into a plain text file. To do so, I can use the following stylesheet:

```
<!-- coffee-copy_elementcontent.xsl -->
<xsl:stylesheet
    xmlns:xsl="http://www.w3.org/1999/XSL/Transform"
    version="1.0">

  <!-- Show just prices -->
  <xsl:template match="coffees">
     <xsl:apply-templates select="region/coffee/price"/>
  </xsl:template>

  <!-- Add price content -->
  <xsl:template match="price"><xsl:text>
</xsl:text>
    <xsl:apply-templates/>
  </xsl:template>

</xsl:stylesheet>
```

Looking at the stylesheet, here are the steps that are taken:

✦ **Narrow the results.** The first template rule narrows the results of the transformation to deal only with the price element rather than all the elements in the document. To do so, the xsl:apply-templates instruction is applied only to the price element by using region/coffee/price as the select attribute value.

However, if I simply used the built-in template of price, the output text would look jumbled together:

```
11.9912.9914.999.99
```

✦ **Modify output.** A second template rule modifies the output of the price element's content. Using the xsl:text instruction, a line break is added before each line to separate the numbers that are generated in the transformation.

The resulting text document that is generated is as follows:

```
11.99
12.99
14.99
9.99
```

Tags only

You can use the xsl:copy instruction to copy the tags of an element without its attributes and, by default, its content as well. For example, suppose I'd like to output just the tags of the price element, but no content. To do so, I can write a stylesheet such as following:

```
<!-- coffee-copy_elementcontent.xsl -->
<xsl:stylesheet
    xmlns:xsl="http://www.w3.org/1999/XSL/Transform"
    version="1.0">

  <!-- Copy just tag -->
  <xsl:template match="price">
    <xsl:copy/>
  </xsl:template>

  <!-- Add parent, run on just price -->
  <xsl:template match="coffees">
    <prices>
      <xsl:apply-templates select="region/coffee/price"/>
    </prices>
  </xsl:template>

</xsl:stylesheet>
```

Dissecting this stylesheet, I perform two tasks:

+ **Copy tags.** The `price` template rule uses an empty `xsl:copy` instruction to tell the XSLT processor to copy just the tags.

+ **Narrow the results.** Because I don't want any other parts of the `coffee.xml` document added to the resulting XML document, I need to add a similar template rule for `coffees` that I used in the previous content only example.

When this stylesheet is applied, the result document is as follows:

```
<?xml version="1.0" encoding="utf-8"?>
<prices>
  <price/>
  <price/>
  <price/>
  <price/>
</prices>
```

Copy both content and tags

You can use two methods for copying complete elements to the result document: using the `xsl:copy-of` and copy by reconstruction.

Using xsl:copy-of

You can use the `xsl:copy-of` instruction to copy an entire element — tags, attributes, and content. For example, to copy both the tags and content of the `price` element, the stylesheet shown below can be used:

```
<!-- coffee-copy_elementfull.xsl -->
<xsl:stylesheet
    xmlns:xsl="http://www.w3.org/1999/XSL/Transform"
    version="1.0">

  <!-- Copy price element -->
  <xsl:template match="price">
    <xsl:copy-of select="."/>
  </xsl:template>

  <!-- Add parent, run on just price -->
  <xsl:template match="coffees">
    <prices>
      <xsl:apply-templates select="region/coffee/price"/>
    </prices>
  </xsl:template>

</xsl:stylesheet>
```

The two primary tasks of the stylesheet are:

✦ **Copy context node.** The first template uses `xsl:copy-of` with a `select` attribute value of `.`, which tells the processor to copy the context node.

✦ **Narrow the results.** The second template adds the `prices` element and limits the result document to deal only with the `price` element.

The XML output produced is shown here:

```
<?xml version="1.0" encoding="utf-8"?>
<prices>
  <price>11.99</price>
  <price>12.99</price>
  <price>14.99</price>
  <price>9.99</price>
</prices>
```

Copying through reconstruction

You can also copy an element to the result document by reconstructing it inside a template rule. You can reconstruct an element by using literal text and `xsl:value` instructions to piece together the various parts of the element. Consider the following stylesheet. The `price` template rule reconstructs the element to get the same results as the preceding `xsl:copy-of` example:

```
<!-- coffee-copy_elementrecreate.xsl -->
<xsl:stylesheet
    xmlns:xsl="http://www.w3.org/1999/XSL/Transform"
    version="1.0">

  <!-- Recreate element -->
  <xsl:template match="price">
    <price><xsl:value-of select="."/></price>
  </xsl:template>

  <!-- Add parent, run on just price -->
  <xsl:template match="coffees">
    <prices>
      <xsl:apply-templates select="region/coffee/price"/>
    </prices>
  </xsl:template>

</xsl:stylesheet>
```

Table 6-1 summarizes the different techniques to use to copy elements.

Table 6-1	Copying Elements
Part to Copy	*Instruction*
Content only	`xsl:apply-templates`
Tags only	Empty `xsl:copy` instruction (`<xsl:copy />`)
Tags, attributes, and content	`xsl:copy-of` or (literal text + `xsl:value-of`)

Copying an entire document

If you'd like to copy the entire document, you can use `xsl:copy-of`, but use it to copy the root node (using / as the match pattern). The stylesheet would look like:

```
<!-- coffee-copy_tree.xsl -->
<xsl:stylesheet
    xmlns:xsl="http://www.w3.org/1999/XSL/Transform"
    version="1.0">

  <xsl:template match="/">
    <xsl:copy-of select="."/>
  </xsl:template>

</xsl:stylesheet>
```

When this stylesheet is applied, the output will look absolutely identical to the original `coffee.xml` document tree.

Adding a new element

You can add a new element to the result document by adding the element as literal text or using the `xsl:element` instruction.

Using literal text

The most straightforward way to add a new element in your result document is to create the element as literal text inside of your template rule, so that it is output when the rule is applied.

For example, suppose I want to add an `online` element as a child of the `coffee` element:

```
<online>Yes</online>
```

To do so, I can use the following stylesheet:

```
<!-- coffee-addelement_literal.xsl -->
<xsl:stylesheet
    xmlns:xsl="http://www.w3.org/1999/XSL/Transform"
    version="1.0">

  <!-- Add new element -->
  <xsl:template match="coffee">
    <coffee>
      <xsl:apply-templates/>
      <online>Yes</online>
    </coffee>
  </xsl:template>

  <!-- Copy everything else over -->
  <xsl:template match="@*|node()">
    <xsl:copy>
      <xsl:apply-templates select="@*|node()"/>
    </xsl:copy>
  </xsl:template>

</xsl:stylesheet>
```

This stylesheet performs the following tasks:

✦ **Add elements:** Because the coffee tags will be stripped away by the built-in template rules when the template rule is applied, the `coffee` template rule adds the `coffee` element tags back again as literal text and then adds the new `online` element as the last child. During the transformation process, these literal text nodes are added to the result tree when `xsl:apply-templates` is executed.

Even though they are XML elements, the `coffee` and `online` tags entered inside the template rule are treated as text by the processor because their namespaces are outside of the `xsl` namespace.

✦ **Copy "dependent" nodes:** The second template rule is a "catch-all" template that copies everything else over — element tags, attributes, and other nodes — into the result tree. This template rule makes sure that the child elements of the coffee element are brought over unchanged into the result document.

After the transformation is performed, the following result is produced:

```
<?xml version="1.0" encoding="utf-8"?>
<coffees>
  <coffee>
    <taste>Curiously Mild And Bland</taste>
    <price>11.99</price>
    <availability>Year-round</availability>
```

```
      <bestwith>Breakfast</bestwith>
      <online>Yes</online>
   </coffee>
   <coffee>
      <taste>Exotic and Untamed</taste>
      <price>12.99</price>
      <availability>Year-round</availability>
      <bestwith>Dessert</bestwith>
      <online>Yes</online>
   </coffee>
   <coffee>
      <taste>Exotic and Untamed</taste>
      <price>14.99</price>
      <availability>Limited</availability>
      <bestwith>Chocolate</bestwith>
      <online>Yes</online>
   </coffee>
   <coffee>
      <taste>Solid Yet Understated</taste>
      <price>9.99</price>
      <availability>Year-round</availability>
      <bestwith>Elephant Ears</bestwith>
      <online>Yes</online>
   </coffee>
</coffees>
```

Using xsl:element

The other way to add elements to your result document is to use the
xsl:element. Its syntax is:

```
<xsl:element name="elementName">elementContent</xsl:element>
```

The name attribute identifies the element's name and the content of the
instruction determines the content of the new element. For example:

```
<xsl:element name="drink">Latte</xsl:element>
```

This code produces the following element:

```
<drink>Latte</drink>
```

Use xsl:element, I can get the same result as with literal text, simply by
substituting the text with an xsl:element instruction, as shown here:

```
<!-- coffee-addelement_instr.xsl -->
<xsl:stylesheet
    xmlns:xsl="http://www.w3.org/1999/XSL/Transform"
    version="1.0">
```

```
<!-- Add new element using xsl:element -->
<xsl:template match="coffee">
  <coffee>
    <xsl:apply-templates/>
    <xsl:element name="online">Yes</xsl:element>
  </coffee>
</xsl:template>

<!-- Copy everything else over -->
<xsl:template match="@*|node()">
  <xsl:copy>
    <xsl:apply-templates select="@*|node()"/>
  </xsl:copy>
</xsl:template>

</xsl:stylesheet>
```

Adding a new attribute

Just like with elements, you can add attributes to your result document using literal text or an XSLT instruction, xsl:attribute.

Using literal text

You can add an attribute by simply entering in literal text within the desired element tag. For example, suppose I want to add a currency attribute to the price element of the coffee-light.xml document. I could do so using the stylesheet that follows:

```
<!-- coffee-addattribute_literal.xsl -->
<xsl:stylesheet
   xmlns:xsl="http://www.w3.org/1999/XSL/Transform"
   version="1.0">

  <!-- Add currency attribute -->
  <xsl:template match="coffee">
    <coffee>
      <taste><xsl:value-of select="taste"/></taste>
      <price currency="$US"><xsl:value-of
  select="price"/></price>
      <availability><xsl:value-of
  select="availability"/></availability>
      <bestwith><xsl:value-of select="taste"/></bestwith>
    </coffee>
  </xsl:template>

</xsl:stylesheet>
```

When the stylesheet is applied to the XML file shown in Listing 6-2, the following document is the result:

```
<?xml version="1.0" encoding="utf-8"?>
<coffee>
  <taste>Curiously Mild And Bland</taste>
  <price currency="$US">11.99</price>
  <availability>Year-round</availability>
  <bestwith>Curiously Mild And Bland</bestwith>
</coffee>
```

Using xsl:attribute

The xsl:attribute instruction is a second method of adding a new attribute to the result document. For example, suppose I want to add a salesevent element as a child of the coffee element, which has quarter, usregion, and supplier attributes. The stylesheet I can use is shown below:

```
<!-- coffee-addattribute_inst.xsl -->
<xsl:stylesheet
    xmlns:xsl="http://www.w3.org/1999/XSL/Transform"
    version="1.0">

  <!-- Add attribute using xsl:attribute instruction -->
  <xsl:template match="coffee">
    <coffee>
      <taste><xsl:value-of select="taste"/></taste>
      <price currency="$US"><xsl:value-of
  select="price"/></price>
      <availability><xsl:value-of
  select="availability"/></availability>
      <bestwith><xsl:value-of select="taste"/></bestwith>
      <xsl:element name="salesevent">
        <xsl:attribute name="quarter">Q3</xsl:attribute>
        <xsl:attribute name="usregion">New
  England</xsl:attribute>
        <xsl:attribute name="supplier">Horacio
  Zeeman</xsl:attribute>
      </xsl:element>
    </coffee>
  </xsl:template>
</xsl:stylesheet>
```

After the transformation, the result document that is generated is as follows:

```
<?xml version="1.0" encoding="utf-8"?>
<coffee>
```

```
<taste>Curiously Mild And Bland</taste>
<price currency="$US">11.99</price>
<availability>Year-round</availability>
<bestwith>Curiously Mild And Bland</bestwith>
<salesevent quarter="Q3" usregion="New England"
  supplier="Horacio Zeeman"/>
</coffee>
```

Renaming an element

If you want to rename an element, you'll typically want to add the new element name as literal text (or using xsl:element) and then copying over the value using xsl:value-of.

Consider the following example. Suppose I'd like to rename the taste element to description in the coffee-light.xml. The following stylesheet is used to perform this transformation:

```
<!-- coffee-rename.xsl -->
<xsl:stylesheet
   xmlns:xsl="http://www.w3.org/1999/XSL/Transform"
   version="1.0">

  <!-- Rename taste to description -->
  <xsl:template match="taste">
    <description><xsl:value-of select="."/></description>
  </xsl:template>

</xsl:stylesheet>
```

I can also use xsl:element in place of literal text:

```
<xsl:stylesheet
   xmlns:xsl="http://www.w3.org/1999/XSL/Transform"
   version="1.0">

  <!-- Rename taste to description -->
  <xsl:template match="taste">
    <xsl:element name="description"><xsl:value-of
    select="."/></xsl:element>
  </xsl:template>
```

The result is the following document:

```
<?xml version="1.0" encoding="utf-8"?>
<coffee name="Guatemalan Express" origin="Guatemala">
   <description>Curiously Mild And Bland</description>
   <price>11.99</price>
```

**Book IV
Chapter 6**

**The Output Side
of XSLT**

```
      <availability>Year-round</availability>
      <bestwith>Breakfast</bestwith>
</coffee>
```

Okay, okay. To be technically accurate, rather than actually renaming the element, the stylesheet shown in this example removes the original element tags and replaces them with the desired new names.

Deleting an element

If you read Book IV, Chapter 2, you know that built-in template rules will automatically add the content of elements to the result tree when the template rule is applied using `xsl:apply-templates`. Therefore, if you want to delete an element from the result document, you can use one of two routines.

Using an empty template rule

You can explicitly delete an element from the result tree by using an empty template rule and using the element you wish to delete as the rule's match pattern. An *empty template rule* is one that has a match pattern defined but no accompanying template. For example:

```
<xsl:template match="drink"/>
```

When an empty template rule is encountered by the processor, the result set is selected, but because there is no template instructions concerning how the node set should be output, nothing is done, removing the element and its children.

For example, suppose I want to create a result document that removes the `taste` and `bestwith` elements as part of the `coffee` element. Using empty template rules for the two elements I wish to delete, the stylesheet looks like:

```
<!-- coffee-remove.xsl -->
<xsl:stylesheet
    xmlns:xsl="http://www.w3.org/1999/XSL/Transform"
    version="1.0">

    <!-- Remove taste element -->
    <xsl:template match="taste"/>
    <xsl:template match="bestwith"/>

    <!-- Copy everything else over -->
    <xsl:template match="@*|node()">
      <xsl:copy>
```

```
      <xsl:apply-templates select="@*|node()"/>
    </xsl:copy>
  </xsl:template>

</xsl:stylesheet>
```

The result document is shown below, the same document but without the taste and bestwith elements:

```
<?xml version="1.0" encoding="utf-8"?>
<coffees>
 <region name="Latin America">
  <coffee name="Guatemalan Express" origin="Guatemala">
    <price>11.99</price>
    <availability>Year-round</availability>
  </coffee>
  <coffee name="Costa Rican Deacon" origin="Costa Rica">
    <price>12.99</price>
    <availability>Year-round</availability>
  </coffee>
 </region>
 <region name="Africa">
  <coffee name="Ethiopian Sunset Supremo" origin="Ethiopia">
    <price>14.99</price>
    <availability>Limited</availability>
  </coffee>
  <coffee name="Kenyan Elephantismo" origin="Kenya">
    <price>9.99</price>
    <availability>Year-round</availability>
  </coffee>
  </region>
</coffees>
```

Removing during element reconstruction

You can implicitly remove an element by essentially neglecting it when you create the document structure for output. For example, suppose that you want to create a new selectcoffees structure that removes several of the elements (region, taste, and bestwith). The stylesheet that can use to perform this transformation is shown below:

```
<!-- coffee-remove2.xsl -->
<xsl:stylesheet
   xmlns:xsl="http://www.w3.org/1999/XSL/Transform"
   version="1.0">

  <xsl:template match="/">
    <selectcoffees>
      <xsl:apply-templates/>
```

```
    </selectcoffees>
  </xsl:template>

  <!-- Copy coffee and its price and availability
    children -->
  <xsl:template match="coffee">
    <coffee>
      <price><xsl:apply-templates select="price"/></price>
      <availability><xsl:apply-templates
    select="availability"/></availability>
    </coffee>
  </xsl:template>

</xsl:stylesheet>
```

Looking at the stylesheet, note that I am performing the following steps:

+ **Create root element.** The first template creates a new root element and uses xsl:apply-templates on the entire document.

+ **Reconstruct the element.** The second template rule is used to recreate the coffee element manually, adding the desired elements (price and availability) but leaving off the "undesirables" (taste and bestwith).

  The region elements of the coffee.xml (Listing 6-1) contain child elements, but no text content. Therefore, I can let the built-in template rule do its thing and remove the region elements from the result document.

The result document is shown below:

```
<?xml version="1.0" encoding="utf-8"?>
<selectcoffees>
  <coffee>
    <price>11.99</price>
    <availability>Year-round</availability>
  </coffee>
  <coffee>
    <price>12.99</price>
    <availability>Year-round</availability>
  </coffee>
  <coffee>
    <price>14.99</price>
    <availability>Limited</availability>
  </coffee>
  <coffee>
    <price>9.99</price>
    <availability>Year-round</availability>
  </coffee>
</selectcoffees>
```

Deleting an attribute

You can delete attributes from the result document by using one of two methods, each of which is explained below.

Removing during a copy operation

The first way to remove an attribute is to explicitly remove all attributes during a copy operation. For example, imagine that I want to delete all the attributes from the region element in my result document. Using the following stylesheet, I can perform this operation:

```
<xsl:stylesheet
   xmlns:xsl="http://www.w3.org/1999/XSL/Transform"
   version="1.0">

  <!-- Copy region, but not its attributes -->
  <xsl:template match="region">
    <xsl:copy>
     <xsl:apply-templates select="*|node()"/>
    </xsl:copy>
  </xsl:template>

  <!-- Copy everything else over -->
  <xsl:template match="@*|node()">
    <xsl:copy>
      <xsl:apply-templates select="@*|node()"/>
    </xsl:copy>
  </xsl:template>

</xsl:stylesheet>
```

The first template uses xsl:copy to duplicate the region element in the result document, but notice that the xsl:apply-templates instruction selects elements and other nodes for the copy operation, but not attribute nodes.

The result document created using this stylesheet is shown below:

```
<?xml version="1.0" encoding="utf-8"?><coffees>
 <region>
  <coffee name="Guatemalan Express" origin="Guatemala">
    <taste>Mild and Bland</taste>
    <price>11.99</price>
    <availability>Year-round</availability>
    <bestwith>Breakfast</bestwith>
  </coffee>
  <coffee name="Costa Rican Deacon" origin="Costa Rica">
    <taste>Solid Yet Understated</taste>
```

Book IV
Chapter 6

The Output Side
of XSLT

```
      <price>12.99</price>
      <availability>Year-round</availability>
      <bestwith>Dessert</bestwith>
   </coffee>
 </region>
 <region>
  <coffee name="Ethiopian Sunset Supremo" origin="Ethiopia">
     <taste>Exotic and Untamed</taste>
     <price>14.99</price>
     <availability>Limited</availability>
     <bestwith>Chocolate</bestwith>
  </coffee>
  <coffee name="Kenyan Elephantismo" origin="Kenya">
     <taste>Thick And Chewy</taste>
     <price>9.99</price>
     <availability>Year-round</availability>
     <bestwith>ElephantEars</bestwith>
  </coffee>
  </region>
</coffees>
```

Removing during element reconstruction

You can also remove an attribute by ignoring it when an element is being reconstructed in a template rule. For example, using the following stylesheet, I can output a result document based on coffee-light.xml (Listing 6-2) that leaves off the origin attribute from the coffee element:

```
<xsl:stylesheet
    xmlns:xsl="http://www.w3.org/1999/XSL/Transform"
    version="1.0">

   <!-- Copy coffee but don't include the origin attribute -->
   <xsl:template match="coffee">
     <coffee name="{@name}">
       <xsl:apply-templates/>
     </coffee>
   </xsl:template>

   <!-- Copy everything else over -->
   <xsl:template match="@*|node()">
     <xsl:copy>
       <xsl:apply-templates select="@*|node()"/>
     </xsl:copy>
   </xsl:template>

</xsl:stylesheet>
```

The result document is as follows:

```
<?xml version="1.0" encoding="utf-8"?>
<coffee name="Guatemalan Express">
  <taste>Mild and Bland</taste>
  <price>11.99</price>
  <availability>Year-round</availability>
  <bestwith>Breakfast</bestwith>
</coffee>
```

Moving an attribute to another element

You can move an attribute from one element in the source document to another element in the result document. Consider the following example. Suppose I want to get delete the region element in the coffee.xml document (Listing 6-1) and place the value of the name attribute inside the coffee element as a new region attribute. I could use the stylesheet shown below:

```
<!-- coffee-move_attr.xsl -->
<xsl:stylesheet
   xmlns:xsl="http://www.w3.org/1999/XSL/Transform"
   version="1.0">

  <!-- Move region name to be an attribute of coffee -->
  <xsl:template match="coffee">
    <coffee region="{../@name}">
      <xsl:copy-of select="@*|node()"/>
    </coffee>
  </xsl:template>

  <!-- Add coffees element as container -->
  <xsl:template match="coffees">
    <coffees>
      <xsl:apply-templates/>
    </coffees>
  </xsl:template>

</xsl:stylesheet>
```

This stylesheet is designed to do the following objectives:

✦ **Add attribute in new location.** The first template rule recreates the coffee element using literal text and adds the region attribute using literal text for its name and an attribute value template for its value. The xsl:copy-of instruction is used to bring over all other nodes of coffee into the result document, including child elements and attributes.

✦ **Add root element.** The second template adds the coffees element tags as the root element of the document. The results are shown below:

```xml
<?xml version="1.0" encoding="utf-8"?>
<coffee>
  <coffee region="Latin America" name="Guatemalan Express"
    origin="Guatemala">
    <taste>Mild and Bland</taste>
    <price>11.99</price>
    <availability>Year-round</availability>
    <bestwith>Breakfast</bestwith>
  </coffee>
  <coffee region="Latin America" name="Costa Rican Deacon"
    origin="Costa Rica">
    <taste>Exotic and Untamed</taste>
    <price>12.99</price>
    <availability>Year-round</availability>
    <bestwith>Dessert</bestwith>
  </coffee>
  <coffee region="Africa" name="Ethiopian Sunset Supremo"
    origin="Ethiopia">
    <taste>Exotic and Untamed</taste>
    <price>14.99</price>
    <availability>Limited</availability>
    <bestwith>Chocolate</bestwith>
  </coffee>
  <coffee region="Africa" name="Kenyan Elephantismo"
    origin="Kenya">
    <taste>Solid yet Understated</taste>
    <price>3.99</price>
    <availability>Year-round</availability>
    <bestwith>Elephant Ears</bestwith>
  </coffee>
</coffees>
```

Converting elements into attributes

You can convert elements from the source document into attributes in the result document. For example, suppose I'd like to output a modified structure to coffee.xml (Listing 6-1) so that the price element is an attribute of coffee rather than a child element. At the same time, I'd like to add a new descriptions element that moves the taste and bestwith elements into attributes that describe coffee. The stylesheet below performs this task:

```xml
<!-- coffee-convert_to_attr.xsl -->
<xsl:stylesheet
    xmlns:xsl="http://www.w3.org/1999/XSL/Transform"
    version="1.0">

  <xsl:template match="coffee">
    <coffee name="{@name}" origin="{@origin}"
    price="{price}">
```

```
      <availability><xsl:value-of
  select="availability"/></availability>
      <descriptions taste="{taste}" bestwith="{bestwith}"/>
    </coffee>
  </xsl:template>

  <!-- Add coffees element as container -->
  <xsl:template match="coffees">
    <coffees>
      <xsl:apply-templates/>
    </coffees>
  </xsl:template>


</xsl:stylesheet>
```

The first template rule recreates the attributes of the `coffee` element and adds the new description element by using the values of the elements as attribute values instead. Specifically:

+ **Reconstruct existing attributes.** The `name` and `origin` attributes are simply reconstructed by referencing their values in attribute value templates (`name="{@name}" origin="{@origin}"`).

+ **Add new attribute.** The new `price` attribute is added using the value of the price child element in the attribute value template (`price="{price}"`).

+ **Add new element.** The new `descriptions` element uses the values of the `taste` and `bestwith` elements in attribute value templates.

The results are shown below:

```
<?xml version="1.0" encoding="utf-8"?>
<coffees>
  <coffee name="Guatemalan Express" origin="Guatemala"
    price="11.99">
    <availability>Year-round</availability>
    <descriptions taste="Curiously Mild And Bland"
    bestwith="Breakfast"/>
  </coffee>
  <coffee name="Costa Rican Deacon" origin="Costa Rica"
    price="12.99">
    <availability>Year-round</availability>
    <descriptions taste="Solid Yet Understated"
    bestwith="Dessert"/>
  </coffee>
  <coffee name="Ethiopian Sunset Supremo" origin="Ethiopia"
    price="14.99">
```

```
    <availability>Limited</availability>
    <descriptions taste="Exotic and Untamed"
  bestwith="Chocolate"/>
  </coffee>
  <coffee name="Kenyan Elephantismo" origin="Kenya"
  price="9.99">
    <availability>Year-round</availability>
    <descriptions taste="Thick And Chewy" bestwith="Elephant
  Ears"/>
  </coffee>
</coffees>
```

Converting attributes into elements

An attribute of an element in the source document can be transformed into
an element in the result document. For example, suppose I'd like to take the
original `coffee.xml` document (Listing 6-1) and make the following changes
to it:

✦ Transform the `region` element's `name` attribute into a new `name` child
  element.

✦ Add a new `source` element as a child of `coffee` that receives its value
  based on the `region` element's `name` and the `coffee` element's `origin`
  attribute.

✦ Change the content of the `price` element to be the value of a new
  `retail` attribute and add a new `wholesale` attribute to `price` that
  is 60 percent of the `retail` value.

The following stylesheet sets up these conversions:

```
<!-- coffee-convert_to_elem.xsl.xsl -->
<xsl:stylesheet
   xmlns:xsl="http://www.w3.org/1999/XSL/Transform"
   version="1.0">

  <!-- Move region name to be a child element of region -->
  <xsl:template match="region">
    <region>
      <xsl:element name="name"><xsl:value-of
  select="@name"/></xsl:element>
      <xsl:apply-templates/>
    </region>
  </xsl:template>

  <!-- Convert coffee element -->
  <xsl:template match="coffee">
    <coffee>
```

```
      <price retail="{price}" wholesale="{format-number(
price*.6, '##.##' )}"></price>
      <source><xsl:value-of select="../@name"/>|<xsl:value-of
select="@origin"/></source>
      <availability><xsl:value-of
select="availability"/></availability>
      <xsl:apply-templates/>
    </coffee>
  </xsl:template>

  <!-- Remove elements -->
  <xsl:template match="taste"/>
  <xsl:template match="price"/>
  <xsl:template match="availability"/>
  <xsl:template match="bestwith"/>

</xsl:stylesheet>
```

When this stylesheet is applied to the `coffee.xml` file, the following result
is generated:

```
<?xml version="1.0" encoding="utf-8"?>
 <region>
   <name>Latin America</name>
   <coffee>
     <price retail="11.99" wholesale="7.19"/>
     <source>Latin America|Guatemala</source>
     <availability>Year-round</availability>
   </coffee>
   <coffee>
     <price retail="12.99" wholesale="7.79"/>
     <source>Latin America|Costa Rica</source>
     <availability>Year-round</availability>
   </coffee>
 </region>

 <region>
  <name>Africa</name>
  <coffee>
    <price retail="14.99" wholesale="8.99"/>
    <source>Africa|Ethiopia</source>
    <availability>Limited</availability>
  </coffee>
  <coffee>
    <price retail="9.99" wholesale="5.99"/>
     <source>Africa|Kenya</source>
     <availability>Year-round</availability>
  </coffee>
 </region>
```

Combining elements

Elements from the source document can be combined together to construct new combined elements in the result document. Suppose, for example, I'd like to add a new `tagline` child element to the `coffee` element in `coffee-light.xml` (Listing 6-2) by combining the `taste` and `bestwith` elements.

To do so, the stylesheet is shown below:

```
<!-- coffee-merge.xsl -->
<xsl:stylesheet
    xmlns:xsl="http://www.w3.org/1999/XSL/Transform"
    version="1.0">

  <!-- Merge elements to create tagline element -->
  <xsl:template match="coffee">
    <coffee>
      <tagline>This Coffee Is <xsl:value-of select="taste"/>
    And Best Enjoyed With <xsl:value-of
    select="bestwith"/></tagline>
      <taste><xsl:value-of select="taste"/></taste>
      <price><xsl:value-of select="price"/></price>
      <availability><xsl:value-of
    select="availability"/></availability>
      <bestwith><xsl:value-of select="taste"/></bestwith>
    </coffee>
  </xsl:template>

</xsl:stylesheet>
```

The `tagline` element is created using a combination of literal text and `xsl:value-of` instructions to get the values of the `taste` and `bestwith` elements.

The result is as follows:

```
<?xml version="1.0" encoding="utf-8"?>
<coffee>
  <tagline>This Coffee Is Curiously Mild And Bland And Best
    Enjoyed With Breakfast</tagline>
  <taste>Curiously Mild And Bland</taste>
  <price>11.99</price>
  <availability>Year-round</availability>
  <bestwith>Curiously Mild And Bland</bestwith>
</coffee>
```

Rearranging elements in a document

Elements of the source document can be rearranged in the result document by reconstructing the structure of the XML elements according to your new needs. Consider the following example, in which I reorganize the child elements of the `coffee` element in the `coffee-light.xml` document (Listing 6-2) using the stylesheet that follows:

```
<!-- coffee-reorder.xsl -->
<xsl:stylesheet
    xmlns:xsl="http://www.w3.org/1999/XSL/Transform"
    version="1.0">

  <!-- Reorder elements -->
  <xsl:template match="coffee">
    <coffee>
      <availability><xsl:apply-templates
    select="availability"/></availability>
      <price><xsl:apply-templates select="price"/></price>
      <bestwith><xsl:apply-templates
    select="bestwith"/></bestwith>
      <taste><xsl:apply-templates select="taste"/></taste>
    </coffee>
  </xsl:template>

</xsl:stylesheet>
```

The elements are recreated using literal text and individual `xsl:apply-templates` instructions.

The result document follows:

```
<coffee>
  <availability>Year-round</availability>
  <price>11.99</price>
  <bestwith>Breakfast</bestwith>
  <taste>Curiously Mild And Bland</taste>
</coffee>
```

Adding comments

The `xsl:comment` instruction can be used to add an XML comment to your result document and has the following syntax:

```
<xsl:comment>CommentText</xsl:comment>
```

After transformation, the comment text you provide becomes surrounded by a $<!-$ and $->$. For example, suppose I'd like to output a note inside the result document using the following stylesheet:

```
<xsl:stylesheet
    xmlns:xsl="http://www.w3.org/1999/XSL/Transform"
    version="1.0">

  <xsl:template match="/">
    <xsl:comment>**** MARTY: Please process this at 6pm! ****
    <xsl:comment>
    <xsl:copy-of select="."/>
  </xsl:template>

</xsl:stylesheet>
```

When applied to the coffee-light.xml document (Listing 6-2), the following output is generated:

```
<?xml version="1.0"?>
<!-- **** MARTY: Please process this at 6pm! **** -->
<coffee name="Guatemalan Express" origin="Guatemala">
    <taste>Curiously Mild And Bland</taste>
    <price>11.99</price>
    <availability>Year-round</availability>
    <bestwith>Breakfast</bestwith>
</coffee>
```

Avoid adding a double hyphen $(-)$ in your comment text or ending your text with a single hyphen $(-)$. These special characters are used to indicate an end of comment tag and so could potentially cause problems in the resulting document output. Some XSLT processors are sophisticated enough to handle this syntax issue by padding an extra space to the last dash to prevent an error, but other processors will generate a runtime error during transformations.

Preserving PIs and comments

During the transformation process, all processing instructions and comments contained in the source document are stripped out. However, you can override this behavior and copy PIs and comments from the source to the result document by using the following template rule:

```
<xsl:template match=
    "processing-instruction()|
    comment()">
  <xsl:copy/>
</xsl:template>
```

Adding processing instructions

A processing instruction (PI) in XML is used to instruct the processor to perform a particular task. For example, following PI links an XML document to an external Cascading Style Sheet (CSS) stylesheet for formatting:

```
<?xml-stylesheet href="defaultstyles.css" type="text/css"?>
```

Processing instructions stand apart from other XML elements due to their `<?` prefix and `?>` suffix.

You can add a PI to your result document using the `xsl:processing-instruction` element. Its syntax is:

```
<xsl:processing-instruction
    name="name">Content</xsl:processing-instruction>
```

For example, to add the stylesheet linking PI shown above to your result document, I'd use the following statement:

```
<xsl:processing-instruction name="xml-
    stylesheet">href="defaultstyles.css"
    type="text/css"</xsl:processing-instruction>
```

The symbol `?>` is reserved for the ending of a PI. As a result, don't include `?>` as part of your PI declaration or you'll receive an error when you transform the stylesheet.

Outputting HTML Documents

If you read Book I, Chapter 1, you discover that while XML and HTML share a common markup language ancestry, there are definite syntactical differences that exist between the two languages. Fortunately, if you want to output an HTML as the result of the transformation, you can let the XSLT processor do the hard conversion work for you.

To illustrate how to output to HTML format, consider the `quotes.xml` file shown in Listing 6-3.

**Book IV
Chapter 6**

**The Output Side
of XSLT**

Listing 6-3   quotes.xml

```
<?xml version="1.0"?>
<filmquotes>
  <quote>
    <spokenby>Buzz Lightyear</spokenby>
```

(continued)

Listing 6-3 *(continued)*

```
    <source>Toy Story</source>
    <text>To infinity, and beyond!</text>
  </quote>
  <quote>
    <spokenby>Sam</spokenby>
    <source>Bennie and Joon</source>
    <text>It seems to me that, aside from being a little
  mentally ill, she's pretty normal.</text>
  </quote>
  <quote>
    <spokenby>Sabrina</spokenby>
    <source>Sabrina</source>
    <text>More isn't always better, Linus. Sometimes it's
  just more.</text>
  </quote>
  <quote>
    <spokenby>Rick Blaine</spokenby>
    <source>Casablanca</source>
    <text>Who are you really, and what were you before? What
  did you do, and what did you think, huh?</text>
  </quote>
  <quote>
    <spokenby>Phil Connors</spokenby>
    <source>Groundhog Day</source>
    <text>Well, it's Groundhog Day... again...</text>
  </quote>
  <quote>
    <spokenby>Wesley</spokenby>
    <source>Princess Bride</source>
    <text>To the pain...</text>
  </quote>
  <quote>
    <spokenby>Delmar</spokenby>
    <source>O Brother, Where Art Thou</source>
    <text>We thought you was a toad.</text>
  </quote>
  <quote>
    <spokenby>Inigo Montoya</spokenby>
    <source>Princess Bride</source>
    <text>Hello. My name is Inigo Montoya. You killed my
  father. Prepare to die.</text>
  </quote>
</filmquotes>
```

In order to transform this source file to an HTML document, I need to perform the following steps:

◆ **Specify HTML output.** By default, the XSLT processor outputs to an
   XML file. But you can use the `xsl:output` instruction to specify that

the result document should be written in HTML. To do so, use
`xsl:output` and define its `method` attribute to `html`:

```
<xsl:output method="html"/>
```

✦ **Add html container.** In order to output XML to HTML, I need to use the
transformation process to shed XML tags and replace them with appropriate HTML formatting tags to accompany the element content.

In this example, I change the `filmquotes` root element into an the `html`
container element and add the `head` and `body` elements. The `xsl:apply-
templates` instruction ensures that all children of the root element are
applied:

```
<xsl:template match="filmquotes">
  <html>
    <head>
      <title>Film Quotes</title>
    </head>
    <body>
      <xsl:apply-templates/>
    </body>
  </html>
</xsl:template>
```

✦ **Add content and formatting instructions.** For each `quote` element, I
prepare a formatted "template" to house its contents. The values of the
three children elements are formatted in this example:

```
<xsl:template match="quote">
  <h2><font color="#000099" face="Arial, Helvetica, sans-
  serif"><xsl:value-of select="source"/></font></h2>
  <font face="Georgia, Times New Roman, Times, serif">
  <p><xsl:value-of select="spokenby"/> said the following
  memorable line in <i><xsl:value-of
  select="source"/></i>:</p>
  <p>"<xsl:value-of select="text"/>"</p></font>
  <hr></hr>
</xsl:template>
```

The entire stylesheet is shown below:

```
<xsl:stylesheet version="1.0"
  xmlns:xsl="http://www.w3.org/1999/XSL/Transform">

<xsl:output method="html"/>

<!-- Wrap html and body elements around rest of
  document -->
```

```
<xsl:template match="filmquotes">
  <html>
    <body>
      <xsl:apply-templates/>
    </body>
  </html>
</xsl:template>

<!-- Render each quote as HTML -->
<xsl:template match="quote">
  <h2><font color="#000099" face="Arial, Helvetica, sans-
  serif"><xsl:value-of select="source"/></font></h2>
  <font face="Georgia, Times New Roman, Times, serif">
  <p><xsl:value-of select="spokenby"/> said the following
  memorable line in <i><xsl:value-of
  select="source"/></i>:</p>
  <p>"<xsl:value-of select="text"/>"</p></font>
  <hr/>
</xsl:template>

</xsl:stylesheet>
```

Check out the HTML that is generated by the transformation:

```
<html>
  <body>

    <h2><font color="#000099" face="Arial, Helvetica, sans-
serif">Toy Story</font></h2><font face="Georgia, Times
New Roman, Times, serif">
    <p>Buzz Lightyear said the following memorable line
in <i>Toy Story</i>:
    </p>
    <p>"To infinity, and beyond!"</p></font><hr>

    <h2><font color="#000099" face="Arial, Helvetica, sans-
serif">Bennie and Joon</font></h2><font face="Georgia,
Times New Roman, Times, serif">
    <p>Sam said the following memorable line in
<i>Bennie and Joon</i>:
    </p>
    <p>"It seems to me that, aside from being a little
mentally ill, she's pretty normal."</p></font><hr>

    <h2><font color="#000099" face="Arial, Helvetica, sans-
serif">Sabrina</font></h2><font face="Georgia, Times New
Roman, Times, serif">
    <p>Sabrina said the following memorable line in
<i>Sabrina</i>:
```

```
      </p>
      <p>"More isn't always better, Linus. Sometimes it's
just more."</p></font><hr>

    <h2><font color="#000099" face="Arial, Helvetica, sans-
serif">Casablanca</font></h2><font face="Georgia, Times
New Roman, Times, serif">
      <p>Rick Blaine said the following memorable line in
<i>Casablanca</i>:
      </p>
      <p>"Who are you really, and what were you before?
What did you do, and what did you think,
huh?"</p></font><hr>

    <h2><font color="#000099" face="Arial, Helvetica, sans-
serif">Groundhog Day</font></h2><font face="Georgia,
Times New Roman, Times, serif">
      <p>Phil Connors said the following memorable line in
<i>Groundhog Day</i>:
      </p>
      <p>"Well, it's Groundhog Day...
again..."</p></font><hr>

    <h2><font color="#000099" face="Arial, Helvetica, sans-
serif">Princess Bride</font></h2><font face="Georgia,
Times New Roman, Times, serif">
      <p>Wesley said the following memorable line in
<i>Princess Bride</i>:
      </p>
      <p>"To the pain..."</p></font><hr>

    <h2><font color="#000099" face="Arial, Helvetica, sans-
serif">O Brother, Where Art Thou</font></h2><font
face="Georgia, Times New Roman, Times, serif">
      <p>Delmar said the following memorable line in <i>O
Brother, Where Art Thou</i>:
      </p>
      <p>"We thought you was a toad."</p></font><hr>

    <h2><font color="#000099" face="Arial, Helvetica, sans-
serif">Princess Bride</font></h2><font face="Georgia,
Times New Roman, Times, serif">
      <p>Inigo Montoya said the following memorable line
in <i>Princess Bride</i>:
      </p>
      <p>"Hello. My name is Inigo Montoya. You killed my
father. Prepare to die."</p></font><hr>

  </body>
</html>
```

The XSLT processor formats the HTML markup document and converts it to syntax that even older browsers can understand. For example, the ⟨hr/⟩ element I defined in my template was converted to ⟨hr⟩.

Working with Whitespace

When you begin to work with XSLT, you quickly start to notice "whitespace" issues in your result documents: an extra line here or there or an unexpected indentation in your XML code. The term *whitespace* is used to describe invisible characters inside a document, such as spaces, tabs, carriage returns, and line feeds.

For XML documents, extra whitespace is often something you can ignore because spacing or line breaks between XML elements won't impact how it is processed. Nonetheless, when you output to text or if the whitespace is part of the element content, then knowing how to work with whitespace is important as you transform your XML documents.

Whitespace in your result document comes from the source XML document, the XSLT stylesheet, or a mixture of both.

Whitespace in the XML document

When an XML document is processed by any XML or XSLT processor, all whitespace outside the start and end tags of the XML elements is preserved. For example, suppose I have an XML document with the following structure:

```
<topfilms createdby="AFI">
  <film place="1" date="1941">Citizen Kane</film>
          <film place="2" date="1942">Casablanca</film>

  <film place="3" date="1972">The Godfather</film>

              <film place="4" date="1939">Gone With The
  Wind</film><film place="5" date="1962">Lawrence Of
  Arabia</film>
  <film place="6" date="1939">The Wizard Of Oz</film>

   <film place="7" date="1967">The Graduate</film><film
   place="8" date="1954">On The Waterfront</film>

   <film place="9" date="1993">Schindler's List</film>


    <film place="10" date="1952">Singin' In The Rain</film>
</topfilms>
```

The whitespace between the elements in this source file is carried over automatically to the result document. I can test this by creating a simple stylesheet:

```
<xsl:template match="film">
  <xsl:apply-templates/>
</xsl:template>
```

After transformation, the output look like:

```
Citizen Kane
        Casablanca

The Godfather

            Gone With The WindLawrence Of Arabia
The Wizard Of Oz

 The GraduateOn The Waterfront

Schindler's List



Singin' In The Rain
```

Removing whitespace with xsl:strip-space

To shed this extra whitespace, I can use the xsl:strip-space instruction. This element has a single required attribute named elements:

```
<xsl:strip-space elements="elementName"/>
```

The elements attribute is used to list the names of elements containing whitespace that you want to strip out during transformation. To add more than one name, separate each name with a space, or use * to specify all elements.

In the example shown above, I specify the topfilms element because the extra whitespace is wholly part of its content:

```
<xsl:strip-space elements="topfilms"/>
```

The xsl:strip-space instruction is a top-level element for a stylesheet and must appear directly below the xsl:stylesheet element in your stylesheet.

When this element is added to the stylesheet, the new result is much different than before:

```
Citizen KaneCasablancaThe GodfatherGone With The WindLawrence
    Of ArabiaThe Wizard Of OzThe GraduateOn The
    WaterfrontSchindler's ListSingin' In The Rain
```

Unlike many other XSLT instructions, xsl:strip-space is not applied to children of elements specified in the elements attribute. Therefore, to remove any whitespace in the film element, I must add it to the elements attribute value: elements="topfilms film".

Maintaining whitespace with xsl:preserve-space

The xsl:preserve-space element is used to preserve whitespace in the source XML document. As you've seen already, XSLT preserves whitespace by default, so xsl:preserve-space is needed only when you need to turn off xsl:strip-space or make an exception to it. For example, suppose I want to remove all the whitespace in the source XML file, except for the whitespace inside the film element. I'd use the following instructions to specify this rule:

```
<xsl:strip-space elements="*"/>
<xsl:preserve-space elements="film"/>
```

Like xsl:strip-space, xsl:preserve-space is a top-level element for a stylesheet.

Preserving whitespace with xml:space attribute

You can also preserve whitespace in the source document by adding the xml:space attribute to one or more of the elements in your source XML file. The xml:space attribute has two possible values:

✦ xml:space="preserve" informs the processor to maintain the whitespace for this element.

✦ xml:space="default" instructs the processor to return to its default whitespace setting.

When added to an element in your XML document, xml:space is applied to that element as well as to its descendants.

Whitespace in XSLT stylesheets

Whitespace in the XSLT stylesheet is generally removed prior to the transformation itself. However, you can tweak how the processor deals with whitespace based on the way in which you handle text nodes and xsl:text instructions.

Whitespace in text nodes

Whitespace in text nodes (see Book V, Chapter 1 for more on text nodes) is ignored by default. However, when a text node contains non-whitespace characters, then whitespace characters are preserved. To demonstrate how this works, consider the afifilms.xml document shown in Listing 6-4:

Listing 6-4   afifilms.xml

```
<topfilms createdby="AFI">
  <film place="1" date="1941">Citizen Kane</film>
  <film place="2" date="1942">Casablanca</film>
  <film place="3" date="1972">The Godfather</film>
  <film place="4" date="1939">Gone With The Wind</film>
  <film place="5" date="1962">Lawrence Of Arabia</film>
  <film place="6" date="1939">The Wizard Of Oz</film>
  <film place="7" date="1967">The Graduate</film>
  <film place="8" date="1954">On The Waterfront</film>
  <film place="9" date="1993">Schindler's List</film>
  <film place="10" date="1952">Singin' In The Rain</film>
</topfilms>
```

To create a simple text list of these films and their dates, I can create the following template rule to achieve this result:

```
<xsl:template match="film">
 <xsl:apply-templates/>
 <xsl:value-of select="@date"/>
</xsl:template>
```

When the XML document is transformed, the text result is as follows:

```
Citizen Kane1941
Casablanca1942
The Godfather1972
Gone With The Wind1939
Lawrence Of Arabia1962
The Wizard Of Oz1939
The Graduate1967
On The Waterfront1954
Schindler's List1993
Singin' In The Rain1952
```

The film names are generated from the xsl:apply-templates while the dates are output using the xsl:value-of instruction. Although you can't see it, a text node actually separates these two instructions because they are separated in the stylesheet by a carriage return and linefeed. However, because the text node just has whitespace in it, this text node has no impact on the result document.

However, suppose I add a connector phrase between the xsl:apply-templates and xsl:value-of instructions:

```
<xsl:template match="film">
 <xsl:apply-templates/> was made in
 <xsl:value-of select="@date"/>
</xsl:template>
```

In this case, because I have non-whitespace between the instructions, the carriage return and line feed characters now cannot be ignored and show up in the result document:

```
Citizen Kane was made in
1941
Casablanca was made in
1942
The Godfather was made in
1972
Gone With The Wind was made in
1939
Lawrence Of Arabia was made in
1962
The Wizard Of Oz was made in
1939
The Graduate was made in
1967
On The Waterfront was made in
1954
Schindler's List was made in
1993
Singin' In The Rain was made in
1952
```

However, by getting rid of the line between instructions and text, I can make the list more readable using the following stylesheet:

```
<xsl:template match="film">
 <xsl:apply-templates/> was made in <xsl:value-of
 select="@date"/>
</xsl:template>
```

The results are shown here:

```
Citizen Kane was made in 1941
Casablanca was made in 1942
The Godfather was made in 1972
Gone With The Wind was made in 1939
Lawrence Of Arabia was made in 1962
The Wizard Of Oz was made in 1939
The Graduate was made in 1967
On The Waterfront was made in 1954
Schindler's List was made in 1993
Singin' In The Rain was made in 1952
```

Whitespace inside xsl:text

When you use the xsl:text instruction in a template rule, any whitespace appearing inside of it is preserved.

Suppose, for example, I decide to add an XML comment before each item in a list using the xsl:comment instruction. Because xsl:text is not used, the results are placed on the same line.

```
<xsl:template match="film">
  <xsl:comment>List entry</xsl:comment>
  <listitem><xsl:apply-templates/> was made in <xsl:value-
  of select="@date"/></listitem>
</xsl:template>
```

The result is:

```
<!--List entry--><listitem>Citizen Kane was made in
  1941</listitem>
<!--List entry--><listitem>Casablanca was made in
  1942</listitem>
<!--List entry--><listitem>The Godfather was made in
  1972</listitem>
<!--List entry--><listitem>Gone With The Wind was made in
  1939</listitem>
<!--List entry--><listitem>Lawrence Of Arabia was made in
  1962</listitem>
<!--List entry--><listitem>The Wizard Of Oz was made in
  1939</listitem>
<!--List entry--><listitem>The Graduate was made in 1967
<!--List entry--><listitem>On The Waterfront was made in
  1954</listitem>
<!--List entry--><listitem>Schindler's List was made in
  1993</listitem>
<!--List entry--><listitem>Singin' In The Rain was made in
  1952</listitem>
```

Because whitespace is ignored between `</xsl:comment>` and `<xsl:apply-templates>` tags, I need to use `xsl:text` to add a line break between the comment and line text:

```
<xsl:template match="film">
<xsl:comment>List entry</xsl:comment><xsl:text>
</xsl:text><listitem><xsl:apply-templates/> was made in
 <xsl:value-of select="@date"/><xsl:text></listitem>
</xsl:text>
</xsl:template>
```

The generated result document follows:

```
<!--List entry-->
<listitem>Citizen Kane was made in 1941</listitem>

<!--List entry-->
<listitem>Casablanca was made in 1942</listitem>

<!--List entry-->
<listitem>The Godfather was made in 1972</listitem>

<!--List entry-->
<listitem>Gone With The Wind was made in 1939</listitem>

<!--List entry-->
<listitem>Lawrence Of Arabia was made in 1962</listitem>

<!--List entry-->
<listitem>The Wizard Of Oz was made in 1939</listitem>

<!--List entry-->
<listitem>The Graduate was made in 1967</listitem>

<!--List entry-->
<listitem>On The Waterfront was made in 1954</listitem>

<!--List entry-->
<listitem>Schindler's List was made in 1993</listitem>

<!--List entry-->
<listitem>Singin' In The Rain was made in 1952</listitem>
```

Book V

Working with the Rest of the X-Team

The 5th Wave   By Rich Tennant

SNOW GLOBE DATA STORAGE

Okay let's shake this thing and see what we come up with.

Contents at a Glance

Chapter 1: XLink — Linking XML Documents

In This Chapter

✔ Discovering how XLink differs from traditional HTML hyperlinks

✔ Exploring how to create multi-directional links using XLink

✔ Discovering simple-type and extended-type links

✔ Finding out how to add navigation rules to links

A link is a link is a link. Right?

That adage may have been true in the HTML world, but it sure doesn't apply to XML documents. I know what you may be thinking: "What else can a link do besides connect A to B? After all, links aren't rocket science."

You surely don't need a degree in rocket propulsion to understand links in XML, but there are more to links than you may realize if you are used to working with HTML. Suppose you want to bring multiple resources together using a single link. Or, perhaps you want to specify the details of how the link should be presented to the user. Impossible ideas in HTML, but altogether possible with XML.

In this chapter, you'll explore XML Linking Language, more commonly known as XLink, and discover that you can use this emerging technology to perform linking beyond your wildest imaginations. Although actual implementations of XLink are few in number today, the technology will continue to become increasingly important with the rapid spread of XML in browser environments on your desktop, cell phone, handheld, and beyond.

Linking 'Til Your Heart's Content

By itself, XML describes data and, as a result, contains no built-in ability to link XML documents and other external resources together. However, recognizing this shortcoming, the W3C defined XLink, which is the standardized way in which you can create links inside XML.

In HTML, you can create hyperlinks by using the anchor element (`<a>`). For example, if you'd like to display the text `See a dummy` as a hyperlink that sends the user to `www.dummies.com`, you could use the following HTML code:

```
<a href="http://www.dummies.com">See a dummy</a>
```

When an HTML document containing the preceding code is displayed in a browser, the text `See a dummy` appears as a hyperlink. When you click the link, you are directed to the Dummies Web site.

Although XLink does allow you to link in the same way in which HTML does, as you'll discover in this chapter, XLink also allows you to do far more than the familiar `<a>` element.

XLink is different than most other XML technologies, such as XSLT or XML Schemas, in which you have a defined set of elements that you use to perform an intended action. Rather than having a distinctive library of elements, XLink is implemented through attributes. As a result, XLink acts more like an *add-in* to an existing document, giving your existing documents instant linking capabilities. The reason for this is quite apparent: hyperlinks in HTML are defined using such predefined presentation elements as `<a>` or `<img>`, but in XML where data is king, you'll typically want to directly link one of your existing elements to another.

To enable linking elements in your XML document, you begin by declaring the XLink namespace to the root or another element in your document. For example, consider the following vanilla element:

```
<vanilla>

</vanilla>
```

To make it a linking element, add the XLink namespace:

```
<vanilla xmlns:xlink="http://www.w3.org/1999/xlink">

</vanilla>
```

You can then add various XLink attributes to your elements depending on the type of links that you want to set up. These different link types are shown in Table 1-1 and are discussed in the remaining sections of the chapter.

Table 1-1		XLink Link Types		
Link Type	**Used For**	**Required Attributes**	**Optional Attributes**	**Permissible XLink Child Elements**
`xlink:type ="simple"`	Defines a simple 1:1 link from a local resource to a remote resource	`type`	`href`, `role`, `arcrole`, `title`, `show`, `actuate`	
`xlink:type ="extended"`	Declares a wrapper element that houses a complex link using locator, arc, and resource types	`type`	`role`, `title`	`locator`, `arc`, `resource`, `title`
`xlink:type ="locator"`	Identifies a remote resource	`type`, `href`	`role`, `title`, `label`	`title`
`xlink:type ="arc"`	Connects resources using the `to` and `from` attributes	`type`	`arcrole`, `title`, `show`, `actuate`, `from`, `to`	`title`
`xlink:type ="resource"`	Identifies a local resource	`type`	`role`, `title`, `label`	
`xlink:type ="title"`	Alternative way to provide a descriptive title for extended, locator, and arc linking elements	`type`		

Creating Simple-Type Links

A *simple-type link* is just like the common HTML link you probably know so well, in which you create link from a *local resource* (a linking element) to a *remote resource* (an identifiable resource referenced by a URI). With a simple-type link, you start the link at an element with a `xlink:type="simple"` attribute defined and end the link at the destination specified by a `href` attribute:

```
<myElement xlink:type="simple" href="URI"/>
```

For example, consider the following `actors` structure in which you'd like to link-enable:

```
<actors>
  <actor>
    <firstname>Kevin</firstname>
    <lastname>Bacon</lastname>
  </actor>
  <actor>
    <firstname>Tom</firstname>
    <lastname>Hanks</lastname>
  </actor>
</actors>
```

Suppose you'd like to link each `actor` element to an external HTML file that provides a biography. To do so, you first add the XLink namespace to the actors element and then add simple link attributes to each `actor` element:

```
<actors xmlns:xlink="http://www.w3.org/1999/xlink">
  <actor xlink:type="simple" href="kbacon_bio.xml">
    <firstname>Kevin</firstname>
    <lastname>Bacon</lastname>
  </actor>
  <actor xlink:type="simple" href="hbogart_bio.xml">
    <firstname>Humphrey</firstname>
    <lastname>Bogart</lastname>
  </actor>
</actors>
```

The XML application then navigates to the XML files specified by the `href` attribute when that link is triggered.

Figure 1-1 shows a visual representation of the two simple links.

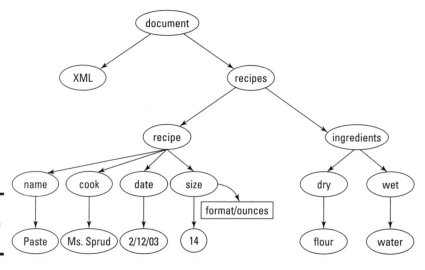

Figure 1-1:
Simple-type
links.

What happens next?

Sometimes emerging XML technologies, such as XLink, are harder to fully comprehend simply because of the lack of implementations on the market today.

For example, if you want to understand what happens when you create a link in HTML, you can get out Notepad, define an <a> element in an HTML file, and then instantly see the results of your code by previewing the file in a Web browser. What's more, you know that the presentation is fixed: When your document is viewed, the browser displays the link text as underlined and jumps to the Web address specified by the `href` attribute.

XLink, however, doesn't enforce behavior of the link like HTML does. Therefore, exactly what happens with the link depends entirely on the application that processes the XML data. A browser that supports XLink may treat a simple XML link in the same manner as a normal HTML hyperlink. But another XML application may want to do something else to represent the link. Additionally, viewing and testing of XLink links are harder today because implementations are only starting to get on the market.

Creating Extended-Type Links

Simple-type links provide basic "two-dimensional" functionality for connecting a local resource with an external resource, but there are many instances in which you may want greater linking power. XLink enables you to create links between multiple local and remote resources to enable "three-dimensional" links.

Linking external resources

Suppose, for example, you have actors.xml and films.xml external resource files and you'd like to bring together an actor, the films in which the actor has starred, and the coactors with whom he or she has worked. The limited nature of HTML links obviously wouldn't be able to handle such a complex task, but XLink provides this support through *extended-type links*.

To create an extended-type link, you add the `xlink:type="extended"` attribute to your element.

```
<myElement xmlns:xlink="http://www.w3.org/1999/xlink"
   xlink:type="extended">
  <!-- Define link here -->
</myElement>
```

This extended-type link element is often in a different location than the resources that it associates. In the actors/film example, suppose that you have a separate linkage.xml file that stores the link structure that is defined below.

Resources and arcs

The `xlink:type="extended"` attribute itself isn't used to define the details of the link you want to set up. Instead, it declares a wrapper element that you can use to house the three link types that actually define the nitty gritty details of the multi-dimensional link. These three link types include the following:

+ **A locator-type link** (defined by `xlink:type="locator"`) identifies a remote resource to which you want to link via a URI.

+ **A resource-type link** (`xlink:type="resource"`) identifies a local resource to which you want to link.

+ **An arc-type link** (`xlink:type="arc"`) serves as the connector or bridge between two resources, telling how to traverse a pair of resources, including the direction and optionally the behavior of the application.

Traversal attributes

In order for an extended-type link to be able to connect all of the dots together, three *traversal attributes* are used to navigate from a link's origin (called a *starting resource*) to the link's destination (called an *ending resource*). These three attributes are as follows:

+ `xlink:label` provides a label to identify a resource. The label should be an `NCName` type string (see Book I, Chapter 2 for more on the `NCName` type), which essentially means that it should be a string without spaces or tabs. The `xlink:label` attribute is used with locator-type and resource-type elements.

+ `xlink:from` identifies the starting resource of an arc-type link. This attribute, used only with arc-type links, has a value that corresponds to the value of an `xlink:label` from a resource or locator element.

+ `xlink:to` identifies the ending resource of an arc-type link. This attribute, used only with arc-type links, has a value that corresponds to the value of an `xlink:label` from a resource or locator element.

Combining XLink parts into an extended-type link

Returning to the actors/films example, suppose that you create an element called `sixDegrees` that serves as the extended link element:

```
<sixDegrees xmlns:xlink="http://www.w3.org/1999/xlink"
    xlink:type="extended">

</sixDegrees>
```

To bring all of the resources together into this structure, you use a combination of locator-type and arc-type elements:

```
<sixDegrees xmlns:xlink="http://www.w3.org/1999/xlink"
   xlink:type="extended">

  <!-- Actor resource -->
  <actorInfo xlink:type="locator" xlink:label="actor"
    xlink:href="kbacon.xml"/>

  <!-- Film resources -->
  <filmInfo xlink:type="locator" xlink:label="film"
    xlink:href="apollo13.xml"/>
  <filmInfo xlink:type="locator" xlink:label="film"
    xlink:href="footloose.xml"/>

  <!-- Coactor resources -->
  <coactorInfo xlink:type="locator" xlink:label="coactor"
    xlink:href="thanks.xml"/>
  <coactorInfo xlink:type="locator" xlink:label="coactor"
    xlink:href="jlithgow.xml"/>

  <!-- Bridge to connect resources -->
  <connector xlink:type="arc" xlink:from="film"
    xlink:to="actor"/>
  <connector xlink:type="arc" xlink:from="coactor"
    xlink:to="actor"/>

</sixDegrees>
```

The `actorInfo` element is defined as a locator-type link to identify the specific external XML resource containing the actor information. The `xlink:label` attribute is used to provide a name that you reference when you create arcs between resources.

The `filmInfo` elements define locator-type links to identify the specific external resources that contain film-related data you need to bring in. Each element uses the same `xlink:label` attribute, because the resources are of the same class of data.

The `connector` elements define the arc-type links that connect the `actor` to both the `film` and the `coactor`. In this example, it joins together Kevin Bacon, his films, and his coactors to give you the "Six Degrees of Kevin Bacon" that you were looking for.

Figure 1-2 illustrates the linking of various remote resources.

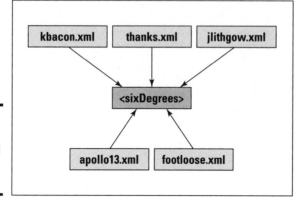

Figure 1-2:
Multi-
dimensional
extended-
type links.

Linking local resources

The locator-type elements reference information from an external XML file. However, suppose that the elements are local and contained within the same structure. If so, you would use a resource-type element (using xlink:type= "resource") to identify the element instead. For example, the following modified code snippet now incorporates the actor data inside the actorInfo element. As a result, I changed its type to be a resource-type element:

```
<sixDegrees xmlns:xlink="http://www.w3.org/1999/xlink"
   xlink:type="extended">

   <!-- Actor local resource -->
   <actorInfo xlink:type="resource" xlink:label="actor">
     <firstName>Kevin</firstName>
     <lastName>Bacon</lastName>
     <bio>Kevin was born in 1958...</bio>
   </actorInfo>

   <!-- Film resources -->
   <filmInfo xlink:type="locator" xlink:label="film"
     xlink:href="apollo13.xml"/>
   <filmInfo xlink:type="locator" xlink:label="film"
     xlink:href="footloose.xml"/>

   <!-- Bridge to connect resources -->
   <connector xlink:type="arc" xlink:from="actor"
     xlink:to="film"/>

</sixDegrees>
```

Matchmaker, matchmaker, make me a match

You may find it helpful to think of the arc-type link as a sort of "matchmaker," joining two different types of resources that are identified by the xlink:to and xlink:from attributes.

Therefore, this link is just like a matchmaker of a couple, who isn't involved in the marriage itself, but instead only serves to connect a man and woman together for the purposes of marriage.

Adding Navigation Rules to Arcs

XLink also enables you to add instructions to arcs that specify how the link should be navigated using the xlink:show and xlink:actuate attributes.

✦ The xlink:show element specifies the way in which the ending resource should be presented. Possible values include the following:

- xlink:show="new" to open a new window.

- xlink:show="replace" to open the ending resource in the same window.

- xlink:show="embed" to embed the ending resource in the current window.

- xlink:show="none" to not restrict any presentation option.

- xlink:show="other" to not restrict any presentation option, but the processing application should look to a child element for more information.

✦ The xlink:actuate element declares the timing of navigating to the ending resource. Possible values include the following:

- xlink:actuate="onLoad" to load the ending resource as soon as the starting resource is located.

- xlink:actuate="onRequest" to load the ending resource only when an event after loading is triggered. The specific events depend entirely on the application, but possible request events could be a button click or a timer being set.

- xlink:actuate="none" to not restrict any timing option.

- xlink:actuaute="other" to not restrict any timing option, but the processing application should look to a child element for more information.

You can use these attributes to further specify the type of arc you want to declare. For example, the following arc-type elements specify that the `actor` resource should be displayed in a new window as soon as the `film` or `coactor` resource is loaded:

```
<connector xlink:type="arc"
  xlink:from="film" xlink:to="actor"
  xlink:show="new" xlink:actuate="onLoad"/>
<connector xlink:type="arc"
  xlink:from="coactor" xlink:to="actor"
  xlink:show="new" xlink:actuate="onLoad"/>
```

Tacking On Descriptions

Three *semantic attributes* are used to provide descriptive information about an XLink link. They are explained in the following list:

✦ The `xlink:title` is an optional attribute that contains a string that describes the link. By itself, this attribute is not functional. However, specific XLink implementations can choose to do what they want with an `xlink:title` if one is present. For example, the following `xlink:title` describes the locator-type element:

```
<filmInfo xlink:type="locator" xlink:title="Apollo 13
  film"
    xlink:href="apollo13.xml"/>
```

The title attribute can be included with any of the XLink type attributes (simple, extended, locator, resource, arc).

✦ `xlink:role` is an advanced attribute that is used to identify a property that the link has. Its value must be a URI.

✦ The `xlink:arcrole` attribute is another attribute used for advanced purposes and also identifies another type of property that the link has. Its value must also be a URI.

Looking at a More Comprehensive Example

Putting all of the XLink capabilities together, the following code listing shows a `sixDegrees` element that is defined as an extended-type link that houses a set of `actor` and `film` locator-type elements as well as `degree` arc-type elements:

```
<sixDegrees xmlns:xlink="http://www.w3.org/1999/xlink"
  xlink:type="extended">

  <!-- Actor locator elements -->
```

```
<actors>
  <actor xlink:type="locator" xlink:label="act100"
    xlink:href="pub/actors/kbacon.xml" xlink:title="Kevin
Bacon"
    xlink:role="http://www.sixdegrees.com/actor"/>
  <actor xlink:type="locator" xlink:label="act101"
    xlink:href="pub/actors/thanks.xml" xlink:title="Tom
Hanks"
    xlink:role="http://www.sixdegrees.com/actor"/>
  <actor xlink:type="locator" xlink:label="act102"
    xlink:href="pub/actors/jlithgow.xml" xlink:title="John
Lithgow"
    xlink:role="http://www.sixdegrees.com/actor"/>
</actors>

<!-- Film locator elements -->
<films>
  <film xlink:type="locator" xlink:label="film101"
    xlink:href="pub/films/apollo13.xml"
    xlink:title="Apollo 13"/>
  <film xlink:type="locator" xlink:label="film102"
    xlink:href="pub/films/footloose.xml"
    xlink:title="Footloose"/>
</films>

<!-- Degree arc elements -->
<degree xlink:type="arc" xlink:title="Kevin's first major
  movie"
  xlink:from="act100" xlink:to="film101"
  xlink:show="new"
  xlink:actuate="onRequest"/>

<degree xlink:type="arc" xlink:title="Kevin as supporting
  actor"
  xlink:from="film102" xlink:to="act100"
  xlink:show="new"
  xlink:actuate="onRequest"

  xlink:arcrole="http://www.sixdegrees.com/supportingrole"/>

<degree xlink:type="arc" xlink:title="Tom Hanks, one degree
  of separation"
  xlink:from="act100" xlink:to="act101"
  xlink:show="new"
  xlink:actuate="onRequest"/>

</sixDegrees>
```

The actors element houses the actor locator elements. Each actor element references an external XML file and uses an xlink:label attribute to uniquely identify the specific actor element. An xlink:title attribute is added to provide descriptive information about the name of the actor. Finally, an xlink:role references a URI that can provide more insight into the nature of the actor role. The films element houses the film locator elements, each of which mirrors the pattern of the actor elements.

The three degree elements connect the pieces together. The first degree element traverses from Kevin Bacon's actor element to the Footloose film element. The second degree element navigates from the Apollo 13 film element to Kevin Bacon's actor element. Finally, the third degree element traverses from Kevin Bacon's actor element to Tom Hanks's actor element.

Chapter 2: XPointer — Pointing to Resources

In This Chapter

✔ Comparing XPointer to HTML's named anchors

✔ Pointing to resources by unique identifier

✔ Navigating to resources using a stepwise approach

✔ Pointing to resources using XPath expressions

✔ Working with XPointer built-in functions

Some people love details. Some don't. Different personality types pay differing amounts of attention to the particulars. Some people like to chart out a course in a broad direction, but they don't like to worry about the minute details of how to get there. Other people relish the particulars, enjoy taking the wide objective defined by the "big picture guy," and figure out the way to carry it out.

If you had to personify XML technologies, XLink (discussed in Book V, Chapter 1) is that stereotypical "big picture guy," because it does a great job of linking to resources. However, XLink always stops at the document level and doesn't dive any further inside of a document. Carrying on where XLink leaves off, XPointer serves as the "details guy," starting at the document that XLink provides and locating a specific resource inside of it.

This chapter introduces you to XPointer and shows you how to combine XLink and XPointer to locate the exact information you want to find inside of your XML documents.

Understanding XPointer

If you read Book II, Chapter 1, you discovered that XLink is XML's "next generation" version of HTML's <a> element, enabling you to link to an external resource from within an XML structure — and do a whole lot more. Similarly, XPointer can be considered the XML enhanced version of HTML's *named anchors*.

HTML uses named anchors to reference a specific location in an HTML document. For example, to define an anchor inside of a document, you use an explicitly named <a> element:

```
<a name="pointToMe">
```

This anchor can then be called from inside the same HTML file, by using the <a> element with an href attribute value that points to it:

```
<a href="#pointToMe">
```

The pound sign (#) is used to denote that pointToMe is a named anchor.

Or, if you want to point to the named anchor from an external HTML file, you prefix the URI of the source document prior to the anchor name:

```
<a href="http://pointtome.com/index.html#pointToMe">
```

XPointer takes the basic concept of named anchors, but builds upon it for XML documents. Like XLink does, XPointer doesn't require pointing to a specific element name (<a>), but instead enables you to find any given resource in your document, whether it be an element or an attribute, and even a range of elements or resources.

XPointer is not only closely associated with the XPath language but, in fact, is built on top of it. (See Book IV, Chapter 3 for the nitty gritty on XPath.) If you read about XPath before, you know that XPath is a language designed to locate nodes inside of an XML tree. XPointer locates nodes, but it also enables you to locate other parts or ranges of a document in addition to nodes. XPointer returns a *location*, which can be a specific non-node *point* in a document (such as a character), a *range* (defined by starting or ending points), or a familiar node or node-set (such as an element or attribute).

Like XPath, XPointer remains an emerging technology at this — pardon the pun — point in time, but it is expected to grow increasingly important as more and more software solutions begin to adopt support for it and the W3C concludes its work on the recommendation.

Each of the XPointer examples in this chapter are based on the coffee.xml file shown in Listing 2-1.

Listing 2-1:   coffee.xml

```
<?xml version="1.0"?>
<coffees>
 <region id="LA" name="Latin America">
  <coffee id="GUA392" name="Guatemalan Express"
   origin="Guatemala">
   <taste>Mild and Bland</taste>
   <price>11.99</price>
   <availability>Year-round</availability>
   <bestwith>Breakfast</bestwith>
  </coffee>
  <coffee id="COS120" name="Costa Rican Deacon" origin="Costa
   Rica">
   <taste>Exotic and Untamed</taste>
   <price>12.99</price>
   <availability>Year-round</availability>
   <bestwith>Dessert</bestwith>
  </coffee>
 </region>
 <region id="AF" name="Africa">
  <coffee id="ETH129" name="Ethiopian Sunset Supremo"
   origin="Ethiopia">
   <taste>Exotic and Untamed</taste>
   <price>14.99</price>
   <availability>Limited</availability>
   <bestwith>Chocolate</bestwith>
  </coffee>
  <coffee id="KEN647" name="Kenyan Elephantismo"
   origin="Kenya">
   <taste>Solid yet Understated</taste>
   <price>3.99</price>
   <availability>Year-round</availability>
   <bestwith>Elephant Ears</bestwith>
  </coffee>
  <coffee id="BUR111" name="Burundi Legolasan"
   origin="Burundi">
   <taste>A Taste Only A Wood Elf Would Like</taste>
   <price>33.99</price>
   <availability>Very Limited</availability>
   <bestwith>Lembas Bread</bestwith>
  </coffee>
  </region>
</coffees>
```

Pointing to Elements by ID

The simplest way to point to specific parts of an XML document is to reference a specific ID value of an element. This *bare name* method of pointing works if your XML document has an ID attribute defined for your XML elements that you wish to point to. Therefore, to refer to a specific part of a document, start with a URI to the document name and then add a pound sign (#) and an XPointer expression to point to the desired part. When you wish to reference an ID, use the following expression:

```
URI#xpointer(id("id-value"))
```

`xpointer()` denotes that the expression is an XPointer expression. The `id()` location term selects the element in the document that has `ID` provided in quotation marks.

To illustrate, each of the `coffee` elements shown in coffee.xml (see Listing 2-1) has an ID attribute defined. To point to the Kenyan Elephantismo coffee, the XPointer expression would look like the following:

```
coffee.xml#xpointer(id("KEN647"))
```

Because XPointer is typically used in combination with XLink, the following code snippet shows the XPointer expression tagged onto the end of an XLink simple link:

```
<coffeeOfTheDay xlink:type="simple"
  xlink:href="http://www.dummycoffee.com#xpointer(id(&apos;
  COS120&apos;)"/>
```

In the preceding code, the quotation marks that surround the ID value are replaced with `&apos;` because the XPointer expression is already inside of quotes.

When you point to a resource by ID, XPointer provides an abbreviated syntax to simplify the expression. Rather than using the `xpointer(id("ID"))` expression, you can simply reference the value of the ID. Therefore, to reference the Kenyan Elephantismo coffee, your expression can be simplified to the following:

```
<coffeeOfTheDay xlink:type="simple"
  xlink:href="http://www.dummycoffee.com#COS120"/>
```

In order to use the bare names method of XPointer, your XML document needs to have a DTD or XML schema that defines an attribute as an ID type. Otherwise, XPointer will not be able to determine whether or not an attribute is an ID.

In addition, the ID attribute doesn't necessarily need to be named `ID` to be used by XPointer. Instead, regardless of the name, define the attribute as an ID type in your DTD or XML Schema and call it anything you wish.

Escape from Alcatraz?

When you use an XPointer expression inside of an XML document, you need to know how to escape. No, escaping in XML doesn't mean breaking out of an island compound, but it does mean you know how to deal with special characters, such as <, &, (, or), in your expressions.

To use < or & in your XPointer expression, escape them using < and &. XPointer also requires that you have balanced parentheses, so that any unbalanced parenthesis must be escaped using ^. For example, to escape the right parenthesis, you use ^). Finally, when you need to use an XPointer expression inside of an XML attribute value, you need to escape quotation marks using " (double quotation mark) and ' (single quotation mark).

As you can see, the shorthand method of pointing to an ID looks very similar to referencing a named anchor in HTML.

Using IDs is the safest and surest way to address a particular point in an XML document. Most of the other ways of pointing to an XML resource (discussed in the rest of this chapter) depend on the surrounding structure of the particular resource.

Pointing by Step-by-Step Navigation

When you are looking for a specific element that has a unique identifier, referencing by ID is often the quickest way to access the resource. However, in many instances, you may not have the luxury of working with an XML structure that has unique IDs or even knowing the particular ID you wish to access.

XPointer provides a *child sequence* method of pointing to resources to locate an element based on a step-by-step approach to navigating the XML document. The syntax used by this method involves using integers separated by forward slashes (/). A forward slash represents a level of nesting in the document. An integer represents the position of an element in the nested level.

To point to the root element of a document, use the following syntax:

```
URI#xpointer(/1)
```

However, like the ID method mentioned earlier, you can shorten the expression to the following:

```
URI#/1
```

Or, to reference the `coffees` element of coffee.xml, use the following:

```
coffee.xml#/1
```

The Kenyan Elephantismo `coffee` element is the second `coffee` element, inside the second `region` element, inside the root `coffees` element. To point to this element, the expression is as follows:

```
coffee.xml#/1/2/2
```

Plugging in that XPointer expression into an XLink reference looks like this:

```
<coffeeOfTheDay xlink:type="simple"
  xlink:href="http://www.dummycoffee.com#/1/2/2"/>
```

In addition to starting at the root element, you can also start at an ID value and begin the step-by-step navigation. For example, both of the following two XPointer expressions locate the Ethiopian Sunset Supremo `coffee` element:

```
coffee.xml#AF/1
coffee.xml#/1/2/1
```

Pointing through XPath Expressions

XPointer is closely associated with XPath. In fact, it is an extension built on top of the core XPath language. (See Book IV, Chapter 3 for the nitty-gritty on XPath.) Just as XPath can be used to locate specific elements in an XSLT transformation, you can use an XPath expression to identify a specific resource to point to in a document.

To point to all of the `region` elements inside of the root element, use the following expression:

```
coffee.xml#xpointer(/child::region)
```

Or, because XPath allows you to imply the `child::` axis, you can leave it off and simply use the following:

```
coffee.xml#xpointer(/region)
```

To point to the Kenyan Elephantismo `coffee` element, which is the second `coffee` element inside of the second `region` element, use the following:

```
coffee.xml#xpointer(/region[2]/coffee[2])
```

Or, to point to the `name` attribute of the Kenyan Elephantismo `coffee` element, use the following expression:

```
coffee.xml#xpointer(/region[2]/coffee[2]/@name)
```

Nesting XPointer Expressions

If you are uncertain whether or not a DTD or schema is available, you can use an alternative syntax to ensure that the resource you want is identified by XPointer. For example, you could use a two-part expression, in which the second part is attempted only if the first part fails:

```
xpointer(id("COS120"))xpointer(//*[@id="COS120"])
```

In the preceding code snippet, the first part looks for a resource with an ID value of `COS120`. If a DTD is not present, this expression will fail. Therefore, the second part of the expression is tried, which uses an XPath expression to locate an element that has an `id` attribute that is `COS120`.

Working with XPointer Functions

XPointer defines several built-in functions that enable you to find point and range locations within a document. Typically, the functions you will use the most include `range-to()`, `string-range()`, `origin()`, and `here()`. These functions are explained in the following sections.

range-to ( ) function

The `range-to()` function is used when you want to return a range inside your XML document. You typically add `range-to()` to the end of an XPointer expression, so that the starting point of the range is determined by the first expression and the ending point of the range is determined by the result of the `range-to()` function.

To illustrate, suppose you want to return the range starting at Ethiopian Sunset Supremo element through the Burundi Legolasan element. You could use the following expression:

```
coffee.xml#xpointer(id("ETH129")/range-to(id("BUR111"))
```

You could also retrieve the same range using the following expression:

```
coffee.xml#xpointer(//*[@id="ETH129"]/range-
    to(following::coffee[2]))
```

string-range ( ) function

The string-range() function returns a range based on the results of a string search in the XML document. For example, the following XPointer searches for a string Exotic in the location set returned by the XPointer expression //coffee/taste:

```
coffee.xml#xpointer(string-range(//coffee/taste, "Exotic"))
```

If the string is located, the starting and ending character points returned by the function are *character points*, or indexes into the characters of the string value of the node.

In this example, the starting point would be the E character point and the ending point would be the c character point for each instance of Exotic, as shown in the following code:

```
<?xml version="1.0"?>
<coffees>
 <region id="LA" name="Latin America">
  <coffee id="GUA392" name="Guatemalan Express"
    origin="Guatemala">
    <taste>Mild and Bland</taste>
    <price>11.99</price>
    <availability>Year-round</availability>
    <bestwith>Breakfast</bestwith>
  </coffee>
  <coffee id="COS120" name="Costa Rican Deacon" origin="Costa
   Rica">
    <taste>Exotic and Untamed</taste>
    <price>12.99</price>
    <availability>Year-round</availability>
    <bestwith>Dessert</bestwith>
  </coffee>
 </region>
 <region id="AF" name="Africa">
  <coffee id="ETH129" name="Ethiopian Sunset Supremo"
    origin="Ethiopia">
    <taste>Exotic and Untamed</taste>
    <price>14.99</price>
    <availability>Limited</availability>
    <bestwith>Chocolate</bestwith>
  </coffee>
  <coffee id="KEN647" name="Kenyan Elephantismo"
    origin="Kenya">
    <taste>Solid yet Understated</taste>
    <price>3.99</price>
    <availability>Year-round</availability>
    <bestwith>Elephant Ears</bestwith>
  </coffee>
```

```
<coffee id="BUR111" name="Burundi Legolasan"
  origin="Burundi">
  <taste>A Taste Only A Wood Elf Would Like</taste>
  <price>33.99</price>
  <availability>Very Limited</availability>
  <bestwith>Lembas Bread</bestwith>
</coffee>
</region>
</coffees>
```

The `string-range()` function also takes two optional number arguments.
The third argument specifies the position of the first character in the resulting range relative to the start match. The final argument specifies the
number of characters in the resulting range.

For example, consider the following XPointer expression:

```
coffee.xml#xpointer(string-
    range(//coffee[@id="COS120"]/taste, "Exotic", 1, 7 ))
```

That expression would return the following range:

```
Exotic and
```

origin ( ) function

The `origin()` built-in function refers to the current element in a document.
For example, use the `origin()` location term when you want to select the
next element of the current element or the parent element of the current
element, like this:

```
coffee.xml#xpointer(origin()/ancestor[2])
```

here ( ) function

The `here()` function is quite different from the other XPointer functions
because it returns the element that contains the XPointer expression that is
being evaluated. Using this function, you can point to other locations that
are relative to the XPointer's location in the pointing documents. Consider
the following XPointer expression:

```
<inStoreCoffees>
  <coffeeOfTheDay xlink:type="simple"
    xlink:href="#xpointer(here()/ancestor[1])">
    Traditionally Bland
  </coffeeOfTheDay>
</inStoreCoffees>
```

The preceding code illustrates the usage of XPointer with XLink. The `here()` function is used with the `coffeeOfTheDay` element and returns this element. The XPointer expression returns the first ancestor of the `coffeeOfTheDay` element. In this way, XPointer enables you to navigate across the document tree and locate the `inStoreCoffees` element.

Chapter 3: XForms — Processing Forms

In This Chapter

✔ Differences between HTML forms and XForms

✔ Exploring how data is separated from the form controls

✔ XForms controls

The Web enjoys its incredible popularity in large part because it is an interactive medium. You don't just view Web pages, but you communicate with the people or companies behind the site through the Web itself. If you and I were limited to only viewing static Web pages, I think the Web would be considered to be "brochureware" by most people rather than a tool that one can live by.

By and large, the manner in which you interact with other services or people on the Web is through the HTML form. Using a form, you can do a Google search, make a one-click Amazon.com order, check your order status from Best Buy, post a message on a Yahoo message board, and so on.

Yet, as XML emerges as a replacement for HTML for many tasks on the Web, the interactive form was one area in particular that needed complete rethinking rather than simply "XMLizing" the form controls of HTML. XForms is the XML-based solution to forms that was devised by the W3C and is the focus of this chapter. In this chapter, you'll survey XForms and work to understand the basics of this emerging technology.

XForms usage is in early-adopter mode right now. Not only is software support for XForms very early on, but the Recommendation from the W3C is only in the stages of being finalized.

HTML Forms on Steroids

Like all other XML technologies, XForms has the benefit of hindsight. It can take what worked with HTML forms and duplicate it, while replacing the shortcomings of HTML forms with something better. That was exactly the attitude that the W3C had in developing XForms.

XForms differs from HTML forms in the following ways:

✦ **XForms separates form data from the user interface.** If you recall back in Book I, I discussed that one of the limitations of HTML is its blending together of data and the formatting instructions, causing the data itself to lose its identity. The data simply becomes part of the presentation to the user, and trying to extract the data again is painful and difficult.

Nowhere is this more evident in HTML than when you work with forms, causing developers to do many crazy workarounds to try and work with complex data structures but effectively map this information to a form on a Web page.

XForms separates the XML data you work with from the actual form controls, enabling you to manage the data, yet link in the form controls to allow users to view and edit the data.

✦ **XForms allows you to work directly with XML data.** HTML requires data to be transported as name-value pairs, but XForms enables you to work with form data as XML data structure. The result is three advantages:

• You can transport an XML structure, making it easier to process on the server-side.

• Rather than treating everything as text, you can work with explicit data types in your forms. These types are the same ones used by XML schemas (see Book II, Chapter 4).

• XForms uses XPath to connect parts of your XML data to form controls, giving you considerable flexibility and power in defining your forms. (See Book IV, Chapter 3 for more on XPath.)

✦ **XForms can be easily viewed on different devices and platforms.** HTML form controls were heavily focused on being able to work within the traditional desktop computer browser. However, with the rapid spread of Web form use on cell phones and PDA devices, some of these small devices with limited space to display controls had a hard time dealing with HTML forms. XForms allows you to tailor the presentation of the form data in a manner that works best for the given device.

✦ **XForms enables you to add logic without scripting.** In HTML, one of the most common purposes of JavaScript is validating data entered by the user in forms or for calculations based on user-defined data. XForms provides some instructions that can be added to the control declaration to perform the most common tasks done by scripting.

Separating Data from the Presentation

At the heart of XForms is the separation of the data from the form controls that you work with in the browser. As a point of contrast, consider the way in which HTML works with forms. A form element in HTML contains form controls that allow users to view and enter data. This form data is then sent to a server process (defined by the form's action attribute) as a series of name-value pairs. In other words, all of the data and formatting for a given form are jam packed inside of the form element. Figure 3-1 shows a summary of this process.

HTML Form

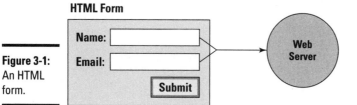

Figure 3-1:
An HTML
form.

In contrast, XForms separates the data definition and transmission from the form controls themselves. The *data model* is used to store the data definition, transmission details, and instructions on binding the data to form controls within the Web page. The *presentation controls* are linked to the data model to provide a way for users to interact with this data within the Web page. Figure 3-2 displays a summary of the separation of data model from presentation controls.

XForms

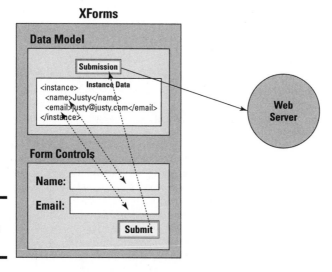

Figure 3-2:
An XForms
form.

One of the most significant aspects of XForms is your ability to read and write XML data when working with forms. With HTML, in order to work with XML in a form, you would need to do a lot of mapping from the HTML form name-value pair structure to the relevant parts of the XML document. In contrast, XForms collects form data and stores it as instance data, which is part of the data model. This instance data is XML and can be any XML structure you want.

Working with XForms

In order to work with XForms in a Web page, you have to add the XForms namespace, define the data model, and add the XForms controls. These are discussed in this section.

XForms namespace

In order to enable XForms in your document, you need to declare the XForms namespace in its root element. XForms uses the `http://www.w3.org/2002/xforms/cr` namespace (see Book I, Chapter 4 for more on namespaces) and typically has `xforms:` as the namespace prefix, as in the following example:

```
<html xmlns:xforms="http://www.w3.org/2002/xforms/cr">
```

XForms data model elements

The XForms data model is declared in the `head` element of the HTML or XHTML document (see Book V, Chapter 4 for more on XHTML). The data model consists of the following elements:

✦ The `xforms:model` element is the container for all data model-related elements (required).

✦ The `xforms:submission` element is used to specify the details of where the XForms form is submitted to and what method is used (required).

✦ The `xforms:instance` element contains or references the instance data of an XForms form (optional, but almost always used).

✦ The `xforms:bind` element is used to apply properties to a nodeset of the instance data (optional).

For example, consider the following XForms data model, contained within the head of an XHTML document:

```
<xforms:model id="Member">
```

```
<xforms:submission id="submit" action="http://www.
  dosomething.com/something.exe" method="post"/>

<xforms:instance xmlns="">
  <memberData>
    <firstName></firstName>
    <lastName></lastName>
    <address></address>
    <city></city>
    <state>MA</state>
    <zipCode></zipCode>
    <subscriptionType>d</subscriptionType>
    <comments></comments>
  </memberData>
</xforms:instance>

<xforms:bind ref="/memberData/firstName"
  constraint="string-length(.)&gt;0"/>
<xforms:bind ref="/memberData/lastName" constraint="string-
  length(.)&gt;0"/>
<xforms:bind ref="/memberData/state" required="true()"/>

</xforms:model>
```

Consider the following components of the data model:

✦ The xforms:model element serves as the container. The optional id
  attribute allows you to reference this data model by ID if needed,
  because multiple data models can be in each document.

✦ The xforms:submission element declares a fictional server-based
  process called http://www.dosomething.com/something.exe that
  would be used to process the XForms form.

✦ The xforms:instance element houses the XML structure that I want
  to work with as instance data. Because you are not adding a namespace
  for the instance data structure, you need to declare an empty namespace
  using xmlns="" in the xforms:instance element.

  As far as the memberData instance data itself, it is a basic XML structure
  used to track members of the fictional organization. The form controls
  will update the values of the instance data and send them back to the
  server-side process specified by the xforms:submission element.

✦ The xforms:bind elements attach certain properties or rules to elements
  in the instance data structure. In the first two examples, the bind statements ensure that the values of firstName and lastName have a value
  greater than 0 characters. The final one classifies the state required.

  If you read "XPath: Scouting Out XML Data" (Book IV, Chapter 3), the
  syntax of the ref attribute values will look familiar to you. That's
  because XForms uses XPath expressions to bind together a rule or control to a specific node or nodeset in the instance data.

XForms controls

In order for the user to work with the instance data, you need to have form controls on your Web page to interact with. If you worked with HTML forms before, several of the names of the XForms controls resemble their HTML counterparts. Table 3-1 shows the common controls that you'll use.

Table 3-1		XForms Controls	
Control	*Usage*	*HTML Equivalent*	*Example*
input	Standard text edit box (1-line)	<input type="text">	<xforms:input ref="name">
			<xforms:label>Name </xforms:label>
			</xforms:input>
textarea	Multi-line text box	<textarea>	<xforms:textarea ref="description">
			<xforms:label>Enter description here:</xforms:label>
			</xforms:textarea>
select1	Selection of one option from a list of options	<input type="radio"> or <select>	<xforms:select1 ref= "subscriptions">
			<xforms:label>Choose one subscription level</xforms: label>
			<xforms:choices>
			<xforms:item>
			<xforms:label>Monthly </xforms:label>
			<xforms:value>m </xforms:value>
			</xforms:item>
			<xforms:item>
			<xforms:label>Weekly</xforms: label>
			<xforms:value>w</xforms:value>
			</xforms:item>
			<xforms:item>

Control	Usage	HTML Equivalent	Example
`select1` (continued)			`<xforms:label>Daily</xforms:label>`
			`<xforms:value>d</xforms: value>`
			`</xforms:item>`
			`</xforms:choices>`
			`</xforms:select1>`
`select`	Selection of multiple options from a list	`<select multiple>` `<input type="checkbox">`	`<xforms:select ref="subscriptions">`
			`<xforms:label>Choose all subscription choices you desire</xforms:label>`
			`<xforms:choices>`
			`<xforms:item>`
			`<xforms:label>Monthly</xforms:label>`
			`<xforms:value>m</xforms:value>`
			`</xforms:item>`
			`<xforms:item>`
			`<xforms:label>Weekly</xforms:label>`
			`<xforms:value>w</xforms:value>`
			`</xforms:item>`
			`<xforms:item>`
			`<xforms:label>Daily</xforms:label>`
			`<xforms:value>d</xforms:value>`
			`</xforms:item>`
			`</xforms:choices>`
			`</xforms:select>`

(continued)

Table 3-1 *(continued)*

Control	Usage	HTML Equivalent	Example
submit	Submit button for form	\<input type="submit"\>	\<xforms:submit submission= "member"\> \<xforms:label\>OK\</xforms: label\> \</xforms:submit\>
trigger	Generic button	\<button\>	\<xforms:trigger\> \<xforms:label\>Advanced\< /xforms:label\> \</xforms:trigger\>
output	Read-only display of form data	None	Your specified name is \<xforms:output ref="member/ name"/\>
secret	Password-type edit box	\<input type= "password"\>	\<xforms:secret ref= "password"\> \<xforms:label\>Enter password: \</xforms:label\> \</xforms:secret\>
range	Sliding scale control for selecting a value among a range	None	\<xforms:range ref="height" start="4.0" end="7.0" step="0.1"\> \<xforms:label\>Height (ft.)\</ xforms:label\> \</xforms:range\>
upload	Control for uploading a file or other data	\<input type="file"\>	\<xforms:upload ref="member/ photo" mediatype="image/*"\> \<xforms:label\>Select image of yourself:\</xforms:label\> \</xforms:upload\>

To add form controls that support the data model created in the previous section, add the following controls to the body element of the document.

```
<xforms:input ref="/memberData/firstName">
  <xforms:label>First Name:</xforms:label>
</xforms:input>

<xforms:input ref="/memberData/lastName">
```

```
    <xforms:label>Last Name:</xforms:label>
</xforms:input>

<xforms:input ref="/memberData/city">
  <xforms:label>City:</xforms:label>
</xforms:input>

<xforms:input ref="/memberData/state">
  <xforms:label>State:</xforms:label>
</xforms:input>

<xforms:input ref="/memberData/zipCode">
  <xforms:label>Zip Code:</xforms:label>
</xforms:input>

<xforms:select1 ref="/memberData/subscriptionType">
  <xforms:label>Subscription choices</xforms:label>
  <xforms:choices>
    <xforms:item>
      <xforms:label>Monthly</xforms:label>
      <xforms:value>m</xforms:value>
    </xforms:item>
    <xforms:item>
      <xforms:label>Weekly</xforms:label>
      <xforms:value>w</xforms:value>
    </xforms:item>
    <xforms:item>
      <xforms:label>Daily (Email) </xforms:label>
      <xforms:value>d</xforms:value>
    </xforms:item>
  </xforms:choices>
</xforms:select1>

<xforms:textarea ref="/memberData/comments">
  <xforms:label>Please enter your comments
  here:</xforms:label>
</xforms:textarea>

<xforms:submit name="Submit" submission="submit">
  <xforms:hint>Click to submit</xforms:hint>
  <xforms:label>OK</xforms:label>
</xforms:submit>
```

Consider the various controls used in this example:

✦ xforms:input provides a standard one-line edit box for entering text. This control is bound to a piece of the instance data, as defined by the ref attribute using an XPath expression. The required xforms:label element is nested inside of this element to provide a text label for the control.

✦ xforms:select1 provides a list of options to choose from. The xforms:choices contains the individual xforms:item elements that serve as the list of choices.

✦ `xforms:textarea` serves as a multi-line box for entering text.

✦ `xforms:submit` acts as the trigger to submit the form data. The button is linked using the `submission` attribute to the `xforms:submission` element defined in the data model.

Listing 3-1 shows the entire members XHTML file.

Listing 3-1:   members.xhtml

```
<?xml version="1.0" encoding="utf-8" ?>
<html xmlns="http://www.w3.org/1999/xhtml"
      xmlns:xforms="http://www.w3.org/2002/xforms/cr">
<head>

  <link href="default.css" rel="stylesheet" type="text/css"/>

  <title>Member profile</title>

  <xforms:model id="Member">

    <xforms:submission id="submit"
    action="http://www.dosomething.com/something.exe"
    method="post"/>

    <xforms:instance xmlns="">
      <memberData>
        <firstName>Rich</firstName>
        <lastName></lastName>
        <address></address>
        <city></city>
        <state>MA</state>
        <zipCode></zipCode>
        <subscriptionType>d</subscriptionType>
        <comments></comments>
      </memberData>
    </xforms:instance>

    <xforms:bind ref="/memberData/firstName"
    constraint="string-length(.)&gt;0"/>
    <xforms:bind ref="/memberData/lastName"
    constraint="string-length(.)&gt;0"/>
    <xforms:bind ref="/memberData/state" required="true()"/>

  </xforms:model>
```

```
</head>

<body>

  <xforms:input ref="/memberData/firstName">
    <xforms:label>First Name:</xforms:label>
  </xforms:input>

  <xforms:input ref="/memberData/lastName">
    <xforms:label>Last Name:</xforms:label>
  </xforms:input>

  <xforms:input ref="/memberData/city">
    <xforms:label>City:</xforms:label>
  </xforms:input>

  <xforms:input ref="/memberData/state">
    <xforms:label>State:</xforms:label>
  </xforms:input>

  <xforms:input ref="/memberData/zipCode">
    <xforms:label>Zip Code:</xforms:label>
  </xforms:input>

  <xforms:select1 ref="/memberData/subscriptionType">
    <xforms:label>Subscription choices</xforms:label>
    <xforms:choices>
      <xforms:item>
        <xforms:label>Monthly</xforms:label>
        <xforms:value>m</xforms:value>
      </xforms:item>
      <xforms:item>
        <xforms:label>Weekly</xforms:label>
        <xforms:value>w</xforms:value>
      </xforms:item>
      <xforms:item>
        <xforms:label>Daily (Email) </xforms:label>
        <xforms:value>d</xforms:value>
      </xforms:item>
    </xforms:choices>
  </xforms:select1>

  <xforms:textarea ref="/memberData/comments">
    <xforms:label>Please enter your comments
  here:</xforms:label>
```

(continued)

Listing 3-1 *(continued)*

```
</xforms:textarea>

<xforms:submit name="Submit" submission="submit">
  <xforms:hint>Click to submit</xforms:hint>
  <xforms:label>OK</xforms:label>
</xforms:submit>


</body>

</html>
```

X-Smiles is an open source browser that provides early support for XForms. (See www.x-smiles.org to download a copy.) Figure 3-3 shows the finished form in this browser.

If you recall, the xforms:bind elements that were defined in the data model add validity checking to the form without the need of scripting. To demonstrate how this works, check out the feedback shown in Figure 3-4 that is provided to the user when the Submit button is clicked before entering a first name.

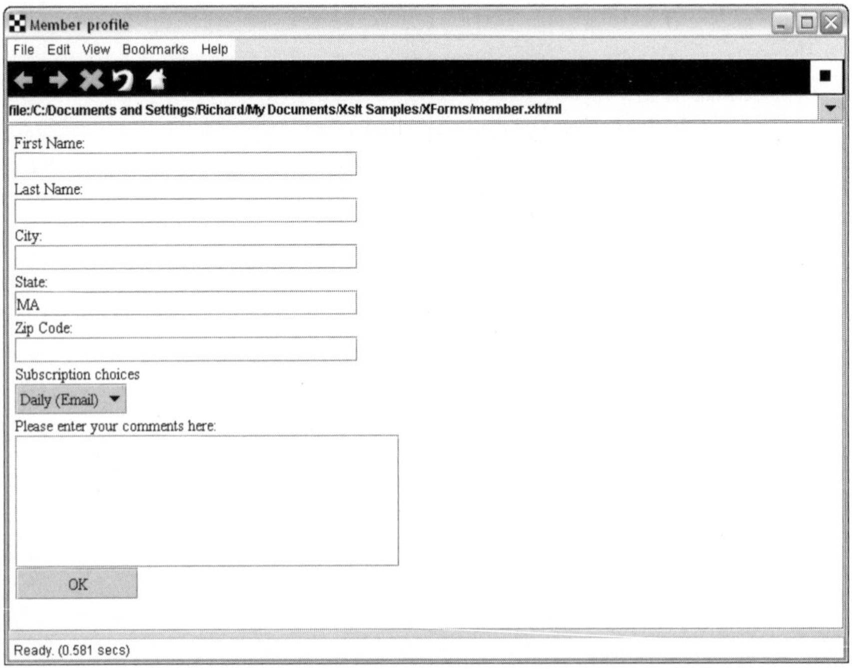

Figure 3-3:
An XForms
form in the
X-Smiles
browser.

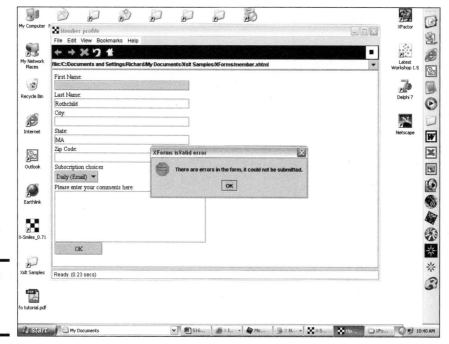

Figure 3-4:
Validation
without
scripting.

Chapter 4: XHTML — Next-Generation HTML

In This Chapter

✔ **Exploring the structure of an XHTML document**

✔ **Discovering the syntax differences between HTML and XHTML**

✔ **Migrating an HTML document to XHTML**

Waaah, do I have to? That may sound like the response of a boy being asked to clean his room, but it is also the typical reply of a browser programmer after he or she has been asked to account for some new HTML eccentricity.

You've discovered by now that XML is a logical, ordered, and structured language. Think of some examples: Every start tag must have an end tag, the case of element names must be consistent, the document must be well-formed, and so on.

But if you've worked with HTML before, you'll probably agree that it is quite the opposite. A quirky language, HTML throws in a lot of exceptions and peculiarities that may have worked well for HTML's original modest goals. But these quirks have grown to look sloppy as people work to design mission-critical solutions built on top of the Web's standard markup language.

HTML ended up becoming something of a behemoth, cumbersome compared to its nimble relative, XML. For example, W3C found it difficult to introduce new elements into the language given the ripple effects. So too, browser companies struggled with rendering HTML Web pages on new devices, such as cell phones or handhelds, given the nature of the language.

As a result, *XHTML* (Extensible Hypertext Markup Language) was introduced by the W3C as the successor to HTML 4.0 as a way to bridge HTML and XML: Take the widespread popularity of HTML and mix it with the soundness and discipline of XML to form a new standard markup language for the Web.

In this chapter, you discover how XHTML works and how you can migrate an existing HTML page to be XHTML compliant.

Structuring the XHTML Document

Although the text and formatting instructions of any given Web page will vary, the core structure of any XHTML document must be consistent in order for it to be handled correctly by a browser or other XHTML processor. There are four major parts to any XHTML document:

✦ doctype declaration

✦ html **root element**

✦ head **element**

✦ body **element**

Each of these is explained in the sections that follow.

doctype declaration

The *doctype declaration* is used to specify the Document Type Definition (DTD) that the document conforms to. (See Book II, Chapter 2 for more information on DTDs.) This declaration must be at the top of the document, appearing *before* the html element. There are three different declarations that you can use:

✦ Strict. **The strict** doctype **declaration is used when formatting for the document is done strictly using Cascading Style Sheets (CSS) rather than the formatting tags of XHTML. The declaration syntax is as follows:**

```
<!DOCTYPE html
    PUBLIC "-//W3C//DTD XHTML 1.0 Strict//EN"
    "http://www.w3.org/TR/xhtml1/DTD/xhtml1-
    strict.dtd">
```

Use the Strict declaration when you want to minimize the amount of formatting instructions that are inside of the XHTML itself, relying instead on external CSS stylesheets.

✦ Transitional. **The** Transitional doctype **declaration is used when formatting for the document is done using XHTML markup tags. The declaration syntax is as follows:**

```
<!DOCTYPE html
    PUBLIC "-//W3C//DTD XHTML 1.0 Transitional//EN"
    "http://www.w3.org/TR/xhtml1/DTD/xhtml1-
    transitional.dtd">
```

Use the Transitional declaration when you want to create a typical Web page, one that combines presentation and data together in one document. Even older browsers that don't support CSS stylesheets should be able to fairly accurately render XHTML documents.

✦ `Frameset`. The final `doctype` declaration should be used when you need to use a frameset in your document. The declaration syntax is as follows:

```
<!DOCTYPE html
      PUBLIC "-//W3C//DTD XHTML 1.0 Frameset//EN"
      "http://www.w3.org/TR/xhtml1/DTD/xhtml1-
      frameset.dtd">
```

The `Strict` declaration is a purist favorite because this method better separates formatting logic (in an external stylesheet) from the information being presented (in the body of the XHTML document). However, the `Transition` declaration is the one that is more widely used in many real world situations today.

Unless you plan to use CSS for all formatting, you need to use the `Transitional` or `Frameset` declarations.

html root element

The `html` element serves as the root element of an XHTML document. HTML recommended the use of `html` tags, but it didn't require the container element to be present in order to display properly. In contrast, the `html` element is required for an XHTML document to be considered valid.

The `html` element must also declare the XSLT namespace, as in the following example:

```
<html xmlns="http://www.w3.org/1999/xhtml">
```

```
<html>
```

See Book I, Chapter 4 for more information on namespaces.

I declare (maybe)

In its XHTML recommendation, the W3C urges developers to start an XHTML document with a standard XML declaration. However, the problem is that some older browsers may not know what to do with the declaration (or any processing instruction for that matter) and display it as text. Therefore, I recommend avoiding an XML declaration if legacy browsers will be used in your environment.

head element

The required head element is used to contain "metadata" pertaining to the document, including title, keywords, and other document-level information. Elements defined inside of the head block are used when processing the document, but they are not displayed on the page.

Common head-level elements include the following:

- ✦ The title element provides a descriptive title of the document, usually displayed in the window caption of the browser.

  The title element is required in XHTML.

- ✦ The link element links external CSS stylesheets and other documents with the XHTML document.

- ✦ The meta element contains meta data describing the document (such as keywords, copyright notices, and so on).

For example, consider the following head element:

```
<head>
  <title>European Explorer</title>
  <link rel="STYLESHEET" type="text/css" href="europe.css"/>
  <meta name="Keywords" content="Europe,Explore"/>
  <meta name="Copyright" content="2003, EE, Inc."/>
</head>
```

body element

The body element is used as a container for all displayable content of the document.

Putting these four parts of the XHTML document together, the following is an example shell XHTML document:

```
<!DOCTYPE html
    PUBLIC "-//W3C//DTD XHTML 1.0 Transitional//EN"
    "http://www.w3.org/TR/xhtml1/DTD/xhtml1-
  transitional.dtd">
<html xmlns="http://www.w3.org/1999/xhtml">
<head>
  <title>European Explorer</title>
</head>
<body>
  <p>I am going to Liechtenstein.</p>
</body>
</html>
```

Migrating from HTML to XHTML

Here is a concise, yet fairly accurate definition of XHTML:

HTML + XML = XHTML

In other words, you take the basic page layout and data presentation capabilities of HTML and add the rigid XML language requirements to it. What comes out of that process is XHTML. Therefore, if you know HTML, you don't have to deal with many new elements or attributes. The <b> tag is still used to bold text, and the <p> tag is used for paragraphs.

Indeed, HTML and XHTML have the same purpose — rendering Web pages — and the same general structure as a markup language. However, there are important syntax-level differences that you need to account for as you move from HTML to XHTML. In order to migrate from HTML to XHTML, you need to consider the following rules of XHTML:

✦ Element and attribute names must be lowercase.

✦ Elements must close properly.

✦ Elements must not overlap.

✦ Attributes values must be quoted.

✦ Attribute values can't be "minimized."

✦ Script and style elements must be classified as CDATA.

These are discussed in the sections that follow.

The XHTML document must also adhere to structural requirements noted in the "Structuring an XHTML document" section.

Element and attribute names must be lowercase

Case of the element and attribute names is a non-issue in HTML, so much so that each of the following tags are considered the same:

```
<BODY></body>
<Body></BODY>
<BoDY></BoDY>
```

In contrast, XHTML requires all element and attribute names to be lowercase. Therefore, consider the following HTML:

```
<BODY BGCOLOR="#000000">
  <P>I am going to Liechtenstein.</P>
</BODY>
```

This code would need to be converted to the following XHTML:

```
<body bgcolor="#000000">
  <p>I am going to Liechtenstein.</p>
</body>
```

Elements must close properly

One of the well-known traits of HTML is its flexibility on the requirement of closing tags for certain elements, such as the paragraph (p) element. In contrast, XHTML requires that all elements close, regardless of whether or not it contains content. Specifically, the following rules apply:

✦ **Non-empty elements:** Elements with content must have a closing tag, as in the following code:

```
<!-- Valid HTML, invalid XHTML -->
Are you going to Liechtenstein?<p>
I am going to Liechtenstein:<p>
<ul>
  <li>Today
  <li>Tomorrow
  <li>I am not going
</ul>

<!-- Valid XHTML -->
<p>Are you going to Liechtenstein?</p>
<p>I am going to Liechtenstein: </p>
<ul>
  <li>Today</li>
  <li>Tomorrow</li>
  <li>I am not going</li>
</ul>
```

The following elements are impacted by this change: html, body, head, p, colgroup, li, tfoot, dd, option, dt, thead, tbody, td, th, and tr.

✦ **Empty elements:** Elements that have no content need to be closed, either with a closing tag or with a trailing forward (/) slash placed before the end bracket, as in the following example:

```
<!-- Valid HTML, invalid XHTML -->
<hr>
I am going to Liechtenstein.<br>

<!-- Valid HTML, invalid XHTML -->
<hr />
I am going to Liechtenstein.<br />
```

The following attributes are impacted by this change: `area`, `base`, `basefont`, `br`, `col`, `frame`, `hr`, `img`, `input`, `isindex`, `link`, `meta`, and `param`.

To ensure backward compatibility with some browsers, I recommend adding a space before the `/>`. In other words, `<br />` is often more backward compatible than `<br/>` is.

Elements must not overlap

HTML isn't strict on enforcing overlapping of elements, but XHTML is. Therefore, all elements need to adhere to the "last opened, first closed" rule as shown in the following example:

```
<!-- Valid HTML, invalid XHTML -->
<p>I am going to <b><i>Liechtenstein</p></b></i>.

<!-- Valid XHTML -->
<p>I am going to <i><b>Liechtenstein</b></i></p>.
```

Attributes values must be quoted

HTML permits attributes without quotes, but XHTML requires that all attribute values be contained within single or double quotation marks, as in the following example:

```
<!-- Valid HTML, invalid XHTML -->
<tr align=left>Liechtenstein</tr>

<!-- Valid XHTML (either) -->
<tr align="left">Liechtenstein</tr>
<tr align='left'>Liechtenstein</tr>
```

Attribute values can't be "minimized"

HTML allows attributes to be minimized when there is one possible value. When you minimize an element, you use the attribute name without a corresponding value, like this:

```
<td nowrap>Liechtenstein</td>
```

However, XHTML does not permit minimized values. As a result, you need to transform it to a standard name-value pair, using the attribute name as the value. Therefore, the preceding minimized attribute is modified to be the following:

```
<td nowrap="nowrap">Liechtenstein</td>
```

Can I see your ID please?

HTML developers have used both the `name` and `id` attributes as a way to uniquely identify an element. However, with XHTML, you are asked to move away from the `name` attribute and use the `id` attribute instead.

Script and style elements must be classified as CDATA

If you use any `script` or `style` elements in your document, you need to declare their content to be of type `CDATA` to ensure that `<` and `&` characters are treated properly by the processor. To do so, place the content within the special `CDATA` brackets:

```
<![CDATA[Content]]>
```

Here is an example:

```
<style type="text/css">
<![CDATA[
  A:hover { color: #941810 }
]]>
</style>

<script language="JavaScript" type="text/javascript">
<![CDATA[
  function changeImages() {
    if (document.images && (preloadFlag == true) )
    {
      for (var i=0; i < changeImages.arguments.length; i+=2)
      {
      document[changeImages.arguments[i]].src =
        changeImages.arguments[i+1];
      }
    }
  }
]]>
</script>
```

Alternatively, you can avoid adding the `CDATA` qualifier if you use external script files (.js) or stylesheets (.css).

```
<!-- Load external script -->
<script language="JavaScript" src="loadimg.js"/>

<!-- Load external stylesheet -->
<link href="hoover.css"/>
```

Paragraph mind bending

In addition to the syntax differences in XHTML, some HTML developers will also need to make a mind shift concerning the use of the paragraph (p) element. Because the closing tag was not required, many HTML developers treated the p element as a *separator* of paragraphs rather than as a *container* of a paragraph.

Instead of converting all of your HTML documents manually into XHTML, I recommend letting HTML Tidy do the work for you. HTML Tidy is a handy utility freely available for converting HTML documents into XHTML. You can download it at `tidy.sourceforge.net`.

XHTML checklist

When you create an XHTML document, make sure you consider the following to-do items:

✦ Doctype **declaration:** Start off by adding a `doctype` declaration (strict, traditional, or frameset) to the top of the document.

✦ `html` **element:** Add an `html` element and use it as the root element of the document.

✦ **XHTML namespace:** Add the XHTML namespace (`http://www.w3.org/1999/xhtml`) to the html element as the default namespace.

✦ `head` **element:** Add the `head` element to contain any document-level (non-visual) elements.

✦ `title` **element:** Add a `title` element inside of the head describing the document.

✦ `body` **element:** Add a `body` element to contain all of the document's displayable content.

✦ **Lowercase:** Make sure that all element and attributes names are lowercase.

✦ **Well-formedness:** Make certain that all elements close, either with a close tag or with the shortcut (`/>`) method. Also, make sure you follow the "last open, first closed" mantra to ensure that no overlapping of elements occurs.

✦ **Attribute values:** Ensure that all attribute values are quoted using single or double quotes and that you don't minimize any attribute values.

✦ `script` **or** `style` **elements:** Use external script files or stylesheets, or else classify their content as `CDATA`.

Book VI

Processing XML

The 5th Wave   By Rich Tennant

They're moving on to the XML APIs section. That should daze and confuse them enough for us to finish changing the tire and get the heck out of here.

ANSI
Document
Publishers

Contents at a Glance

Chapter 1: Introduction to XML APIs

XML, a descendant of HTML, shares HTML's inability to compute. They are fundamentally *markup* languages — describing how things look or how information should be arranged, but not how information can be processed.

Information processing is the definition of computing, but by themselves languages such as HTML and XML cannot even add 2 + 2.

Why APIs Are Needed

APIs to the rescue. An API is an *Application Programmer's Interface*. It is a collection of prewritten procedures. (A *procedure* is a segment of code that performs a job, such as addition, by processing information.)

When you add an API to XML, you give XML the ability to add numbers together, to search documents for a particular piece of data, and to save files and otherwise manage information. If you want to extend XML's abilities to permit it to actively process the information it packages, you need an API (or several APIs) to support the base XML language.

Understanding DOM

Two primary APIs are used today with XML: DOM (Document Object Model) and SAX (Simple API for XML). Both of them add capabilities to XML, but DOM is the "heavier" of the two because it requires that the entire XML document be held in memory while being processed. By contrast, SAX is "lighter" — and can be used on a *stream* of XML, which need not be held entirely in memory at one time.

Think of SAX as having the ability to survey a document in a linear fashion (from start to finish), just the way that you would view a long freight train as it passed you while you sat at a crossing. DOM, however, can move around, go back and forth, and otherwise access an XML document in a random fashion — as if you were walking wherever you wanted around a train while it was stopped in a station.

Both DOM and SAX have their special uses, so you choose which API to employ based on the job at hand.

XML is an unusual language in several respects. For one thing, as you know, it attempts to be self-describing (without waiting until computers are smart enough to analyze descriptions through artificial intelligence). Perhaps even more interesting is the fact that most computer languages start out as a series of procedures: functions that display text, do math, and so on. Then, later, sophisticated ways to structure data are added to the language. Visual Basic, for example, was used for years before several advanced data structures — the user-defined types, variants and such — were included. XML, by contrast, started as a data structure (information organizing) technology and has since added APIs to process those structures. In XML, data processing has followed after data structure.

Using DOM

You can use a parser to load an XML document into memory; then you can retrieve information from the document and manipulate (process) that information using the DOM.

After an XML document is placed into memory, you can use DOM to simply read it or to change it. Other utilities, such as the XMLReader, permit you to view the contents of a document, but they do not allow you to insert or delete nodes, nor do they allow you to change the values of elements or attributes. It is just such editing that is the main purpose of the DOM.

DOM employs a particular way of looking at an XML document called a *tree view.* Here is a typical XML data structure:

```
<?xml version="1.0"?>
  <recipes>
    <recipe>
    <name>Paste</name>
    <cook>Mrs. Sprud</cook>
    <date>2/12/03</date>
    <size format="ounces">14</size>
    <recipe>
    <ingredients>
    <dry>flour</dry>
```

```
<wet>water</wet>
</ingredients>
</recipes>
```

When this data is put into memory in a DOM structure, it looks like the structure shown in Figure 1-1.

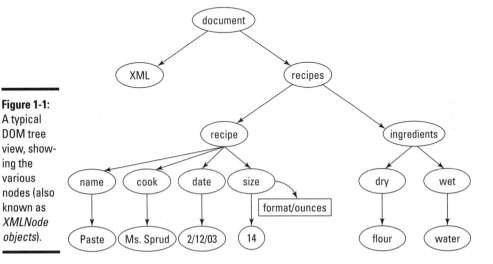

Figure 1-1:
A typical DOM tree view, showing the various nodes (also known as *XMLNode* objects).

Just like objects in traditional Object-Oriented Programming (OOP), nodes (node *objects* as they are called in DOM) can have methods and properties.

If you look at the diagram in Figure 1-1, notice several features. Objects can contain other objects (the Document object contains XMLNode objects). The main object in DOM is the XMLNode, and you can see many different nodes in Figure 1-1. Nodes can have relationships to each other, based on their relative positions within the tree-hierarchy in a DOM document. A node above another node is a *parent.* (The Ingredients node in Figure 1-1 is a parent of the Wet node.) A node beneath another node is a *child.* (The Wet node is a child of Ingredients.) A single node can be both parent and child. (Ingredients is a parent of Wet, but also a child of Recipes.) And nodes on the same level are called *siblings.* (Dry and Wet are siblings.) All nodes (other than the top *document* node) have a parent, but are allowed only *one* parent. A node can have several children.

Attributes: The odd duck

You may have noticed the odd bird in Figure 1-1, the *attribute.* It's in a square box and is divided into two sections: the name of the attribute and the *value* (the variable content) of the attribute. For example, a format attribute name may be paired with a variety of different possible values: ounces, pounds, liters, and so on. But what makes an attribute a special kind of node isn't that it's inside a box or has a strange, circular arrow popping it out the side of a normal node. What's strange is that it is always dual (made up of a name/value pair) and that it is not part of the usual parent-child-or-sibling relationship pattern within a DOM document. Instead, an attribute is considered a *property* of the node it's associated with. If you're really on your toes, you might be saying: Well, why isn't Cook|Mrs. Sprud an attribute of the recipe node? Or Wet|Water an attribute of the ingredients node? Good question. Now, please be seated.

All too often, the distinctions that we make in our minds aren't reflected in messy real-world programming situations. Sometimes what seems like a property is really a method, and what seems like a clear name/value pair relationship is cast as a parent-child relationship. You just have to be a bit flexible about these things. The more you work with XML, the more you'll gain a sense of how the categories and types of nodes work together.

A short review of objects

To understand the XML object model as embodied in the DOM, you need to know about a few key qualities of objects. An object's characteristics and behaviors are based on the description of that object. This description can be found in an XML document (or document fragment).

You can divide computing into two broad categories: information and processing (activities that manipulate the information). Similarly, objects are made up of two broad categories of components: properties and methods. Properties are similar to *information:* Properties describe an object's characteristics, like the format of an attribute (format=ounces, for example). Methods are similar to *processing.* A method is a *behavior* or *job* that an object knows how to perform, like the XMLNode object's ReplaceChild method that, as you probably guessed, can be used to modify a child

node. Another way to look at this distinction is that properties are similar to what a programmer thinks of as traditional variables, and methods are similar to traditional functions. Collectively, an object's methods and properties are called its *members.* (There can also be additional members, such as fields and events, but never mind that for now.)

These distinctions between object, properties, and methods are hardly new to computer programming, much less an invention of OOP or XML. Instead, they are built into reality and can be found in the simplest childhood grammar: "Black storm go boom!" is more than a two-year-old's poetic description of thunder. It reveals the fundamental nature of object/ member relationships: Black (property), storm (object), go boom (method).

Types of nodes

When an XML document is read into memory by the DOM, it builds the various nodes and assigns a *node type* to each node. An element node type, for example, is handled differently when it is processed in the DOM than a document node type is handled. Different node types follow different rules and use different syntax.

Here is a list of the various types of DOM nodes, divided into two categories: the nodes that can have children, and those that can't. The uses of these various types of nodes are discussed in detail in Book V, Chapter 3.

These types of nodes can have child nodes:

 + Attribute
 + Document
 + DocumentFragment
 + EntityReference
 + Element
 + Entity

And these types of nodes cannot have child nodes:

 + CDATASection
 + Comment
 + DocumentType
 + Entity
 + Notation
 + ProcessingInstruction
 + Text
 + XmlDeclaration

Everything You Ever Wanted to Know about SAX

If DOM is the heavier, more powerful and flexible XML-processing technology, SAX is its lighter and more supple cousin. One isn't *better* than the other — they're complementary. Chose the one that suits your needs at the time. Or, just use them both at the same time if you wish!

SAX is most useful when your job doesn't demand random-access to the XML data — when you want to search rather than modify data. To be more

specific: Use SAX for searching large documents using relatively straightforward search criteria (simple queries) for small portions of data.

You'll hear techno-speak descriptions of SAX such as "events-based parsing," "linear sequencing," "area 51," "magic pyramid," and so on. I suggest
you ignore this kind of chatter (unless you already have a propeller
attached to your hat). Instead, just remember the following simple
distinctions:

✦ **SAX is useful for *reading* and *searching* XML data; not for *modifying*
or *creating* new data.** With DOM, you can create a new XML document
in memory, modify a document, or read a document from a file (or other
stream source). So, DOM is certainly your choice if you want to modify
an XML document and then save the results.

✦ **Use DOM when your XML job is complex.** DOM is best for random
access to XML data, or when the XML itself is complicated with many
internal cross-reference structures (ID and IDREF, for example). *Random
access* means you can jump to any location (node) within the XML document. It's the way you can jump immediately to any song on a CD. SAX
involves *serial* or *linear access,* so you have to go from the start through
each section of the data to get to a particular node. SAX is similar to the
way you have to fast-forward through a music cassette tape to get to a
particular song.

✦ **DOM creates a big, fat navigable tree structure in memory.**
(Remember that, among other things, DOM creates a type description
for each node in a document and XML is filled with nodes.) SAX documents are not held in memory; rather they are streamed (fast-forwarded)
through a small pair of buffers. So SAX is usually your best choice when
you have a huge XML document to search through. Hand a 200K XML
document to SAX, and it simply streams it through your computer, without demanding lots of memory. DOM, by contrast, is like setting off an
airbag: XML data (which is already quite verbose all by itself) positively
swells into colossal proportions when DOM expands it in memory. The
XML after DOM gets through with it can grow by an order of magnitude,
from 200K to over 2,000,000K. If memory is an issue, you might want to
stick with the lighter load imposed by SAX processing.

✦ **SAX is usually best for *searching* through XML data, especially if you
are merely interested in retrieving a specific, small piece of information, rather than *changing* data.** With SAX, you can quickly scan through
a huge requisition list, get the specific data you are looking for, and
simply stop processing right there. However, if your query (your search
specification) is relatively complex (such as "Find all widgets made in
Holland between 1996-1997, and any books about those widgets written
in Japan or Canada"), you're better off using DOM instead. SAX can rapidly scan through XML without forcing you to store the entire document
in memory. Then, when SAX finds the piece of info you're after, it can

hand you a partial document structure (DocumentFragment) containing only the data you needed.

✦ **DOM should be used for more technical jobs such as sophisticated XPath filtering**. With SAX, you would be responsible for somehow preserving context information, but with DOM the context is already sitting there in memory. DOM is also used for XSLT transformations, for similar reasons.

To summarize: Both SAX and DOM have their strength and weaknesses. What's more, they aren't mutually exclusive: You can use them harmoniously together on the same job, if you wish — letting each do what it does best. For example, you can use SAX to build a DOM tree-structure in memory. Or you can emit a SAX stream from a DOM tree. And until you've seen a tree emitting a SAX stream, I'd say you haven't really lived.

Chapter 2: Reading XML with SAX and XMLReader

In This Chapter

✓ Working with SAX

✓ Understanding SAX events

✓ Using the XMLTextReader

Although XML has been available to programmers of all stripes and persuasions — from Open Source (free software) hackers to corporate group programmers — until recently there was no comprehensive IDE supporting XML.

An IDE (Integrated Design Environment) is a suite of programming tools. It includes an editor for writing programs, plus many other features such as debugging tools, automated translators, code libraries, and so on. All of these features can interact, so you have a synergy within an IDE that you don't get when using separate tools from various sources.

Just as Windows is the standard operating system today, so too has Microsoft's Visual Studio become the standard IDE, particularly for programmers making the transition from traditional Windows-based, local-machine programming to Internet-based, distributed programming. Visual Studio .NET is built upon XML and is stuffed with XML classes and XML tools.

Because Visual Studio is by far the most popular programming environment, this and several following chapters use Visual Studio as the laboratory in which to experiment with XML programming. However, if you don't have Visual Studio, most of the concepts, and some of the source code, are still usable.

Inside the Machine

It's time to go through the magic black doors and enter the machine. So far in this book, you've trustingly handed XML over to a processor from time to time, and simply accepted the result that dropped out the other side.

Inquiring programmers want to know: What exactly happens inside an XML processor, and how can I do my own processing? (*Processing* here is just another word for *programming*.)

The first job of an XML processor is to understand the XML itself, so a *parser* is always there just inside the entrance to the machine. Parsers look over information and divide it up into manageable pieces. In XML, these pieces are called nodes (or sometimes, *tokens*). Most elements of an XML document are nodes: a processing directive, a text string, the start tag of an element, and so on. You get the idea. The parser is dividing things into small units — or what professors today like to call *deconstructing*.

Just next to the parser, a bit further down the assembly line, is the *event switcher*. It watches the stream of nodes that the parser spits out, and it puts the nodes into categories — something like a postman sorting mail into a wall of boxes. This switcher is particularly interested in *events*, which isn't surprising considering that its name is *event* switcher.

In programming, as in life, an event is something that *happens*. It's an action, such as a mouse click, that usually is supposed to cause a reaction. When a user clicks a button, the programmer thinks of that as the button's *click event*. So the programmer writes some source code to handle that event. If the button is captioned *End*, the programmer probably writes code that shuts down the program, but perhaps saves something to a disk file first — whatever is needed to handle the event.

In XML processing, too, an event is something that requires some response from the event handler. For example, if a `<Title>` element node comes down the assembly line, the event switcher knows that a font change is probably needed. The event switcher then sends this node (and associated text between the start tag and end tag) to a procedure that actually does the work of changing fonts. The procedure (a sub or function) is called an *event handler*.

A DOM XML processor includes additional components beyond the parser and switcher, but that's the subject of the following chapter. For now, you can focus on the SAX processor's job.

Your Own SAX

You can write your own SAX processor if you're brave, or you can use the full MSXML parser built into Visual Studio .NET. You can find other sources of XML processors, too, so you can pick and choose what you want.

Parsing, though, isn't usually all that difficult a job: You just search through the XML text, looking for the basic XML units (elements, tags, attributes, and so on). In many cases, you're searching for some specific information, such as the cost of a screwdriver or the number of elements in the document.

To understand the basics of SAX parsing, you can now build a limited little parser for yourself. XML follows regular, predictable patterns, so it's not hard to parse (as long as the XML is *well formed* as they say — meaning that it doesn't violate rules, such as leaving off an end tag). In this example, your goal is to get a report telling you how many elements and attributes are in the XML document.

Using Visual Studio .NET

To see how to parse an XML document, run Visual Studio and choose Visual Basic, the most popular computer language in use today. (VB is also the most productive language — not coincidentally because it's the easiest to use — but in its new version, VB.NET, it has all the power of competing languages such as C++ and other C-derivatives such as Java, J++, and C#.)

Now choose New Project (either click the button on the bottom of the Visual Studio start page, or choose File⇨New⇨Project). Then double-click the Windows Application icon in the dialog box.

Saving the sample XML document

You now need a sample XML document to practice with. Here's a sample document that is included in Visual Studio so that programmers like us can experiment with XML. You use this sample in various examples in several of the chapters in the rest of this book, so it's a good idea to save it to your hard drive right now. Save it in a file named *books.xml* on your C:\ drive, so that you can always find it later as `C:\books.xml`. It comes in handy when you explore the programming examples in this chapter and in later chapters.

You probably don't want to type all the books.xml code by hand, so choose Help⇨Run the Visual Studio Help⇨Index in VB.NET, and then type this address into the address field at the top of the Help window:

```
ms-help://MS.VSCC.2003/MS.MSDNQTR.2003FEB.1033/xmlsdk/
    htm/sdk_booksxml_30rw.htm
```

Or you can use the Help Search feature (click the Search tab at the bottom of the Help window) and search for the following:

```
<author>Gambardella, Matthew</author>
```

You see the sample, as shown in Figure 2-1.

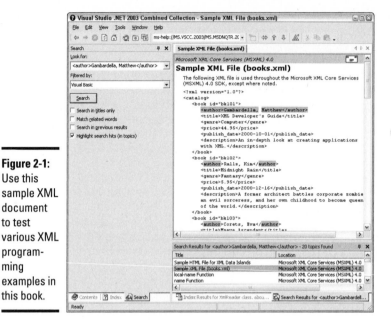

Figure 2-1:
Use this
sample XML
document
to test
various XML
program-
ming
examples in
this book.

In either case, you can now copy the entire XML sample document by dragging your mouse across it to select it in Help, pressing Ctrl+C to copy it,
opening Windows Notepad, and pressing Ctrl+V to paste it into Notepad.

To help you identify it, the sample begins like this:

```
<?xml version="1.0"?>
<catalog>
   <book id="bk101">
      <author>Gambardella, Matthew</author>
      <title>XML Developer's Guide</title>
      <genre>Computer</genre>
      <price>44.95</price>
```

and it ends like this:

```
   <description>Microsoft Visual Studio 7 is explored in
   depth,
      looking at how Visual Basic, Visual C++, C#, and ASP+
   are
      integrated into a comprehensive development
      environment.</description>
   </book>
</catalog>
```

When the entire sample is in Notepad, save it to the hard drive by choosing File⇨Save As in Notepad and then saving it to this path: `C:\books.xml`.

Go back now to the VB.NET IDE. You started a new project, so you see Form1 ready for you to add components to it. But this parsing experiment requires no components (or *controls* as they're often called, such as TextBoxes or buttons). So just double-click Form1 and a `Form_Load` event is displayed in the code window. This code window is where you write your programming. (`Form_Load` is the VB equivalent of `Sub Main` in C-type languages — it executes first automatically when the program runs, so it's the best place to put some code that you want to test.)

Using namespaces

Type in these two import statements at the very top of the code window, above `Public Class Form1`:

```
Imports System.Xml
```

This XML *namespace* adds lots of cool functions that you can use to manage and manipulate XML. In the .NET world, you often add namespaces to a code window. These `Imports` statements don't actually add code libraries; those libraries are always present underneath Visual Studio, like a vast underground resource. All that happens when you import a namespace is that you can then refer to procedures and classes in its library without having to repeat the namespace in your code. For example, without `Imports System.XML`, you have to write this:

```
New System.XML.XmlTextReader("c:\books.xml")
```

But after using the `Imports` statement, you can simplify your code by writing this:

```
New XmlTextReader("c:\books.xml")
```

Now type in the little parser, inside the `Form1_Load` event handler:

```
Private Sub Form1_Load(ByVal sender As System.Object, ByVal e
    As System.EventArgs) Handles MyBase.Load

Dim Xreader = New XmlTextReader("c:\books.xml")
Dim elements, attributes As Integer

        While Xreader.Read()

            If Xreader.nodetype = XmlNodeType.Element Then
                elements += 1
```

```
            If (Xreader.HasAttributes) Then
                  attributes += Xreader.AttributeCount
            End If
        End If

    End While


    Dim t As String

    t &= "Number of Elements: " & elements
    t &= "   Number of Attributes: " & attributes

    MsgBox(t)


End Sub
```

Press F5 to see the results. F5 executes the current program in Visual Studio. If you see an error message like the one shown in Figure 2-2, it means that you didn't save the books.xml file to your C:\ drive correctly, as described earlier in this chapter. Or you mistyped the path `c:\books.xml` in your source code. Fix the problem and press F5 again.

Figure 2-2:
Most error messages in Visual Studio are quite specific and helpful.

After declaring a new XMLTextReader (which is pointed to the sample books.xml file), you are able to use this XMLReader object to do your job of parsing.

The XMLReader is quite like the classic SAX parser, but with the XMLReader you can modify its behavior to suit your purposes. The XMLReader is an abstract class that offers three useful inherited classes: XMLTextReader, XMLNodeReader, and XMLValidatingReader. In this chapter, you explore the XMLTextReader.

Understanding node types

You used the reader's .Read method in this example, but you ignored much of the information the method provides. You looked for elements and attributes, but here are the other node types that the reader can tell you about: CDATA, comment, Document, DocumentFragment, Document-Type, EndElement, EndEntity, Entity, EntityReference, Notation, ProcessingInstruction, SignificantWhitespace, Text, Whitespace, and XmlDeclaration. That should meet any needs you may have.

This example simply loops through the sample XML (while something is left to read). As it parses, it keeps a count of all element and attribute nodes it finds. Then it displays the results in a messagebox.

When you first use the XMLTextReader's Read method, the parsing begins and a virtual "finger" moves down through the document, like a cursor, one node at a time. Each time the Read method is used in your code, it moves to the next node, at which point you can examine the XML with the Reader's properties and methods, such as HasAttributes in this example.

Instead of providing the name of a stream or a local file path as you did in this example, you can alternatively supply an Internet address, like this:

```
Dim Xreader = New XmlTextReader(http://www.manx/sample.xml")
```

Should You Use SAX Itself?

As you see, using the XMLReader class is extremely flexible. You can customize it to your heart's content.

However, SAX and the XMLReader have a great deal in common. Both only move forward through the XML text, reading it like a stream. They are also both read-only, meaning you can't modify the XML text. No edits, inserts, or deletes are allowed. However, you can easily add some code to any project that you create that uses the XMLReader to modify the source file or source stream. Also, both SAX and XMLReader are light and fast: They don't cache the stream (store it in memory, like DOM does); they read the stream on the fly.

The big difference between SAX and XMLReader is in the way they handle the XML: SAX *pushes* the events into your source code (notifying you each time a node is read). XMLReader takes a different *pull* approach. Pulling gives you more flexibility in how you work with XML text. For example, the XMLReader easily permits you to mix more than one input stream (or source file). With SAX, that's not easy at all: It's like driving with your legs crossed — it can be done, but it's dangerous. Also, the XMLReader works more efficiently, avoiding duplicated caching, for example.

Perhaps the biggest advantage is that the XML Reader offers a little random access: You can skip nodes and other content that is not of interest to you, zeroing in more quickly on your target data. Check out the XMLReader's `Skip` and `MoveToContent` methods.

Should you use SAX? My advice is no. XMLReader is faster, lighter, and easier to work with and customize. What's more, the Visual Studio .NET IDE is solid and highly efficient. Only if you're burdened with a boss who goes to any length to avoid Microsoft products (or you are of that political persuasion yourself) should you try to cobble together XML programming solutions outside the Visual Studio .NET platform.

If you do want to work with SAX, visit this excellent Web site:

`http://www.saxproject.org`

You'll discover that although SAX was originally available only to Java programmers, it can now be used with several programming languages (C, C++, and so on). SAX also appeals to those who belong to the Open Source movement because SAX is in the public domain and there is no charge for using it.

An implementation of SAX can also be used within the Visual Studio .NET environment, with a little bit of extra effort on your part. To see how to make it work, visit this location within the Microsoft Web site:

`http://msdn.microsoft.com/library/default.asp?url=/library/`
`    en-us/xmlsdk30/htm/sax2_com_vb_interfaces.asp`

Deeper into XMLReader

Simply providing a count of elements or attributes, as you did in the previous example, is only a part of the XMLReader's capabilities. I encourage you to use the Visual Studio .NET Help system to explore this tool's features further. This chapter concludes with a few additional XML parsing techniques that you may want to employ.

Here's a common scenario. Someone sends you an XML file and you want to read it node by node to find some information. First, though, you want to ensure that no simple errors are in the XML, such as a missing end tag. The XMLReader automatically generates an error message (*throws an exception as the latest lingo calls it*) if it finds a problem in the XML. (This check doesn't validate the XML by checking it against a schema; it merely locates simple internal inconsistencies.)

Parsing for errors

To see how to get specific details from an incoming XML file and how to report an error, try the following example code. First, switch to Design View in the IDE by clicking the Form1.vb(Design) tab at the top of the IDE code window. Choose View⇨Toolbox and then double-click the TextBox icon in the Toolbox to add a TextBox to your form. Press F4 to see the Properties window and double-click the `MultiLine` property so that you can view more than one line at a time in the TextBox. Also click the `ScrollBars` property in the Property window and choose Vertical, so that you can scroll through the results.

Switch to the code window by clicking the tab Form1.vb at the top of the design window. Replace the source code from the previous example in the Form_Load event with the following new code:

**Book VI
Chapter 2**

**Reading XML
with SAX and
XMLReader**

```
Private Sub Form1_Load(ByVal sender As System.Object, ByVal e
    As System.EventArgs) Handles MyBase.Load

        Dim Xreader = New XmlTextReader("c:\books.xml")
        Dim t As String, cr As String = ControlChars.CrLf
'carriage return

        Try
            'The Read method moves to the next node in the
document automatically
            'if you are at the end (there are no more nodes),
Read will return
            'false
            While Xreader.Read()
                t &= Xreader.readouterXML & cr
                MsgBox(t)
            End While

            'Display any errors to the user
        Catch xmlErr As XmlException
            MsgBox("This file contained an error in the XML:
(" & xmlErr.Message & ")." & _
                cr & cr & "    Also look at line number: " &
_
                Xreader.LineNumber & cr & "    position: " &
_
                Xreader.LinePosition - 1)
        End Try

        TextBox1.Text = t
End Sub
```

Press F5, and you see that the entire XML file has been transferred as a string into the TextBox. Note that in the sample books.xml file, the entire text between `<catalog>` and `</catalog>` is seen as single node and is read in one big gulp. The `ReadOuterXML` method sends back a string containing the entire contents of the current node and all its children. In this case, the current node is the outermost node: `<catalog>`.

Introducing an error

To see what happens if the XML isn't well-formed (contains an error), open the sample file `c:\books.xml` in Notepad, and remove the `</author>` end tag following `Ralls, Kim` in the XML text. Now choose File⇨Save to put this error into the sample file.

Press F5 to re-run the program, and you should see the error message displayed in Figure 2-3.

Figure 2-3:
The
XMLText
Reader
can locate
errors and
report them
to you.

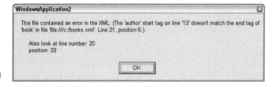

The `Try...End Try` code in this example is an error-trapping structure and, if the `XMLTextReader` notices an error, the `Catch` portion of the structure executes. In this case, it displays two pieces of information. First, you see a highly specific error description, telling you the actual line where the problem happened, the error (missing end tag), and a second line number (21) that revealed to the parser that there was an error. (Until the parser finds the `</Book>` end tag, it can't know that the `</author>` end tag is actually missing. It's possible that all those other elements were properly contained within the `<author></author>`element.)

Just to illustrate a couple of other error messages you can provide, the Reader's current `LineNumber` and `LinePosition` properties are also displayed.

Fixing the sample

Now restore the sample file `c:\books.xml` to good health by fixing the bad line so that it looks like this: `<author>Ralls, Kim</author>`. Then choose File⇨Save in Notepad.

Parsing XML More Closely

As you likely suspected, the XMLTextReader can provide all kinds of information about each node it reads. Table 2-1 shows you XMLTextReader properties that provide node data:

Table 2-1	XMLTextReader **Properties That Return Node Information**
Property	*Description*
AttributeCount	How many attributes are contained within the current node
BaseURI	The base URI. Duh.
Depth	The depth of the current node (how many parent-child nests down it is) within the documents structure
Encoding	The encoding attribute
HasAttributes	A boolean (true or false) value specifying if the node has any attributes
HasValue	A boolean value specifying if the node has any "value" (contents, such as text or numeric data)
IsDefault	A boolean value signifying whether the node's value is the default value specified in a DTD or XSD file
IsEmptyElement	A boolean value indicating if the node contains no data
LocalName	The name of the current node, but leaves off any namespace prefix
Name	The "fully qualified" name of the node, including any namespace prefix
NodeType	The type of the current node (using the XmlNodeType constants — see " XmlNodeType enumeration" in Visual Studio Help, and see the section earlier in this chapter titled "Understanding node types.")
Prefix	The namespace prefix of the node
Value	The text value of the node

If you need the XMLTextReader to examine a document node by node, providing all the tiny details of each node, use code similar to the following example. Type this into the Form_Load event:

```
Private Sub Form1_Load(ByVal sender As System.Object, ByVal e
    As System.EventArgs) Handles MyBase.Load

        Dim Xreader = New XmlTextReader("c:\books.xml")
        Dim t As String, cr As String = ControlChars.CrLf
    'carriage return
```

```
        Dim nodeType As XmlNodeType
        Xreader.WhitespaceHandling = WhitespaceHandling.None
'ignore blanks

    Try

        While Xreader.Read()

            t &= "Node: " & Xreader.Name & cr
            t &= "Type: " & _
                nodeType.GetName(nodeType.GetType(), _
            Xreader.NodeType()) & cr
            t &= "Number of Attributes: " & _
                Xreader.AttributeCount & cr
            t &= "Are there Attributes?: " &
Xreader.HasAttributes & cr
            t &= "Depth in Document: " & Xreader.Depth &
cr
            t &= "Is it empty?: " &
Xreader.IsEmptyElement & cr
            t &= "Is there a value?: " & Xreader.HasValue
& cr
            t &= "Name: " & Xreader.Name & cr
            t &= "Value: " & Xreader.Value & cr
            t &=
"......................................" & cr & cr

        End While

        'Dislay any errors to the user
    Catch xmlErr As XmlException
        MsgBox("This file contained an error in the XML:
(" & xmlErr.Message & ").")
    End Try

    TextBox1.Text = t

End Sub
```

Try This

Before leaving this chapter, it's hard for me to resist demonstrating a little .NET magic. Open Windows Explorer and double-click your sample XML file: c:\books.xml. Internet Explorer opens with the XML displayed as a formatted outline. Now for the real fun: Choose File➪Edit with Microsoft Visual Studio .NET. An XML view is displayed, which is somewhat similar to the IE version. Now, though, click the Data tab at the bottom of the .NET IDE window. You see your XML transformed automatically into the neat editable data table shown in Figure 2-4.

Now, right-click anywhere in the data set shown in Figure 2-4 and choose Create Schema from the context menu. You may get an error message saying "not enough room" or something, but don't be fooled. Look in the c:\ drive for a file named c:\books.xsd, open it in Notepad, and you should see the schema (structure) that Visual Studio has constructed out of your raw XML text. It begins like this:

```
<?xml version="1.0"?>

<xs:schema id="catalog"
    targetNamespace="http://tempuri.org/books.xsd"
    xmlns:mstns="http://tempuri.org/books.xsd"
    xmlns="http://tempuri.org/books.xsd"
    xmlns:xs="http://www.w3.org/2001/XMLSchema"
    xmlns:msdata="urn:schemas-microsoft-com:xml-msdata"
    attributeFormDefault="qualified"
    elementFormDefault="qualified">

  <xs:element name="catalog" msdata:IsDataSet="true"
      msdata:EnforceConstraints="False">

    <xs:complexType>
      <xs:choice maxOccurs="unbounded">
        <xs:element name="book">
          <xs:complexType>
```

**Book VI
Chapter 2**

**Reading XML
with SAX and
XMLReader**

Figure 2-4:
Just one of the benefits of using a powerful IDE, this data set is automatically created for you by Visual Studio.

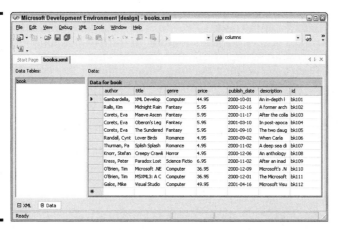

Also, remember from the previous example in this chapter (refer to Figure 2-3) that you got an error message specifying a line number in the XML source text where the error could be found. Do you want to have to count down 21 lines in the source file? Or do you prefer to have the lines numbered for you?

Choose Tools⇨Options and then click the Text Editor node in the left pane of the Options dialog box. Click the check box next to Line Numbers. Click OK to close the dialog box. Now you can immediately locate lines 13 and 21, as reported by the error message.

This is just a little sample of some of the ways that Visual Studio can assist with XML projects. You certainly don't want to have to figure out and then type in the schema file yourself, do you? And how useful is it that Visual Studio can instantly transform an XML document into a database-ready data set for you? Quite useful, indeed.

Moving Up to DOM

As you see, SAX or XMLTextReader are both high-speed *readers*. They're fine when all you want to do is move through a document, forward-only, to scan or parse it. But what happens if you want to be able to move around, back and forth perhaps, among the nodes in a document? In other words, what if you need to maintain the entire document context and explore it both forward and backward (random access)?

What if you want to locate all books whose prices are higher than $30? You could do that with forward-reading SAX or XMLTextReader techniques, but it's difficult and clumsy. You would have to "maintain state," as they say, meaning that you would need to get a node, store it, look at its price value, and then go back programmatically (by writing your own programming code) to find out the node's <author> or <title> value. There is an easier way. Perhaps you've guessed it: Store the entire document in memory; then skipping around to get information, compare nodes, or even *modify* the XML rather than simply *read* it becomes much simpler. Storing the whole thing in memory calls for the Document Object Model, the subject of the following two chapters.

Chapter 3: Understanding the XML DOM

In This Chapter

✔ What is DOM?

✔ Taking a look at document structure with DOM

✔ Understanding fundamental and extended DOM interfaces

*1*s DOM (Document Object Model) a set of usable classes? No. It's a set of specs, not actual code.

Technically, DOM, at its most basic level, isn't a library of working procedures. Instead, it is made up of *interfaces* only. An interface, in this context, means merely a sketch, not a set of classes. An interface contains no code in its methods, events, or properties — just the names and parameters of the members. Interfaces are primarily used when a committee or someone in power wants to specify a standardized set of commands that accomplish a particular job. Because XML DOM is an empty shell of specifications, you or anyone else can write the code that implements these interfaces, thereby creating actual usable classes. Or, you can do what I and most other programmers do: Use the Microsoft implementation of the DOM.

The Microsoft .NET implementation of the DOM specification is tightly modeled on the official W3C DOM interfaces. The .NET `XMLNodeList` and `XMLDocument` classes — and associated classes — offer both the fundamental and extended technologies specified by W3C. If you've worked with W3C DOM, you'll feel quite at home with its .NET implementation. And you'll likely appreciate the additional features available in .NET to make your XML less error-prone and to make it work more easily.

The .NET XMLDocument object represents a document as a node tree. In this tree are (among other types of nodes) element and attribute nodes, along with their contents (their values, or data). In addition to the contents, added to each node is any *relational* information, which specifies child, parent, or sibling relationships.

The `XMLDocument` object permits you to manage XML documents in many different ways. For example, you can add new objects to the document by employing a set of *create* methods (`CreateNode`, `CreateAttribute`, `CreateElement` and so on). What's more, most of these methods are overloaded: `CreateElement` has these three versions, for example:

```
Public Function CreateElement(ByVal name As String) As
    XmlElement

Public Function CreateElement(ByVal qualifiedName As String,
    ByVal namespaceURI As String) As XmlElement

Overridable Public Function CreateElement(ByVal prefix As
    String, ByVal localName As String, ByVal namespaceURI As
    String) As XmlElement
```

Overloading means collapsing multiple functions into a single function that takes several different argument lists. The differences in the argument lists can be different data types, a different order of the arguments, or a different number of arguments — or two or three of these variations at once. The VB.NET compiler can then tell which version of this function should be used by examining the arguments accepted by the function in its argument list.

.NET is overflowing with many tens of thousands of built-in functions. Who can remember them all? Nobody. One way to reduce the overhead of so much functionality is to make a single function (or property or method) capable of doing various different things — *overloading* the function. That way, you have to remember only one function name and, thanks to the Intellisense that's built into .NET, you see all of its variations when you type its name into the code window. Under Tools⇨Options⇨Text Editor⇨All Languages⇨General, you want to select Auto List Members and Parameter Information (unless you have a photographic memory and have read through the entire .NET class documentation and know everything by heart). These two Intellisense features are, for most of us, essential: As you type in your source code, they display the properties and methods (with their arguments and their various alternative parameters) for each VB.NET function.

After you use one of the create methods, you then insert them into the document using one of the XMLNode class's node insertion methods:

```
Overridable Public Function InsertAfter(ByVal newChild As
    XmlNode,
        ByVal refChild As XmlNode) As XmlNode

Overridable Public Function InsertBefore(ByVal newChild As
    XmlNode,
        ByVal refChild As XmlNode) As XmlNode

Overridable Public Function ReplaceChild(ByVal newChild As
    XmlNode,
        ByVal oldChild As XmlNode) As XmlNode
```

You practice manipulating XMLDocuments in all kinds of ways in Book VI, Chapter 4. This chapter focuses on an overview of the XMLDocument implementation of the DOM.

Discovering the DOM

The Document Object Model is logical and hierarchical. It's a *tree* after all, and that's a hierarchy that employs branches and a root — concepts everyone easily understands.

The XMLTextReader described in the previous chapter is just fine for reading or parsing XML documents, but the DOM's job is to provide a more hands-on approach. Because DOM sits in memory, it's easier to use it when you want to add a node (or delete one), locate sub-trees, find nested nodes, and other manipulations of the XML document.

Your first job when accessing DOM is to actually put the document into memory. For this, you use the XMLDocument class, like this:

```
Dim myXMLDocument As New XmlDocument
```

The variable name you use can be any name you prefer, but I always prefer to be as descriptive as practical when naming variables; that makes it easier to read the code later if you have to track down bugs or modify the program. So here I chose myXMLDocument as the variable name.

Understanding the Fundamental and Extended DOM Interfaces

Object models are an effort to standardize a technology. (By the way, there are other DOMs, too, including a DOM for HTML.) Unfortunately, standardization is usually merely a brief phase, a short pause before the object model starts rapidly forking in all directions and unraveling.

In the fast-moving world of computers, very few standards remain intact for long. The term *forking* is used by Open Source (free software) hackers to describe the almost guaranteed proliferation of incompatible versions of any language, operating system, or, indeed, object model.

Despite heavy breathing on the part of the techie crowd and quite a bit of positive publicity in the press, all previous efforts to maintain standards have failed. Even a simple character code like ASCII is being eclipsed by a new code, UNICODE. Unfortunately, standards must make provision for new features, but you do see that the idea of *flexible* standards is oxymoronic.

It's an impossibly idealistic, contradictory goal: *extensible standards.* So far computing has suffered from a Tower of Babel effect.

Linux aficionados call this effect *forking.* By this, they mean that an IT department can easily lose control of a Linux-based project because it's all too easy to create a "fork" in the code base. Precisely because the central source code is open to anyone's fiddling, the fundamental core (code base) of Linux can divide into two incompatible code bases, which can't ever be reconciled. This effect is not accidental or rare. Forking becomes a tree of forks rather rapidly. Indeed, forking always seems to happen to extensible languages, such as Forth, and to extensible operating systems, such as BSD. (BSD has bifurcated into multiple forks: NetBSD, FreeBSD, OpenBSD, and so on.)

Even XML itself is forking rapidly into incompatible versions for bankers, bakers, and candlestick makers. Efforts are usually made to enforce conformity (for example, XML standards committees, Linus Torvald's and Alan Cox's attempts to act as a central authority for adding and accessing the Linux kernel, and so on). Nonetheless, these efforts at keeping open source or extensible languages and platforms "closed" are by definition paradoxical. How can something be simultaneously "open" and "closed"?

This brings us to extensibility provisions within the XML DOM specs. Wisely, or perhaps resignedly, those in control of the W3C DOM specification divided XML management classes into two categories. The *fundamental* classes contain the essential functionality needed to read and write XML. The *extended* classes are not absolutely necessary, but are useful because they assist programmers. Think of the extended classes as similar to the mirrors on a car — not essential, but certainly helpful.

Table 3-1 shows you the fundamental classes as implemented in the .NET framework, and Table 3-2 shows the implementation of the extended classes.

Table 3-1	The .NET DOM Fundamental Classes
Class	*Description*
XmlNode	A node in an XML document
XmlNodeList	A collection of nodes
XmlNamedNodeMap	A collection of nodes that can be accessed directly from code using their node names

Table 3-2	The .NET DOM Extended Classes
Class	*Description*
XmlDocument	An entire XML document (the top node and all the child nodes)
XmlAttribute	An XML attribute
XmlAttributeCollection	A collection of attributes (all attributes are associated with a single XML element)
XmlCDataSection	A CDATA section in a document
XmlCharacterData	Offers several text-manipulation methods
XmlComment	An XML comment
XmlDeclaration	An XML declaration
XmlDocumentFragment	A section from a full XML document (not a complete document)
XmlDocumentType	A DOCTYPE declaration
XmlElement	An XML element
XmlEntity	An <!ENTITY ... > declaration
XmlEntityReference	An entity reference node
XmlImplementation	A definition of the context for a set of XMLDocument objects
XmlLinkedNode	A node just before (such as a parent) or after (such as a child) the currently referenced node
XmlNotation	A notation declaration in a DTD or XSD file
XmlProcessingInstruction	A processing instruction
XmlSignificantWhitespace	Whitespace in an element or attribute
XmlText	The value (the text content) of an element or attribute

When you work with the DOM, you are working with several .NET classes in the System.XML namespace. The XMLNode class contains a variety of other classes, including the XMLDocument. Before you actually write some programming to manipulate a document using DOM (in the following chapter), it's worth your time to take a look at the most important (or, at least, most often used) members of the XMLNode and XMLDocument classes. These are your tools for programmatic access to your XML documents.

XMLNode Class

This class is virtual, which means you can't directly instantiate it in your code; instead, you have to get to it indirectly via the XMLDocument class (which can be instantiated). You work with these classes in the examples in the following chapter. For now, just familiarize yourself with the tools available through these classes: their properties and methods.

Properties

The type of node

These properties of the XMLNode class tell you information about a node in a document: `Prefix`, `Name`, `BaseURI` and `NamespaceURI`, and `NodeType`. The `NodeType` is an enumerated value (a list of possible values, including comment, attribute, element, and so on), which is used in code like this, for example:

```
Select Case xmlnode.NodeType
     Case XmlNodeType.Element
```

Value

`Value` (such as the contents of an attribute, or some text in an element), `InnerXml` (the current node's child nodes), `OuterXml` (read-only, includes both the current node and its children), `InnerText` (all the contents of all the children of the current node)

Moving through the nodes

`Attributes` (only used within elements, returns an `XMLAttribute` collection), `HasChildNodes` (does the current node have children?), `ChildNodes` (an `XMLNodeList` collection), `OwnerDocument` (the document the node is in), `ParentNode`, `FirstChild`, `LastChild`, `PreviousSibling`, `NextSibling`, `Item(name)` (the child node that matches the name argument).

Methods

Searching

`SelectNodes (xpath)`, `SelectSingleNode(xpath)`

Cloning, inserting, and deleting

`Clone` (creates a duplicate of the current node), `CloneNode` (clones the current node and all child nodes), `InsertBefore`, `InsertAfter`, `AppendChild`, `PrependChild`, `ReplaceChild`, `RemoveChild`, `Removeall`.

Writing

`WriteContentTo` (saves all child nodes to an `XMLWriter` object), `WriteTo` (writes the current node).

XMLDocument Class

The XMLDocument class is the class you actually instantiate (it inherits from the XMLNode class).

Properties

Comparing strings

NameTable returns an XMLNameTable, a list of all atomized strings in your document, so that you can quickly compare them. The XMLDocument class stores element and attribute names in an XMLNameTable, but if a particular name occurs more than once, it is stored only once (so that XML's famous redundancy is thus avoided), and you can do a fast search for the existence of a particular string. The names are stored in a way that avoids some of the less-efficient string comparison methods built into .NET. Strings held in this format are called *atomized* strings.

Information

DocumentElement (the root element of the document), DocumentType(the DOCTYPE declaration), PreserveWhiteSpace (is formatting preserved?).

Methods

Creating new XML

CreateAttribute, CreateCDataSection, CreateComment, CreateDocumentFragment, CreateDocumentType, CreateElement, CreateEntityReference, CreateNavigator, CreateNode, CreateProcessingInstruction, CreateSignificantWhitespace, XmlSignificantWhitespace, CreateTextNode, CreateWhitespace, CreateXmlDeclaration.

Searching

GetElementById, GetElementsByTagName, GetEnumerator, GetHashCode, GetNamespaceOfPrefix, GetPrefixOfNamespace, GetType, ImportNode, InsertAfter, InsertBefore.

I/O

Load (used to load from streams, disk files, TextReaders, or XMLReaders), LoadXml (loads directly from a string, such as TextBox.Text contents), Save.

Chapter 4: Processing XML Using the DOM

In This Chapter

✔ **Programmatically accessing an XML document**

✔ **Formatting (or not)**

✔ **Accessing a single node**

✔ **Accessing a node list**

✔ **Removing a node**

✔ **Replacing a node**

✔ **Inserting a node**

✔ **Creating a node**

✔ **Appending nodes**

✔ **Using recursion to atomize a document**

*I*n this chapter, you experiment directly with the DOM, discovering how to manipulate XML programmatically. Before you can manipulate it, though, you must first put some XML into a DOM object. But after that, the sky's the limit!

Loading into DOM

DOM can be loaded in two ways: The Load method accepts an argument describing the source, and the source can be a disk file, a stream, or an `XMLReader` or `TextReader` object. The `LoadXML` method also accepts an argument, but in this case you directly load a literal string or string variable into the document.

First, at the very top of the VB.NET code window, type these `Imports` statements to bring in the necessary code namespaces:

```
Imports System.Xml
Imports System.Xml.Xsl
```

Now, to load a literal string, type the following into the `Form_Load` event in the code window:

```
Private Sub Form1_Load(ByVal sender As System.Object, ByVal e
    As System.EventArgs) Handles MyBase.Load
        Dim myXMLdoc As XmlDocument

    Try
        myXMLdoc = New XmlDocument
        myXMLdoc.LoadXml("<Cookie><Name>Chocolate
Chip</Name></Cookie>")

    Console.WriteLine(myXMLdoc.DocumentElement.OuterXml)

    Console.WriteLine(myXMLdoc.DocumentElement.InnerXml)
        Catch ex As Exception
            MsgBox(ex.Message)
        End Try

End Sub
```

When you press F5, you see the following result in the output window (press Ctrl+Alt+O):

```
<Cookie><Name>Chocolate Chip</Name></Cookie>
<Name>Chocolate Chip</Name>
```

Or you can load from a file. (If you haven't yet saved the sample XML file, follow the instructions in Book V, Chapter 2 in the section titled "Saving the sample XML document."

Make the following change to the previous example. You simply change `LoadXml` to `Load`, and replace the string with a file path to an XML file. Here's the code that loads in the XML sample file named `c:\books.xml`:

```
myXMLdoc.Load("c:\books.xml")
```

Press F5 and notice the two large chunks of information now visible in the Output window. The only difference is that the first one includes the `<catalog>` tags because it displays the "outer" XML.

Preserving Formatting

We poor humans need a little help when reading documents. We need some variety on the page. In particular, we depend on white space to separate words, paragraphs (using tabs, and sometimes a blank line), headlines, and other elements of a page. The computer doesn't need all this whitespace.

So if you're just sending some XML to another computer, you don't need to preserve the formatting. As you saw in the first example code in this chapter, you can dump the entire XML document to the Visual Studio Output window as a single giant string of data.

However, often you want to use whitespace to subdivide the data, making it more palatable for people. Formatting XML over multiple lines makes the data much easier for us to deal with.

If you want to preserve formatting, you can use the PreserveWhitespace property to control whether or not formatting is retained in the XmlDocument. False removes all spaces (except those within element text), tabs, and all the rest of the formatting information.

For example, the following code produces a formatted result (by preserving the whitespace "tabs" in the original XML file):

```
Private Sub Form1_Load(ByVal sender As System.Object, ByVal e
    As System.EventArgs) Handles MyBase.Load
        Dim myXMLdoc As XmlDocument
        myXMLdoc = New XmlDocument

        myXMLdoc.PreserveWhitespace = True

        myXMLdoc.Load("c:\books.xml")
        Console.WriteLine(myXMLdoc.DocumentElement.OuterXml)

End Sub
```

Press F5 and you see the following formatted, indented result (I'm only reproducing the first node here):

```
<catalog>
   <book id="bk101">
      <author>Gambardella, Matthew</author>
      <title>XML Developer's Guide</title>
      <genre>Computer</genre>
      <price>44.95</price>
      <publish_date>2000-10-01</publish_date>
      <description>An in-depth look at creating applications
      with XML.</description>
   </book>
```

But change the line that specifies what to do with whitespace, and you get a different result — stripped of all but the essential characters:

```
myXMLdoc.PreserveWhitespace = False
```

Here's the result:

```
<catalog><book id="bk101"><author>Gambardella,
    Matthew</author><title>XML Developer's
    Guide</title><genre>Computer</genre><price>44.95</price><
    publish_date>2000-10-01</publish_date><description>An
    in-depth look at creating applications with
    XML.</description></book>
```

Searching

You've probably been wondering: Well, how about fetching particular information from the XML? After all, searching is one of the fundamental jobs of any data management system, and XML is a data storage (and transmission) scheme, so I have to know how to search it.

Just in time. You can get the entire document, as illustrated in the previous section, or you can use the GetElementsByTagName method to get a list of just what you want. In the following example, you get an XmlNodeList object that contains all the author elements. Type the following into the Form_Load event:

```
Private Sub Form1_Load(ByVal sender As System.Object, ByVal e
    As System.EventArgs) Handles MyBase.Load
        Dim myXMLdoc As XmlDocument

        myXMLdoc = New XmlDocument

        myXMLdoc.Load("c:\books.xml")

        Dim nodes As XmlNodeList =
    myXMLdoc.GetElementsByTagName("author")
        Dim i As Integer
        For i = 0 To nodes.Count - 1
            Console.WriteLine(nodes(i).InnerXml)
        Next i

End Sub
```

After getting the list of all the nodes matching the tag name author, this code then writes the entire list from zero to Count-1. Notice that the XmlNodeList count property is one higher than the number you must loop up to. That's because the XmlNodeList starts counting with item *zero* and counts up to one less than the actual total of the list. This peculiarity is common in programming when using collections (of which this list is merely one of many examples). However, not all collections begin with a "zeroth" item; some begin with one (just to make our programming lives a little more interesting and our debugging jobs a little more time-consuming). You just have to live with it and remember to subtract 1 from Count.

I did not use the `Try...Catch...End Try` error-trapping structure in this example. It wastes space in the book to repeat that structure for each example, so I'll leave it off from now on. But I do assume that you will use it whenever importing (reading) or saving (writing) data. It lets you know if there was a problem with the disk drive, for example, or, perhaps a badly-formed XML file was aborted before being read in.

Displaying Nodes

In the following example, you display the outermost node (the document itself) and its child nodes. The document in the book's sample file contains two children: `XML` and `Catalog`. You also see how to pass an entire document as a node. (Remember that almost everything in XML is considered a node of one kind of another, so a node is essentially as ubiquitous as an *object* in modern programming languages, and about as useless as a description. Because it's so useless, you need to have a second description, the *nodetype*.)

Book VI Chapter 4

Processing XML Using the DOM

XML nests its nodes within each other, so you can move through the XML document tree in various ways. You can run through the `ChildNodes` collection (using an index number). You can employ the `FirstChild` and `NextSibling` properties. You can use the dreaded *recursion* (an example of this terrifying and risky technique is offered at the end of this chapter). Or you can manage an individual node. This example illustrates how you can pass an entire document as an `XmlNode` object to a subroutine and then have that subroutine display any child nodes and attributes.

First, type the following into the `Form_Load` event:

```
Private Sub Form1_Load(ByVal sender As System.Object, ByVal e
    As System.EventArgs) Handles MyBase.Load
        Dim myXMLdoc As XmlDocument

        myXMLdoc = New XmlDocument

        myXMLdoc.Load("c:\books.xml")


        Dim i As Integer

        shownodes(myXMLdoc)


        If myXMLdoc.HasChildNodes Then
            Console.WriteLine("Child Nodes")

            For i = 0 To myXMLdoc.ChildNodes.Count - 1
                shownodes(myXMLdoc.ChildNodes.Item(i))
            Next
```

```
        End If

    End Sub
```

Then, immediately below the `Form_Load` event (right after the `End Sub` line), type the following subroutine:

```
Sub shownodes(ByVal node As XmlNode)

    Dim i As Integer


    Console.WriteLine("Node Name: " & node.Name)
    Console.WriteLine("    Type: " & node.NodeType)
    Console.WriteLine("    Node Value: " & node.Value)

    Console.WriteLine("_____")

End Sub
```

This `shownodes` procedure accepts a document and a child node (or any other node); then it displays the name, type, and value of the node. Press F5 and you should see the following output, the main node and the two children:

```
Node Name: #document
    Type: 9
    Node Value:
_____
Child Nodes
Node Name: xml
    Type: 17
    Node Value: version="1.0"
_____
Node Name: catalog
    Type: 1
    Node Value:
_____
```

This document node has no attributes, but if the node passed to the `shownodes` procedure does have some attributes, here's how you can display them:

```
' display any attributes

        Dim Xattr As XmlAttribute

    If Not node.Attributes Is Nothing Then
        If node.Attributes.Count > 0 Then
            For i = 0 To node.Attributes.Count - 1
                Xattr = node.Attributes.Item(i)
```

```
                    Console.WriteLine("    attribute: " &
    Xattr.Name)
                    Console.WriteLine("         type: " &
    Xattr.Value)
                    Console.WriteLine("    Attribute value: "
    & Xattr.Specified)
                Next
            End If
        End If
```

Finding Specific Nodes with XPath Expressions

You can use the XPath language to access individual nodes that interest you. See Book I for an in-depth exploration of XPath and the many expressions you can specify to track down the node, or nodes, that interest you.

Using SelectNodes and SelectSingleNode

The `XmlNode` class offers two methods that retrieve nodes based on XPath expressions you provide. The `SelectSingleNode` method gets the first node that matches the expression; the `SelectNodes` method gets an `XmlNodeList` containing all matches.

Type in the following code to see how to use both methods:

```
Private Sub Form1_Load(ByVal sender As System.Object, ByVal e
    As System.EventArgs) Handles MyBase.Load

        Dim myXMLdoc As New XmlDocument
        myXMLdoc.Load("c:\books.xml")

        Dim node As XmlNode
        Dim nodes As XmlNodeList

        node = myXMLdoc.SelectSingleNode("//book/author")
        MsgBox(node.InnerText)

        nodes = myXMLdoc.SelectNodes("//book/author")
        Dim i As Integer
        For i = 0 To nodes.Count - 1
            Console.WriteLine(i & ". " & nodes(i).InnerText)
        Next
    End Sub
```

When you press F5 to run this, you see a messagebox displaying `Gambardella, Matthew`, which is the name of the first author in the document. Then in the Output window, you see a list of all 12 authors in the document.

This example illustrates two primary ways that .NET programmers test their code. After entering the code in the `Form_Load` event (so that it automatically runs when you press F5 to execute the program), a single result is most conveniently displayed in a messagebox. However, a multiple result (like the entire contents here of an `XMLNodeList`) is best displayed in the Output window using the `WriteLine` method to place each result on its own line. Multiple results are confusing when viewed within a messagebox.

Using the Item property

Another way to get child data from within a node is to use the `Item` property of the `XMLNode` class. You pass the node name to the `Item` property and it returns the first matching child node. Here's an example:

```
Private Sub Form1_Load(ByVal sender As System.Object, ByVal e
    As System.EventArgs) Handles MyBase.Load

        Dim myXMLdoc As New XmlDocument
        myXMLdoc.Load("c:\books.xml")

        Dim node As XmlNode

        node =
myXMLdoc.Item("catalog").Item("book").Item("title")
        MsgBox(node.OuterXml)

        node =
myXMLdoc.Item("catalog").Item("book").Item("genre")
        MsgBox(node.OuterXml)

    End Sub
```

Yet another way to access individual nodes is by using the `GetElementsByID` method.

Changing a Document and Saving It

So far in this chapter, you've seen various ways to access parts of a document. But now it's time to see how to edit a document: add, remove, or change parts of the document. Also, you see how to use an `XmlTextWriter` object to save an XML file to the hard drive.

Removing attributes and saving a new .XML file

To remove a node, use the `RemoveChild` method of its parent node (the parent element). Therefore, before you can remove the child, you must search the document for its parent.

In this next example, you decide that you want to delete all the id attributes from the book elements. You simply loop through the XmlElements, stopping at each child node (in other words, all nodes within the general, outermode node <catalog>). For each child node, you remove any attribute named id:

```
Private Sub Form1_Load(ByVal sender As System.Object, ByVal e
    As System.EventArgs) Handles MyBase.Load

        Dim myXMLdoc As New XmlDocument
        myXMLdoc.Load("c:\books.xml")

        Dim XElement As XmlElement

        For Each XElement In
myXMLdoc.DocumentElement.ChildNodes
            XElement.RemoveAttribute("id")
        Next

        Dim writer As XmlTextWriter = New
XmlTextWriter("c:\bookschanged.xml", Nothing)
        myXMLdoc.Save(writer)

        End

End Sub
```

Press F5 and then use Windows Explorer to locate the new file you just created: c:\bookschanged.xml. Double-click this filename in Windows Explorer to display it in Internet Explorer. Using the End command forces the file to be saved and the writer and document objects to be destroyed. This prevents confusion if you use Windows Explorer to try to view the file c:\bookschanged.xml while your VB.NET program is still running. Until the VB.NET program ends, you can't view the new file.

Here's a sample showing how your XML looks in the books.xml file, before you attack it and remove all the id attributes:

```
<?xml version="1.0" ?>
 <catalog>
    - <book id="bk101">
      <author>Gambardella, Matthew</author>
  <title>XML Developer's Guide</title>
  <genre>Computer</genre>
  <price>44.95</price>
  <publish_date>2000-10-01</publish_date>
  <description>An in-depth look at creating applications with
    XML.</description>
 </book>
  <book id="bk102">
  <author>Ralls, Kim</author>
```

And here's how it looks with the id attributes stripped out and saved to the new bookschanged.xml file:

```
<?xml version="1.0" ?>
<catalog>
 <book>
  <author>Gambardella, Matthew</author>
  <title>XML Developer's Guide</title>
  <genre>Computer</genre>
  <price>44.95</price>
  <publish_date>2000-10-01</publish_date>
  <description>An in-depth look at creating applications with
    XML.</description>
 </book>
 <book>
  <author>Ralls, Kim</author>
```

Removing elements

You can use a similar For Each structure to delete elements. In the following example, you delete all description elements:

```
Private Sub Form1_Load(ByVal sender As System.Object, ByVal e
    As System.EventArgs) Handles MyBase.Load

    Dim myXMLdoc As New XmlDocument
    myXMLdoc.Load("c:\books.xml")

    Dim XElement As XmlElement
    Dim i As Integer


    For Each XElement In myXMLdoc.DocumentElement.ChildNodes

        Dim xmlList As XmlNodeList =
    XElement.GetElementsByTagName("author")

        For i = 0 To xmlList.Count - 1
            XElement.RemoveChild(xmlList(0))
        Next

    Next

        Dim writer As XmlTextWriter = New
    XmlTextWriter("c:\bookschanged.xml", Nothing)
        myXMLdoc.Save(writer)
    End

End Sub
```

Notice here that after you create a list of all the elements named description, you remove the first child (xmlList(0)) from each item in the list.

The XmlElement object has many useful methods, including the RemoveChild method you just used and the ReplaceChild method you use next to modify XML documents. The member list for the XmlElement class is extensive, and when you type the period (.) following an XmlElement object, the Intellisense list pops out, as shown in Figure 4-1.

**Book VI
Chapter 4**

Processing XML
Using the DOM

Figure 4-1:
The Xml-
Element
object has
many
members.

Replacing elements

To replace an element, use the ReplaceChild method, as shown in the following example. Type the following into the Form_Load event:

```
Private Sub Form1_Load(ByVal sender As System.Object, ByVal e
    As System.EventArgs) Handles MyBase.Load

        Dim myXMLdoc As New XmlDocument
        myXMLdoc.Load("c:\books.xml")

        Dim root As XmlNode = myXMLdoc.DocumentElement

        'Create a new node.
        Dim Xelement As XmlElement =
    myXMLdoc.CreateElement("price")
        Xelement.InnerText = "99.99"

        'Replace the first element (book ID = 101) with this
    new element
        root.ReplaceChild(Xelement, root.FirstChild)

        myXMLdoc.Save(Console.Out)
        End

End Sub
```

You should notice several tricks used here. The DocumentElement property contains the root element of a document. In this case, the root element is the entire `<catalog>` element (the entire document, in effect). You next build a new node using the `CreateElement` method of the document. What's also interesting here is that you can describe a new piece of XML by just assigning a name to the new element (`"price"`) and whatever `InnerText` you want to provide. Then you use the `ReplaceChild` method to remove the first `<book>` element and add your new `<price>` element. Finally, you "save" the entire document to the console (the Output window), so that you can see the results (without having to iterate through all the individual nodes using `Console.WriteLine` inside a loop, as you did in previous examples). The End command shuts down the program without requiring you to locate `Form1` and close it. These final two techniques are useful testing techniques.

After you run this example, the Output window displays the document, showing that the new `<price>` element has replaced the first `<book id = "bk101">`. The first few lines in the changed document look like this:

```
<?xml version="1.0" encoding="Windows-1252"?>
<catalog>
  <price>99.99</price>
  <book id="bk102">
    <author>Ralls, Kim</author>
```

Adding elements

As you probably expect, you need not replace an existing element if you are simply trying to add new elements to a document, using the `InsertAfter` or `InsertBefore` methods. Just delete the following line from the previous example:

```
root.ReplaceChild(Xelement, root.FirstChild)
```

And replace it with this new line:

```
root.InsertAfter(Xelement, root.FirstChild)
```

Your results now illustrate that your new element `<price>` has been inserted after the first `<book>` element:

```
<?xml version="1.0" encoding="Windows-1252"?>
<catalog>
  <book id="bk101">
    <author>Gambardella, Matthew</author>
    <title>XML Developer's Guide</title>
    <genre>Computer</genre>
    <price>44.95</price>
    <publish_date>2000-10-01</publish_date>
    <description>An in-depth look at creating applications
      with XML.</description>
```

```
</book>
<price>99.99</price>
<book id="bk102">
```

You have a choice when adding elements. The DOM objects have four methods from which you can choose: `InsertAfter`, `InsertBefore`, `AppendChild`, and `PrependChild`.

Adding a New Element with Sub-elements and Attributes

Now that you understand how to modify a document, it's useful to work with a longer example that illustrates how to add a complete main node with attributes and sub-elements.

In the following example, you build and add an entire `<book>` element with all its contents. This is the equivalent of adding an entire new record to a table in a database. Type the following into the `Form_Load` event:

```
Private Sub Form1_Load(ByVal sender As System.Object, ByVal e
    As System.EventArgs) Handles MyBase.Load

        Dim myXMLdoc As New XmlDocument
        myXMLdoc.Load("c:\books.xml")

        ' Create a new Book element
        Dim XElement As XmlElement =
myXMLdoc.CreateElement("book")
        ' Append it to the collection of children of the
document's root element (<catalog>).
        myXMLdoc.DocumentElement.AppendChild(XElement)

        ' Set the ID attribute of this new Book element.
        XElement.SetAttribute("id", "2009")

        ' Now create all the sub-elements that belong within
a <book> element.
        Dim XChildElement As XmlElement

        ' Create the author sub-element.
        XChildElement = myXMLdoc.CreateElement("author")
        'Add the text (the value) to this element, and append
it to the new <book> element:

XChildElement.AppendChild(myXMLdoc.CreateTextNode("Pennis
s, Mandy"))
        ' Append this author element to the new book element.
        XElement.AppendChild(XChildElement)
```

```
        ' Repeat the process to build all the rest of the
    sub-elements:

        XChildElement = myXMLdoc.CreateElement("title")

    XChildElement.AppendChild(myXMLdoc.CreateTextNode("Seems
    to Me!"))
        XElement.AppendChild(XChildElement)


        XChildElement = myXMLdoc.CreateElement("genre")

    XChildElement.AppendChild(myXMLdoc.CreateTextNode("Pointl
    ess Self-help"))
        XElement.AppendChild(XChildElement)


        XChildElement = myXMLdoc.CreateElement("price")

    XChildElement.AppendChild(myXMLdoc.CreateTextNode("$4.95"
    ))
        XElement.AppendChild(XChildElement)

        XChildElement =
    myXMLdoc.CreateElement("publish_date")

    XChildElement.AppendChild(myXMLdoc.CreateTextNode("2003-1
    0-03"))
        XElement.AppendChild(XChildElement)

        XChildElement = myXMLdoc.CreateElement("description")

    XChildElement.AppendChild(myXMLdoc.CreateTextNode("This
    book is indescribable"))
        XElement.AppendChild(XChildElement)

        myXMLdoc.Save(Console.Out)
        End

    End Sub
```

Press F5 and notice that the following new record has been added to the bottom of your XML document:

```
<book id="2009">
    <author>Penniss, Mandy</author>
    <title>Seems to Me!</title>
    <genre>Pointless Self-help</genre>
    <price>$4.95</price>
    <publish_date>2003-10-03</publish_date>
    <description>This book is indescribable</description>
```

```
</book>
</catalog>
```

This example is heavily commented, so you should have no trouble seeing what's happening at each step.

Recursion, Recursion

Recursion... How to explain it? In a few special programming situations, employing recursion is the most efficient technique you can use. But what can I compare it to? It's like the chicken that laid the same egg *twice* during a thunderstorm, or the way that cows eat and swallow the same food four or five times before finally sending it down to the next stomach.

Professors of programming have been known to slap the blackboard with their pointer and scream "Verboten!" when the topic of recursion comes up.

It can create an "endless loop" if you aren't careful to ensure that an exit condition is satisfied at some point, in order to halt the recursing.

What does recursion mean? It means a procedure that calls itself. Somewhere within the procedure is a call to itself. When you're searching a tree structure like the Windows folder, subfolder, and file system, or an XML document with its elements, sub-elements, and attributes, using recursion can be your most effective (if somewhat perplexing) tactic.

When traversing a tree, you look at each node to see if it has any children, and then you deal with any children. Then you repeat the same process for each child of the node, repeat it with any children of the children, and on and on until you finish with the whole tree.

In the following example, recursion does the job of walking through the entire XML document, node by node, allowing you to intercept any of the atomized individual items and process them as you will. It also loops through any attribute list, attribute by attribute. So, in effect, you're able to view and manipulate each of the smallest pieces of this document, in order.

Add a TextBox from the Toolbox to your form. Using the Properties window, change the TextBox's `MultiLine` property to `True` and its `ScrollBars` property to `Vertical`. Then type the following into your code window:

```
Imports System.Xml

Public Class Form1
    Inherits System.Windows.Forms.Form

    Dim s As String
```

```
Dim cr As String = ControlChars.CrLf
Dim quot As String = ControlChars.Quote


Private Sub Form1_Load(ByVal sender As System.Object, ByVal e
    As System.EventArgs) Handles MyBase.Load

        Dim xmldoc As New XmlDocument
        xmldoc.Load("c:\books.xml")

        ShowElements(xmldoc) 'pass the document to the
    recursive subroutine

        TextBox1.Text = s 'display the whole, finished string
        TextBox1.SelectionLength = 0 'turn off the selection

End Sub
```

The Form1_Load event starts the action off by loading the document and
then passing it to the recursive subroutine. Because recursion repeats itself,
it's easier to place the recursive code in a procedure all by itself. (You don't
want to keep loading the document over and over, for example.) After the
recursion is finished (after it finds Nothing when using the NextChild
method), execution returns to this Form_Load event and displays the
results (accumulated in string variable s). Note the final line: One kink in
.NET is that text placed into a TextBox is by default *selected* (white text
on black background). Therefore, you always have to deselect it so that it
doesn't look weird to users. Just set the SelectionLength property to zero.

Now just below the End Sub that concludes the Form_Load event, type in
this new recursive procedure:

```
Sub ShowElements(ByVal XNode As XmlNode)

        Static c As Integer 'counter
        c += 1 'raise count each time through the recursion

        If XNode.Name = "book" Then 'major node
            s &= "_____Major Parent
Node _____" & cr
            s &= c & ". Name of this Node: " & XNode.Name &
cr

        ElseIf XNode.Name <> "#text" Then 'show the name of
the other children except text
            s &= c & ". " & XNode.Name & cr
        End If

        Select Case XNode.NodeType
            Case XmlNodeType.Element
                ' Are there attributes inside this element?
```

```
If XNode.Attributes.Count > 0 Then 'yes
    s &= ".........Attributes:"

Dim XAttribute As XmlAttribute

' find and display each attribute
For Each XAttribute In XNode.Attributes
    s &= XAttribute.Name & " = " & quot &
XAttribute.Value & quot & cr & cr
    Next
End If
Case XmlNodeType.Text 'show only the contents of
a text node
    s &= c & ".             " & XNode.Value & cr
Case Else
    ' ignore other types of elements
End Select

' Keep calling this same ShowElements Sub until you
run out of child elements:
Dim XChild As XmlNode = XNode.FirstChild
Do Until XChild Is Nothing
    ShowElements(XChild) 'call yourself
    XChild = XChild.NextSibling 'move further
Loop

End Sub
```

This entire procedure repeats itself for each node (each element) in the entire document. It begins when the whole document is passed (and is seen as a single big element) from the Form_Load event. Each element (node) is handled a little differently. Each element is given a number, showing its position within the entire document.

The <book> element is the primary parent in this document, so it's offset by a line drawn onscreen, thereby visually cuing the user to each major record as it is listed. A <text> element's name (#text) isn't displayed, but its value is displayed (later on in the Select Case structure). All other child elements are displayed by their name, followed by their value (tabbed over a bit for formatting reasons). Any attributes are listed; then the Do...Loop continues on, moving each time to the NextSibling, until it finds Nothing, which ends the recursion process and returns execution to Form_Load.

The results are shown in Figure 4-2.

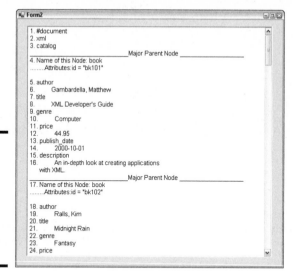

Figure 4-2:
Recursion
can be
the best
solution
to parsing
a tree
structure.

Book VII

XML Web Services

The 5th Wave — By Rich Tennant

"Great goulash, Stan. That reminds me, are you still scripting your own Web page?"

Contents at a Glance

Chapter 1: Introduction to XML Web Services

In This Chapter

✔ **What is a Web Service?**

✔ **Discovering the XML role in distributed computing**

✔ **Building a working Web Service**

✔ **Testing a Web Service**

✔ **Calling Web Services**

*Y*ou'll find considerable confusion about Web Services. How do they differ from traditional programming? What need do they fill? Just what *are* they?

You do need to understand them because Web Services could prove to be the single most important programming technology in the coming years.

It all started in the late '90s when the Internet began to gather momentum. People began to look outward from their personal computers, and they began to increasingly rely on information (and processing that information) on the Web. Both data storage and computing began a migration from local hard drives to servers that could be located anywhere in the world.

This migration continues to gain momentum, and it's possible that when the process of transferring computation from local, personal machines to Internet-based servers is complete, you'll be left with a mere shell on your desktop. *Dumb terminals* is the technical name for devices that have a monitor, a keyboard, and a mouse but are nearly empty-headed (possessing very little memory or intelligence). You look around and you don't see the actual computer anywhere; that familiar tan desktop case is simply missing. (As a side effect of this transfer of power, there may also no longer be application software as we think of it today; procedures may fly away across the Internet, and your word processor may be a set of distributed objects, located in various remote servers. What's more, you may have to subscribe to software, rather than buying it in a shrink-wrapped box. We'll see.)

Although nobody can yet predict the final equilibrium that will be reached between local and Web-based computing, it's now clear that a considerable and increasing amount of "personal" computing is no longer personal: It's located elsewhere and the results are sent back to your local machine from somewhere out there on the Internet.

Obviously this migration from local to Web-based computing has a major impact on programmers. The old, reliable solutions are giving way to new techniques. Everything from managing state (preserving variables) to debugging has to undergo a more or less radical change.

One implication of the migration is that information must be processed on remote computers, so these processing "services" must solve some communication problems.

Bridging the Gap

Web Services — along with XML and related technologies — are the latest effort to bridge the communication gap between applications, operating systems, and platforms. Sometimes called *platform independence*, this communication problem has proven surprisingly difficult to solve. But unlike previous attempts, which have all more or less failed, Web Services just may actually succeed.

In the past 20 years, many initiatives have been proposed to assist computer applications in communicating with each other. Back in the early '80s, for example, a suite of applications named *Symphony* (harmonizing was the idea) were able to share data. What you wrote in Symphony's word processor could be read and stored by its database application. It worked fairly well, but failed to solve the underlying problems: incompatible platforms, legacy data held in proprietary formats, the graphic department using Macs while everyone else in the company uses PCs, and so on.

Incommunicado

Computing suffers from a Tower of Babel problem. The Windows Clipboard is one way to transfer data between applications, but it's inefficient and does, after all, only work within Windows. (A small but vocal group of programmers and businesses insist on having nothing to do with Microsoft.)

OLE (object linking and embedding) was another "solution" that fell short. Two recent attempts were named COM and CORBA. They permit applications to share processes and data. However, they have two fundamental weaknesses: They require a *state* (a stable, persistent environment), and they package their communications in a binary format (which is unreadable by humans).

Web Services are stateless (which solves several communication and timing problems), and they also communicate via ordinary text (which obviously simplifies searching, programming, and just plain understanding the messages). Being stateless and text-based also makes Web Services fundamentally platform-independent. In theory — and usually in practice — Web Services freely communicate between Macs and PCs, between contemporary data formats and legacy structures, between local processes and remote ones, between *your* database format and *mine*.

A Web Service, however, involves more than just sending a message from one computer, requesting that a remote computer perform a job (process some data).

Distributed Computing

When you divide data and processing between more than one machine, you face some very important adjustments. You could compare it to the adjustment you must make when you get married. It's like figuring out how to manage your money jointly with your new spouse. A joint checking account forces you to behave differently than you did when you were single. It's more complicated.

You have to share data, to synchronize your deposits and withdrawals (to avoid bouncing checks). You may even have to figure out some security measures, ways to communicate about your finances without letting others in on your secrets. What was once merely a computation job within your single checkbook now becomes a communication problem between two checkbooks.

Likewise, in traditional computing, a programmer writes procedures knowing various facts about the environment in which the procedures operate: which operating system is being used; the language in which other procedures were written; and the location and structure of any data used by the procedures. In other words, the programmer works within a predictable, stable, fundamentally *local* environment.

Distributed computing does not offer the programmer that kind of predictability. The data may reside in Des Moines, on a machine running Linux, but the procedure that processes that data may sit on a computer in London running Windows. Web Services exchange information between distributed computers.

Web Services employ XML and other technologies to solve the communication and security problems associated with today's Internet-based computing.

Here's a typical business scenario that can benefit from Web Services. Say that your local computer holds the data about the customers you've signed up, but you are just one of a dozen salespeople in a company. The actual inventory management software used by all the salespeople resides in a remote location like Des Moines (remote from you, anyway). The problem is this: Your local computer in, say, Santa Barbara needs to join together somehow with the remote computer — so that they can exchange messages.

How do you send your local customer data to the remote inventory software so that it can process orders and send information back to you about prices, availability, and so on? The best solution so far is Web Services.

Visual Studio to the Rescue

Web Services themselves are designed to be platform-independent — to run on virtually all computer systems and to embrace all computer languages. Nonetheless, programmers must depend on a particular platform and, usually, a single language during the process of *creating* the Web Services. Programmers and developers need to work within an environment that offers them a rich set of useful and familiar tools: debugging features, pop-up lists of methods, an effective help system, and so on.

Web Services make a special demand on the programmer: Exchanged information must be translated into XML and communicated via SOAP (Simple Object Access Protocol) calls, a subset of XML. (Don't be fooled by the hopeful, but often misleading, use of the word *simple* here.)

Fortunately, there is an answer: Visual Studio .NET (VS .NET). It's likely that the majority of Web Services programmers will choose Microsoft's VS .NET as their programming environment. VS .NET also supports multiple languages. And even though it isn't the only Web Services programming environment, it appears destined to be the dominant one. Also, it features many useful tools, including the ability to automatically generate SOAP envelopes — lifting that significant burden from the programmer.

VS .NET includes other important tools. ASP .NET facilitates the creation of Web-based programming. ADO .NET brings database programming up to speed with its support for disconnected DataSets and automatic data packaging into XML. In sum, VS .NET boasts a powerful set of tools to assist programmers and developers in creating and maintaining Web Services.

An Overview

Here are the main points to remember about Web Services:

✦ **Web Services are free of physical (geographical) and computer language constraints.** Web Services are made available on the Internet, but you can also keep them on your local hard drive or on a server for an intranet. Therefore, they can be accessed from *anywhere*: from within your local intranet or from Zambia, it makes no difference.

✦ **Web Services are written as functions (or a collection of functions).** Therefore, they do not include a user interface — no textboxes, buttons, and so on for people to interact with. In this sense, they are similar to traditional code libraries (such as DLLs, or *assemblies*).

✦ **Web Services communicate with applications and with one another using the XML-based technology SOAP.** It eliminates the difficulties that have traditionally hampered computer-to-computer communications. In the past, proprietary database structures, unique object models, and incompatible computer languages have made life very difficult for programmers trying to reach out and touch a computer beyond the one they are working on. All too often, even the various applications on the same computer's hard drive could not efficiently communicate.

✦ **Because a Web Service merely sends text (XML) over the Internet (rather than executable code), a Web Service can't transmit a virus.** Firewalls are designed to block executables, but to permit text to pass right through — so that firewalls do not block Web Service communications. (Some hackers, though, have taken advantage of the fact that executable binary data can be loaded into a string.)

✦ **Web Services are based on a universal standardized language: XML.** Because they are communicated via XML, any application that is able to deal with XML can access any Web Service.

✦ **Web Services permit applications to consume the methods that the Web Service exposes.** In this way, a Web Service is just like a traditional object. However, unlike traditional objects, Web Services do not require that the consumer application employ the same object model as the Web Service. Both the Web Service and its consumers rely instead on XML as their shared protocol. Traditional objects are said to be tightly coupled to specific object models. Web Services are not.

✦ **Possibly important in the long run, Web Services can potentially circumvent traditional inefficiencies within organizations.** A salesman in Santa Barbara should be able to pretty easily access the data and software at the home office in Des Moines, thanks to the relative simplicity and universality offered by the Web Services communication model. (This is the theory, anyway.)

Book VII Chapter 1

Introduction to XML Web Services

Predictions

Many believed that 2002 would be the *Year of the Web Services*, but that didn't happen. And I doubt that 2003 will see a serious increase in Web Service traffic either. This should not discourage you. It took a few years for wireless technologies to catch on, but few computers in the coming years will be shipped without BlueTooth or 811. Sometimes technology takes a little while.

I suspect that 2004 or 2005 will see the fruition of the concept of Web Services. IT departments, developers, and programmers need to adjust to .NET and other Internet-centric environments.

One of the main drags on Web Services are security problems inherent in Internet communications. XML (and SOAP) are the communication tools used to send messages over the Internet, but XML is plain text. Anybody can read it. So you have to find ways to hide sensitive data (information such as credit card numbers, for example) in plain sight.

A bit more work needs to be done to improve Web Services' authentication, validation, and encryption techniques before corporations can entirely trust the Web Services' communication model. Actually, the security features are already in place. .NET includes highly secure versions of both asymmetric and symmetric encryption, for example. It's just that most programmers don't yet know how to use it with Web Services.

Web Services allow you to effectively *wrap* already tested corporate solutions (systems, databases, and so on) and expose them in a standardized, understood fashion. Nothing else competes with the features offered by Web Services. So I agree with many experts in predicting the eventual victory of Web Services as the standard for future Internet communications.

I also agree with most experts that both internal corporate database and related systems, as well as corporate portals and external Web Services communications, will eventually be managed by in-house developers using Microsoft's Visual Studio .NET. There's no significant competition to .NET either.

The Great Migration

Most programmers now face a daunting task: migrating from traditional Windows-based programming to Internet-based programming.

For many programmers, this migration is as challenging as anything they will face in their entire career. Not only must they cope with a new platform (or, more precisely, collection of platforms) — the Internet — but they must also learn to employ novel technologies to ensure the stability and security of their distributed applications.

And, ideally — but perhaps too idealistically — some have suggested that Web Services may permit many of today's non-programmers to join in the fun. Web Service programming can be quite high-level and relatively easy to use — particularly for people using Visual Basic .NET. Web Services can be assembled as objects into modular applications that, it is hoped, many business people will be able to fashion themselves rather than relying on overworked, understaffed, chronically behind IT staffs. After all, who is in a better position to know what's needed and to update a business or e-business utility than the business people who use it daily?

Perhaps IT employees can generate sufficiently well-designed and clearly described Web Service objects so that the actual applications employing those objects can be put together by business people. Salespeople, department managers, analysts, and so on could then join in the effort to improve a company's efficiency. In the Internet Age, most businesses must try to be as agile as possible — and Web Services offer great agility to a company transitioning to e-business.

However it eventually turns out, it nonetheless appears to many experts that Web Services may just be, at long last, the solution to one of computing's most serious problems. And if Web Services do solve the backward compatibility, messaging security, and cross-platform communication difficulties — the Tower of Babel that has plagued programmers and developers for decades — you'll certainly want to be among the early adopters who start converting soon to this new paradigm.

Remember, in the fast-moving information economy, agile companies (and programmers) are the most successful. Until quite recently, Xerox and Polaroid were among the bluest of the blue chip stocks. Nothing was ever supposed to happen to them.

Deeper into Web Services

What exactly do Web Services have to do with XML? They employ XML to do the important job of communication. It's basically a three-step process:

1. An XML message (a document) is composed and then sent as a request to a Web Service located on the Internet (or sometimes to a local service within an intranet, although this stretches the definition of *Web Service*).

2. The Web Service does whatever processing is necessary to satisfy the request it received. Any computer language, working within any operating system, can be used for this processing.

3. The Web Service composes an XML document containing its response and sends it back to the caller. (A response isn't always required.)

Creating Your First Web Service

TIP

If you don't have access to Visual Studio .NET, it's widely available in stores and online, and it's easy to install. You most likely want to get the Professional version; it has all the features that most people need, especially if you're learning. And if your company can't provide a copy for you, the Professional version of Visual Studio .NET can usually be found on eBay for a very reasonable price.

To see how to create a Web Service in Visual Studio, start Visual Studio. Choose File⇨New⇨Project; then click Visual Basic Projects in the left pane of the New Project dialog box. In the right pane of the dialog box, double-click the ASP.NET Web Service icon. A new project is created. (If the new project can't be created, you may need to use Visual Studio Help to see how to install IIS for ASP.NET.)

You first see a design window, and you can add controls to this window. But remember that a Web Service doesn't display any user interface, so it would be rather eccentric of you to add a button that no one will ever see. However, you may want to use some non-visible controls, such as the data connection controls. That's why a design window is made available.

Click the "click here to switch to code view" link in the center of the design window. You now see the basic Web Service template. When VB.NET first creates a Web Service template for you, it provides this source code in the code window. Don't worry if your Namespace is slightly different from this one — the latest version of Visual Studio .NET adds the name of your Web Service to *tempuri.org*, but this won't affect the example:

```
Imports System.Web.Services

<WebService(Namespace := "http://tempuri.org/")> _
Public Class Service1
    Inherits System.Web.Services.WebService

" Web Services Designer Generated Code "

    ' WEB SERVICE EXAMPLE
    ' The HelloWorld() example service returns the string
    Hello World.
```

```
' To build, uncomment the following lines then save and
build the project.
' To test this web service, ensure that the .asmx file is
the start page
' and press F5.
'
'<WebMethod()> Public Function HelloWorld() As String
'        HelloWorld = "Hello World"
' End Function
```

```
End Class
```

To write your own Web Service, replace the WEB SERVICE EXAMPLE (all those commented lines that begin with the ' character) with your own code.

To see how you write a Web Service and then test it, try creating a new Web Service that provides the current time and date. Delete the commented lines and then type the following source code, shown in boldface:

```
Imports System.Web.Services
```

Imports System

```
<WebService(Namespace := "http://tempuri.org/")> _
Public Class Service1
```

```
        Inherits System.Web.Services.WebService
```

```
" Web Services Designer Generated Code "
```

<WebMethod()> Public Function WhatTimeIsIt() As String

Dim s As String

s = Now.ToString

Return s

```
End Function
```

```
End Class
```

**Book VII
Chapter 1**

**Introduction to
XML Web Services**

The <WebService(Namespace:="http://tempuri.org/")> element specifies that this is a special kind of class, a Web Service. Notice the < > symbols, which traditionally enclose an element in HTML. This WebService element can be omitted because ASP.NET understands that you are writing a Web Service (its file extension is .ASMX, which makes that clear). However, the element has its uses. It can include various attributes, including the namespace and also a Description attribute, like this:

```
<WebService(Description:="Provides the current date and
    time", Namespace:="http://tempuri.org/")> Public Class
    Service1
```

Also, you use the `<WebMethod()>` element to make it clear that the function is part of a Web Service. (You can include a `Description` attribute in this element, too.) The `<WebMethod()>` element is not optional. You must include it because it's the only way that a remote client can see and access your function (method) from the outside.

This mingling of HTML-style source code (elements and attributes) with VB.NET code may seem a bit awkward at first, but you get used to it. Aside from those elements, the source code in this function is typical, familiar VB.NET.

Now press F5 to test this Web Service. You should see your browser fire up and display the information shown in Figure 1-1. (If you are using Visual Studio .NET version 1, ignore the information about tempuri and changing the default namespace. That's information you must deal with when deploying a real Web Service on the Internet. At this point, you are merely testing the service.)

The name of your Web Service is displayed as a hyperlink, as shown in Figure 1-1. (If you provide a `Description` attribute for your WebMethod, it is displayed just above the link.) Click the link and you see the Invoke button, as shown in Figure 1-2.

Figure 1-1:
Notice that if you've included a `Descrip-tion` attribute, it will be displayed at the top of this page ("Provides the current date and time").

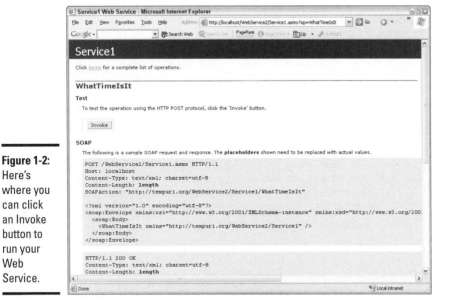

Figure 1-2:
Here's where you can click an Invoke button to run your Web Service.

Click the Invoke button to imitate a request to your Web service — as if someone had sent the request over the Internet — and your service responds. You see the result shown in Figure 1-3.

Figure 1-3:
There you are! Your Web Service "sent back" the date and time as a string in XML format to the remote client.

Testing Multiple Methods and Passing Parameters

In the previous example, you created a Web Service that has a single method and didn't have any arguments (meaning that it didn't receive passed data — parameters). Of course, Web Services can accept passed parameters and expose multiple methods. The next example shows you how to test this more complex type of Web Service, "passing" parameters by posing as the remote client.

This example exposes two methods: One accepts a string and responds to the caller by sending back the length of the string. The other method accepts two strings and then concatenates them and returns the result. Replace the code (shown in boldface) from the previous example in the Visual Studio code window. Then type the following into the code window:

```
Imports System.Web.Services
Imports System

<WebService(Description:="Counts characters, or concatenates
    two strings", Namespace:="http://tempuri.org/")> Public
    Class Service1

    Inherits System.Web.Services.WebService

<WebMethod(Description:="Please supply a string")> Public
    Function CountChars(ByVal s As String) As Integer

        Return s.Length

End Function

<WebMethod(Description:="Please supply two strings")> Public
    Function Concat(ByVal s As String, ByVal s1 As String) As
    String

        Return s & s1

End Function

End Class
```

Press F5 to test this Web Service. As shown in Figure 1-4, now you see two links, one for each exposed method.

Figure 1-4: In this example, your Web Service exposes two functions to clients.

Click the Concat link. You now see that in addition to the Invoke button, two Textboxes appear, where you can provide the two strings required by the Concat method, as shown in Figure 1-5. Notice that by providing a Description attribute, you are describing what parameters each method requires.

Type in two strings, click the Invoke button, and see the XML response that is sent back to the client:

```
<?xml version="1.0" encoding="utf-8" ?>
<string xmlns="http://tempuri.org/">Mary Queen of
    Scots</string>
```

Figure 1-5: Textboxes are automatically provided when parameters need to be passed to test a Web Service.

You may have noticed in the various Web Service browser testing pages in these examples that you see SOAP code and links that you can click to see "a complete list of operators" and a "service description." These XML files are essential to the communication process between a client and your Web Service. Fortunately, though, you can generally ignore them and let ASP.NET translate your VB.NET source code into the necessary XML. SOAP and its features are discussed in depth in Book VII, Chapter 3.

How to Call a Web Service

Now that you've seen how to create and test a Web Service, it's useful to go to the other side of the connection and see how you can use (consume) a Web Service from within VB.NET.

The idea is that more and more organizations will make Web Services available for various purposes. You need to know how to write source code that takes advantage of those services. Follow these steps to add a Web reference to a Windows project:

1. **Shut down Visual Studio.**

2. **Answer *yes* if you are asked whether you want to save changes to your Web Service project or whether you want to "stop debugging."**

3. **Restart VB.NET.**

4. **Choose File⇨New⇨Project.**

You see the New Project dialog box.

5. **Double-click the Windows Application icon.**

The New Project dialog box closes, and a new Windows-style application is available to you.

6. **Double-click the TextBox icon in the Toolbox twice.**

Two TextBoxes are added to your form.

7. **Double-click the background of the form.**

The code window opens and your insertion cursor is in the Form_Load event.

8. **Choose Project⇨Add Web Reference.**

The Add Web Reference dialog box opens, as shown in Figure 1-6.

The dialog box shown in Figure 1-6 is actually a pared down browser window, featuring a URL address Textbox, plus Back and Forward buttons and other features.

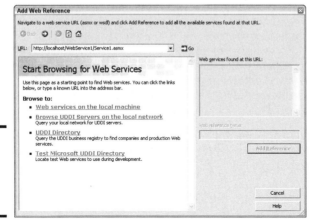

Figure 1-6:
Use this
browser to
test Web
Services.

9. **Into the Address Textbox shown in Figure 1-6, type the path to your "local host" (simulated Web site) Web Service. The Address will be something like this (depending on what you named your Web Service project and your Web Service). If you let VB.NET automatically name your project, it is probably named** `WebService1` **and the actual WebService is named** `Service1`**. In that case, you can type this into the Address TextBox:**

```
http://localhost/WebService1/Service1.asmx
```

(If you have created previous Web Services, the default name may be `WebService2` or `WebService3`, for example.)

10. **Click the arrow icon (Go) to the right of the Address Textbox.**

You see the result shown in Figure 1-7.

Book VII
Chapter 1

Introduction to
XML Web Services

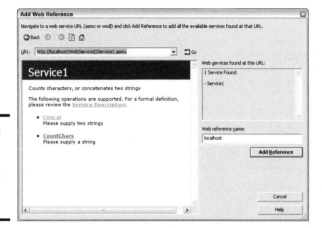

Figure 1-7:
Add this
Web
Reference
to your
project.

***11.* Click the Add Reference button.**

The Add Reference browser window closes, a reference to this Web Service is added to your project (you can see it in the Solution Explorer), and you are returned to the code window. By adding this reference, you simulate a location on the Internet. (However, in this case, the Web Service is located on your computer, on the *local* host, because you are still testing it.)

Now you want to write code that connects your Windows project to the Web Service, uses its methods, and displays the results that are returned from the Web Service.

Type the following line into the Form_Load event, noticing that as you type the period after localhost, the .NET Intellisense feature lists for you any Web Services available at the "Web site" (as shown in Figure 1-8). In this case, the only service is named Service1:

```
dim WebServiceAnswer as New localhost.Service1
```

Figure 1-8:
The excellent auto-list-members Intellisense feature shows you the Web Service's name.

```
dim WebServiceAnswer as New localhost.
                                      Service1
   End Sub
```

Now finish typing the following code into the Form_Load event to complete the Web Service access:

```
Private Sub Form1_Load(ByVal sender As System.Object, ByVal e
    As System.EventArgs) Handles MyBase.Load

        Dim WebServiceAnswer As New localhost.Service1()

        Dim param As String = TextBox1.Text

        TextBox2.Text = WebServiceAnswer.CountChars(param)

End Sub
```

Press F5 and notice that `Textbox1` contains the default `Text` value: `TextBox1`. `Textbox2` contains 8, the character count of the text in `TextBox1`. The Web Service did its job. (If you have a firewall running on your machine, it may display a message when you press F5 to run this example. It may want to know if you will grant permission for this service to connect to local host port 80. Go ahead and give permission. You know what's going on.)

If you make any changes to a Web Service in the code window, you must then *rebuild* it before you can retest it. (In the previous example, you added a Web Reference for a Windows-style client application, so you have to rebuild in that situation.) To rebuild, right-click *localhost* in the Solution Explorer. Then choose *Update Web Reference* in the context menu. That rebuilds your Web Service. (If the context menu doesn't offer this option, you are still in debug mode — meaning that your test program is still running. Choose Debug⇨Stop Debugging, and then try right-clicking *localhost*.)

Chapter 2: XML-RPC — Simple Distributed Computing

In This Chapter

✔ **Understanding RPCs**

✔ **Discussing parameters**

✔ **Forking the technology**

✔ **Sending structures and arrays**

✔ **Sending a fault response**

*T*raditional computing is undergoing a phase-shift, or as professors are fond of saying, a paradigm shift. In other words, a sea-change, a big move, a different way of looking at things, a major change.

You are adding a world of hard drives to what was previously just your own little personal hard drive, as a repository of data. Your primary source of information — of stored data — is increasingly the Internet rather than your local computer's disk drives. And, not far behind, is another trend: Your primary source of information processing (computing) is increasingly the Internet rather than your local computer's microprocessor and its stored procedures. When you go to your accounts page on your online broker's Web site, the broker's server, not your computer, calculates your current investment profit or loss.

Computing is essentially conducted by the passing of messages, called *procedure calls*. If you press the Enter key, a string of whatever text you just typed in is passed as a *parameter* to a *procedure* located in whatever software you are currently using. For example, if you are working in a word processor, it is filled with thousands of procedures, one of which may be called:

```
TheyHitTheEnterKey (TextLine as string)
```

This is a *procedure call*. The names `TheyHitTheEnterKey` and `TextLine` are merely names made up by the programmer who wrote the software, but `string` is a variable type, identifying the contents of the `TextLine` parameter. When the `TheyHitTheEnterKey` procedure receives the value in the

TextLine parameter, it moves the cursor visible on your monitor down by one line and prepares to accept more keystrokes from you (some other procedure does this).

A *remote* procedure call is pretty much the same thing as a procedure call, except it isn't *local*. It isn't a message sent from your keyboard triggering a procedure in your software on your hard drive. The "remote" part of this is that some software in your computer sends a procedure call across the Internet (or some other network) and (usually) gets a response sent back.

When you leave your local machine, a few important issues relating to communication must be solved:

✦ **Interoperability:** Can the procedure call's programming language be understood by the recipient, and can the recipient return a response understandable by the caller?

✦ **Security:** Can the request and response be hidden from prying eyes?

✦ **Authenticity:** Is the request and response coming from a trusted, authentic source, or have they been fabricated by an intruder up to no good?

✦ **Speed:** Remote calls are necessarily far slower to execute than local calls — so a few time-intensive behaviors are never used with RPCs. For example, in a local (Windows) graphics application, you can drag your mouse pointer to draw a line or to pick up and drop an icon in a different location on the monitor. Visible dragging requires pixel-by-pixel call/response traffic between each new mouse position and the application tracking it and redisplaying the line or moved icon. Given current bandwidth, such an intense communication loop can't be accommodated on an Internet connection. That's why you can click a button on a Web page (which generates a single RPC between your browser and the Web page server), but you can't drag that same button across a Web page (which generates hundreds of rapid calls — too many, too fast to allow *remote* procedure calls to be involved).

These same issues bedevil Web Services in general, and SOAP in particular, as you see throughout this book. The first issue, interoperability, is greatly ameliorated by the fact that XML is designed to be platform and language agnostic: It's supposed to be plain-text information.

Security (encryption, verification, and authentication) is another game altogether and security issues are probably the primary reason that remote procedure calls and Web Services are not yet dominating computer activity. Nonetheless, computing marches forward and many talented people are trying to solve these problems today. So it's worth your time to get on board. This train may just be leaving the station rather slowly now, but it will almost certainly pick up speed in the coming years. And, to best understand the nature and uses of SOAP and Web Services, it's helpful to go back to SOAP's older siblings (1998-today), Remote Procedure Calls (RPCs).

Understanding XML-RPCs

Sorry about all the parentheses in the next paragraphs, but as you doubtless know by now, computing, and especially programming, is filled with jargon. Sometimes they come up with five ways to describe the same thing. You just have to live with it. Computer languages have given us humans the second opportunity in history to design a language from the ground up — to make up the grammar, diction, syntax, and punctuation. Unfortunately, we're making rather a mess of things so far. (The first designed language was Esperanto, and it never caught on.)

XML-RPC (Remote Procedure Call) offers one way to access a remote object (an object that is not on your hard drive). If the object offers (exposes) public methods (procedures) or properties (variables), you can use XML-RPC as a way of communicating with the remote object and using (consuming) its public members.

Microsoft's older DCOM and Sun's RMI technologies both incorporated RPC support, though generally limited to C language implementations. XML-RPC is, of course, language-independent, like all XML. XML-RPC — in its various proprietary forked flavors — is relatively widely employed throughout businesses today.

XML-RPC attempts to free us from the main drawback of previous RPC implementations: They were highly language-specific (tightly coupled, and language- and platform-dependent).

Just like SOAP (described in the following chapter), XML-RPC is transmitted as an HTTP POST request, and the return message is transmitted as an ordinary HTTP response.

The first attempt to employ XML-RPCs took place in 1998. RPCs and XML-RPCs predate Web Services technology, but these RPCs themselves are a useful introduction to the efforts currently underway to bring Web Services to critical mass — to the point where they are as ubiquitous, as convenient, and as secure as possible.

Think of RPCs this way: They were the first and most successful effort to give the Internet some brains. Until PRCs (of one kind or another) came along, the World Wide Web was just a World Wide Bulletin Board — a collection of pages where people pinned messages and graphics. It had no more computing power than your morning newspaper. Add *procedures*, however, and the Internet becomes far more powerful — capable of making decisions and processing information, rather than merely displaying information.

Simpler than SOAP, XML-RPC lacks some of SOAP's sophistication, but XML-RPC is efficient. Unfortunately, though, XML-RPC has forked and there are now dozens of flavors of this "standard."

Here's a typical method call using XML-RPC:

```
<?xml version="1.0"?>
<methodCall>
    <methodName>users.getUserDebt</methodName>
  <params>
      <param>
          <value><i4>1255</i4></value>
          </param>
  </params>
</methodCall>
```

This is an ordinary XML document (I've left off the header here), and it merely contains two items of data: the methodName, `users.getUserDebt`; and the passed parameter, which is the user ID number, `1255`.

The `<methodCall>` must contain at least one `methodName` sub-item, which must be a string data type. Notice that within the `<methodName>` tag, you are required to use a fully qualified method name (you must include the object name, followed by the method name). You can use the following characters: uppercase or lowercase A to Z, digits (0 to 9), underscore, dot, colon, or slash. However, just what this "method" amounts to can be quite various: It may be a typical method (a procedure within an object), or it may be a script's filename, a stored procedure within a database, a record in a table, and so on. In other words, once you get down to the `methodName` level, it's up to the programmer exposing the method to decide just exactly what that "method" is and what it does.

Parameters Passed and Passing

You can send as many parameters as you want within the `<params>` tag pair, with each parameter enclosed by a `<param>` tag pair. You can optionally specify the data type of the parameter if you wish, like this:

```
<value><string>Tortillas</string></value>
```

XML-RPC permits a variety of data types (remember XML-RPC has *forked* into various versions). The default data type is, as you may have guessed, a *string* type. After all, XML is based on the notion that all its information is functionally just plain text.

Here is a subset of the typical data types you can send via XML-RPC:

+ **i4 (or *int*):** A four-byte signed integer (32-bit).

+ **base64:** Base64-encoded binary.

+ **Boolean:** Binary, two-states: 0 (false) or 1 (true).

+ **single:** A single-precision signed floating point number (range unspecified, implementation-dependent).

+ **double:** A double-precision signed floating point number (range unspecified, implementation-dependent).

+ **datetime:** Date and time.

+ **string:** An ASCII string. (You can use any characters in a string except < and &, which can be expressed as < and &. Also, you can store binary data within a string. Hackers take advantage of this fact to slip executables past firewalls.)

Forking the Technology

You are free to extend the data types to more advanced constructions, such as structures or arrays, or arrays-of-arrays, or anything else you may dream up. In fact, given the extensibility of XML, you're pretty much free to define whatever user-specified constructs are useful to you or your business partners. Nonetheless, you can find specifications for XML-RPC data types as well as other elements of these procedure calls. As usual, you can't have your cake and eat it too, but when people get together in specification committees to think up the rules for their new technology, they regularly act as if they've discovered a magic way to go in both directions at once, like quantum particles. Spec committees often claim that their new language is extensible, yet users must follow specifications.

In practice, some people follow the specs, but others ignore them and customize their RPC's, thereby *forking* the technology.

Sending Structures

Here's a typical structure (which sticks to the XML-RPC specifications), with individual members subdivided into the user name/value pairs that are found in constants and variables throughout the computing language world:

```
<struct>
   <member>
      <name>taco price</name>
      <value><single>.95</single></value>
      </member>
   <member>
      <name>enchilada price</name>
      <value><single>1.49</single></value>
      </member>
   </struct>
```

The preceding example code illustrates the fundamental difference between XML and traditional data storage and transmission tactics: XML is *verbose* in an effort to be clear. XML doesn't mind using up lots of extra memory in its effort to clearly define the meaning of each piece of data.

In traditional programming, you normally find data stored as a name/value pair (StateTax=.07, EmployeeID=1227, SamsDaughter="Ashley", and so on). XML takes this at least one step further by enclosing each data pair within an envelope of tags that clearly identify which item is the name and which is the value: <name>StateTax</name><value>.07</value>. XML sometimes goes even further than this by adding more tag envelopes to describe the data type of the value (<value><single>.07</single></value>), and to define a set of nested categories (the tree structure) that illustrates elementary relationships between the data items.

XML makes clear the basic relationships between the pieces of data (primary/subordinate/sibling, parent/child/sibling, or put another way, larger/smaller/equal). It builds the tree structure by nesting: In the preceding example, each name/value item is nested within a <member>, and those same <member> elements are themselves nested within a <struct>.

All these efforts, and this XML verbosity, are an attempt to improve what's called *discoverability*. This means that a programmer getting an XML-RPC POST or response should be able to easily read the XML text message and discover (figure out) the meaning of the message. If necessary, this programmer can then write a script or otherwise deal with the message programmatically. (Some people think that applications can themselves "discover" the meaning of "self-describing" data, without the help of human assistance.

I've never seen this in practice and doubt it can work on any meaningful scale until computers become artificially intelligent.)

Sending Arrays

Here's one way to transmit an array via XML-RPC. You're free to mix and match variable types, but like any typical computer language array, index numbers (the item's position within the array, such as the fifth item) identify the various values instead of variable names:

```
<array>
   <data>
      <value><string>barium</string></value>
      <value><string>engines</string></value>
      <value><int>55</int></value>
   </data>
   </array>
```

XML-RPC Responses

After having received the request in the previous code example, here is an example of a response returned to the caller:

```
<?xml version="1.0"?>
<methodResponse>
   <params>
      <param>
         <value><string>Bob Jones owes $166</string></value>
         </param>
      </params>
</methodResponse>
```

**Book VII
Chapter 2**

**XML-RPC — Simple
Distributed
Computing**

Here's the response header:

```
HTTP/1.1 200 OK
Connection: close
Content-Length: 265
Content-Type: text/xml
Date: Wed, 22 Jan 2003 22:35:36 GMT
Server: DaraData/7.2.2-WinXP
```

A header is sent, of course, with the message it describes. This is a return message, so you find no POST keyword, but both return and original XML-RPC message headers contain the content specifier text/xml. Firewall software takes a look at the Content-Type and, finding that it's harmless text/xml, allows the message to pass through.

A Bit More about Headers

The URI in the first line of the header has no particular specification. You can use whatever URI makes sense to you. Nonetheless, the connection, length of content, type of content, and server must be specified.

Headers are necessary because as soon as a Web browser such as Internet Explorer gets any document, it looks at the header for information about the document. (*Metadata* is the name sometimes given to information-about-information, such as a header.) The header specifies how (or if) the message should be displayed. An ordinary Web page, intended for display, has a content type text/html. You don't see the header; it's not displayed, but when the browser notices the text/html specification, the browser hands the page to its HTML parser, which then renders the contents on the user's monitor.

The first line in the header in the previous code example contains the "all clear, everything worked" signal 200 OK that you also see in a successful SOAP response message.

Sending a Fault Response

If there were a problem in the procedure's efforts to respond accurately (the parameter passed was the wrong data type, for example), a <fault> element would be returned (instead of any <params> element), like this:

```
HTTP/1.1 200 OK
Connection: close
Content-Length: 512
Content-Type: text/xml
Date: Wed, 22 Jan 2003 22:35:36 GMT
Server: SanaTatTech/7.4.2-WinXP
<?xml version="1.0"?>
<methodResponse>
  <fault>
    <value>
      <struct>
        <member>
          <name>faultCode</name>
          <value><int>9</int></value>
        </member>
        <member>
          <name>faultString</name>
          <value><string>
            Wrong data type: require integer.
```

```
        </string></value>
      </member>
    </struct>
  </value>
</fault>
</methodResponse>
```

No official standardized list of error codes or error strings exists. Creating those lists is up to you or someone interested in generating a standard.

Note here that you still get an all-clear HTTP code (200 OK). That's because the problem wasn't in the HTTP transmission itself, but instead in the application trying to process the RPC request. If an HTTP protocol error had occurred, you would get an HTTP error 400 or 500.

A response XML-RPC message must contain either a <params> structure or, if there was a problem, a <fault> structure (some C programmers like to call structures *structs*). The XML-RPC specifications insist, however, that you can't extend a <fault> structure to include additional members. Only the <fault> struct is permitted (along with its sub-items <faultCode> and <faultString>). According to those in charge, you can't start making up such items as <SolutionToErrorString> or <ErrorType>. In fact, the spec people say you can't add *any* new items to any part of the XML-RPC standard unless you first get them to agree. So much for extensibility.

As you know, XML-RPC, like everything else XML, has forked into various "implementations." If you want to see a list of 73 various "language-related" implementations of XML-RPC, look here:

```
http://www.xmlrpc.com/directory/1568/implementations" \t
    "_blank"
```

So much for language-agnostic. To be fair, most of us instinctively know that when someone tells you that "one size fits all," you're probably getting a lowest-common-denominator item — an item that needs some personalizing and modifying before it really fits your needs.

Chapter 3: SOAP — Accessing Web Services the Clean and Slippery Way

SOAP is similar to the XML-RPC technology described in the previous chapter. However, SOAP expands on the capabilities of XML-RPC. SOAP includes remote procedure call facilities, but is more generic.

SOAP is a general-purpose messaging technique that you can use to send information of any kind, for any purpose, over the Internet (or simply between computers connected by any kind of networking).

Like XML-RPC, a SOAP message usually includes a header and a body, but SOAP adds an *envelope*. In SOAP, the envelope and body are required, but you can leave out the header if you wish.

Before going any further, you can now create a SOAP message to get your feet wet. I think it's usually helpful to get down to cases quickly so that you can get familiar with an actual example of the topic under discussion. After you see a real example, generalizations and abstractions make more sense. At least that's the way I learn new things best.

So, before going into some of the details of SOAP, you can create an example now. Microsoft's Visual Studio .NET includes a SOAP serializer, which saves structures in text format, like all XML. SOAP serialization ignores any private fields (the alternative *binary* serialization saves both private and public fields). If you aren't familiar with streaming or serialization, take a look at the following section of this chapter before going on with the SOAP serialization example.

Understanding Streams and Serialization

Streams are flows of data, to or from your application. In .NET, streams replace traditional Visual Basic communication techniques between applications and files on a hard drive. What mainly distinguishes the concept of streaming from traditional approaches is that streaming isn't limited to communication with disk files. In the new world of distributed programming (typical of Web programming), data can be stored in multiple locations. In addition to files, for example, incoming streams can contain data from a Web source. Or computer memory itself can be considered a data store. For example, in .NET you can bind an array to a ListBox — treating the array that resides in memory as if it were a database. This, too, is a non-traditional source of "database" connections.

So, to take into account the various places where you may get or send data, the idea of *streaming* permits connections between all kinds of data sources (known as *data stores*). It's even possible to connect one data stream to another. One example of this is storing a secret message in memory, sending that message via a memorystream into a cryptostream to encrypt it, and finally sending it via a filestream into a file on your drive.

When you grasp the concept of streams and learn how to use them to send or receive data, you can then employ the same techniques no matter what data stores are involved. In theory, getting data from a remote computer in Peking should be no different from getting data off your own hard drive. I say "in theory" because — although you may wish it were so — it's not possible to do everything the same way in all situations. For example, when you're working with a file on your local hard drive, you can ask the stream to tell you the length of that file — how much data is stored there. But when working with a remote file coming in from Peking, you can't query a `Length` property; no such property is automatically available. (You probably recall that this problem is solved in XML-RPC by including a Content-Length element in the header.) Nonetheless, streaming is an improvement over the havoc of previous data-access technologies. Improved consistency is preferable to no consistency.

Related to streaming is the concept of *serialization*. Simple data types, like the string or byte or integer, are easy enough to store and retrieve. Only three things need to be stored per variable: its name, its type, and its value. Because of their simplicity, these simple variable types can be directly streamed without any special handling.

However, other kinds of data are also used — more complex data structures, such as arrays or objects. Increasingly, programmers have embraced a trend toward grouping related data into *packages* or *structures*. These structures can have a fairly intricate internal organization (parent, child, or sibling, for example). And the structure is often user-defined (you, the programmer create the structure of an object you define when you create a class). For these reasons, information describing a structure's organization must be stored when structures are sent to a stream.

Before a data structure is sent into a stream, it must be deconstructed into its structural components. This deconstruction is called *serialization*. Serialization is the process of breaking down a complicated structure into bytes that can be streamed, yet preserve the original structural organization. For example, an object can contain public and private properties and functions, can belong to a particular assembly (library of code), has a name, and so on. Each of these elements must be identified by name, internal order within the structure, individual data type, scope, contents, and other details about the structure, which must all enter the stream and be saved.

Serializing SOAP

To see a SOAP message, follow these steps to try this example of SOAP serialization.

1. **Start Visual Studio .NET.**

A Start Page is displayed.

2. **Click the New Project button on the Start Page (or choose File⇨ New⇨Project).**

The New Project dialog box appears.

3. **Click Visual Basic Projects in the left pane of the New Project dialog box.**

This selects VB.NET as your programming language.

4. **Double-click the Windows Application icon in the right pane of this dialog box.**

A new Windows-style project starts, the dialog box closes, and you see the design view in your editor.

5. **Choose Project⇨Add Reference.**

The Add Reference dialog box appears.

6. **Scroll down the list of components (under the default .NET tab) until you locate System.Runtime.Serialization.Formatters.Soap, and then double-click it.**

This namespace is added to the Selected Components window.

7. **Click OK.**

   The dialog box closes and you can see that the System.Runtime.
   Serialization.Formatters.Soap reference has been added in the Solution
   Explorer.

   Oddly, some namespaces must be added in this way (as a "reference")
   to a project rather than by simply typing in the usual Imports statements. The distinction between which namespaces are imported and
   which are added as "references" escapes me.

8. **Double-click the form in the Design window.**

   You see the Code window.

9. **Type in the following Imports statements at the very top of your code
   window, above the line Public Class Form1:**

   ```
   Imports System.IO
   Imports System.Runtime.Serialization.Formatters
   ```

10. **Now create a serializable class by typing this at the very bottom of
    your code window (below the line End Class, which concludes the
    Form1 class):**

    ```
    <Serializable()> Public Class MyObject

        Public a As String = "Now to disk"
        Public b As String = "....and back."
        Public c As Integer = 120

    End Class
    ```

11. **Finally, type this into the Form1_Load event:**

    ```
    Private Sub Form1_Load(ByVal sender As System.Object, _
        ByVal e As System.EventArgs) Handles MyBase.Load

            Dim obj As New MyObject

            Console.WriteLine(obj.a)
            Console.WriteLine(obj.b)
            Console.WriteLine(obj.c)
            Console.WriteLine()

            obj.a = "this test"
            obj.b = "is now over."
            obj.c = 44
            Dim fs As New FileStream("c:\test.txt", _
        FileMode.Create, FileAccess.Write)
            Dim XMLf As New Soap.SoapFormatter
    ```

```
XMLf.Serialize(fs, obj)
fs.Close()

'read it back

Dim XMLf1 As New Soap.SoapFormatter
Dim fs1 As New FileStream("c:\test.txt",
FileMode.Open, FileAccess.Read)

obj = XMLf1.Deserialize(fs1)
fs1.Close()

Console.WriteLine(obj.a)
Console.WriteLine(obj.b)
Console.WriteLine(obj.c)

End Sub
```

In this example, you create an object and display three of its properties in the output window, just to show that it exists. Then you change those properties, serialize the object, and stream it to a SOAP file. Finally, you read the object back from the SOAP file, deserialize it, and display the new properties in the output window to demonstrate that everything went well.

No hand soap

Press F5 to run this example. You should see two sets of properties displayed in the Output window, but the interesting thing is to examine the c:\test.txt file created by the XML serialization. You see the usual, verbose, XML SOAP formatting. The file is entirely text, and you can see tags aplenty:

```
<SOAP-ENV:Envelope
    xmlns:xsi="http://www.w3.org/2001/XMLSchema-instance"
    xmlns:xsd="http://www.w3.org/2001/XMLSchema" xmlns:SOAP-
    ENC="http://schemas.xmlsoap.org/soap/encoding/"
    xmlns:SOAP-
    ENV="http://schemas.xmlsoap.org/soap/envelope/"
    xmlns:clr="http://schemas.microsoft.com/soap/encoding/clr
    /1.0" SOAP-
    ENV:encodingStyle="http://schemas.xmlsoap.org/soap/encodi
    ng/">

<SOAP-ENV:Body>
<a1:MyObject id="ref-1"
    xmlns:a1="http://schemas.microsoft.com/clr/nsassem/Window
    sApplication2/WindowsApplication2%2C%20Version%3D1.0.1122
    .17619%2C%20Culture%3Dneutral%2C%20PublicKeyToken%3Dnull"
    >
```

Book VII
Chapter 3

SOAP — Accessing
Web Services

```
<a id="ref-3">this test</a>
<b id="ref-4">is now over.</b>
<c>44</c>
</a1:MyObject>
</SOAP-ENV:Body>
</SOAP-ENV:Envelope>
```

You find out the details of this strange-looking text later in this chapter, but at least you now know what a SOAP message looks like, and, probably more important, you know how you can transform an object into SOAP automatically using .NET's SoapFormatter. The fact that this can be done is, for now, all you need to know to give yourself hope, to reassure yourself that creating SOAP doesn't have to be done by hand.

Back up into the clouds

Now that you have seen a real, live SOAP message, you can go back up into some abstractions, some general concepts that underlie the SOAP technology.

SOAP, made public in 1999, grew out of the XML-RPC specification. People still use XML-RPC, but SOAP is gaining ground because it is more sophisticated and more flexible.

As you probably expect, the official XML Protocols Working Group at the W3C (World Wide Web Consortium) moved gradually forward from the original (v1) specs for SOAP to the slightly different v1.1, and as we speak they are busy at work debating the issues of v1.2. This process will, of course, continue until the problem is solved or until a different technology becomes popular, whichever comes first.

An important distinction: The W3C does not refer to its specifications as *standards*; rather, they are called *recommendations*. This is a distinction that the group insists on making, and you better make it too.

More forking

In spite of academic hair-splitting and the heady debates over the possibility of extending the permitted elements of a `<header>` section, SOAP plays an important role in the evolution of Web services. But wherever you find specifications (er...recommendations, I mean), you also find lots of forking going on under the table.

Estimates vary, but more than 90 different, independent implementations of the SOAP specification have been identified so far. Compatibility is stronger than in most spec forking, though, so you can sometimes expect a message from one implementation to be usable by a different implementation (with maybe a little tweaking here and there). All popular modern computer languages now have a SOAP implementation, and some unpopular ones (Perl, Python) do too. They are able to communicate via SOAP messages surprisingly often.

Areas where interoperability (the ability to actually work together) breaks down in the various SOAP implementations include various higher-level jobs, such as making sure that a usable reply is constructed in the same "flavor" as the original request message.

The Basics of SOAP

At its most elementary level, a SOAP message is divided into four fundamental parts (or *blocks*):

✦ **A way to bind to HTTP (the standard Web messaging protocol) to make sure that the SOAP message gets to its destination.** SOAP messages are dealt with by *processors,* which are utility programs that handle the message and perhaps modify it or otherwise respond to it.

You also usually need to ensure that a SOAP processor on the recipient's computer is alerted that SOAP is on the way and needs to be parsed, interpreted, and handled. This can be ensured by repeating the word soap 11 times (give or take a few), as in the following example:

```
<SOAP-ENV:Envelope
    xmlns:xsi="http://www.w3.org/2001/XMLSchema-
    instance"
    xmlns:xsd="http://www.w3.org/2001/XMLSchema"
    xmlns:SOAP-
    ENC="http://schemas.xmlsoap.org/soap/encoding/"
    xmlns:SOAP-
    ENV="http://schemas.xmlsoap.org/soap/envelope/"
    xmlns:clr="http://schemas.microsoft.com/soap/encodi
    ng/clr/1.0" SOAP-
    ENV:encodingStyle="http://schemas.xmlsoap.org/soap/
    encoding/">
```

✦ **An envelope (an element, a pair of tags) that specifies the start and end of the SOAP message.** Technically, in XML, this is called the *top element* in the same sense that a <document> is the top element in an XML document — it means the outermost container, or the root of the tree structure, depending on which metaphor you prefer. The main job of the envelop tags themselves is to tell the receiver when the message begins, and when it has all been received:

```
<SOAP-ENV:Envelope

. . .

</SOAP-ENV:Envelope>
```

✦ **Within the envelope is the <body> section of a SOAP message, the place where the meat of the message resides.** The body can contain pretty much anything, as long as it is represented in a text format. Remember, you can stream even binary graphics files into a string, thereby preserving the requirement that XML always be "text." However, large amounts of data, such as image files, are not usually sent via XML because XML itself is already pretty verbose. Here's an example of a typical SOAP body section:

```
<SOAP-ENV:Body>
<a1:MyObject id="ref-1"
    xmlns:a1="http://schemas.microsoft.com/clr/nsassem/
    WindowsApplication2/WindowsApplication2%2C%20Versio
    n%3D1.0.1122.17619%2C%20Culture%3Dneutral%2C%20Publ
    icKeyToken%3Dnull">
<a id="ref-3">this test</a>
<b id="ref-4">is now over.</b>
<c>44</c>
</a1:MyObject>
</SOAP-ENV:Body>
```

✦ **An optional header that can contain additional information or schemas, such as ways to coordinate the messaging (process flow, RSVP, routing), how to ensure security, manage transactions, the names of the sender and recipient, the length of the message, and such.** Essentially, the header block was tacked onto the SOAP specs to provide for a way of gracefully specifying extensions to the SOAP specs themselves. Here's a typical SOAP header:

```
POST /TimeFrame HTTP/1.1
Host: www.Timeserver.com
Content-Type: text/xml; charset="utf-8"
Content-Length: 352
SOAPAction: "http://RunTimeserver.com/2003/09/respo"
```

This header specifies an HTTP POST operation, and the TimeFrame mentioned in the header refers to a utility program that is supposed to be executed at the Timerserver.com Web site. Headers, if used, are supposed to be the first child element within an <envelope>, and you can use multiple headers if you wish. Typically, a description of the header is provided in an associated XML schema, and there may be other schemas as well, such as the one described here by SOAPAction, which is an "actor" that verifies the message for security purposes.

The idea of permitting optional headers resulted from some bad behavior on the part of some XML-RPC users. Often a business needs to identify the language used in a message, authenticate the message, indicate about how many times this request was made (keeping track of "sessions" for example), or send other data that's not really part of the body of the message, but must be transmitted anyway. (Actually, there's no compelling reason why application-specific information can't be transmitted as part of the body block, but some people think that causes confusion between "meta data" and ordinary "data data." Whatever.)

Anyway, some badly behaved users were stuffing this extra data into HTTP blocks in their XML-RPC messages. (Here's an example of HTTP stuffing: `http://www.MyServer.com/flavors", "Flavor", "Berry", true)` This makes communication highly implementation-specific and works against the goal of interoperability. To solve this problem, the SOAP specs permit the optional `<header>` block, which can include all kinds of special information without mangling the message structure. The Berry Flavor info example can now be properly sent within a SOAP header, preserving interoperability, like this:

```
SOAP-ENV:Header>
    <ns:Flavor
        xmlns:ns="http://www.MyServer.com/flavors"
        SOAP-ENV:mustUnderstand="1">
    </t:Flavor>
</SOAP-ENV:Header>
```

Using an actor

SOAP messages, like any other Internet transactions, may travel through various in-between processors before arriving at the ultimate destination (the recipient's SOAP processing utility). Web Services involve *distributed* computing, after all, so a message may be routed through several different processes. It may be necessary, for example, for an intermediate process to provide some inventory information from a database at the home office in Detroit before the fulfillment house in Pasadena can send a catalog order to the distribution center in Indianapolis. You get the idea.

To identify which process in a distributed application is supposed to handle which part of the SOAP message, you can use the `actor` attribute. Each actor identifies the URI of the processor that is supposed to handle this portion of the message. (Remember that there can be multiple headers within a SOAP message, and each can specify a different actor.) An actor's value is simply the URI:

```
<soap:Header>
  <TransactionId ss:mustUnderstand="1"
    actor="urn:CheckAvailability>123</TransactionId>
</soap:Header>
```

In this example, the processor is told that if it doesn't understand how to handle this section of the message, it must raise an error. Otherwise, the CheckAvailability process looks at the inventory and gives a go-ahead (or a warning that the requested product is currently out of stock).

Alternatively, if you are certain of the order in which the various distributed processes are going to handle the message, you can use the next value rather than specifying the exact URI:

```
http://schemas.xmlsoap.org/soap/actor/next
```

As messages are passed from processor to processor, headers are removed. In other words, each processor in a chain of intermediate processors removes its header. It can optionally add a new header before sending the message on to the next processor in the chain. For example, the inventory processor removes the CheckAvailability URI before sending the message on to the fulfillment processor. The same inventory processor also removes the TransactionID header. When the ultimate recipient gets the message, it can see if the TransactionID has, in fact, been removed — thereby ensuring that the intermediate processor has looked at the message and had its chance to process it. (Intermediate processors are supposed to modify the header, but not the body, of a SOAP message.)

This is all a bit reminiscent of the gossip game: You pass a message to Betty that "the party is at seven," who tells Joy, who tells Sam, who tells Josh, who ends up telling Angie that "Kevin is arty."

The problem with messages going through multiple processors — each having the ability, indeed the *duty*, to modify the message — is that the final recipient has a difficult time ensuring the accuracy of the message, and that it has successfully been through all necessary previous processes STET in the correct order. The SOAP specifications do not provide any protocols or recommendations about how such problems are to be prevented or resolved. This rather touchy job is left up to each implementation (to each individual Web service provider).

A confession

Truth be told, SOAP header blocks are simply undefined and largely unspecified (few attributes are recommended). You put into the headers whatever you feel doesn't belong in the body. You can find no actual rules (or even many recommendations) about what should go into headers, or how it should go in. Consider the `MustUnderstand` attribute. It is (sometimes) found in a header to provide a way to manage a communication between users of older SOAP implementations when they message with users of newer implementations. If a consumer receives a message it doesn't entirely understand, it checks to see if complete understanding is necessary (=`"1"`) or not necessary (=`"0"`). In the previous example, the sender says that this message must be entirely understood, so a recipient that doesn't understand must return a SOAP fault and reject the message. (More about SOAP faults later in this chapter.) Nonetheless, various programmers make various uses of header blocks, which is in the spirit of SOAP extensibility but works against the spirit of interoperability. You always find that ancient tug-of-war between flexibility and conformity.

Two envelope recommendations (so far)

Alas, the best laid schemes o' mice and men gang aft a-gley. Here I am talking about platform independence, implementation-agnostic interoperability, and so on, and no sooner do you start to relax than you find out that even the `<envelope>` block of SOAP messages comes in two versions — two incompatible versions. Something's a-gley.

SOAP spec V1:

```
SOAP-ENV="http://schemas.xmlsoap.org/soap/envelope/"
```

SOAP spec V1.2:

```
<SOAP-ENV:Envelope
    xmlns:xsi="http://www.w3.org/2001/XMLSchema-instance"
```

Send V1 to a receiver expecting V1.2 (or vice versa) and the receiving parser throws up a `VersionMatch` error, chokes, and rejects the job. A programmer on the receiving end of this mismatch must do a little tweaking here, too, to handle this error within the parser, if possible.

You can also include within the envelope block a URL that defines a specialized (non-SOAP spec) encoding style, if you wish. This is one way to specify the namespace for a set of encoding rules that are to be applied to the message:

```
SOAP-ENV:encodingStyle="http://schemas.xmlsoap.org/soap/
    encoding/"
```

If you do point to a special encoding namespace, you are expected to still rely on the "standard" XML schema for simple data types, but you are free to specify your own complex objects, structures, and so on. Also, as new envelopes and other specs emerge, they are planned to ensure that they are backward compatible.

Both sender and recipient (or *publisher* and *consumer* to use the technical terms) must have agreed in advance to use any special encoding. Such custom encoding schemas are usually downloaded via a URL pointed to in the envelope. Note that there can be a different schema used to define the elements of the envelope from the schema used to define the encoding of the body.

Here is a list of the recommended SOAP namespaces (for V1.2):

+ `www.w3.org/2001/12/soap-envelope`: This namespace describes elements and attributes used in the *required* parts of a message.

+ `www.w3.org/2001/12/soap-encoding`: This namespace describes elements and attributes specifying the data types used in serialization (serialization of the data is optional).

+ `www.w3.org/2001/12/soap-faults`: This namespace describes the error code names used in error (fault) messages.

+ `www.w3.org/2001/12/soap-upgrade`: This namespace describes the SOAP versions that a particular SOAP processor supports.

You can actually just type these URLs into your browser's address field and then click the Go button to read the namespaces (it's mostly just XML text). As an example, take a look at the faults page. (I can't reproduce it here because it is copyrighted by MIT, the Institut National de Recherche en Informatique et en Automatique, and Keio University.) When you look at the faults page, you find a very brief system for dealing with what is called the `Misunderstood` element.

The Body Itself

Now you come to the primary reason for SOAP messages — the actual contents. If the `<header>` is similar to an address you write on an envelope before mailing it, and the `<envelope>` is similar to, well, an envelope, the <body> is the actual message — the information that you really want to convey in the message. Just like living people, each SOAP message is required to have a body.

Most SOAP bodies can be divided into two basic varieties: document-style (simply transmitted data) or procedure-style (some data processing is expected to take place, and a response is often expected back). Here is a document-style message example: A traveling salesman sends in his itinerary and contact list, but expects no reply. Here is an example of a procedure-style message: A salesman sends in an order, expecting a confirmation reply that includes a predicted date of delivery.

In the SOAP body, you find a true free-for-all. There simply are no rules, specs, recommendations, or suggestions at all. It can be XML, with its tree structure and its internal elements and attributes. Or it may be a structure, an object, a serialized array, or even just a string. (By the way, remember that security people are always aware that a string can contain a binary executable encoded within the string. Strings seem innocent enough, but aren't.) Nonetheless, the SOAP specs do include a suggested way of serializing data within the body.

You must enclose the body in the envelope, and the body must come after any headers used in the message. (The body is a child element of the envelope, in other words.)

The following are two examples of typical bodies. The first is a request that uses the "www.mysite.com/InventoryQueries" namespace to specify the element tag names and attributes that are application-specific. In other words, non-standard elements are "qualified" (described) by the XML located at this Web address:

**Book VII
Chapter 3**

**SOAP — Accessing
Web Services**

```
<SOAP-ENV:Envelope
  . . .
    <SOAP-ENV:Body>
      <m:CheckInventory
      xmlns:m="www.mysite.com/InventoryQueries">
          <partID>33552244</partID>
          <partName>Those Big Donut Cutters</partName>
      </m:CheckInventory>
    </SOAP-ENV:Body>

</SOAP-ENV:Envelope>
```

And the following is an example of a response:

```
<SOAP-ENV:Envelope
  . . .
    <SOAP-ENV:Body>
      <m:SendInventoryAnswer
      xmlns:m="www.theirsite.com/InventoryResponses">
          <inventoryResponse>True</inventoryResponse>
          <inventoryQuantity>152</inventoryResponse>
      </m:SendInventoryAnswer>
    </SOAP-ENV:Body>

</SOAP-ENV:Envelope>
```

Or, the body of a request could simply look like this:

```
<SOAP-ENV:Body>
"Have you got any of those big donut cutters left?"
</SOAP-ENV:Body>
```

The SOAP processor takes the incoming message and maps (translates) it to whatever application or object is used to manage the information.

You hear the term *map* more and more in programming circles. It means that you take one set of vocabulary words and create a one-to-one relationship between that set and a different set. It's somewhat like what happens when you study French: You learn to map the English word *goodbye* to the French equivalent *adieu*. When a soap body contains, say, the term `m:` if your processor is translating the incoming message into .NET terminology, it maps `m:` to the equivalent .NET term, which is `Function`.

Whose Fault Is It?

In the SOAP world, errors are called *faults*. (In languages derived from C, errors are called *exceptions*, which is certainly more politically correct because it attempts to disguise the fact that someone made a mistake.)

I prefer the honest word *error*, but it seems to be disappearing even from languages like Basic, which have always called things by their real names in the past. So when talking about XML, *fault* it is.

All computer languages — and SOAP is a language, albeit rather specialized and small — must have a way of handling errors. When an error occurs during the processing of a SOAP message by the recipient Web service (or by an intermediate process), the message is returned to the caller with a fault element inserted into the response message body. (However, if an error occurs while processing the header block, that error information must be placed within the header block itself before the response message is returned.)

Typically, computer error messages have two parts: an error number (or error "code") that is paired with an error message, and a string that describes the error. Recall that transmission errors are handled by HTTP and the error messages use error codes between 200 and 299. SOAP errors, or, excuse me, *faults*, use error codes between 500 and 599.

A SOAP response message can contain a response or a fault block, but not both. Also, there can be only one SOAP fault block in a SOAP message, and the fault block is supposed to include what is confusingly called the

`<faultcode>`. It's confusing because it's not a number; it's a string (such as `"VersionMismatch"`). Also, an actual error code (500-599) exists.

In addition to the "faultcode" (not the 500-599 code, the string code), you have `<faultstring>`, which is an error description string. You can also optionally include (within a `<detail>` element) any processor- or application-generated error messages if the error occurred while the message was being processed or handled. Finally, you can also provide the URI of the processor where the fault occurred (within a `<faultactor>` element).

Here's a simple example of a fault:

```
HTTP/1.1 500 Internal Server Error
...
  <env:Body>
    <env:Fault>
      <faultcode>env:InvalidParameter</faultcode>
      <faultstring>This service requires two
  strings</faultstring>
    </env:Fault>
  </env:Body>
</env:Envelope>
```

This is a list of the fault sub-elements:

✦ `<faultcode>` is actually not a numeric code at all. It's a fault name and is supposed to include information about whether the error is from the sender or the receiver. This determines whether an error was embedded in the message itself upon receipt (a `sender` fault), or whether an error occurred while the message was being processed (a `receiver` fault). However, this information isn't always used (again, the SOAP "recommendations" are evolving and many variations are currently in use). Here's an example of a value attribute specifying receiver:

```
<faultcode value='soap:Receiver' >
```

Some have suggested that you can use the dot (.) convention to add your own details to make fault codes more meaningful:

```
<faultcode>Server.RegionalDatabase.Overflow</faultcode>
```

In this example, the error was not a problem contained within the message, but rather was a problem on the server's database. Notice that this second example doesn't use a value attribute, and it uses the term `Server` rather than `Receiver`. You can almost always find many ways to transmit SOAP.

✦ `<faultstring>` is a "fuller" description explaining the error in more detail (a little more anyway) than the `faultcode`.

The fault string should be an understandable, descriptive message to the programmer, as in the following example:

```
<faultstring>Could not store your data. The database is
    closed.</faultstring>
```

✦ `<faultactor>` is a URI providing the address of the processor where the fault was generated. This element is included only if an intermediate processor generated the fault. If the final recipient of the message generates the fault, the `<faultactor>` element is not used (though some experts on SOAP say it's always optional).

✦ `<detail>` is an explanation of the fault provided by the processor or the application that handled the message. The `<detail>` element is included only if the message could not be processed successfully, and only if the error occurred within the body itself. The detail section looks like this:

```
<soap:Envelope
    xmlns:soap="http://schemas.xmlsoap.org/soap/envelop
    e/">
  <soap:Body>
   <soap:Fault>
      <soap:faultcode>Server.Security</soap:faultcode>
      <soap:faultstring>Improper Validation
    String</soap:faultstring>

      <soap:faultactor>http://myserver.com</soap:faultact
    or>
       <soap:detail>
         <SevError>
           <Originator>Distribution Verification
    App</Originator>
           <Resource>Test.txt</Resource>
         </SevError>
       </soap:detail>
     </soap:Fault>
   </soap:Body>
</soap:Envelope>
```

I've found various suggestions on various Internet sites — some "sanctioned," some not — that list fault codes and other elements of the SOAP fault system, but I have found no actual official list. In fact, at most you find only four "codes:" VersionMismatch, MustUnderstand, Client, or Server. (Client and Server are evidently equivalent to sender and receiver.) As you can see, the status of SOAP error handling is rather ill-defined at this point, if not actually best described as *havoc*.

A procedure-type message (which expects action to be taken on the message and a response to be sent back) is sometimes called an RPC message.

Mapping is often simplified, or even eliminated, because the name of the object sent can be identical to the method used to process the object on the receiving end. Also, any parameters passed can also be named identically, can be in the same order, and can be of the identical data type. This tightly coupled arrangement is preferred in many situations, although it obviously can't work across platforms or languages where, at the very least, data type specs vary. (The maximum size of the integer variable, for example, can differ in different languages, or even in different versions of the same language.)

Sending Your SOAP

SOAP messages are intended to be sent, so they must be transported via some protocol (some set of transmission rules). To see how a message is "bound" to a transport mechanism, use the automatic SOAP-generating features in Microsoft .NET to create a Web service template in Visual Basic .NET. (If you don't recall how to do this, follow the steps in Book VII, Chapter 1.)

After you've created a new Web Service template, delete the Web Service Example code in the code window (delete all the lines colored green in Public Class Service1). Now type this into Public Class Service 1 (type what's shown in boldface):

```
Imports System.Web.Services

<System.Web.Services.WebService(Namespace :=
    "http://tempuri.org/WebService4/Service1")> _
Public Class Service1
    Inherits System.Web.Services.WebService

" Web Services Designer Generated Code "

    <WebMethod()> _
    Public Function Discount(ByVal Retail As Single) As
    Single
        Return Retail * 0.7 'return the wholesale price
    End Function

End Class
```

Now press F5 to test this Web service. Internet Explorer starts running, and you see the Discount method listed. Click the link in Internet Explorer that says Service Description.

You now see this service description. Notice the `binding` element here in boldface:

```xml
<?xml version="1.0" encoding="utf-8" ?>
<definitions
    xmlns:http="http://schemas.xmlsoap.org/wsdl/http/"
    xmlns:soap="http://schemas.xmlsoap.org/wsdl/soap/"
    xmlns:s="http://www.w3.org/2001/XMLSchema"
    xmlns:s0="http://tempuri.org/WebService4/Service1"
    xmlns:soapenc="http://schemas.xmlsoap.org/soap/encoding/"
    xmlns:tm="http://microsoft.com/wsdl/mime/textMatching/"
    xmlns:mime="http://schemas.xmlsoap.org/wsdl/mime/"
    targetNamespace="http://tempuri.org/WebService4/Service1"
    xmlns="http://schemas.xmlsoap.org/wsdl/">
<types>
<s:schema elementFormDefault="qualified"
    targetNamespace="http://tempuri.org/WebService4/Service1"
    >
<s:element name="Discount">
<s:complexType>
<s:sequence>
  <s:element minOccurs="1" maxOccurs="1" name="Retail"
  type="s:float" />
  </s:sequence>
  </s:complexType>
  </s:element>
<s:element name="DiscountResponse">
<s:complexType>
<s:sequence>
  <s:element minOccurs="1" maxOccurs="1"
  name="DiscountResult" type="s:float" />
  </s:sequence>
  </s:complexType>
  </s:element>
  </s:schema>
  </types>
<message name="DiscountSoapIn">
  <part name="parameters" element="s0:Discount" />
  </message>
<message name="DiscountSoapOut">
  <part name="parameters" element="s0:DiscountResponse" />
  </message>

<portType name="Service1Soap">
<operation name="Discount">
  <input message="s0:DiscountSoapIn" />
  <output message="s0:DiscountSoapOut" />
  </operation>
  </portType>
```

```
<binding name="Service1Soap" type="s0:Service1Soap">
  <soap:binding
    transport="http://schemas.xmlsoap.org/soap/http"
    style="document" />
<operation name="Discount">
  <soap:operation
    soapAction="http://tempuri.org/WebService4/Service1/Disco
    unt" style="document" />
<input>
  <soap:body use="literal" />
  </input>
<output>
  <soap:body use="literal" />
  </output>
  </operation>
  </binding>

<service name="Service1">
<port name="Service1Soap" binding="s0:Service1Soap">
  <soap:address
    location="http://localhost/WebService4/Service1.asmx" />
  </port>
  </service>
  </definitions>
```

SOAP messages are, after all, *messages*, so they must be transported. By itself, SOAP is not a transmission protocol, but it can include information describing how it is to be sent. In other words, a SOAP message can ride on other protocols in its trip to and from a Web service. SOAP is sent via HTTP most often, but it can also be sent via SMTP or other methods. (SMTP is Simple Mail Transfer Protocol, a server-to-server technique, and the main protocol used for delivering Internet e-mail, but it is also used on other TCP/IP networks as well.)

In the preceding example code, you can see that the transport method is HTTP:

```
<soap:binding
    transport="http://schemas.xmlsoap.org/soap/http"
```

A Web service must, of course, communicate over the Internet, but sometimes Web services are also used internally by a company within its own local area network (LAN). Therefore, the transport mechanism must be capable of working in both areas. The most common choice for Web services is HTTP, a long-established messaging protocol, but SMTP is field-proven as well.

Both HTTP and SMTP are widely used (in browsers and e-mail applications, respectively), and therefore programmers and developers involved in computer communications are familiar with them and know how to manage them. Another possible transmission choice is the venerable FTP (File Transfer Protocol), but it is less useful because it lacks the more advanced error-handling abilities of HTTP and SMTP.

An HTTP session is designed to be quite flexible. If connections are intermittent or go down, HTTP tries again, routing the message (or parts of it) in a different way. HTTP is stateless (it doesn't maintain variables or other data in a continuous, global fashion — other than indirectly via such techniques as cookies). HTTP is discontinuous (it doesn't use a constant connection between sender and receiver — but it can break a message into various packages and send them by different paths). One advantage of SMTP over HTTP, though, is that a company's local mail server can accept SMTP messages within the firewall and, the local server can itself attempt retries at delivery.

If you need a two-way communication, such as verifying a bank transfer, HTTP is an excellent solution because it rests on a request-response communication model (unlike SMTP, which does not require a reply). SMTP, though, is good for situations similar to mail delivery: If your Web site offers a hot new robot doll and suddenly you get thousands of orders, SMTP is prepared to simply let those orders pile up until you are ready to process them. SMTP doesn't ask for a response.

Chapter 4: WSDL — Telling the World about Your Web Services

In This Chapter

✔ **Understanding WSDL**

✔ **Diving into WSDL syntax**

✔ **Elements of WSDL**

✔ **Understanding overloading**

✔ **Binding**

XML messages attempt to be self-describing as much as possible. They are often called *verbose* because they often contain a considerable amount of repetitious information included in an XML document, in an attempt to ensure that it's clear what each part of the document does and how it should be used.

Nonetheless, people are continually trying to make XML less platform- and language-specific. The goal is that you should be able to send a message from a Java script inside a Macintosh and have it be automatically understood by a Visual Basic process within a PC.

One attempt to improve the self-describing capabilities of XML messages is a separate language dedicated to describing Web services. WSDL (Web Services Description Language) attempts to standardize the job of describing the formats, responses, and protocols employed by Web services.

WSDL can be used to describe several primary qualities of a Web service message:

+ The type of data being sent between client and server during a Web service message exchange.

+ The type of processing that is to be carried out on the data.

+ The type of exchange (one-way, multicast, solicit/response, response/request).

+ The type of message used for input and output (procedure-style or document-style).

+ Error information.

✦ The protocol used to send the message(s).

✦ The address of the Web service.

The WSDL description is written in XML, of course, and is generally located within an XML schema or set of schemas. Both the sender and receiver in a Web service message exchange use the same schema(s) to agree on how the outgoing message is to be formatted and how the incoming message is to be processed. WSDL, therefore, allows for a variety of different implementations to be employed — COM, ERP, and so on.

Is WSDL Necessary?

You may be thinking: This all sounds familiar. Can't most — perhaps all — of this information be transferred using XML schemas and SOAP? Indeed, it can. In fact, the information can be transmitted in simple text strings. The idea, though, is to provide increasing levels of abstraction to facilitate interoperability. For example, XML-RPC and SOAP messages can include information that describes data types. This specifies a string data type, for example:

```
<value><string>
  Wrong data type: require integer.
</string></value>
```

However, using a procedure (many Web services make functions available to the client, which is the sender) involves more than simply knowing the correct data type to send. You must also know the name of the function you want to use and the parameters that you must pass to that function. In addition, parameters must be sent in the correct order and be of the correct data type or the function can't do its job. This information can be sent on paper via U.S. mail, via e-mail, or just by a phone call between the Web service sender and receiver. But that's the old-fashioned way; it's neither platform- and language-independent, nor is it self-describing. It requires some form of human intervention. WSDL is sometimes called a "contract" between the sender and receiver of a Web service message, and in this contract is all the machine-readable information necessary to correctly process the message. The theory is that people don't have to get involved, after things are correctly set up via the contract.

The WSDL Document

As is true of all XML-based communications, WSDL documents include a tree structure that helps sort out the parent/child/sibling relationships between the document's elements.

A WSDL document can include several sets of abstract definitions (which are general, non-specific definitions, found within element blocks in the document):

+ **Messages:** Document descriptions or function parameters (uses definitions from the following Types section).

+ **Types:** Variable type definitions (which are supposed to be language-independent). There can be only one Types section, or it can be omitted.

+ **PortTypes:** Message definitions (see the first item in this list) that describe the name and parameters for the functions.

And a WSDL document can include two specific descriptions (which are language-specific, concrete details):

+ **Bindings:** The specific binding or bindings of each operation described in the PortTypes definition.

+ **Services:** The specific port address or addresses for each binding described in the previous Bindings section. This isn't the same meaning of the word *port* that people have been using in computing for several decades. Instead, it actually means the URL address.

Table 4-1 outlines the elements, attributes, and child elements used in a WSDL document:

Book VII
Chapter 4

WSDL — Telling the World about Your Web Services

Table 4-1	WSDL Document Elements, Attributes, and Child Elements	
Elements	*Attributes (if any)*	*Children (if any)*
<definitions> (This is the base element; the entire WSDL message is enclosed within it.)	Name targetNamespace xmlns (alternative namespaces)	<types> <message> <portType> <binding> <service> (These are the primary blocks, or divisions, within the entire WSDL document.)
<types>		<xsd:schema>
<message>	Name	<part>
<portType>	Name	<operation>
<binding>	Name type	<operation>
<service>	Name	<port>

(continued)

Table 4-1 *(continued)*

Elements	Attributes *(if any)*	Children *(if any)*
<part>	Name type	
<operation>	Name parameterOrder	<input> <output> <fault>
<input>	name message	
<output>	name message	
<fault>	name message	
<port>	name binding	<soap:address>

Exploring WSDL Syntax

It's easy to see a WSDL service description using Visual Studio .NET. Start a Visual Basic .NET ASP.NET Web Service-style project in Visual Studio .NET by choosing File⇨New⇨Project. In the New Project dialog box, name your new ASP.NET Web Service WebService2.

At the very top of the code window, type these two Imports statements:

```
Imports System.Web.Services
Imports System
```

Adjust the line just beneath the Imports statements so that it includes a Description attribute, like this:

```
<System.Web.Services.WebService(Description:="Counts
    characters, or concatenates two strings",
    Namespace:="http://tempuri.org/WebService2/Service1")> _
```

Finally, delete the green code lines in the Service1 Class, and replace them by typing in these two functions:

```
    <WebMethod(Description:="Please supply a string")> Public
    Function CountChars(ByVal s As String) As Integer

        Return s.Length
```

```
End Function

<WebMethod(Description:="Please supply two strings")>
Public Function Concat(ByVal s As String, ByVal s1 As
String) As String

        Return s & s1

End Function
```

This Web service exposes (*publishes* or, put more simply, *makes available*) two different functions. Press F5 to test this Web service, and Internet Explorer starts running, displaying the new Web service. To see the WSDL file, click the Service Description link. You see the following description of your Web service and its two functions (with the major sections separated by blank lines):

```
<?xml version="1.0" encoding="utf-8" ?>

<definitions
    xmlns:http="http://schemas.xmlsoap.org/wsdl/http/"
    xmlns:soap="http://schemas.xmlsoap.org/wsdl/soap/"
    xmlns:s="http://www.w3.org/2001/XMLSchema"
    xmlns:s0="http://tempuri.org/WebService2/Service1"
    xmlns:soapenc="http://schemas.xmlsoap.org/soap/encoding/"
    xmlns:tm="http://microsoft.com/wsdl/mime/textMatching/"
    xmlns:mime="http://schemas.xmlsoap.org/wsdl/mime/"
    targetNamespace="http://tempuri.org/WebService2/Service1"
    xmlns="http://schemas.xmlsoap.org/wsdl/">

<types>
<s:schema elementFormDefault="qualified"
    targetNamespace="http://tempuri.org/WebService2/Service1"
    >
<s:element name="CountChars">
<s:complexType>
<s:sequence>
  <s:element minOccurs="0" maxOccurs="1" name="s"
  type="s:string" />
  </s:sequence>
  </s:complexType>
  </s:element>
<s:element name="CountCharsResponse">
<s:complexType>
<s:sequence>
  <s:element minOccurs="1" maxOccurs="1"
  name="CountCharsResult" type="s:int" />
  </s:sequence>
  </s:complexType>
  </s:element>
```

```
<s:element name="Concat">
<s:complexType>
<s:sequence>
  <s:element minOccurs="0" maxOccurs="1" name="s"
   type="s:string" />
  <s:element minOccurs="0" maxOccurs="1" name="s1"
   type="s:string" />
  </s:sequence>
  </s:complexType>
  </s:element>
<s:element name="ConcatResponse">
<s:complexType>
<s:sequence>
  <s:element minOccurs="0" maxOccurs="1" name="ConcatResult"
   type="s:string" />
  </s:sequence>
  </s:complexType>
  </s:element>
  </s:schema>
  </types>

<message name="CountCharsSoapIn">
  <part name="parameters" element="s0:CountChars" />
  </message>
<message name="CountCharsSoapOut">
  <part name="parameters" element="s0:CountCharsResponse" />
  </message>

<message name="ConcatSoapIn">
  <part name="parameters" element="s0:Concat" />
  </message>
<message name="ConcatSoapOut">
  <part name="parameters" element="s0:ConcatResponse" />
  </message>

<portType name="Service1Soap">
<operation name="CountChars">
  <documentation>Please supply a string</documentation>
  <input message="s0:CountCharsSoapIn" />
  <output message="s0:CountCharsSoapOut" />
  </operation>

<operation name="Concat">
  <documentation>Please supply two strings</documentation>
  <input message="s0:ConcatSoapIn" />
  <output message="s0:ConcatSoapOut" />
  </operation>
  </portType>

<binding name="Service1Soap" type="s0:Service1Soap">
```

```
  <soap:binding
    transport="http://schemas.xmlsoap.org/soap/http"
    style="document" />
<operation name="CountChars">
  <soap:operation
    soapAction="http://tempuri.org/WebService2/Service1/CountC
    hars" style="document" />
<input>
  <soap:body use="literal" />
  </input>
<output>
  <soap:body use="literal" />
  </output>
  </operation>
<operation name="Concat">
  <soap:operation
    soapAction="http://tempuri.org/WebService2/Service1/Concat
    " style="document" />
<input>
  <soap:body use="literal" />
  </input>
<output>
  <soap:body use="literal" />
  </output>
  </operation>
  </binding>

<service name="Service1">
  <documentation>Counts characters, or concatenates two
    strings</documentation>
<port name="Service1Soap" binding="s0:Service1Soap">
  <soap:address
    location="http://localhost/WebService2/Service1.asmx" />
  </port>
  </service>
  </definitions>
```

The first line beginning with ?XML specifies that this is, indeed, an XML document. This line is optional, but you usually see it included. The second line begins the huge root element <definitions> that encloses all the rest of the entire document.

Namespaces

Following that is a series of namespace abbreviation definitions. These abbreviations are used throughout the rest of the document to identify the location of the schema containing the definitions of the elements in a particular block within the document.

For example, here the abbreviation `xmlns:s` is identified as located at this URI: `http://www.w3.org/2001/XMLSchema`.

Then, later, in the `<types>` block, the abbreviation is used to specify the schema location:

```
<s:element name="CountCharsResponse">
<s:complexType>
<s:sequence>
```

Or, elsewhere, the `s0` abbreviation is used, as shown here:

```
<input message="s0:CountCharsSoapIn" />
```

This assignment of abbreviations is simply for convenience — to avoid having to repeat the entire lengthy URI for each element or attribute in the document. It's similar to the efficiencies achieved when using the `Imports` statement in Visual Basic .NET code. The abbreviations work only within the element in which they are assigned (in this case, the entire `<definitions>` element).

Namespaces are a clerical feature — preventing "name collision" if you use, for example, the same name (such as `CountChars`) for two different functions. How can the processor know which function to execute? This is the same problem solved by the post office when it gets dozens of letters every day to *John Smith* in New York City. By adding an address and zip code to the name *John Smith*, the letters are correctly delivered to their intended recipient. Programmers speak of *qualifying* functions and other programming components. This means the same thing as *specifying* in the sense of adding an address or adding some adjectives to a noun (the "fully qualified" phrase "the red-headed boy in the back of the room," versus the "unqualified" phrase, "the boy"). Recall that URIs are not necessarily a Web address (a URL). Instead, you can provide an internal address or a GUID (described in the following chapter).

The `targetNamespace` is a more general definition, specifying a container namespace (a more general one) to which all components of the element (`<definitions>`, in this example) belong. In other words, all names declared in this document belong, in this example, to your WebService at "tempuri" (your computer's internal "site"):

```
targetNamespace="http://tempuri.org/WebService2/Service1"
```

Notice too that below the primary list of namespaces, a second `target Namespace` definition appears within the `<schema>` element. This can differ from the other earlier `targetNamespace`, and this `<schema>` definition specifies the namespace for the names within the `<schema>` element. This `targetNamespace`, therefore, can override the earlier `targetNamespace` specification.

Types

The Types, Messages, and PortType sections within a WSDL each specify the data content of the Web service message. Each performs a (slightly) different job.

The `<Types>` block defines variable types used in the Web service (both the parameters passed to a function and the type of the value passed back in the response). The data types are described by XML schemas, or, optionally, they can be described in some other way.

In this example, the `CountChars` function expects to receive a string parameter from the incoming message:

```
<s:element name="CountChars">
...
  <s:element minOccurs="0" maxOccurs="1" name="s"
   type="s:string" />
```

and to send back an integer in the response:
```
<s:element name="CountCharsResponse">
...
    <s:element minOccurs="1" maxOccurs="1"
   name="CountCharsResult" type="s:int" />
```

Notice that the variable types `string` and `int` are qualified by the abbreviation `s:`. This `s:` is defined at the start of this document as an abbreviation for the URI of the schema (the namespace) where the meaning of these variable types is actually defined:

```
xmlns:s="http://www.w3.org/2001/XMLSchema"
```

**Book VII
Chapter 4**

**WSDL — Telling the
World about Your
Web Services**

You can look at these schemas by simply entering the URL in Internet Explorer's address field and clicking the Go button. However, don't expect to see a simple list of definitions. Many schemas are still under "review" and are not finalized. In fact, you may come across certain links in a schema Web page that are closed to the public. Try one of those links and you may get a long message about passwords and authorization.

Messages

After the types comes a series of `<message>` elements, each defining the abstract parameters that are required (the data type is not included). Here's the abstract description of the `CountChars` function:

```
<message name="CountCharsSoapIn">
  <part name="parameters" element="s0:CountChars" />
  </message>
<message name="CountCharsSoapOut">
  <part name="parameters" element="s0:CountCharsResponse" />
  </message>
```

Each `<part>` element represents a parameter or a value sent back as a response. The data type of each `<part>`, confusingly named the "element" attribute, can be a type defined (as in this example) within the Type block of the document, or it can be found in a schema such as a SOAP-defined type, an XSD base type, or a WSDL-defined type.

These schemas can be extensive. For example, Table 4-2 maps the XSD base types to Visual Basic variables.

Table 4-2	The SOAP Base Variable Types Mapped to VB 6
XSD (Soap) Type	*VB*
anyURI	String
base64Binary	Byte()
boolean	Boolean
byte	Integer
date	Date
dateTime	Date
double	Double
duration	String
ENTITIES	String
ENTITY	String
float	Single
gDay	String
gMonth	String
gMonthDay	String
gYear	String
gYearMonth	String

XSD (Soap) Type	VB
ID	String
IDREF	String
IDREFS	String
int	Long
integer	Variant
language	String
long	Variant
Name	String
NCName	String
negativeInteger	Variant
NMTOKEN	String
NMTOKENS	String
nonNegativeInteger	Variant
nonPositiveInteger	Variant
normalizedString	String
NOTATION	String
number	Variant
positiveInteger	Variant
QName	String
short	Integer
string	String
time	Date
token	String
unsignedByte	Byte
unsignedInt	Variant
unsignedLong	Variant
unsignedShort	Long

Interestingly, the schemas suffer from versioning problems just as do most other aspects of computing. In this case, the mapping of these variable types is not correct for the most recent version of Visual Basic. In fact, the variant variable type has been removed entirely from the 2 1/2 year old Visual Basic .NET language.

If you look around enough on the Internet, you come upon proposed or official schemas. Here's an example of a definition of the string variable type:

```
<xs:simpleType name="string" id="string">
    <xs:annotation>
      <xs:appinfo>
        <hfp:hasFacet name="length"/>
        <hfp:hasFacet name="minLength"/>
        <hfp:hasFacet name="maxLength"/>
        <hfp:hasFacet name="pattern"/>
        <hfp:hasFacet name="enumeration"/>
        <hfp:hasFacet name="whiteSpace"/>
        <hfp:hasProperty name="ordered" value="false"/>
        <hfp:hasProperty name="bounded" value="false"/>
        <hfp:hasProperty name="cardinality" value="countably
  infinite"/>
        <hfp:hasProperty name="numeric" value="false"/>
      </xs:appinfo>
      <xs:documentation
              source="http://www.w3.org/TR/xmlschema-
  2/#string"/>
    </xs:annotation>
    <xs:restriction base="xs:anySimpleType">
      <xs:whiteSpace value="preserve" id="string.preserve"/>
    </xs:restriction>
  </xs:simpleType>
```

Take a look at this Web page, if you're brave:

```
http://www.w3.org/TR/xmlschema-2/
```

Or look at this one:

```
http://www.w3.org/TR/2001/PR-xmlschema-2-20010330
```

You can find several versions of most SOAP schemas; at least four different data type schemas are currently available, and there seems to be a new version every year. In some cases, the schema version is identified by its year in the URI, such as this version from 2001:

```
xmlns:s="http://www.w3.org/2001/XMLSchema"
```

The example WSDL contract I'm using in this chapter contains functions, and is therefore a procedure-style contract. Document-style contracts require less verbosity because they need not define procedures.

When you create an ASP.NET Web service in Visual Studio .NET, pressing F5 creates a WSDL file (as shown in the example code earlier in this chapter), but it also creates a SOAP request and response. Here's the request SOAP message for the CountChars function in the Web service:

```
POST /WebService2/Service1.asmx HTTP/1.1
Host: localhost
Content-Type: text/xml; charset=utf-8
Content-Length: length
SOAPAction:
    "http://tempuri.org/WebService2/Service1/CountChars"

<?xml version="1.0" encoding="utf-8"?>
<soap:Envelope xmlns:xsi="http://www.w3.org/2001/XMLSchema-
    instance" xmlns:xsd="http://www.w3.org/2001/XMLSchema"
    xmlns:soap="http://schemas.xmlsoap.org/soap/envelope/">
  <soap:Body>
    <CountChars
    xmlns="http://tempuri.org/WebService2/Service1">
      <s>string</s>
    </CountChars>
  </soap:Body>
</soap:Envelope>
```

Note that the actual, literal string you send to this function must be put into the message, replacing `<s>string</s>` with, for example, `<s>Arizona</s>`. After making that substitution, your application that's sending this message then must count the characters and replace `Content-Length: length` with the actual count, such as `Content-Length: length 278`.

After the server receives the message and executes the function, it returns this response SOAP message:

```
HTTP/1.1 200 OK
Content-Type: text/xml; charset=utf-8
Content-Length: length

<?xml version="1.0" encoding="utf-8"?>
<soap:Envelope xmlns:xsi="http://www.w3.org/2001/XMLSchema-
    instance" xmlns:xsd="http://www.w3.org/2001/XMLSchema"
    xmlns:soap="http://schemas.xmlsoap.org/soap/envelope/">
  <soap:Body>
    <CountCharsResponse
    xmlns="http://tempuri.org/WebService2/Service1">
      <CountCharsResult>int</CountCharsResult>
    </CountCharsResponse>
  </soap:Body>
</soap:Envelope>
```

Before returning this message, the int in `<CountCharsResult>int-</CountCharsResult>` must be replaced with a literal integer value (the result of executing the function is an integer). Then the character count must again be calculated.

Finally, ASP.NET also provides you with the POST request and response code:

```
POST /WebService2/Service1.asmx/CountChars HTTP/1.1
Host: localhost
Content-Type: application/x-www-form-urlencoded
Content-Length: length
s=string
```

```
HTTP/1.1 200 OK
Content-Type: text/xml; charset=utf-8
Content-Length: length
<?xml version="1.0" encoding="utf-8"?>
<int
    xmlns="http://tempuri.org/WebService2/Service1">int</int>
```

Complex types

You can use more complicated variables, such as your own custom-defined structures (what were called *user-defined types* in previous versions of Visual Basic). For example, you could define the following structure in the Web service:

```
Public Structure MyType
      Public RefNo As Integer
      Public Comment As String
      Public Money As Single
  End Structure

  <WebMethod(Description:="Please supply a string")> Public
    Function CountChars(ByVal s As String) As MyType
      Dim myty As New MyType


      myty.Comment = "sall"
      myty.Money = "12.22"
      myty.RefNo = 12422

      Return myty

  End Function
```

The SOAP message specifying this structure looks like this:

```
<?xml version="1.0" encoding="utf-8"?>
<soap:Envelope xmlns:xsi="http://www.w3.org/2001/XMLSchema-
    instance" xmlns:xsd="http://www.w3.org/2001/XMLSchema"
    xmlns:soap="http://schemas.xmlsoap.org/soap/envelope/">
```

```
<soap:Body>
  <CountCharsResponse
  xmlns="http://tempuri.org/WebService2/Service1">
    <CountCharsResult>
      <RefNo>int</RefNo>
      <Comment>string</Comment>
      <Money>float</Money>
    </CountCharsResult>
  </CountCharsResponse>
</soap:Body>
</soap:Envelope>
```

Notice that the Visual Basic data type `Single` (single-precision floating point) has been mapped to the `float` type. This "language independence" in XML and SOAP is sometimes just a question of the favorite language of the people designing the type schemas. In most cases, their favorite language is C or one of its offspring, so you find a Visual Basic data type such as `single` yielding to the C type `float`. On the other hand, a `long` in C becomes an `int`.

All three variables within the `MyType` structure are represented here, along with their data types. The actual name `MyType` doesn't appear within these SOAP messages, but it does appear in the associated WSDL document, in the form of a complex type defining the entire structure:

```
<s:complexType name="MyType">
<s:sequence>
  <s:element minOccurs="1" maxOccurs="1" name="RefNo"
    type="s:int" />
  <s:element minOccurs="0" maxOccurs="1" name="Comment"
    type="s:string" />
  <s:element minOccurs="1" maxOccurs="1" name="Money"
    type="s:float" />
</s:sequence>
</s:complexType>
```

Enums

Another kind of complex data "type" contains a variety of possible values. Enumerations are also expressible in SOAP and WSDL. Here's an enum in VB.NET:

```
Public Enum DaysOfTheWeek
    Sunday
    Monday
    Tuesday
    Wednesday
    Thursday
```

```
      Friday
      Saturday
End Enum

<WebMethod(Description:="Please supply a string")> Public
    Function CountChars(ByVal s As String) As DaysOfTheWeek

    Dim e As New DaysOfTheWeek
    Return e

End Function
```

This translates into the following SOAP:

```
<soap:Envelope xmlns:xsi="http://www.w3.org/2001/XMLSchema-
    instance" xmlns:xsd="http://www.w3.org/2001/XMLSchema"
    xmlns:soap="http://schemas.xmlsoap.org/soap/envelope/">
  <soap:Body>
    <CountCharsResponse
    xmlns="http://tempuri.org/WebService2/Service1">
      <CountCharsResult>Sunday or Monday or Tuesday or
    Wednesday or Thursday or Friday or
    Saturday</CountCharsResult>
    </CountCharsResponse>
  </soap:Body>
</soap:Envelope>
```

And in the `Type` section, this is how an enumeration is expressed in the WSDL file:

```
<s:complexType>
<s:sequence>
  <s:element minOccurs="1" maxOccurs="1"
    name="CountCharsResult" type="s0:DaysOfTheWeek" />
  </s:sequence>
  </s:complexType>
  </s:element>
<s:simpleType name="DaysOfTheWeek">
<s:restriction base="s:string">
  <s:enumeration value="Sunday" />
  <s:enumeration value="Monday" />
  <s:enumeration value="Tuesday" />
  <s:enumeration value="Wednesday" />
  <s:enumeration value="Thursday" />
  <s:enumeration value="Friday" />
  <s:enumeration value="Saturday" />
</s:restriction>
</s:simpleType>
```

portType

The `portType` section is yet another abstraction of the Web service. It includes the names of the functions, any documentation provided by the Web service author, and references to schemas that describe any incoming and outgoing parameters. In some implementations of WSDL, the data types are also included within the operation elements, but not in the current .NET implementation:

```
<portType name="Service1Soap">

<operation name="CountChars">
  <documentation>Please supply a string</documentation>
  <input message="s0:CountCharsSoapIn" />
  <output message="s0:CountCharsSoapOut" />
</operation>
```

Understanding overloading

For most Visual Basic programmers — and indeed COM programmers — overloading is a new idea. It makes its first appearance in .NET. Overloading means that a function (or a method, sub, property, or constructor) behaves differently based on what data is passed to it. The data passed is technically called its *parameter signature*. It's similar to the way that a bank teller behaves differently depending on whether you hand her a deposit slip or a note saying "This is a holdup!"

You overload a function by writing several versions of that function. Each different version of the function uses the same function name but has a different argument list (in other words, different parameters are passed to each version).

Why bother? Why not create various different functions? It's convenient sometimes to allow various kinds of parameters to be passed. For example, say that you write a function to add two numbers together. You could overload it so that it accepted integers, long integers, or floating point variable types. What's more, you could even include a version that accepted strings, such as "12" rather than numeric types. In all these cases, you are simply adding two numbers, but your function is more useful if it can accept a variety of types.

Another way to view overloading is that you have multiple procedures that do different things but share the same name. Typically, these various procedures do related but somewhat different variations on the same task.

The argument lists must differ among the overloaded variations on the function — after all, that's how the compiler determines which variation you want to execute. The differences in the argument list can be different data types, a different order of the parameters, or a different number of parameters — or two or three of these variations at once. The compiler can then tell which version of this function should be used by examining the arguments passed to the function, the argument list. Technically, VB.NET creates unique "signatures" for overloaded functions. These signatures are based on the name of the function and the number, order, and types of the arguments.

```
<operation name="Concat">
  <documentation>Please supply two strings</documentation>
  <input message="s0:ConcatSoapIn" />
  <output message="s0:ConcatSoapOut" />
  </operation>

</portType>
```

An operation element contains an abstract definition of the what must be done to the message. It can be the name of a method, a business process, or even a message queue.

You can include as many portType elements in a WSDL document as needed. Multiple portType elements perform a little clerical job, grouping multiple functions into logical categories. In a WSDL document, Web service functions' syntax is specified in other blocks in addition to this portType block. The primary reason for including yet another set of definitions of the Web service functions here in portType is that you can specify overloaded functions here (functions that share the same name, but accept varying parameters).

Binding

The binding element within a WSDL document specifies how the message is to be transmitted. Protocol, encoding, and any serialization are all specified.

```
<binding name="Service1Soap" type="s0:Service1Soap">
  <soap:binding
    transport="http://schemas.xmlsoap.org/soap/http"
    style="document" />
<operation name="CountChars">
  <soap:operation
    soapAction="http://tempuri.org/WebService2/Service1/Count
    Chars" style="document" />
<input>
  <soap:body use="literal" />
  </input>
<output>
  <soap:body use="literal" />
  </output>
  </operation>
<operation name="Concat">
  <soap:operation
    soapAction="http://tempuri.org/WebService2/Service1/Conca
    t" style="document" />
<input>
```

```
    <soap:body use="literal" />
    </input>
<output>
    <soap:body use="literal" />
    </output>
    </operation>
    </binding>
```

First, the binding element is named (here it's called `Service1Soap`). This name is used by the `<port>` element. Also included is a type attribute that refers to a `portType` in the document.

The `<soap:binding>` element includes a `<style>` attribute (normally `"document"` or `"rpc"`) and a transport description, which is included in a namespace (in this example, the HTTP SOAP protocol). Note that the WSDL technology is usually, but not limited to, facilitating SOAP messages transmitted via HTTP. WSDL can just as easily describe more esoteric transmission protocols such as HTTP-POST, HTTP-GET, FTP, SMTP, or others.

The `<style>` attribute, when set to *document* as it is here, causes the message to be transmitted in document format rather than with function signatures.

The function names are listed in the operation elements, and the `soapAction` attribute points to the Web service's URI. Experts differ on just what the `soapAction` attributes contribute here in the binding block. Some have suggested that they assist somehow with overloaded functions (which the previous example doesn't include). Nonetheless, they are here. Because with .NET you need not hand-code the WSDL document, you can just relax and let .NET decide what should or shouldn't be included. Some experts recommend that `soapAction` attributes must only be used with HTTP, never with other protocols.

The `<operation>` element can contain `<input>`, `<output>`, and `<fault>` (optional) elements, and the same elements are echoed from the identical elements in the `PortTypes` block.

The `<soap:body>` element (which oddly has no close tag) is intended to specify what must be included in the body of the soap message. This element has three attributes. The `use` attribute can be either "encoded" or, as in this example, "literal." If encoded, an `encodingStyle` attribute specifies the encoding to be used; if literal, the data is to be formatted as described in the previous `Types`, `Messages`, and `portTypes` blocks. An optional namespace attribute is not used in this example code, but it can be used to ensure that the body of the message has a unique set of names.

Service

Finally, the WSDL `<definitions>` element (in other words, the entire WSDL document) concludes with a service element:

```
<service name="Service1">
  <documentation>Counts characters, or concatenates two
    strings</documentation>
<port name="Service1Soap" binding="s0:Service1Soap">
  <soap:address
    location="http://localhost/WebService2/Service1.asmx" />
  </port>
  </service>
  </definitions>
```

The service block includes the final destinations (the actual location of the ultimate Web service). There can be a collection here of alternative service elements, each mapping the binding to a port and also including any extensibility definitions.

In plain English: Within the service element is a `port name` child element that describes the URL where the service is located. There can be more than one Web service in a WSDL document, and, if so, the users of the Web service can choose between various options based on which service they access (such as choosing different transmission protocols other than HTTP or including variations on the service at different URLs).

Where to Go from Here?

You are probably hoping that you'll never have to actually write a WSDL document, and with .NET, you won't have to. Fortunately, you can follow the step-by-step procedure of creating a Web service, as described earlier in this chapter, and .NET generates an associated WSDL document for you.

You may have to edit a WSDL document, though, or more likely, write a utility that analyzes a WSDL document and handles it appropriately. Hence, the reason for this chapter's existence with its explanation of the inner workings of WSDL documents.

If you are assigned the job of writing WSDL from scratch, you can find some editors that lift some of the burdens of hand-coding. Check out Altova's XML Spy (www.altova.com) or OmniOpera (www.omniopera.com). Also take a look at Cape Clear's free WSDL editor (www.capescience.com/downloads/wsdleditor).

Chapter 5: UDDI — Finding Web Services

In This Chapter

✔ **What is UDDI?**

✔ **Accessing local Web services programmatically**

✔ **Deconstructing a Web service**

✔ **Consuming a Public Web service**

✔ **Understanding DISCO**

So far in this book, you've seen how to change an ordinary function into an XML-RPC function for a Web service, explain the service with SOAP, and describe the whole package in a WSDL contract. You have your Web service all ready for the world to see and use. You're ready for your close-up.

How do you let the world know of the existence of your service? UDDI (Universal Description, Discovery, and Integration) actually describes two things. It's similar to the relationship between class and object. UDDI itself is merely a specification telling how to build a directory of Web services and the businesses that offer them. In this sense, UDDI is like a class (a blueprint).

Growing out of this specification is the UDDI Business Registry (also known as *cloud services* and UBR) that brings the UDDI specs to life as a real-world registry. The UDDI registry makes it possible to search existing UDDI information, and it also allows any company to register its Web services. The UDDI Registry is similar to an object (it's the realization or instantiation of the UDDI "class").

In any case, I use the term *UDDI* to refer to the specs, and I use the term *UDDI Registry* to refer to the real-world implementation — the actual registry you can use to look up businesses and their Web service offerings.

The Three Parts of UDDI

Information stored in a UDDI Registry entry describes a Web service in three ways:

✦ **White pages:** General information about the company offering the Web service (such as its contact people, its products, addresses, phone number, and so on).

✦ **Yellow pages:** A more abstract classification of a company's category or the Web service being offered (such as "construction/earth movers," "Northeast telecommunications," or product codes, and so on).

✦ **Green pages:** The specifications that detail the Web service itself. These specs can be pretty much anything, but usually it's a URI to the address of the Web service or its associated SOAP or WSDL files. These specs however need not be SOAP; they can be Java RMI or other descriptions. Also, the Web service need not be as sophisticated as what one normally thinks of as a Web service. Indeed, it could merely be a simple document such as a Web page or even a simple e-mail address.

As you work with Web services, you gradually begin to realize that the term *Web service* itself means many different things. In fact, no accepted standard meaning exists; it's quite generalized by now and people use it to describe programming of wildly different sizes. It is used to refer to something as small and simple as a single e-mail address or something as large as an enterprise-wide solution tying together multiple applications distributed across multiple remote servers.

In a warm, somewhat unusual confab, Microsoft and IBM got together in 2000 to bring UDDI to life, and it went "on air" in 2001.

Microsoft hosts a node of the UDDI Registry. It's free, public, and offers you a way to get information about existing Web services or to "publish" your own Web service. (Other nodes are hosted by IBM, SAP, and NTT. See http://www.uddi.org/register.html for additional information.)

Visual Studio .NET has facilities you can use to search others' Web services, or they publish their own in the UDDI registry maintained by Microsoft. You can search for existing Web services (and add them to your .NET projects) by choosing Project⇨Add Web Reference (or via the Start Page, as explained later in this chapter).

You can register your own service by choosing Help⇨Show Start Page, clicking the Online Resources tab, and then clicking the XML Web services option in the left pane.

When you open the Add Web Reference dialog box, you can access UDDIs in the following ways:

✦ **Browse UDDI Servers on the local network:** This link displays any servers in your LAN (if you're attached to a local area network) that expose UDDI described Web services and associated discovery documents.

✦ **UDDI Directory:** This link lets you search the Microsoft UDDI Registry to locate published, official, Web services that have registered on Microsoft's node.

✦ **Test Microsoft UDDI Directory:** The final link allows you to search for test Web services that have been posted here. These services are not "official" but can be useful for learning how to programmatically access Web services. You can also use this test directory to register your own Web services while you're testing them.

Accessing a Local Web Service Programmatically

To see how to programmatically access a Web service from within an application, follow these steps:

1. **Start VB.NET.**

2. **Choose File⇨New⇨Project.**

The New Project dialog box opens.

3. **Double-click the Windows Application icon.**

A new Windows-style application is created.

You could use a Web application or even a Web service as the consumer for this example — but I think it's nearly always good to keep examples as simple as possible to focus on the actual technology being tested. In this case, you want to find out how to consume a Web service from an application. Windows applications are the most straightforward test ground because, unlike Web applications, they do not require any special communication between the local host (the faux "Web" created inside your machine for Web testing purposes). Nor do Windows applications require display within your browser. Windows applications are the most stable and simple way to test new ideas.

4. **Double-click the form in Design view.**

You are taken to the code view, where you can write a little source code to test a Web service and display the results.

5. **Choose Project⇨Add Web Reference.**

The Add Web Reference dialog box opens, as shown in Figure 5-1.

Figure 5-1:
This dialog
box is your
gateway to
the Web
services on
your local
hard drive,
as well as
the Internet.

6. **Click the Web Services on the local machine link.**

   You see a list of all Web services installed on your computer — either those used in QuickStart tutorials you've copied from the Visual Studio .NET CDs or Web services you have written yourself.

7. **Scroll down the list until you find Service1, as shown in Figure 5-2.**

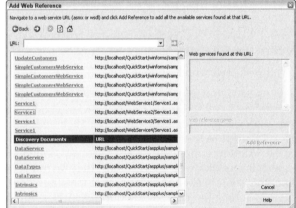

Figure 5-2:
Look for
the Web
Service you
created that
includes the
Concat
function.

   You want to locate the Web service you created in Book VI, Chapter 1. It is most likely listed in the Add Web Reference dialog box as `local-host/WebService1.Service1.asmx`.

8. **Double-click `localhost/WebService1.Service1.asmx` in the Add Web Reference dialog box.**

You now see the service you created in Chapter 1, including the `Concat` function, as shown in Figure 5-3.

Figure 5-3:
This is the Web service you're after.

**Book VII
Chapter 5**

UDDI — Finding
Web Services

9. **If you don't see the `Concat` function displayed in the dialog box, press your Backspace key to return to the list of services and try double-clicking another one until you find the Web service containing the `Concat` function.**

10. **Click the Add Reference button.**

    The dialog box closes and a reference to your Web service is added to your project. Open Solution Explorer and you can see that localhost is now included in your project's references. (References are similar to using namespaces.)

11. **At the very top of your code window (above `Public Class Form1`), type this `Imports` statement:**

    ```
    Imports WindowsApplication1.localhost
    ```

    If your project name isn't `WindowsApplication1`, replace that with your project's name, such as `WindowsApplication3` or whatever. Your application's name is the item in **boldface** in Solution Explorer.

12. **Now you can type in the code that accesses your Web service. Type this into the `Form_Load` event:**

    ```
    Private Sub Form1_Load(ByVal sender As System.Object,
        ByVal e As System.EventArgs) Handles MyBase.Load

        Dim wService As New localhost.Service1

        Dim n As String = "area"
    ```

```
Dim m As String = "code"

n = wService.Concat(n, m)

MsgBox(n)

End Sub
```

In this example code, you first define an object variable wService that points to your Web service. Then you use that variable to access one of the Web service's public functions, Concat, to join together the two strings submitted as parameters to the Web service.

13. **Press F5 to run your project.**

A messagebox appears displaying areacode, showing that your concat Web service received the message and returned the correct response by joining the two strings.

How to Figure Out a Web Service

.NET has just "generated a proxy class" for you! How fortunate for you. Don't worry about it, you can just use it without knowing the complex name for it. One of the best things about VB.NET and Visual Studio in general is that they hide quite a bit of busywork behind the scenes, doing tedious jobs for you so that you can focus on the big picture (namely, getting something to actually work).

Visual Studio downloads the WSDL or "service description" for any Web service that you select. In the proxy class are any methods and properties you can use to access the "exposed members" of the service. However, if you can't figure out how to access the methods and properties of a Web service, you should memorize the following technique. To see how to write code to access a referenced Web service, you really want to lift the curtain and pay attention to the little man behind it. Here's how to take a gander at the proxy class.

In Solution Explorer's title bar, you see several icons. Slowly move your mouse pointer across the icons until you locate the one labeled Show All Files. If the icons are not visible, click the name of your project (which is in boldface) in Solution Explorer. (Solution Explorer, by default, shows you only the files it thinks you'll need to directly work with — and tries to keep the gory details of support files like the proxy class hidden from your tender sensibilities.) Now expand the Web service node (click the + next to your Web service's blue-world icon in Solution Explorer). You see several files. You see the "Disco" (discovery) file, the WSDL file that contains XML information used by .NET to create the proxy class, and (finally) what you're after: the Reference Map. Click the + to expand the Reference Map node and double-click Reference.vb in Solution Explorer. A new code window opens up, displaying something similar to the following:

```
'-----------------------------------------------------------
' <autogenerated>
'     This code was generated by a tool.
'     Runtime Version: 1.1.4322.535
'
'     Changes to this file may_u99 ?ause incorrect behavior
   and will be lost if
'     the code is regenerated.
' </autogenerated>
'-----------------------------------------------------------

Option Strict Off
Option Explicit On

Imports System
Imports System.ComponentModel
Imports System.Diagnostics
Imports System.Web.Services
Imports System.Web.Services.Protocols
Imports System.Xml.Serialization

'
'This source code was auto-generated by Microsoft.VSDesigner,
   Version 1.1.4322.535.
'
Namespace localhost

    '<remarks/>
    <System.Diagnostics.DebuggerStepThroughAttribute(), _
     System.ComponentModel.DesignerCategoryAttribute("code"),
    _

    System.Web.Services.WebServiceBindingAttribute(Name:="Ser
    vice1Soap",
    [Namespace]:="http://tempuri.org/WebService2/Service1")>_
    u32 ?_
     Public Class Service1
         Inherits
    System.Web.Services.Protocols.SoapHttpClientProtocol

        '<remarks/>
        Public Sub New()
            MyBase.New
            Me.Url =
    "http://localhost/WebService2/Service1.asmx"
```

**Book VII
Chapter 5**

**UDDI — Finding
Web Services**

```
        End Sub

        '<remarks/>
        <System.Web.Services.Protocols.
SoapDocumentMethodAttribute("http://tempuri.org/
WebService2/Service1/CountChars", RequestNamespace:=
"http://tempuri.org/WebService2/Service1",
ResponseNamespace:="http://tempuri.org/WebService2/
Service1",
Use:=System.Web.Services.Description.
SoapBindingUse.Literal, ParameterStyle:=System.
Web.Services.Protocols.SoapParameterStyle.Wrapped)>  _
        Public Function CountChars(ByVal s As String)
As String
            Dim results() As Object = Me.Invoke("CountChars",
New Object() {s})
            Return CType(results(0),String)
        End Function

        '<remarks/>

        Public Function BeginCountChars(ByVal s As String,
ByVal callback As System.AsyncCallback, ByVal asyncState
As Object) As System.IAsyncResult
            Return Me.BeginInvoke("CountChars", New Object()
{s}, callback, asyncState)
        End Function

        '<remarks/>

        Public Function EndCountChars(ByVal asyncResult As
System.IAsyncResult) As String
            Dim results() As Object =
Me.EndInvoke(asyncResult)
            Return CType(results(0),String)
        End Function

        '<remarks/>
        <System.Web.Services.Protocols. SoapDocumentMethod
Attribute("http://tempuri.org/WebService2/Service1/
Concat",
RequestNamespace:= "http://tempuri.org/WebService2/
Service1",
ResponseNamespace:="http://tempuri.org/WebService2/
Service1",
Use:=System.Web.Services.Description. SoapBindingUse.
Literal,
ParameterStyle:=System.Web. Services.Protocols.Soap
ParameterStyle.Wrapped)>  _

    Public Function Concat(ByVal s As String, ByVal s1
As  String) As String
```

```
            Dim results() As Object = Me.Invoke("Concat", New
    Object() {s, s1})
            Return CType(results(0), String)
        End Function

        '<remarks/>
        Public Function BeginConcat(ByVal s As String, ByVal
    s1 As String, ByVal callback As System.AsyncCallback,
    ByVal asyncState As Object) As System.IAsyncResult
            Return Me.BeginInvoke("Concat", New Object() {s,
    s1}, callback, asyncState)
        End Function

        '<remarks/>
        Public Function EndConcat(ByVal asyncResult As
    System.IAsyncResult) As String
            Dim results() As Object =
    Me.EndInvoke(asyncResult)
            Return CType(results(0), String)
        End Function
    End Class
End Namespace
```

You can ignore these `Begin` and `End` functions — they're not your concern. The key item in this code that you want to understand is the `Concat` function, which wants you to supply two strings as parameters, and then it returns a string variable. This is an easy way to see how to call the methods of an unknown Web service (how to figure out what parameters and variable types are involved in the call). Here's the key line in this code:

```
Public Function Concat(ByVal s As String, ByVal s1 As String)
    As String
```

That line tells you how to write code that triggers this function, passing two strings and getting one string back:

```
Dim n As String = "area"
Dim m As String = "code"

n = wService.Concat(n, m)
```

Consuming a Published Web Service on the Internet

The same .NET UDDI utility that lists your local Web services also lists many services exposed by others. Some are for testing; some are "official." It's useful to know how to contact someone else's service. In some cases, you can actually *discover* (get it?) how to use their service — what parameters to input (or what properties to assign values to) and the variable types you are supposed to use to get back a response.

Many of the services I've explored are either impossible to figure out or are no longer available. However, some can be used. You should explore the services on your own, attempting to figure out how to use them.

Here's an example of a Web service that I found that worked for me:

1. **Start VB.NET.**

2. **Choose File⇨New⇨Project.**

   The New Project dialog box opens.

3. **Double-click the Windows Application icon.**

   A new Windows-style application is created.

4. **Double-click the form in Design view.**

   You are taken to the code view.

5. **Choose Help⇨Show Start Page.**

   The Start Page is displayed.

6. **Click XML Web Services in the left pane.**

7. **Click the option button Search in UDDI Production Environment.**

8. **Drop the listbox under Category, and choose Miscellaneous.**

9. **Click the Go button.**

   You see a list of various Web services, as shown in Figure 5-4.

10. **Scroll the list of Web services until you locate** `Quote of the Day`.

11. **Click the** `Add as web reference to current project` **link.**

    You can look in the Web References section of Solution Explorer and see that `com.gotdotnet.www` has been added to your project.

12. **Click the Form1.vb(Design) tab.**

    You see the form.

13. **Double-click the form.**

    You go to the code window.

14. **At the very top of the code window (above** `Public Class Form1`**), type this** `Imports` **statement:**

    ```
    Imports WindowsApplication6.com.gotdotnet.www.Quote
    ```

    If your project name isn't `WindowsApplication6`, replace that with your project's name, such as `WindowsApplication2`, or whatever.

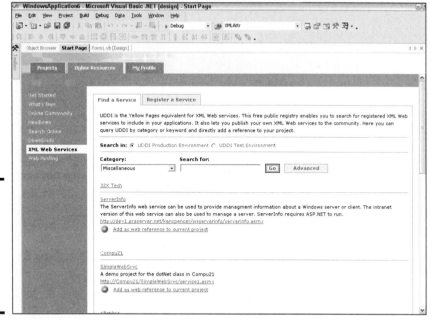

Book VII
Chapter 5

UDDI — Finding
Web Services

Figure 5-4:
Use the
Start Page
to locate
Web
services on
the UDDI
Registry.

15. **Now type in this code that accesses the Web service:**

```
Private Sub Form1_Load(ByVal sender As System.Object,
     ByVal e As System.EventArgs) Handles MyBase.Load

     Dim cService As New com.gotdotnet.www.Quote

     Dim s As String

     s = cService.GetQuote()

     MsgBox(s)

End Sub
```

16. **Press F5 to run this program.**

If all goes well, you get an HTML-formatted message — like a quote-of-
the-day — returned from this Web service.

Understanding DISCO

DISCO (for *disc*overy) is an alternative way to publish and discover (figure
out and use) Web services. DISCO was developed by Microsoft as a protocol
that makes it easier (than UDDI) to figure out what Web services are available

on a particular server. Think of UDDI as a large, Internet-wide registry and DISCO as more local, as an intranet technology.

DISCO gives you a way of quickly discovering what's available locally, within a network. Actually DISCO and UDDI can be thought of as complementary technologies, in the same way that interoffice mail is complementary to the U.S. Postal service.

Because DISCO is local, it's also easier to use among programmers who are still testing their Web services. Without going through the formal process of registering your service under UDDI, you can just "publish" it locally via DISCO and test it locally as well.

For example, type this into the Address field in Internet Explorer:

```
http://localhost/default.vsdisco
```

Now click the Go button. You see the following DISCO file (like most everything else involved with Web services, it's a form of XML):

```
<?xml version="1.0" ?>
<dynamicDiscovery xmlns="urn:schemas-
  dynamicdiscovery:disco.2000-03-17">
<exclude path="_vti_cnf" />
<exclude path="_vti_pvt" />
<exclude path="_vti_log" />
<exclude path="_vti_script" />
<exclude path="_vti_txt" />
</dynamicDiscovery>
```

The `default.vsdisco` file is placed into your "Web server" root directory (`c:\Inetpub\wwwroot`).

In general, you need not *write* DISCO files yourself; VB.NET generates them for you automatically as needed when you use the ASP.NET technology.

If you want to employ DISCO to discover how to use a local Web service (as a substitute for UDDI discovery), here's an example. In VB.NET, choose Project⇨Add Web Reference. The Add Web Reference dialog box opens. Click the arrow next to the URL Listbox, as shown in Figure 5-5, to drop down the list of recently viewed services.

In this list, locate a Web service that includes the Concat function — the service you created in Book VII, Chapter 1. Or, type something similar to this into the URL listbox:

```
http://localhost/WebService1/Service1.asmx
```

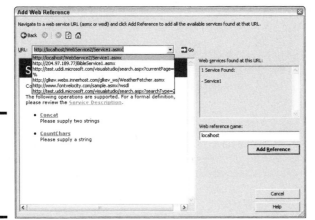

**Book VII
Chapter 5**

**UDDI — Finding
Web Services**

Figure 5-5:
Locate a
local Web
service
in this
browser.

Click the Go button, and then click the Add Reference button to add this
Web service's "proxy class" to your project. Now click the name of your
project (in boldface) in Solution Explorer; then click the Show All Files icon
in Solution Explorer's title bar. In Solution Explorer, expand the localhost
Web reference by clicking the + next to it and double-click `Service1.disco`
to see the DISCO file. It looks something like this:

```
<?xml version="1.0" encoding="utf-8"?>
<discovery xmlns:xsd="http://www.w3.org/2001/XMLSchema"
    xmlns:xsi="http://www.w3.org/2001/XMLSchema-instance"
    xmlns="http://schemas.xmlsoap.org/disco/">
  <contractRef ref="http://localhost/WebService2/Service1.
    asmx?wsdl"
    docRef="http://localhost/WebService2/Service1.asmx"
    xmlns="http://schemas.xmlsoap.org/disco/scl/" />
  <soap address="http://localhost/WebService2/Service1.asmx"
    xmlns:q1="http://tempuri.org/WebService2/Service1"
    binding="q1:Service1Soap"
    xmlns="http://schemas.xmlsoap.org/disco/soap/" />
</discovery>
```

This format should be familiar to you. It's quite similar to a WSDL file, providing XSD schemas and references that help explain where the service is
located, links to other discovery documents, and how it is to be used (service descriptions).

The `contractRef` element refers to a WSDL document and also to the
HTML documentation (the .asmx file) that describes your Web service, as
shown in Figure 5-6.

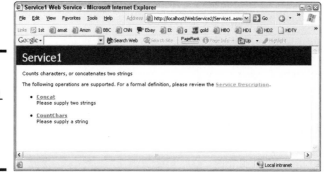

Figure 5-6:
An .asmx
file is HTML
documen-
tation for
a Web
service.

You can also view a DISCO file by appending ?DISCO to its URL in the
Address box in Internet Explorer and then clicking the Go button next to the
address, like this:

```
http://localhost/WebService2/Service1.asmx?DISCO
```

Chapter 6: Voice and Wireless Services

In This Chapter

🗸 **VoiceXML**

🗸 **Wireless Web services**

XML is designed to be flexible enough to prove itself useful in many different kinds of applications. So far in this book, you've seen XML employed in messaging, meta data, Web services, and a variety of other situations. In this chapter, you look a bit into the future: You see how XML can be used with various audio technologies and how it can contribute to wireless Web services.

Audio XML

VoiceXML (Voice Extensible Markup Language) can be used in multiple ways: digital audio, voice recognition, storing recordings of speech, synthesized speech (text to speech), control of dialog flow, and telephony (such as automatic call transfers).

One currently hot application involving VoiceXML is creating speech implementations for Internet communication. You can talk to VoiceXML-ready applications, rather than relying on more traditional input devices such as typing or clicking a mouse.

If you think you've never used this technology, you're wrong. It's at the other end in some cases when you get caught in one of those endless loop voicemail black holes that start with the fake promise: *Your call is very important to us*. (Right. Do the people who say this stuff think we're really, really gullible?)

Phone robot experiences

VoiceXML is also sometimes behind those announcements in the grocery store: "Security scan in section 43!" VoiceXML is the voice on the other end of "phone banking" and other phone-robot experiences so typical of modern life.

Say nine

How do you know when you're in a conversation with VoiceXML? The typical giveaway is a comment like this from a robotic voice: "Say *nine* or press the nine key." When the robot gives you the option of *speaking* a word or two, it's almost certain that you're in a conversation with XML.

Browsing via Voice

Although VoiceXML is used in a variety of Web applications — from assisting the blind and handicapped to digitizing data — perhaps the most promising application is audio Internet browsing. Connection to, and interaction with, the Internet is likely to become less and less keyboard-dependent.

People already access the Internet via cell phone. On a cross-country train trip last year, I was happy to discover that I could check my e-mail and the latest terror warning headlines from pretty much anywhere that I could receive a wireless signal. Just choose Option 4 on the old cell phone and it dials you into the Internet while the train is drifting slowly through Beaumont, Texas.

Of course, I didn't have a keyboard on the cell phone, so I had to resort to clumsy input techniques. I would have been much happier to be able to surf the Web and interact with Web pages by speaking voice commands. Instead, I had to punch in a series of nested menus and awkward *Down-Arrow, Down-Arrow, Enter* maneuvers to get where I was going.

It won't be too long before you can say "Yahoo News" and be taken directly to that home page on your cell phone screen. Many Web pages will be able to accept both traditional HTML Web page input (hyperlink clicks, Submit button clicks, and so on) or voice commands. When that happy day arrives, you can really make good use of your cell phone's Internet capabilities.

The Elements of VoiceXML

What does VoiceXML look like? It's pretty much like ordinary XML, except it is enclosed within `vxml` tags:

```
<?xml version="1.0"?>
<vxml version="2.0">
  <form>
  <field name="stamps">
    <prompt>How many stamps do you want sent to
  you?</prompt>
```

```
    <grammar src="stamps.grxml"
  type="application/grammar+xml"/>
  </field>
  <block>
    <submit
  next="http://www.stamps.sample.com/stampNo4.asp"/>
  </block>
 </form>
</vxml>
```

VoiceXML is contained within a document (or group of documents collectively called an *application*). If more than a single document is involved, the application's set of documents shares a single *application root document*. The application root document is always active.

The application is technically described as maintaining the caller (the person) in a single "dialog" at a time, and potentially transitioning the caller to another dialog. These transitions are specified by URIs. Control flow implementations permit, for example, branching decisions based on caller input. The transitioning ends (meaning that the dialog or call ends) when no further specified transition URI is listed, or when an ending element is included in the VoiceXML document.

A VoiceXML document includes two distinct types of dialogs: menus and forms. The previous example is a form, which gathers data from the user that is placed in field item variables. The field can specify validation (permissible input values) for that particular field. You can also implement larger, form-level grammars that can be used to provide data to several fields simultaneously (the user may say "Greece" and the Continent field could automatically be filled with *Europe*, for example).

Menus, by contrast, operate the way they do normally: The caller gets a list of options, voices his choice, and the VoiceXML transitions based on the user's choice. (Faults are provided for with prepared responses such as "I didn't understand your choice, please repeat it.")

VoiceXML has most of the features of any simple computer language, such as the ability to go to a "subroutine" (called a *subdialog*) and then return to the place in the form where it jumped to the sub. State is preserved during the jump to the sub, as you probably expect. Subroutines are used as they are in other languages — to avoid having to repeat lengthy code in various locations in an application. For example, if users are required to verify information from various different dialogs in a VoiceXML application, there's no reason to repeat the verification process within each dialog.

VoiceXML contains a considerable number of elements, allowing for many kinds of rich audio interactions. Table 6-1 lists all the VoiceXML elements.

**Book VII
Chapter 6**

**Voice and
Wireless Services**

Table 6-1	The Elements of VoiceXML
Element	*Description*
`<assign>`	Assign a variable a value.
`<audio>`	Play an audio clip from inside a prompt.
`<block>`	An envelope containing code that's not interactive with the caller.
`<catch>`	Catches an event.
`<choice>`	Used to specify each menu item.
`<clear>`	Empties a variable or variables within a form.
`<disconnect>`	Ends the session.
`<else>`	Used inside `<if>` elements, just as it's used in VB.NET.
`<elseif>`	Used inside `<if>` elements, just as it's used in VB.NET.
`<enumerate>`	Enumerates choices in a menu element.
`<error>`	Traps an error.
`<exit>`	Exits a session.
`<field>`	An input field within a form element.
`<filled>`	Specifies what to do when fields are filled.
`<form>`	A dialog that gets data from the caller.
`<goto>`	Jumps to a different dialog (within the current document, or in another document). This kind of branching was outlawed years ago in most programming languages because it is believed to cause more problems than it solves.
`<grammar>`	Specifies a speech recognition grammar.
`<help>`	Traps a help event.
`<if>`	Branches to different locations, based on a condition (an expression).
`<initial>`	Declares initial logic when execution enters a form.
`<link>`	Specifies a transition that is used in all the dialogs that are located within the link's scope.
`<log>`	Logs a debugging comment.
`<menu>`	The dialog type that selects among a list of choices.
`<meta>`	Specifies a meta data item (the usual name and value pair).
`<noinput>`	Traps a `noinput` event.
`<nomatch>`	Traps a `nomatch` event.
`<object>`	Provides for interaction with a custom extension.
`<option>`	Specifies an option in a field element.
`<param>`	Specifies a parameter to be sent to an object or subdialog (subdialogs can be functions).
`<prompt>`	Prepares an audio clip that will be sent to the user.
`<property>`	Controls implementation platform settings.

Element	Description
`<record>`	Records an audio clip.
`<reprompt>`	Plays a prompt when, after an event, execution returns to a field element.
`<return>`	Returns from a subdialog.
`<script>`	Encloses a block of ECMAScript, client-side scripting logic.
`<subdialog>`	Invokes another dialog as a subroutine (subdialog).
`<submit>`	Submits variable values to a document server.
`<throw>`	Throws (triggers) an event.
`<transfer>`	Transfers the caller to another location.
`<value>`	Inserts the value of an expression in a prompt.
`<var>`	Declares a variable.
`<vxml>`	This is the top-level element (or "root element") in any VoiceXML document.

VoiceXML includes many refinements and technical details beyond the scope of this book (indeed, an entire book is devoted just to VoiceXML). Nonetheless, VoiceXML is worth getting acquainted with — if only so that you know it's there if you ever need it.

Wireless Web Services

The Internet is already pretty much everywhere, and it keeps spreading to new locations and new devices. As Wi-Fi and other wireless technologies proliferate, it seems likely that the day may come when you can connect to the Internet pretty much anywhere you can receive an over-the-air TV signal — namely: most any, even sparsely populated, area.

Spreading wireless connectivity further afield is relatively inexpensive and relatively easy. The antennae and other hardware are fairly cheap and whole cities may one day be Wi-Fi ready. The hard part is on the other end: Just how do you create a Web page that works equally well on a 19-inch flatscreen and a 2-inch wireless PDA? The short answer is that you can't (see the "Whither WAP" sidebar).

But you must try. This problem is described by XML experts with the quaint phrase "one content — many presentations." Think of it as yet another aspect of scalability, only in this case, it involves finding ways to successfully compress layout and reduce content. Do you rewrite to make the text shorter? Do you crop photos, or just leave graphics out entirely? Is it necessary to divide a single Web page into multiple pages for a pager? What about trying to shove streaming video through the 14.4 BPS pipeline that goes into a cell phone connection?

Whither WAP?

Yet another industry committee ("consortium") gathered in 1997 to figure out how to jam a browser into the small (then black and white) screen on cell phones and PDAs. WAP (wireless application protocol) requires that Web sites be rewritten to conform to WAP, and the HTML of the Web pages must be translated into WML (WAP markup language). If you think this is a little like trying to pass off a cracker as a wedding cake, you're right. But we do what we can. In other words, many sets of Web pages exist — the big normal ones like those for TV and computer monitors, all the way down to the tiny, monochrome ones like cheap Palm PDAs. Bravely, sites like Amazon went ahead and got out their miniature cake-carving tools and crafted little mini-me versions of themselves. Google even attempted to figure out a way to provide Web pages to their wireless users, without having to hand-carve 72 googillion different Web pages into WML. Needless to say, the tiny four-line screens, not to mention a 14.4 BPS bandwidth and battery power constraints, force those who translate HTML pages into WAP pages to toss out most of the HTML data — and pretty much *all* of the multimedia data — in the process. Fortunately, cell phones show signs of merging with PDAs, and both are increasing their screen resolution, improving bandwidth and moving to color. A talent for downgrading information is sometimes admirable, but admirable more for the effort that it requires than the quality of the result. It's like those people who build replicas of the Eiffel Tower out of spaghetti — you marvel at their patience and ingenuity, but you don't confuse it with beauty or art. WAP nonetheless is still alive and weakly kicking — if only barely (it has suffered what some call a collapse of interest). Yet efforts continue to deal with the increases in data capacity of wireless devices. WAP Version 2 was released January 2002. Some hope that WML Version 2 meets with a more generous reception than the thunderclap of silence that greeted Version 1.

And what about the dual aspect ratios you must deal with when displaying Web pages on TV sets? (The new widescreen HDTV shape, versus the traditional box shape, strangely called "fullscreen" by DVD marketers trying to make the limited size of old sets sound good.)

In other words, in the future, you'll likely have to deal with quite a range of user-input methods, CPU power levels, screen sizes, and bandwidths.

XML to the rescue. For one thing, XML anticipates the multiple-devices problem by making provisions for alternative "presentations" of its data. XML is designed to separate content from appearance (as is Visual Studio's ASP.NET Web programming technology). You can create style sheets (CSS) for every occasion, or use XSL and DTD. You can strip out all video and other pictorial content, if necessary, and instead of displaying paragraphs, you can scroll a single line of text. The content layer may be the same for all, but the presentation layer must differ.

Clearly problems remain, though, because although you can fairly easily adjust text content via style sheets, you can't adjust binary content such as music and video. Also, DTDs differ quite a bit among the various parts of an organization. (You need one kind of XML content for the inventory job and an entirely different DTD is used for the display catalog job — so you must generate different style sheets not only for each different markup language variant, but also for each DTD.)

The dumbing down of multimedia can be achieved by removing detail (creating mosaic-like blocks with less color resolution, among other things), by reducing frame-rate (so that motion becomes jumpy), and by limiting the dynamic range of audio. Several schemes achieve these forms of compression, none particularly desirable, and none usable via style sheet techniques. All the decisions about reducing multimedia content must be made individually, by hand. And even the same type of device may require different levels of quality. (Take PDAs. Late model PocketPCs, for example, can handle video with audio pretty well, but Palm-based PDAs often have to display simple, mute slideshows.)

Is there any solution to the "one content — many presentations" problem? Not so far. There have been good intentions, good ideas, and several tries, but automating the process of reducing Web pages to small device screens seems to me to require a level of artificial intelligence that is simply not yet available. Too many essentially aesthetic decisions must be made when reducing content to leave the job to style sheets, however huge those style sheets grow.

Onward and Upward in the Arts

What else is different about writing XML for wireless devices (beyond the scaling problems, and the provisions for speech synthesis and recognition discussed earlier in this chapter)? The only major difference derives from the *wirelessness* of wireless, and it's primarily a security issue.

After all, once you set up a wireless network, you've created what amounts to a radio station, broadcasting your data. Normally, a hacker has to find a way to get physically into your building, or to get electronically past your firewall. But when you're "on the air," you have to wonder who may be listening in. What about that guy on the bus bench in front of your office, the one with the laptop and the big grin? Studies have shown that the security schemes currently built into Wi-Fi equipment are fragile and easily broken with commonly available utilities.

XML itself is deliberately designed to be readable, understandable text. So it is necessary to protect sensitive data in some way or another from eavesdroppers. The best way is encryption, and that's the topic of the next chapter.

Chapter 7: Web Services Security

In This Chapter

✔ Understanding XML security weaknesses

✔ Applying encryption solutions

✔ Choosing passwords wisely

✔ Employing practical XML security practices

*A*ll modern organizations must understand the importance of protecting their data from intruders. Although widely under-reported, computer crime is a significant and increasing cost of doing business.

XML, of course, is designed to be *readable*, to be plain text. A string can be sent via XML, though, which contains encrypted binary data. And, of all the ways to protect your data from prying eyes, encryption is the most secure (as long as you use sufficiently advanced encryption, and protect the secret password or key).

Computer security is a vast and challenging topic. I personally find it fascinating — a kind of spy-versus-spy contest among often highly intelligent competitors. How do you scramble information as completely as possible, while still being able to restore it?

However, given the scope of this book, I can't use the several chapters I would like to spend on the subject. The best I can do is provide you with an overview, a list of common security issues, their solutions, and resources for further reading.

XML and Security

XML SOAP or XML-RPC don't specify security techniques. And the consortia involved in the various Web services protocols have yet to reach agreement on some industry-wide tactics to protect Web service data from prying eyes.

Computer security can be divided into two fundamental issues: *privacy* (hiding your data, or verifying that the message has not been tampered with by changing, say, $100 to $1,000,000) and *authentication* (permitting only the right people to have access to a Web service, or authorizing various levels of access to various locations on a system).

XML Web service messages ride on HTTP (usually), so you can use the Secure Sockets Layer (SSL) technology to encrypt your messages (usually). SSL encryption isn't too difficult to implement. You obtain a *certificate* (or your company does) from a third-party certification authority such as VeriSign. The certificate is a digital signature uniquely identifying your site. SSL employs public key encryption, and your certificate includes the public portion of your key pair. You then send both the certificate and the associated public key to the Web service's server. That server then takes the public key and creates a method to encrypt the messaging.

If you're observant, you may have noticed that sometimes an address in your browser's address field begins with `https://` rather than `http://`. `Https` instructs a browser to automatically send messages via an encrypted channel — as long as Microsoft's IIS (Internet Information Services) is available on both ends of the communication.

SSL does pose a problem, though, because Web services are often distributed among several servers, bouncing the message from the personnel application to the payroll application to the check-writing application, and so on. SSL isn't the ideal solution when you have chained applications because you have to encrypt the message before sending it to each additional application along the call chain. Not only does this slow things down, but it introduces often unacceptable security vulnerabilities.

W3C has developed an Encryption Standard to attempt to address this multiple-node SSL weakness. With the XML Encryption Standard, you can encrypt an entire XML document or only a sensitive portion of the document.

Encryption, when successful, does solve the privacy aspect of security. However, a password must usually be sent, at some point, between the client and server. Authentication is usually handled by requiring an ID/password pair. In both cases, communicating the password is a problem: How do you send a password through the Internet without someone intercepting — and thereby being able to *use* — that password? Generally, this problem is addressed by encrypting the password! As you can see, this quickly becomes a hall of mirrors because if you encrypt a password, you have to send another password to decrypt the first password. Where does it end?

Some password problems can seem solved until you look at them more closely. Consider, for example, the server that offers an encrypted Web service response. The client sends his password to get to use your service, but you don't want to store a list of passwords on your server. What if that list gets hacked? So instead, you decide to hash the password (generate a nonsense version of the password) and store the hash rather than the password. Then, when the password comes in from the client, you hash the incoming password, compare that hash to the stored hash, and if they match, the client gets in. If you use the same hash method on the same text password, you always get the same hash result.

This sounds like a solution, and indeed it does make things more difficult for an intruder. But it's not impossible for an intruder to reverse engineer any application, including the one you use to hash. If you do want to experiment with hashing (which is a quick, and often useful form of encrypting), here's a sub in VB.NET that takes a text password and transforms it into a hash.

At the top of your VB.NET code window, add these `Imports` statements:

```
Imports System.Text
Imports System.Security.Cryptography
```

Invoke the sub from the `Form_Load` event, like this:

```
Private Sub Form1_Load(ByVal sender As System.Object, ByVal e
    As System.EventArgs) Handles MyBase.Load

    CreateKey("Donatull")

End Sub
```

And type in this sub beneath the `Form1_Load` sub:

```
Sub CreateKey(ByVal Password As String) 'password must be 8
   characters

    Dim arrByte(7) As Byte ' Byte array to hold password

    Dim AscEncod As New ASCIIEncoding
    Dim i As Integer = 0
    AscEncod.GetBytes(Password, i, Password.Length,
arrByte, i)


    'Get the hash value of the password
    Dim hashSha As New SHA1CryptoServiceProvider

    Dim arrHash() As Byte = hashSha.ComputeHash(arrByte)

    Console.Write("Hash Result for " & Password & ": ")

    'display the hash value
    For i = 0 To 7
        Console.Write(arrHash(i) & ",") 'display result
    Next i

   End Sub
```

If you submit `"Donatell"` as your password, it hashes to these numbers:

```
Hash Result for "Donatell": 146,250,127,247,59,52,11,178
```

But if you change a single character in the password, submitting for example `"Donatull"` instead of `"Donatell"`, notice how the entire hash changes. This isn't some simple character-substitution encryption — it's sophisticated:

```
Hash Result for "Donatull": 93,145,46,144,229,77,105,10
```

The Main Problem

The fundamental difficulty with security — which is also the reason it's so interesting, to me anyway — is that it is based on a paradox: An absolutely secure messaging system requires that the message itself be destroyed beyond reconstruction.

The only way to be absolutely sure that no one can figure out how to read your diary's secret code is to totally burn the diary. The only way to make absolutely sure no one feeds a poison into your bedroom while you're asleep is to encase yourself in a ten foot thick wall of solid concrete, and suffocate yourself.

Throughout history, people have invented "unbreakable" encryption schemes, only to have them broken, usually rather quickly.

Another way of viewing the security paradox is that when you employ too much security, you end up paralyzed — the protection becomes so cumbersome that it's impractical. A sad situation confronting many elderly people illustrates the "secure walls" paradox. Retired, they have low monthly income and are forced to stay in their paid-off house. They can't sell the house because it's no longer worth very much. Why? Because in the 30 years they've lived there, the neighborhood has collapsed. Years ago this was a nice, quiet, tree-lined street.

Now it's a run-down slum, littered with smoldering abandoned cars and gunfire in the night. What can they do? After a few robberies, they decide to put bars up on all their windows. This has the obvious drawback of preventing them from getting out easily in case of fire. But they're more afraid of the robbers breaking in than they are of fire. After all, fire is relatively rare; but nearly every night, the robbers can be heard outside their windows, trying to find a way in. Of course, an enterprising robber could saw through the bars. To be totally secure, you have to encase the entire house in solid steel — but then how can you breathe? So the old couple deals as best they can with the paradox inherent in securing walls: Make them too strong and you imprison whatever is held within.

And consider this paradox: firewalls are designed to prevent outside messages from executing commands or functions inside the network it protects.

XML-RPC and SOAP are designed to slip past firewalls and execute commands and functions inside the network. Because XML in general (including SOAP messages) is supposedly innocent "text" like HTML — mere documents, rather than executable (and therefore possibly viral) code — firewalls let Web service messages into networks.

Efforts continue — at the deliberative pace of academic committee decision-making — to find a solution to XML security issues. SDKs, kits, APIs, and acronyms are floating up out of committee meetings and marketing departments, always a sign that some progress is being made.

XKMS (XML key management specification) is an effort to standardize and facilitate public key encryption, considered today's strongest encryption technique.

SAML (Security Assertion Markup Language) is being developed by SSTC (the Security Services Technical Committee) and is designed to address the authentication problem (who has permission to access the server?). You send your "identity" credentials, such as your e-mail address and its Internet DNS (Domain Name System) ID. An XML request-response format can be used to accept verification data such as passwords, logon names, and so on. SAML has provisions for signing on once at the beginning of a chain of distributed applications in a Web service and propagating the sign-on automatically down the call chain. That way, you don't have to repeatedly authenticate yourself at each server along the way.

Here's what a SAML request looks like:

```
< ?xml version="1.0" encoding="UTF-8"?>
< Request
  xmlns=" http://www.oasis-
    open.org/committees/security/docs/draft-sstc-schema-
    protocol-19.xsd"
  xmlns:saml="http://www.oasis-
    open.org/committees/security/docs/draft-sstc-schema-
    assertion-19.xsd"
xmlns:xsi="http://www.w3.org/2001/XMLSchema-instance"
  xsi:schemaLocation="http://www.oasis-
    open.org/committees/security/docs/draft-sstc-schema-
    protocol-19.xsdd:/platform/draft-sstc-schema-protocol-
    19.xsd"
  RequestID="String"
  MajorVersion="0" MinorVersion="0" >
< AuthenticationQuery>
  <saml:Subject>
   < saml:NameIdentifier Name="admin"
   SecurityDomain="UserID"/>
   < saml:NameIdentifier Name="admin"
   SecurityDomain="Password"/>
```

```
< /saml:Subject>
< /AuthenticationQuery>
</Request
```

Aside from all the schema URIs you see here, the actual payload in all this code is the familiar, simple user ID and password.

Microsoft has also created a special initiative named GXA (Global XML Web Services Architecture) that adds what Microsoft calls "WS-Security" to SOAP, WSDL, and UDDI. GXA offers what all other XML security solutions offer: both cryptography and authentication capabilities. Read more about GXA at http://msdn.microsoft.com/library/default.asp?url=/library/en-us/dngxa/html/gloxmlws500.asp.

Encryption Solutions

For many companies, the most damaging security failure by far is someone stealing information. A virus can be temporarily inconvenient if it wipes your hard drives (but you do have backups, don't you?). However, if a rival company gets hold of your five-year plan or your new secret formula, it can destroy you.

Your main defense against prying eyes is encryption. Your Web service document (or part of it) is mangled, encrypted — transforming the original, called the *plaintext*, into *cyphertext*. All you need to do is encrypt a string and then send it as a Base64-encoded string (now full of binary, rather than text, information).

When you send something over the Internet, it can quite easily be intercepted. But if your message is encrypted it can be impossible for the interceptor (the *intruder*, or *eavesdropper*, as he or she is called) to understand. Thus, an effectively encrypted message is useless to the intruder. Here's an example of the difference between a plain text XML message and an encrypted one:

The plaintext version:

```
<SOAP-ENV:Envelope
  . . .
    <SOAP-ENV:Body>
      <m:CheckInventory
      xmlns:m="www.mysite.com/InventoryQueries">
        <partID>33552244</partID>
        <partName>Those Big Donut Cutters</partName>
      </m:CheckInventory>
    </SOAP-ENV:Body>

</SOAP-ENV:Envelope>
```

The encrypted version:

```
<SOAP-ENV:Envelope
  . . .
   <SOAP-ENV:Body>
      <m:CheckInventory
      xmlns:m="www.mysite.com/InventoryQueries">
          <partID>aRrs09eWe#@@</partID>
          <partName>O*PIz2Fa+@Gv9</partName>
      </m:CheckInventory>
   </SOAP-ENV:Body>

</SOAP-ENV:Envelope>
```

You can easily encrypt messages (on the client or server) using prewritten TripleDES or RSA classes available from third-party vendors or using the classes in the Microsoft Visual Studio .NET set of security services. This solution, however, does restrict the clients of a Web service to those who can communicate a password and who share the same encryption schemes as the server.

Using the Great DES

Among the various encryption technologies being embraced by Web services security standards initiatives are DES (specifically TripleDES, a newer, stronger version) and public key encryption.

The DES (Data Encryption Standard) encryption technology was created by IBM in the early 1970s. Back then, IBM was one of the few games in town, and the government requested that the brilliant IBM R&D people come up with a way of protecting bank money transfers, government communications, and other sensitive information. In 1972, the National Bureau of Standards asked for a reliable, fast, inexpensive, standardized, very robust United States encryption system. They got what they wanted.

It was clear that computer communications must become increasingly essential in the modern world, and those communications had to be secured in some way. After all, the only difference between $1,000 and $1,000,000 in your savings account is a very tiny magnetic pattern on a hard drive somewhere.

DES was formally introduced in 1976, and to this day it is routinely used for the great majority of business and government encryption. With DES available to Web services security technology, you too can protect your secrets.

Making it public

Strangely, the DES algorithm was made public! Historically, the primary reason that people couldn't crack an encryption scheme was precisely because they didn't know how the scheme worked. If you decide to encrypt by spelling all the words backwards and also substituting x for e, you certainly don't tell people that's what you're doing.

The process used by the DES technique was published so that software could be written to automate the encryption process, and possibly for other more mysterious reasons. The inventors of DES said that knowledge of how a DES message was encrypted did not provide an intruder with a way of decrypting it. IBM's DES system isn't really that tough to understand if you've done any bit-level programming. It's just that DES performs many, many transformations (such as rotation) of the key (password) against the plaintext.

Each individual transformation is simple. A typical rotation left of a 4-bit unit, for example, changes 0101 into 1010, or 1001 into 0011. However, DES does so many transformations, and each one impacts the next one in a domino-like fashion. In this way, a cumulative distortion occurs, a sum-greater-than-the-parts effect. It's as if you started a rumor that was passed along through a million people. You certainly wouldn't recognize your original message when they finished with it.

Can it be cracked?

A dispute among cryptologists concerns whether or not the government (or amateur groups) has secretly cracked DES. (Some even claim that there was always a secret "trap door" built into the DES system right from the start — to permit government agencies access any time they wished. Like most con-spiracy theories, this seems doubtful. Somebody in on the secret would have spilled the beans in the past several decades, no?)

However, if the government has subsequently cracked DES, the public wouldn't likely be told (yet). Some experts claim that the 15th cycle, of the 16 cycles used by DES, has been successfully penetrated. Now and then an amateur group claims to have cracked DES completely. It does seem likely that the basic, 56-bit version of DES is no longer secure from supercomputer (or massive parallel processing) brute force key searches.

For this reason, XML-based Web service security specs call for using Triple-DES, which uses three times as many key bits (but runs three times slower, unfortunately).

Choosing a Good Password

The single greatest weakness in any security system is people. They talk too much, and they usually choose a really lame password if you let them.

DES encryption requires a password. In fact, almost all security measures employ a password — including authentication schemes.

You must be able to remember the password (usually by storing it somewhere), and you must also somehow transmit it to the Web service. This weakens your security because someone can discover the password in its storage location or while it's being transmitted.

The password should include digits (1 through 9) as well as alphabetic characters. What's more, you should choose the most random password that you can remember. No matter how much encryption power you use, if people can guess your password, they're in! Your entire message rolls out for them to read.

Your dog's name is not a good password. Your address, your birthday, your favorite food — all of these would probably be tried by an even moderately motivated, semi-talented intruder. Don't write the password down and stick it in your desk. Memorize it, if possible.

Although computers make it possible to run millions of transformations on a message to encrypt it, computers are value-neutral. A computer doesn't know whether it's running an encryption program written by you (the innocent good person, trying to protect his personal information) or running an intruder's (the bad person trying to get into your bank account) key-testing hacking program that goes through entire dictionaries of possible passwords in a flash.

How does a password work?

A password is some text (often including digits) that you provide as a way of proving you are a legit person: proving that you should be allowed into a server, a database, a Web site, or a message. (The terms *password* and *key* are often used interchangeably.) So assume that you provide a password that is used as a key in the following example.

A key is usually used in encryption to provide a way of distorting the plaintext. A particular key distorts in a particular way, and it also permits the cyphertext to later be restored to the plaintext.

Here's a simple example. Assume that you think up an encryption scheme. Your idea is to drop the password's characters into every other letter of the plaintext, like this:

Password: Mike

Plaintext: Ring of fire.

Encryption: RMiinkge Moifk efMiirkee.

Rotation

Many times, as illustrated here, the password is "rotated," repeated as often as necessary to distort each character in the plaintext. (Although impossible in most situations, it is ideal to use a password that is both entirely random and also as long as the message to be encrypted.)

For illustration purposes, I used alphabetic characters in the previous example. However, with the arrival of the computer, modern encryption generally involves mathematical transformations rather than the simple character substitutions or transpositions characteristic of classic encryption schemes.

Computers are so good at math compared to us, and so much faster at it as well. So, before being used mathematically in a modern encryption scheme like DES, the text password is transformed (hashed, for example) into a numeric value (the *key*) that can then be employed in the mathematical encryption.

Public Key Encryption

RSA public key encryption is also part of the emerging Web services security standards. Stronger than DES but slower, public key encryption employs two keys, one of which is not kept secret. Rather, one key is made *public*.

In this chapter, I explained what is known as *symmetric* encryption (DES). Both the encryption and decryption use the same single key and, functionally, the same algorithm. Techniques like DES are also known as *private key* encryption because you have to keep the key secret or the game is over, and the ciphertext can be unlocked by anyone.

But with *public key*, *asymmetric* encryption, anyone can know the public key, and the encryption process differs from the decryption process. Asymmetric encryption is fascinating, but beyond the scope of this book. If you're interested in experimenting with it, take a look at the RSACryptoServiceProvider class in Visual Studio .NET.

Practical XML Encryption Security

Microsoft's ASP.NET technology has quite a few provisions for both authentication/authorization and encryption security measures. Both a Web service client and the server where the service resides can use SOAP extensions to encrypt or decrypt messages, before or after the serialization phases of the communication.

Of course, XML strategists and consortium members are trying to find ways to make XML security Microsoft-agnostic — in other words, to figure out how security can be platform-independent (namely, Windows-independent). Whether something as complex as security can be generalized to work effectively across competing technologies remains to be seen.

Nonetheless, here in the real world, the great majority of us work within the Microsoft platform. Fortunately for us, quite a bit of implementation has already been dealt with in the .NET framework. All you have to do as a programmer is manage some quite high-level properties and methods. The Microsoft .NET Cryptographic classes are comprehensive, including RC2, TripleDES, and RSA. The classes also include hash functions that are useful for key generation (among other things) such as SHA and MD5.

Microsoft has also introduced the concept of *remoting* — a technology available in the .NET framework that offers security in a systematic way to distributed applications. Remoting provides several hooks permitting access to a serialized message before it is transmitted. In general, remoting is something of an alternative to what you and I think of as "traditional" Web services. If you think it may be a useful alternative, check it out in the .NET framework literature.

Remoting, like any attempt at providing security to distributed applications (including Web services), faces the issue of mutual authentication. Not only must the client authenticate itself throughout the multiple applications that are sometimes required to pass a message from client to the ultimate server, but also the server's response must be authenticated to the client by the server. Both authentication and encryption are necessary to secure this kind of distributed computing. Performance degradation is inevitable with all this security activity riding on top of the execution of applications and transmission of data. How much degradation you can tolerate is up to you, but be aware of the tradeoff between tight security and quick execution.

Whether you employ remoting or more generic Web services techniques, you must deal with several different security threats along the chain of communication. Here are the primary security weaknesses and solutions you can employ:

✦ The Web service has been killed and a false, hacker-written service is residing on the server. How do you know you're using the Web service you expect to use? The server must be authenticated by the client to solve this problem.

✦ An eavesdropper captures your ID/password pair while it travels over the Internet. Solution: Encrypt the password.

✦ An eavesdropper captures your message, changes the auction offer from $200 to $24,000, and sits there laughing as you win the auction by a wide margin. Solution: Encrypt the messages. In many cases, you must encrypt data in both client-server and server-client directions. Sometimes, though, you have no need to encrypt one of the messages. (The response "Congratulations! You won the 1978 vase in the auction" probably doesn't need to be encrypted, for example.)

✦ A DOS attack (denial of service) goes into effect against your Web service. Thousands of RPCs every second are bombarding your server. Both passwords and firewalls can be useful here. You can also specify the frequency of RPC's originating from a single user.

Chapter 8: Implementing Web Services

In This Chapter

✓ Saving state and persisting data

✓ Connecting to databases

✓ Working with the XML Designer

✓ Creating types

✓ Building relational tables

✓ Generating a DataSet

✓ Importing a table from a database into the XML Designer

✓ Using XML Data View

*W*eb services are primarily designed to accept messages from other programs and to, optionally, respond to the other program with an answer to a question, a list of items from a database, or some other information. (Microsoft's Visual Studio .NET also has provisions for creating Web pages — called Web Forms — that *humans*, rather than programs, interact with.)

Although creating elementary Web services in Visual Studio .NET is quite straightforward, you can benefit from exploring techniques that enhance your Web services. In this chapter, you see how to save state, how to establish a connection between a Web service and a database, and how to exploit various features of the XML Designer to easily translate database tables into XML or schemas, and vice versa. Several important tools built into the .NET technology support XML, Web services, and their interaction with traditional programming components such as databases.

Considering State

It's helpful to be flexible when programming. Web services are theoretically supposed to be *stateless* like other aspects of Internet communication. In other words, any necessary information about a client is supposed to be sent to the service (usually as a parameter passed to the Web method). This information is then retained in memory only as long as the service is preparing its response; then the information is discarded. This means that details — such as a client's phone number — are not *retained* anywhere on the server's hard drive. Nor are other details, such as the client's hours of operation, street address, preferences (such as method of payment), or any other information.

Statelessness has its advantages. Clearly, if your Web site is open to the world, you can't afford to, say, store the street address of every visitor to the site. If your site became popular, you could quickly overwhelm the hard drive space on your server. If, like Amazon, you want to provide an Instant Ordering service so that repeat buyers don't have to fill in their address each time they order something, you have to make provisions for storing this huge amount of data.

Likewise, an ordinary Web service doesn't expect to have to store user data. It expects the messages sent to it to remain stateless. Most Web service calls can remain stateless. If your service gets location data and then responds with the current weather forecast for that town, there's simply no need to store the location data.

In other cases, though, Web services can be more efficient if they store data or state. Some Web services benefit if you preserve state or *persist* (retain) other data when using Web services. If you sell the products of a basket weaving commune in Taos, NM, for example, you don't want to have them send you their phone number as an argument each time they access your service. This is not only unnecessarily repetitious, but it can also slow down your server if you are handling many Web service requests simultaneously and don't want to have to keep mucking things up by getting repetitive data from all your clients. The solution: Get the information once, and store it.

Using Session State

ASP.NET, Microsoft's Web programming technologies, offer a session object. You can use this object to persist (store) data while a session is active. The session object has scope that includes all the Web pages in a Web site, so you can use session state to even pass data between a Web site's pages.

To see how this works, start a VB.NET, ASP.NET Web Service (choose File⇨New⇨Project in Visual Studio .NET). Click the code view link in the design window. Replace the green (commented) Web Service template with the following code:

```
<WebMethod(Description:="Figures current time.",
    enablesession:=True)> _

    Public Function CountVisits() As Integer

        If Session("counter") Is Nothing Then
```

```
            Session.Add("counter", 1)
        Else
            Session("counter") += 1

        End If

        Return Session("counter")

End Function
```

It's necessary to add the `Description` argument, because the `enablesession` argument can't come first in the argument list.

This example creates a session variable named `counter` to hold the data about how many times this Web method has been invoked (executed). The first time the `CountVisits` function runs, the session variable is created with the `Add` method. And at the same time, a value of 1 is stored in the variable.

Each time thereafter that the `CountVisits` function runs, the counter variable is incremented by 1 (`+= 1`).

Notice that the name within the parentheses is equivalent to an ordinary variable name.

You can also get a unique ID from the session object. To do that, change `As Integer` to `As String`:

```
Public Function CountVisits() As String
```

And change the return line to this:

```
Return Session.SessionID
```

After executing the Web service, you get the ID, which looks something like this:

```
<?xml version="1.0" encoding="utf-8" ?>
  <string
    xmlns="http://tempuri.org/WebService17/Service1">twzbpunm
    0arfqz55sakent55</string>
```

Connecting to Databases

Authorities estimate that more than 80 percent of all computer applications involve a database. That makes sense — computers are, after all, *data* processors, and data is quite frequently stored in a database.

It's important to know how to connect your Web services to databases. Much e-commerce requires a database connection (such as accessing the latest inventory, or retrieving customer records).

Preparing for a Database Connection

To use database connections in Microsoft's .NET, your best bet is to activate SQL Server, a set of utilities from Microsoft that perform a variety of useful database-related jobs. Among other things, SQL Server helps simulate a server computer holding a database with which your "client" computer (your VB.NET Windows, or Web, application) communicates. If you haven't installed SQL Server (or the MSDE, an equivalent testing platform) when you installed VB.NET itself, install it now. (If you've already installed it, but it's not working — perhaps it has a logon failure or whatever — first uninstall it using Control Panel's Add/Remove Programs utility, and then reinstall it.)

To test the following database-related example, you need to have the pubs sample databases stored on your hard drive. Are these databases on your computer? To find out, choose View⇨Server Explorer in the VB.NET editor. Open the various nodes by clicking the + symbols until you locate pubs under the SQL Servers node. If you don't see SQL Server, reboot your computer. If you just installed it, it should show up after a reboot.

If you don't see the pubs database listed in the Server explorer, you need to install the samples that come with VB.NET. To install the sample database, follow these steps:

1. **Choose Start⇨ Programs⇨Microsoft .NET Framework SDK⇨ Samples and Quickstart Tutorials.**

   A file named StartSamples is displayed to you in Internet Explorer.

2. **Click "Step 1: Install the .NET Framework Samples Database" in Internet Explorer.**

3. **Follow the instructions to Save two files to a temporary directory.**

4. **Use Windows Explorer to locate the temporary directory where you saved those two files.**

5. **Double-click the InstMSDE.exe file to install the samples.**

   If this file fails to install, double-click the SQL Server icon on your tray; then click the red button to stop SQL Server from running. Rerun InstMSDE.exe. Then reboot your computer to restart SQL Server.

6. **Double-click the ConfigSamples.exe file in your temporary directory.**

The samples are configured and you should now see the pubs (and Northwind and GrocerToGo database connections) in your Server Explorer. If not, try rebooting.

Finally, you must create a *connection* to the sample pubs database. Click the + next to Data Connections in the Server Explorer. Do you see a connection to Pubs? If not, make those connections right now by following these steps:

1. **Right-click Data Connections in the Server Explorer.**

   A context menu appears.

2. **Choose Add Connection from the context menu.**

   The Data Link Properties dialog box appears.

3. **Click the Provider tab.**

   You see a list of data providers (connection utilities).

4. **Click Microsoft OLE DB Provider for SQL Server in the listbox to select it.**

5. **Click the Next button.**

6. **Open the list under *Select or enter a server name* and choose your SQL Server's name.**

7. **Click the radiobutton next to Use Windows NT Integrated security.**

8. **Drop the list under *Select the database on the server*.**

9. **Choose Northwind (or whatever database you want to create a connection for).**

10. **Click the Test Connection button.**

11. **Click the OK button to close the dialog box.**

Now, with these data connections established, you can use them to quickly bind controls to the databases or to write source code to access the databases programmatically.

Returning an XML dataset

This next example shows how to connect a database to a Web service. To create a Web service-database connection, first you must add a couple of database-related Imports statements to the code window. Then you can create your database connection Web service function and send back information from your database to the remote client requesting it. The database information you request is automatically converted into XML format.

Add these `Imports` statements to the Web service code page:

```
Imports System.Web.Services
Imports System
Imports System.Data
Imports System.Data.SqlClient
```

Now delete any existing Web Service on the VB.NET code page (such as the green lines of template code), and replace it with the following code:

```
<WebService(Description:="Sends back a list of jobs from our
    database", Namespace:="http://tempuri.org/")> Public
    Class Service1

    Inherits System.Web.Services.WebService

Web Services Designer Generated Code

    <WebMethod()> Public Function ShowJobs() As DataSet

        Dim connPubs As New
SqlConnection("server=localhost;Initial
Catalog=pubs;Integrated Security=SSPI")
        Dim Datacmd As New SqlDataAdapter("select * from
Jobs", connPubs)
        Dim ds As New DataSet()
        Datacmd.Fill(ds, "Jobs")

        Return ds

    End Function

End Class
```

Press F5, click the link to your Web service in Internet Explorer, and then click the Invoke button to see the results, as shown in Figure 8-1.

Looking at the results

Briefly examine the XML message that results when this data is retrieved and displayed in the browser (part of which is shown in Figure 8-1). Notice that it is divided into two primary sections. First, the *schema* (structure) describes each field and some details about it, such as its data type. Second comes the dataset itself, with the records and actual values. Be grateful that ASP.NET generates HTML and XML for you when you work with the ASP.NET WebForms and Web Services. Doing those jobs by hand is tedious, to put it mildly.

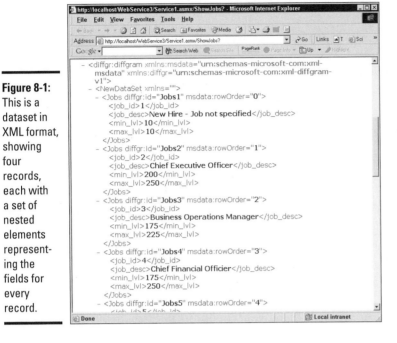

Figure 8-1:
This is a dataset in XML format, showing four records, each with a set of nested elements representing the fields for every record.

Using the XML Designer

Visual Studio .NET includes considerable support for XML — indeed, .NET is built on the XML communication model and employs it extensively. You may find it useful to know how to use the XML Designer built into the .NET editor.

You can begin your exploration of the XML Designer by adding an XML schema to an existing ASP.NET project. Either use the Web service project you started earlier in this chapter, start a new VB.NET Web project, or open an existing one. It doesn't matter. Choose Project⇨Add New Item, and then double-click the XML Schema icon in the Add New Item dialog box, as shown in Figure 8-2.

As soon as you choose the XML Schema icon, you're shown the Design view of the new file (named XMLSchema1.XSD; XSD stands for *XML Schema Definition*). There's nothing to see yet in the Design view, but a message tells you to create a schema by dragging objects from the Server Explorer or the ToolBox. If you want, you can also right-click the designer window to do some lower-level schema designing.

Figure 8-2:
The XML
Schema
icon is your
gateway to
designing
XML.

Before going any further, take a look at the default schema template. Click the XML tab on the bottom of the designer window, and you'll see the frame-work code typical of any schema file:

```
<?xml version="1.0" encoding="utf-8" ?>
<xs:schema id="XMLSchema1"

    targetNamespace="http://tempuri.org/XMLSchema1.xsd"
                elementFormDefault="qualified"
                xmlns="http://tempuri.org/XMLSchema1.xsd"

    xmlns:mstns="http://tempuri.org/XMLSchema1.xsd"

    xmlns:xs="http://www.w3.org/2001/XMLSchema">
</xs:schema>
```

You can see that two local namespaces have been specified, plus the stan-dard XML namespace located at the World Wide Web Consortium (W3C).

Creating Types

Now you're ready to build a schema for an XML type. Click the Schema tab on the bottom of the designer window, and then open the Toolbox. There they are. Metadata items you can add to your schema, as shown in Figure 8-3.

Most of these items should be familiar to you. This database-flavor XML includes two kinds of XML schema types. The *simple* type contains only text content. The *complex* type can contain other types or attributes or both. A complex type can be mapped to a relational table in a database, and when you do that, the simple types (contained sub-types within the complex type) are equivalent to the fields (or columns, as they are sometimes called) in the table.

Figure 8-3:
Here is your set of tools to use when creating XML schema. (Ignore the pointer.)

First, create a simple type, `ZipCode`, and also ensure that the schema specifies that it must not be larger than five characters. Later in this chapter, you use this type as a sub-type by placing it within a complex `Voter` type.

Double-click the SimpleType icon in the Toolbox to place it on the design window. Now click the TextBox containing `simpleType1` and replace the default name (`simpleType1`) with `ZipCode`. Click the word `string` to reveal the down-arrow (indicating that this is a ComboBox, with a list of options). Click the down-arrow symbol to drop the ComboBox list down to see all the variable types you can choose from. Select string as your variable type (it's the default anyway, but you need to see how this works). The list of variable types is shown in Figure 8-4.

**Book VII
Chapter 8**

**Implementing
Web Services**

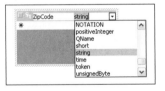

Figure 8-4:
You can select from many variable types.

Now click the XML tab at the bottom of the designer window, and you see that the following lines have been added to the schema:

```
<xs:simpleType name="ZipCode">
    <xs:restriction base="xs:string" />
</xs:simpleType>
```

Click the Schema tab and click the white space just below the ST symbol; then click the white space below the word `ZipCode`. This takes a little practice — it's not Microsoft's ergonomics high-water mark.

Another down-arrow symbol appears! Magic. Click the down arrow to reveal another hidden list; in this case, it's a list of attributes you can specify for your element. Click length to choose it, as shown in Figure 8-5.

Figure 8-5:
Each cell
that you
click reveals
another
drop-down
list.

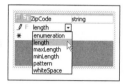

In the cell right next to Length, type **5**, and then press Enter to ensure that your value is added to the underlying XML.

Now check the XML, and you see this code:

```
<xs:simpleType name="ZipCode">
            <xs:restriction base="xs:string">
                    <xs:length value="5" />
            </xs:restriction>
        </xs:simpleType>
```

At this point, it begins to dawn on people why this is named the *XML designer.*

Try clicking the next cell below the length cell (click below the ST symbol first), and you see that each cell within a simple type in the designer contains the list of attributes.

However, in this case, you don't want any further attributes. So click that cell below the length attribute(which should now contain an enumeration attribute) so that you select this unwanted cell. To get rid of an unwanted cell, click it to select it, and then press the Del key. Don't right-click an unwanted cell and choose cut or delete. They remove the entire type, not just a cell within it.

Adding a Complex Type

Now it's time to add a complex type that, among other things, contains the simple ZipCode type that you just defined. Your complex type is going to be named Voter and is going to include several other types. A complex type defines a structure, a hierarchical diagram that specifies relationships between the elements of data it contains. I'm using the data terminology *type* here, but you understand that in XML it means *element*. Likewise, *sub-type* means *child element*.

You want your `Voter` type to include the following sub-types: `FirstName`, `LastName`, `VoterID`, and the simple type you previously defined named `ZipCode`. The Designer can handle this job just fine.

With the Schema tab selected in the Designer, double-click the ComplexType icon in the Toolbox to add it to the Designer window. Rename the default `complexType1` to `Voter`.

Click the first cell on the left under `Voter` (click under the ST first, you know the drill by now), select Attribute, and then type in `FirstName`. Add additional cells for `LastName`, `VoterID`, and `Zip`. Try using the mouse to click cells you want to adjust, or press the Tab and Enter keys to maneuver among these cells.

All the cells can be left to the default string data type, except for Zip, which should be set to the `ZipCode` data type. Wait a minute. There was no `ZipCode` data type earlier when you defined the simple type. Your new data type (the simple type), `ZipCode`, has been included in the drop-down list along with all the usual XSD data types.

Viewing the XML

Now that you've created a complex type, you want to peek at the XML that the Designer has built for you:

```
<?xml version="1.0" encoding="utf-8" ?>
<xs:schema id="XMLSchema1"
    targetNamespace="http://tempuri.org/XMLSchema1.xsd"
    elementFormDefault="qualified"
        xmlns="http://tempuri.org/XMLSchema1.xsd"
    xmlns:mstns="http://tempuri.org/XMLSchema1.xsd"
        xmlns:xs="http://www.w3.org/2001/XMLSchema">
        <xs:simpleType name="ZipCode">
                <xs:restriction base="xs:string">
                        <xs:length value="5" />
                </xs:restriction>
        </xs:simpleType>
        <xs:complexType name="Voter">
                <xs:simpleContent>
                        <xs:restriction
base="xs:string">
                                        <xs:attribute
name="FirstName" type="xs:string" />
                                        <xs:attribute
name="LastName" type="xs:string" />
```

```
                                        <xs:attribute
name="VoterID" type="xs:string" />
                                        <xs:attribute
name="Zip" type="ZipCode" />
                            </xs:restriction>
                    </xs:simpleContent>
            </xs:complexType>
</xs:schema>
```

The parser identifies problems

The Designer has a built-in parser (a utility that reads the XML source code and tells you about any flaws, or as it's called "badly formed XML," that it may find). To see the parser do its thing, add a bad line of code to the preceding example. Type the following boldface line into the XML source code (down near the bottom of the code). This new woof woof is sure to give the parser problems:

```
                    </xs:restriction>
            </xs:simpleContent>
</xs:Woof Woof>
        </xs:complexType>
</xs:schema>
```

Now click the Schema tab in the Designer and instead of a diagram of your schema, you see the following message from the parser:

```
The XML Designer encountered the following error while
    reading this file:

The 'xs:complexType' start tag on line '10' does not match
    the end tag of 'xs:Woof' - line 19, position 3.

Please return to source view and correct these errors.
```

By "source view," this message means: Click the XML tab at the bottom of the design window. Nonetheless, this is pretty good, specific information. (A parser generally relies on the inherent tag/endtag symmetry to discover anomalies in XML source code.) One little annoyance is that, like several features in computer programming languages (arrays, for example), the parser considers the first line to be *line zero*. So when you try to locate line 10, you'll actually count up from line 1 to line 11 rather than line 10.

Remove the offending Woof Woof line in the source code, and when you return to the Schema view, you see the diagram again and no error message appears. If you see a red X in either of your schema boxes, do not panic. Instead, click the XML tab, and then click the Schema tab again. That usually brings the Designer back to its senses.

Building Relational Tables

Although you've created simple and complex *types* so far, recall that they are, in fact, very similar to XML *elements*. A *type* has the same, somewhat ambiguous and fragile relationship to an *element* as a class has to an object that can be instantiated from it. It's like the distinction — and it's a fragile distinction, too — between designtime and runtime.

But, note that a schema is supposed to be metadata, a *design* that is later instantiated when elements are created containing actual data. Given that you have been creating types, aren't you somewhat surprised to see, on the schema Toolbox, an icon representing an *element*?

An element "object" is actually just a `complexType`, or, put another way, a relational table. You create tables with the XML Designer and then create one-to-many relationships between those tables. In this way, you design what eventually becomes a new DataSet. A DataSet can be held in memory, transmitted via XML, or inserted into a database. It's the all-purpose data store in .NET and can be detached from a database for use with Web services. (Current thinking in computer theory circles suggests that because potentially several thousand people during a Christmas buying frenzy may want to interact with a company's order-entry database at the same time, they therefore can't all maintain active connections to that database while they're filling in their order forms. The Access database engine, for example, can't handle more than 10 simultaneous connections. Anyway, for reasons of scalability, theorists say that portions of databases should be detachable. Then, after a customer submits an order, the DataSet can be reattached to the main database — new information integrated into it.)

The XML Designer builds a table by first creating an element containing a complex type, and within that type it places sub-elements corresponding to the fields in the table. Each sub-element contains attributes defining the field's name, data type, and the frequency of occurrence of that field.

A schema doesn't, of course, contain an attribute for each and every feature in an ADO.NET DataSet. So, if there's a quality, such as *read-only*, that isn't part of the schema's vocabulary, an *annotation* is used to note that feature. Annotations look like this:

```
<annotation>
    <appinfo>
        <msdata:readonly="True" />
    </appinfo>
</annotation>
```

A primary key can be specified using XSD. It is indicated with code like this:

```
<key name=" MyKey" msdata:primarykey="True">
    <selector>.</selector>
    <field>VoterRegNum</field>
</key>
```

Adding an element

Continuing with the example schema you've been building in this chapter, double-click the element icon in the Toolbox to add it to your Designer. This is now an unnamed complex type:

```
<xs:element name="element1">
                <xs:complexType>
                        <xs:sequence />
                </xs:complexType>
</xs:element>
```

This is the basis of a database table. You can now add more elements to specify the fields. You can also add unnamed complex types within this relational table, thereby nesting a new relation inside the original container relation. Change the name of the new element from element1 to VoterStats. When you change the name, the variable type (the cell to the right of the *name* cell) automatically fills in with a variable type of the same name (VoterStats). You can leave this as-is.

Now click the first cell in the first row and select element from the drop-down list. Rename this element Frequency. Then add two additional elements named Registration and Party. Leave them all set to the default data type, string.

Now double-click the element icon in the Toolbox to add a second relational table framework. Name it Verification and add two sub-elements: Vcode and BackCodes. Leave both of their data types set to string.

Now drag a Key icon from the Toolbox and drop it on the Verification element. The Edit Key window opens, as shown in Figure 8-6.

Drop down the Fields list by clicking the first cell in the Fields list (you see both Vcode and BackCodes. Choose VCode. Click the Dataset Primary Key checkbox. Click OK to close the dialog box; then notice that a key symbol has been added to the Verification VCode element box in the diagram.

Follow the same steps to add a key to the VoterStats element. Use the Frequency field as the key field.

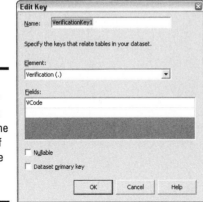

Figure 8-6:
This editor allows you to define the qualities of a key in the XML Designer.

Defining a Relation

Now drag the Relation icon from the Toolbox and drop it on the `Verification` element. You see the Edit Relation dialog box open, as shown in Figure 8-7.

Drop down the list under Child Element (these are actually fields in a DataSet), and choose Verification. Click the New button to choose a new key. In the Fields box, choose Registration, and then click OK. In the Foreign Key Fields, choose `VCode`. Now click OK to close the Edit Relation dialog box. In the Designer, you see a diagrammatic representation of the relation between these two tables, as shown in Figure 8-8.

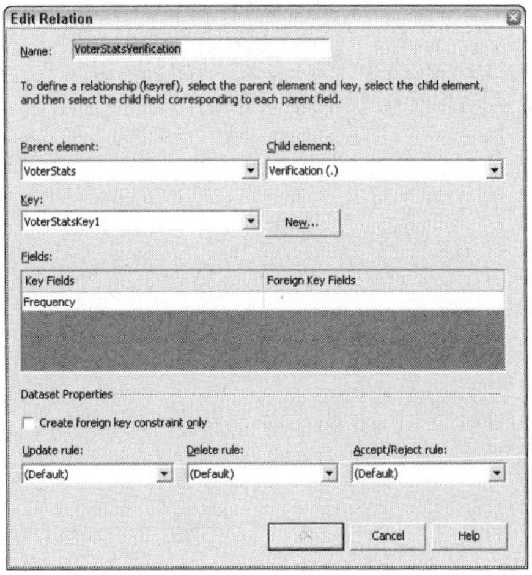

Figure 8-7:
Here's where you can specify the features of a relation.

Figure 8-8:
Notice the
new key
symbol
next to
Registration,
and the
dashed lines
illustrating
the relation.

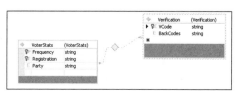

Click the XML tab to see the complete set of table and attribute definitions
the Designer has created for you:

```
<xs:simpleType name="ZipCode">
        <xs:restriction base="xs:string">
                <xs:length value="5" />
        </xs:restriction>
</xs:simpleType>

<xs:element name="VoterStats">
        <xs:complexType>
                <xs:sequence>
                <xs:element name="Frequency"
    type="xs:string" />
                <xs:element name="Registration"
    type="xs:string" />
                <xs:element name="Party" type="xs:string"
    />
                </xs:sequence>
        </xs:complexType>
        <xs:key name="VoterStatsKey1">
                <xs:selector xpath="." />
                <xs:field
    xpath="mstns:Frequency" />
        </xs:key>
        <xs:unique name="VoterStatsKey2">
                <xs:selector xpath="." />
                <xs:field
    xpath="mstns:Registration" />
        </xs:unique>
    </xs:element>
<xs:complexType name="Voter">

<xs:simpleContent>
                <xs:restriction base="xs:string">
        <xs:attribute name="FirstName"
    type="xs:string" />
```

```
                         <xs:attribute name="LastName"
      type="xs:string" />
                         <xs:attribute name="VoterID"
      type="xs:string" />
                         <xs:attribute name="Zip" type="ZipCode"
      />
                    </xs:restriction>
      </xs:simpleContent>

      </xs:complexType>
         <xs:element name="Verification">
             <xs:complexType>
                 <xs:sequence>
                     <xs:element name="VCode" type="xs:string"
      />
                     <xs:element name="BackCodes"
      type="xs:string" />
                 </xs:sequence>
      </xs:complexType>

             <xs:key name="VerificationKey1"
      msdata:PrimaryKey="true">
                 <xs:selector xpath="." />
                 <xs:field xpath="mstns:VCode" />
             </xs:key>
             <xs:keyref name="VoterStatsVerification"
      refer="VoterStatsKey1">
                 <xs:selector xpath="." />
                 <xs:field xpath="mstns:VCode" />
             </xs:keyref>
         </xs:element>
      </xs:schema>
```

If you wish, you can edit this schema (then when you're finished editing, click the Schema tab to see if the parser has any errors to report).

Generating a DataSet

Now you can see how to transform XML into a dataset (a table or group of tables, that can be added to a relational database). Transmitting DataSets (in XML format) is a key technique when sending Web service messages.

You can use a new, simple XML element to see how the transformation from XML element into database table works. Start a new XML Designer window by choosing Project⇨Add New Item and then double-click the XML Schema icon in the Add New Project dialog box.

Double-click Complex Type in the Toolbox to add an element to your design window. In the cells beneath complexType1, add three sub-elements named

One, Two, and Three. Make One and Two string data types, and choose Byte for Three (by dropping the listbox on the cell to the right of Three), as shown in Figure 8-9.

Figure 8-9:
Create a new element, with three sub-elements, that can be transformed into a relational database table.

To create your DataSet, right-click anywhere on the yellow background of the Designer. Choose Generate DataSet from the context menu. The new DataSet is constructed for you. To see it, look up at the top of the Designer window to see the name of your XMLSchema (it's the one in boldface). Then find the .*VB* file in the Solution Explorer (press Ctrl+Alt+L) associated with the name of your XMLSchema. It is likely named XMLSchema2.VB or XMLSchema3.VB, depending on how many XML schemas you've added to this project. (To find the VB file, you may have to click the Show All Files icon in the Solution Explorer title bar, and also click the + symbol next to your XML file.)

Inside the VB file, you find the code that defines your new DataSet's class. It's quite extensive, with serialization instructions, namespaces galore, stream-ing information, debugging technology, inheritance activity, cloning capabili-ties, and what not. The class's name is the same as your XMLSchema, but the sub-element names and data types do not appear in this huge amount of code. That information is read in during runtime from the XMLSchema.

Dropping a Table Into the XML Designer

As you saw in the preceding section, you can transform an XML schema into a database table. In this section, you see how to go the other way. The XML Designer can also accept tables directly from a database and then translate that table's structure into an XML Schema. The table is displayed in the Designer window.

To try this, open the Server Explorer (Ctrl+Alt+S) and locate Servers, find SQL Servers, and finally find the sample pubs database.

Click the Schema tab in the Designer window (you can't add Toolbox controls or other items unless you're in the Design, or Schema, view). Under the Pubs database in the Server Explorer locate the Tables entry and then locate the publishers table. Drag `publishers` from the Server Explorer window and drop it into the XML Designer. You see that it is diagramed, as shown in Figure 8-10.

Click the XML tab to see that the database table has been translated into this XML schema:

```
<?xml version="1.0" encoding="utf-8" ?>
<xs:schema id="XMLSchema3"
    targetNamespace="http://tempuri.org/XMLSchema3.xsd"
    elementFormDefault="qualified"
    xmlns="http://tempuri.org/XMLSchema3.xsd"
    xmlns:mstns="http://tempuri.org/XMLSchema3.xsd"
    xmlns:xs="http://www.w3.org/2001/XMLSchema"
    xmlns:msdata="urn:schemas-microsoft-com:xml-msdata">
    <xs:element name="Document">
        <xs:complexType>
            <xs:choice maxOccurs="unbounded">
                <xs:element name="publishers">
                    <xs:complexType>
                        <xs:sequence>
                            <xs:element name="pub_id"
type="xs:string" />
                            <xs:element
name="pub_name" type="xs:string" minOccurs="0" />
                            <xs:element name="city"
type="xs:string" minOccurs="0" />
                            <xs:element name="state"
type="xs:string" minOccurs="0" />
                            <xs:element name="country"
type="xs:string" minOccurs="0" />
                        </xs:sequence>
                    </xs:complexType>
                </xs:element>
            </xs:choice>
        </xs:complexType>
        <xs:unique name="DocumentKey1"
    msdata:PrimaryKey="true">
            <xs:selector xpath=".//mstns:publishers" />
            <xs:field xpath="mstns:pub_id" />
        </xs:unique>
    </xs:element>
</xs:schema>
```

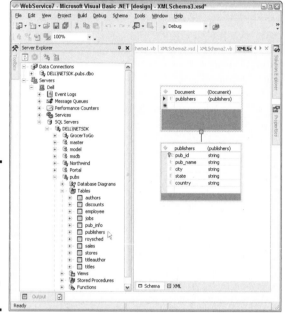

Figure 8-10:
The XML
Designer
accepts
ordinary
database
tables, as
well as XML
controls.

The XML Designer can also work with files having the following extensions:
.TDL (Template Description Language), .WEB, .RESX, and .XSLT.

In addition to the Toolbox, the Server Explorer, and right-clicking the background of the Designer window, you can also manage the XML Designer using the Schema menu and the Schema Toolbar:

The Schema Toolbar offers you most of the options available in the Schema menu or Toolbox.

Using Data View

The XML Designer isn't limited to XML Schemas. It can also provide you with a nice tool for visualizing and manipulating an .XML file (a data file, not just any .XML).

To see how this works, choose Project⇨Add New Item. Then double-click the XML File icon in the Add New Item dialog box. Type this into the new XML file, just below the <?XML Version line that .NET automatically inserts for you:

```
<XML ID="Movies">
<films>
```

```
<film copyrightnumber="133117">
  <name>Annie Hall</name>
  <director>Woody Allen</director>
  <star>Diane Keeton</star>
</film>
</films>
</XML>
```

Notice in Figure 8-11 that the XML Designer now displays two tabs on the bottom of its window, XML and Data (this is not a schema .XSD file, so you see no Schema tab). Click the Data tab to see the diagram shown in Figure 8-11.

Figure 8-11: The XML Designer can also be useful when you're working with an XML data file, rather than a metadata schema.

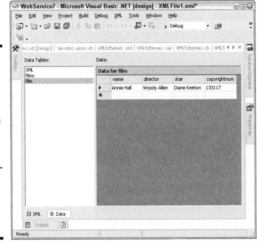

Book VII
Chapter 8

Implementing
Web Services

The Data view offers three views, selected by clicking the items in the left column (in this example, you can choose between XML, *films*, the table, and *film*, one of the records in that table). The Data tab appears when you add an XML data file to your project. In the DataTables column each relation in the XML is displayed in order from highest to lowest of the nesting. Click a table and data is then displayed in the Data zone of the Designer window.

Index

Y

Notes

Notes

Notes

Notes

Notes

Notes

Notes

FOR DUMMIES

The easy way to get more done and have more fun

PERSONAL FINANCE

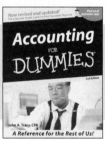

0-7645-5231-7

0-7645-2431-3

0-7645-5331-3

Also available:

Estate Planning For Dummies
(0-7645-5501-4)
401(k)s For Dummies
(0-7645-5468-9)
Frugal Living For Dummies
(0-7645-5403-4)
Microsoft Money "X" For
Dummies
(0-7645-1689-2)
Mutual Funds For Dummies
(0-7645-5329-1)

Personal Bankruptcy For
Dummies
(0-7645-5498-0)
Quicken "X" For Dummies
(0-7645-1666-3)
Stock Investing For Dummies
(0-7645-5411-5)
Taxes For Dummies 2003
(0-7645-5475-1)

BUSINESS & CAREERS

0-7645-5314-3

0-7645-5307-0

0-7645-5471-9

Also available:

Business Plans Kit For
Dummies
(0-7645-5365-8)
Consulting For Dummies
(0-7645-5034-9)
Cool Careers For Dummies
(0-7645-5345-3)
Human Resources Kit For
Dummies
(0-7645-5131-0)
Managing For Dummies
(1-5688-4858-7)

QuickBooks All-in-One Desk
Reference For Dummies
(0-7645-1963-8)
Selling For Dummies
(0-7645-5363-1)
Small Business Kit For
Dummies
(0-7645-5093-4)
Starting an eBay Business For
Dummies
(0-7645-1547-0)

HEALTH, SPORTS & FITNESS

0-7645-5167-1

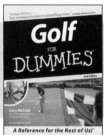

0-7645-5146-9

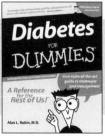

0-7645-5154-X

Also available:

Controlling Cholesterol For
Dummies
(0-7645-5440-9)
Dieting For Dummies
(0-7645-5126-4)
High Blood Pressure For
Dummies
(0-7645-5424-7)
Martial Arts For Dummies
(0-7645-5358-5)
Menopause For Dummies
(0-7645-5458-1)

Nutrition For Dummies
(0-7645-5180-9)
Power Yoga For Dummies
(0-7645-5342-9)
Thyroid For Dummies
(0-7645-5385-2)
Weight Training For Dummies
(0-7645-5168-X)
Yoga For Dummies
(0-7645-5117-5)

Available wherever books are sold.
Go to www.dummies.com or call 1-877-762-2974 to order direct.

FOR DUMMIES®

A world of resources to help you grow

HOME, GARDEN & HOBBIES

Feng Shui
0-7645-5295-3

Gardening
0-7645-5130-2

Guitar
0-7645-5106-X

Also available:

Auto Repair For Dummies
(0-7645-5089-6)

Chess For Dummies
(0-7645-5003-9)

Home Maintenance For
Dummies
(0-7645-5215-5)

Organizing For Dummies
(0-7645-5300-3)

Piano For Dummies
(0-7645-5105-1)

Poker For Dummies
(0-7645-5232-5)

Quilting For Dummies
(0-7645-5118-3)

Rock Guitar For Dummies
(0-7645-5356-9)

Roses For Dummies
(0-7645-5202-3)

Sewing For Dummies
(0-7645-5137-X)

FOOD & WINE

Cooking
0-7645-5250-3

Cookies
0-7645-5390-9

Wine
0-7645-5114-0

Also available:

Bartending For Dummies
(0-7645-5051-9)

Chinese Cooking For
Dummies
(0-7645-5247-3)

Christmas Cooking For
Dummies
(0-7645-5407-7)

Diabetes Cookbook For
Dummies
(0-7645-5230-9)

Grilling For Dummies
(0-7645-5076-4)

Low-Fat Cooking For
Dummies
(0-7645-5035-7)

Slow Cookers For Dummies
(0-7645-5240-6)

TRAVEL

Italy
0-7645-5453-0

Hawaii
0-7645-5438-7

Las Vegas
0-7645-5448-4

Also available:

America's National Parks For
Dummies
(0-7645-6204-5)

Caribbean For Dummies
(0-7645-5445-X)

Cruise Vacations For
Dummies 2003
(0-7645-5459-X)

Europe For Dummies
(0-7645-5456-5)

Ireland For Dummies
(0-7645-6199-5)

France For Dummies
(0-7645-6292-4)

London For Dummies
(0-7645-5416-6)

Mexico's Beach Resorts For
Dummies
(0-7645-6262-2)

Paris For Dummies
(0-7645-5494-8)

RV Vacations For Dummies
(0-7645-5443-3)

Walt Disney World & Orlando
For Dummies
(0-7645-5444-1)

Available wherever books are sold. Go to www.dummies.com or call 1-877-762-2974 to order direct.

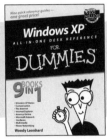

FOR DUMMIES®

Helping you expand your horizons and realize your potential

INTERNET

0-7645-0894-6

0-7645-1659-0

0-7645-1642-6

DIGITAL MEDIA

0-7645-1664-7

0-7645-1675-2

0-7645-0806-7

GRAPHICS

0-7645-0817-2

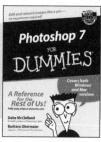

0-7645-1651-5

0-7645-0895-4

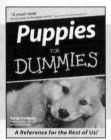

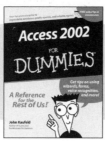